Practical Neo4j

Greg Jordan

Apress®

Practical Neo4j

ISBN-13 (pbk): 978-1-4842-0023-0

ISBN-13 (electronic): 978-1-4842-0022-3

Managing Director: Welmoed Spahr
Acquisitions Editor: Jeff Olson
Developmental Editor: Robert Hutchinson
Technical Reviewers: Kenny Bastani, Jeremy Kendall, Brad Montgomery, Daniel Prichett, Brian Swanson

Coordinating Editor: Rita Fernando
Copy Editor: Laura Lawrie
Compositor: SPi Global
Indexer: SPi Global

Distributed to the book trade worldwide by Springer Science+Business Media New York, 233 Spring Street, 6th Floor, New York, NY 10013. Phone 1-800-SPRINGER, fax (201) 348-4505, e-mail orders-ny@springer-sbm.com, or visit www.springeronline.com. Apress Media, LLC is a California LLC and the sole member (owner) is Springer Science + Business Media Finance Inc (SSBM Finance Inc). SSBM Finance Inc is a Delaware corporation.

For information on translations, please e-mail rights@apress.com, or visit www.apress.com.

Apress and friends of ED books may be purchased in bulk for academic, corporate, or promotional use. eBook versions and licenses are also available for most titles. For more information, reference our Special Bulk Sales–eBook Licensing web page at www.apress.com/bulk-sales.

Any source code or other supplementary materials referenced by the author in this text is available to readers at www.apress.com. For detailed information about how to locate your book's source code, go to www.apress.com/source-code/.

*Dedicated to my beautiful wife, Rachel, and our three amazing boys,
Gregory, Samuel, and Andrew*

Contents at a Glance

Contents

Foreword

The modern world is awash with data. But it's no longer merely gray, pithy views of payroll or accounting information; now it also represents moments in lives, transportation, healthcare, recreation, and finance.

The volume and intricacy of data we are presented with today is wildly different from the data we worked with even just a few decades ago. This means that databases are changing, too.

To wit, in the last decade, we've seen the emergence of a new category of data store under the banner of "NoSQL," whose motivation is to deal with the substantially increased performance demands and dataset sizes of modern applications. To achieve these goals of scale and performance, most NoSQL databases have given up on the relational database notion of building and querying a high-fidelity model. Instead, most NoSQL databases optimize for the symmetric storage and retrieval of individual, disconnected items known as "aggregate data." With most NoSQL stores, it's an easy task to store a customer document and retrieve it, to store a shopping basket and get it back, or to store a vote and count it.

However, for queries of any reasonable complexity, most NoSQL stores switch to a compute-centric approach. To analyze data in depth, subsets are extracted from the store and pumped through some compute infrastructure (typically a MapReduce framework). From the results of that computation, insight arises.

However, connected data poses manifest difficulties for typical NoSQL databases, which manage documents, columns, or key–value pairs as disconnected aggregates. To create a connected worldview using these stores, we as application developers must denormalize data and fake connections within an inherently disconnected model. In turn, renormalizing and reifying connections at query time are vastly more expensive than in a native graph database.

In contrast, graph databases embrace connected data and make querying it rapid and inexpensive—and, dare I say, also pleasurable. Whereas relational databases choke on intermediate sets as data volumes grow and NoSQL stores demand ever-more-elaborate external processing support, graph databases crunch through connected data with the greatest of ease.

This is of great importance because the most interesting questions we want to ask our data require us to understand the things that are connected and the many different meaningful ways in which those things are connected. Graph databases such as Neo4j offer the most powerful and performant means for generating this kind of insight in real time. And since most data is connected, it really is true that graphs are eating the world right now.

While Neo4j has come to prominence alongside other popular NoSQL stores, it is fundamentally dissimilar to them. Neo4j provides traditional database-like support (including transactions) for highly-connected data and orders of magnitude better performance than relational databases. Across numerous domains as varied as social, recommendations, telecoms, logistics, datacenter management, careers management, finance, policing, and geospatial, Neo4j has demonstrated it's the de facto choice for managing complex interconnected data.

Because Neo4j is by far the most popular graph database, it's the one that most developers encounter. First contact with a relatively new technology such as Neo4j can be overwhelming. There are new tools, APIs, query languages, and data modeling to be learned, along with performance tuning, bullet-proof deployments, and new terminology. And let's not forget a whole host of graph theory from nearly 300 years of history!

But don't be daunted. Switching to graphs and Neo4j isn't hard, and with books of the caliber of *Practical Neo4j* at hand as your guide, you'll be building and querying graphs in no time.

Practical Neo4j provides both general and specific guidance based on Greg Jordan's vast Neo4j experience. The general guidance pertaining to graph modeling in comparison to familiar SQL helps provide a great platform for new Neo4j developers to understand the graph paradigm, and it provides a reference even for experienced folks. The specific guidance and extensive worked examples in a variety of programming languages provide a rich basis for developers to build directly upon. The result is a rounded view of Neo4j across the systems development lifecycle for a variety of platforms.

As a Neo4j contributor and author, I am extremely pleased with *Practical Neo4j*'s breadth and depth. Greg is one of the most experienced Neo4j users around, and it's exciting to see his expertise captured for a wide audience.

—Dr. Jim Webber
Chief Scientist
Neo Technology

About the Author

Greg Jordan has been creating software for more than 15 years with a focus on content systems and mobile applications. He is an avid speaker as well as writer on the topic of graph databases and has been working with Neo4j since version 1.5. Greg holds two Master's degrees, is a Ph.D. candidate, and resides in Memphis, Tennessee.

About the Technical Reviewers

Kenny Bastani is a passionate technology evangelist and and open-source software advocate in Silicon Valley. As an enterprise software consultant, he has applied a diverse set of skills needed for projects requiring a full-stack web developer in agile mode. As an entrepreneur, he has managed the software development life cycle of many high-volume and high-availability web applications using the .NET technology stack.

As a developer evangelist for the popular database Neo4j, Kenny has supported developers from globally recognized companies who have inserted the NoSQL graph database product inside their technology stack. As a passionate blogger and open-source contributor, Kenny engages a community of passionate developers who are looking to take advantage of newer graph processing techniques to analyze data.

Jeremy Kendall is a PHP Developer, open-source contributor, founder and former organizer of Memphis PHP, new father, and amateur photographer. Jeremy has been developing for the web in PHP since 2001, and he has a passion for learning, teaching, open source, and best practices. He currently lives in his hometown of Memphis, Tennessee, and is the CTO and Lead Developer for Graph Story.

Brad Montgomery is a software developer and entrepreneur in Memphis, Tennessee. He has worked predominantly on web-based products and is the cofounder of Work for Pie—a company that believes that it can find a better way for companies to recruit software developers. Brad believes in an agile-inspired approach to work, and he prefers open-source tools. He has built a number of products using Python and Django, although he fully believes in using the right tool for the job (whether that's Python, Ruby, Javascript, C, or a bash script). Brad lives in Bartlett, Tennessee, with his wonder wife and two amazing daughters (both of whom are growing up way too quickly).

Daniel Pritchett got his start building financial reports for Fortune 100 companies. He has worked in corporate IT and in consulting application development in Memphis, Tennessee. As a consultant with Rails Dog, Daniel is now focusing on building online stores customized to enable interesting business models. He will happily talk with you about fitness or ukuleles if you catch him at a local meetup.

Brian Swanson is the leader of the Memphis .Net User Group, Cofounder of GiveCamp Memphis, and Co-Chairman of the Memphis Technology Foundation. He embraces all things that help make Memphis, Tennessee, a better place. He's been programming for 25-plus years, and he still continues to learn new things. Brian is an avid runner of marathons and ultramarathons and anything else that gets him outdoors and away from the computers that he spends so much time on.

Acknowledgments

I would like to thank my technical reviewers: Jeremy Kendall, Brian Swanson, Brad Montgomery, Daniel Pritchett, and Kenny Bastani.

A big thank you to the wonderful editors and team at Apress, especially Rita Fernando and Jeff Olson.

I would also like to thank the entire team at Neo Technology, the Neo4j driver developers, especially Michael Hunger, Tatham Oddie, Josh Adell, Nigel Small, and Max De Marzi, as well as the entire Neo4j community. Thank you to Emil Eifrem for providing a great presentation at ApacheCon and kickstarting the journey.

Finally, thank you to Jason Gilmore for the introduction to Apress and advice along the way.

PART 1

Getting Started

CHAPTER 1

Introduction to Graphs

What do Cisco, Walmart, and eBay have in common with many academic and research projects? They all depend on graph databases as a core part of their technology stack.

Why have such a wide range of industries and fields found a common relationship through graph databases? The short answer is that graphs can offer superior and consistent speed when analyzing deep, dense relationships and can do so with a flexible data structure.

As many developers can attest, one of the most tedious pieces of a web application or software project is managing the schema for its database. Although relational databases are often the right tool for the job, certain limitations—particularly the time as well as the risk involved to make additions to or update the model—invite the use or consideration of alternatives and complementary data storage solutions. Enter NoSQL.

When NoSQL databases, such as MongoDB and Cassandra, came along, they brought with them a simpler way to model data, as well as a high degree of flexibility—or even a schema-less approach—for the model. While document and key-value databases remove many of the time and effort hurdles, they were mainly designed to handle simple data structures. However, the most useful, interesting and insightful applications require complex data and yield a deeper understanding of the connections and relationships between different data sets.

Graph databases—another branch of databases in the NoSQL family tree—can offer the blend of simplicity and speed while permitting data relationships to maintain a first-class status. For example, Twitter's graph database, called *FlockDB*, more elegantly solves the complex problem of storing and querying billions of connections than their prior relational database solution. In addition to simplifying the structure of the connections, FlockDB also ensures extremely fast access to this complex data. Twitter is just one use case of many that demonstrates why graph databases have become a draw for many organizations that need to solve scaling issues for their data relationships.

While offering fast access to complex data at scale is a primary driver for adoption of graph databases, they also offer the same tremendous flexibility found in so many other NoSQL options. The schema-free nature of a graph database permits the data model to evolve without sacrificing any of the speed of access or adding significant and costly overhead to development cycles.

Poised at the intersection of graph database capabilities, the growth of interest, and the trend toward more connected large sets of data, this chapter demonstrates how the graph database will affect future web and mobile application development—specifically, how graph databases will grow as a leading alternative to relational databases.

I start with a quick overview of graph theory and a look at the main elements of a graph database. I proceed to show how graph databases compare to relational databases as well as other NoSQL options. I conclude the chapter with a look at use cases for graph databases.

Graph Theory

The history of graph theory begins with Leonhard Euler (pronounced "oiler"), the Swiss mathematician and physicist. Euler made many significant contributions to pure and applied mathematics over a more than 50-year academic career. His solution to the Seven Bridges of Königsberg problem in 1735 is considered to be the first theorem of graph theory and one of his most important contributions.[1]

The Seven Bridges of Königsberg problem was to find a path through the city that would cross each of the seven bridges connecting two large islands. Figure 1-1 highlights the bridges connecting the mainland and the two islands with oval markers.

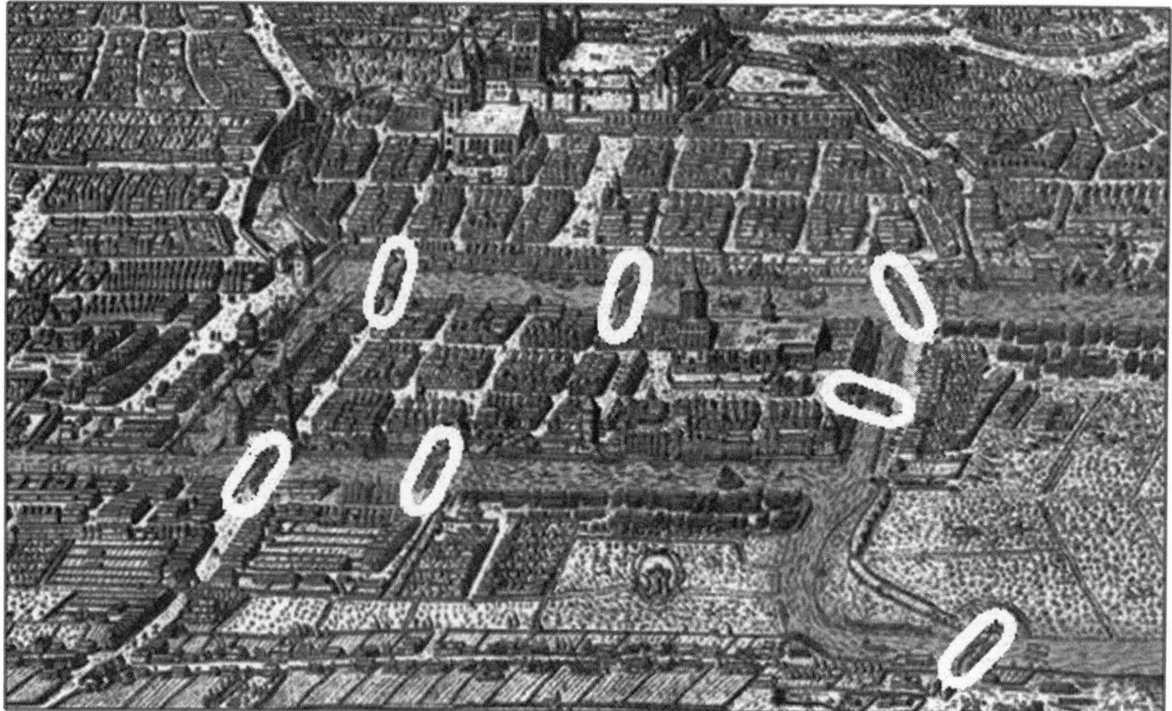

Figure 1-1. *The Seven Bridges of Königsberg*

Other conditions of the problem were that the bridges may not be crossed more than once and each bridge must be crossed completely. Euler's subsequent treatise on the problem was written in 1736 and later published in 1741. Euler proved that the problem could not be solved but, more importantly, noted that the most relevant aspect of the problem is the order in which the bridges were crossed. In creating this singular, fundamental approach, Euler could examine the problem in abstract terms. His more focused methodology considered only the mainland, the islands, and the bridges that connected them.

[1]http://www.ams.org/journals/bull/2006-43-04/S0273-0979-06-01130-X/S0273-0979-06-01130-X.pdf

In graph theory, the mainland and islands are what is referred to as *vertices* (the plural of *vertex*). Each bridge that connects two vertices is known as an *edge*, which, for the purposes of graph theory, serves to identify which pair of vertices is connected by that bridge. As you can see in Figure 1-2, the components of the problem are broken down into four vertices connected by seven edges. The final mathematical structure that represents all the vertices and edges is called a *graph*.

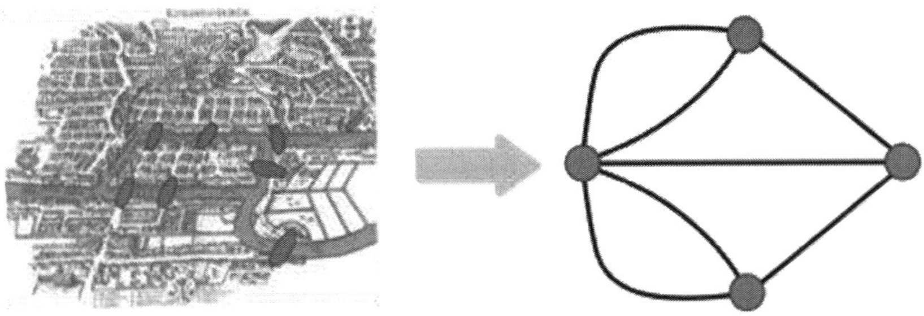

Figure 1-2. *The Seven Bridges of Königsberg problem displayed as Euler's graph representation*

■ **Note** A deep understanding of graph theory is not essential to working with graph databases. For those readers who want to dive further into graph theory, Richard J. Trudeau's *Introduction to Graph Theory* (Dover, 1993) provides a more thorough discussion.

A common mistake is to refer to the item in Figure 1-3, and items similar to it, as a *graph*. Although graph data or diagrams may be contained within a chart, the terms *graph* and *chart* are not synonymous.

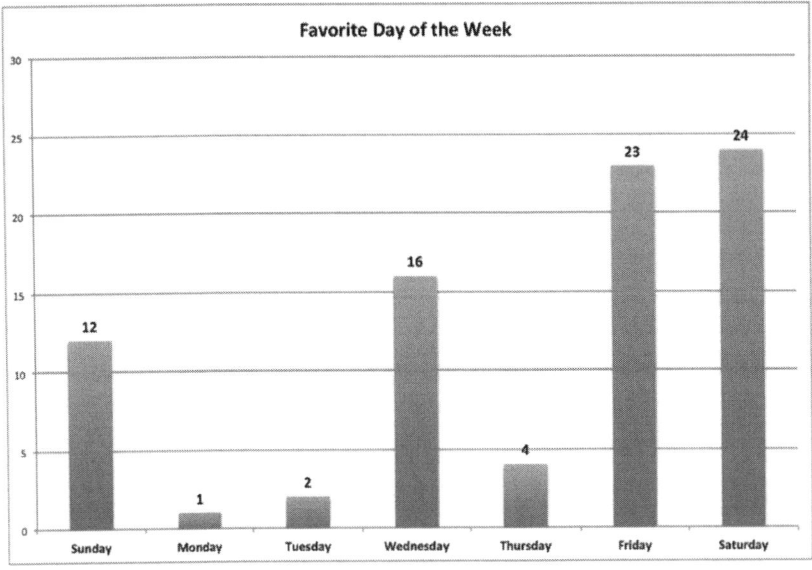

Figure 1-3. *Bar chart*

Graph Databases

In its simplest form, a *graph database* is a set of vertices and edges. Another way to picture graph databases is to view the data as an arbitrary set of objects connected by one or more kinds of relationships. This section defines and expands on the most essential components of a graph database—specifically, how they occur within and apply to the graph database, Neo4j.

Nodes and Relationships

When discussing graph databases, vertices are more commonly referred to as *nodes* and edges are more commonly referred to as *relationships* (Figure 1-4). While these two pairs of terms may be used interchangeably, this book follows the more common usage.

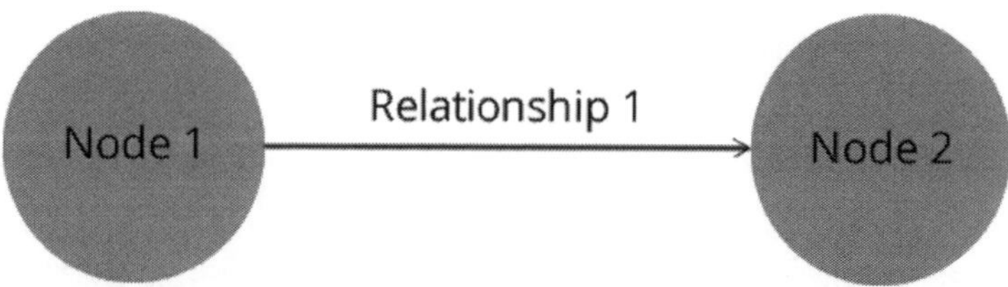

Figure 1-4. *Two nodes connected by a relationship*

A node can be thought of as an object with any number of properties. Unlike the keys that connect rows within a relational database, relationships within a graph database can also have properties.

Labels

Starting with the 2.0 version of Neo4j, the concept of labels was introduced as a way to group nodes. As the example in Figure 1-5 demonstrates, you can define a node as "Person" and then provide additional values for each property of the node as necessary. By grouping nodes in this way, we can query the graph to show common subsets of what are essentially node types. Labeling of nodes also offers a way to enforce modeling constraints when necessary, as well as to increase the speed at which data can be accessed through improved indexing.

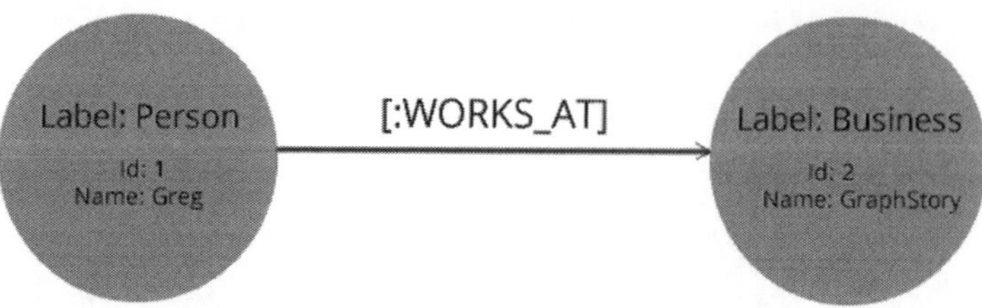

Figure 1-5. *Labels provide a way for nodes to be grouped*

Traversal

The most common method for querying a graph is by performing a *traversal*. In a traversal operation, the query begins with a single node that follows a path of relationships over connected nodes. Neo4j's traversal API allows you specify this path, essentially creating a subgraph of nodes and relationships. The shortest path has a length of zero, which is a single node without returning its relationships as part of the query. When a path has a length of one, the path can contain a relationship to another node or, as shown in Figure 1-6, even back to the same node.

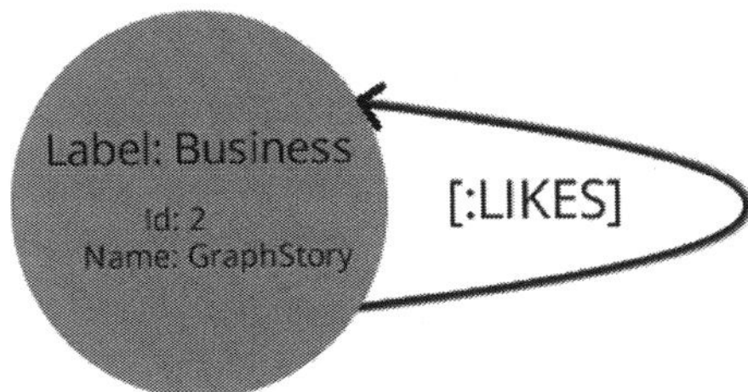

Figure 1-6. *A node that features a relationship back to itself*

Indexes

Like many other databases, Neo4j relies on an index to do an explicit look-up for a specific node or relationship. While it is possible to traverse the graph to find the node or relationship, it is sometimes more performant to allow indexing to handle the request. For example, when looking a specific "Person" node, you could query the index by a unique identifier such as a username or other unique key.

Relational Databases and Neo4j

When comparing graph databases to relational databases, one thing that should be clear upfront is that data affiliation does not have to be exclusive. That is, graph databases or other NoSQL options will likely not take over or replace relational databases. Clear and well-defined use cases will involve relational databases for the foreseeable future. Matt Aslett, research director of data management for 451 Research, has observed the growth of graph databases, specifically Neo4j, in which a relational database might have been otherwise used, and he notes that "there is a tipping point, but that will take some time."[2]

Undertaking the task of transforming an existing functional and manageable relational database into another database type is sometimes necessary. Relational databases may be poor fits for the goals of certain data for a number of reasons and use cases.

For example, the limitation on how a relationship is defined within a relational database is one reason to consider switching to a graph database such as Neo4j. As mentioned earlier in this chapter, relationships in the graph can, like nodes, have properties of their own. With that capability, it would be fairly trivial to add in a property on a graph relationship that was not defined when the relationship began. Although creating a *join table* (as it is known in the relational database world) that brings together two disparate tables is a common practice, doing so adds a layer of complexity. Chapter 3, which addresses data modeling with Neo4j, includes diagrams of graph models and how they compare to modeling with a relational database.

---

[2]`http://techcrunch.com/2014/02/02/neo4j-a-graph-database-for-building-recommendation-engines-gets-a-visual-overhaul/`

Another reason you might consider moving to a graph database is to avoid the half-measures and workarounds you must use to make your model fit within a relational database. A join table is created in order to have metadata that provides properties about relationships between two tables. When a similar relationship needs to be created among other tables, yet another join table must be created. Even if it has the same properties as the first join table, it must be created in order to ensure the integrity of the relationships. A certain type of relationship—such as "LIKES"—can exist among more than just two types of nodes. In fact, the relationship type could be applied to all types of nodes.

Another reason to favor graph databases over relational database is to avoid what might be referred to as "join hell." The joins required to connect two tables are often trivial, but those types of joins provide the least expressive data. When the application requires data that connects several tables, it is then that expense of joins begins to manifest itself in both the complexity and as well as diminished performance. In addition, the nature and depth of the query would need to be known ahead of time, or the query would need to be dynamically generated.

Despite the differences between graph and relational databases, there are a few similarities. A significant similarity is that both can achieve what is known as *ACID compliance. ACID*—Atomicity, Consistency, Isolation and Durability—is a set of principles guaranteeing that transactions completed by the database are processed reliably. In Neo4j, the Enterprise edition is fully ACID in high-availability clustering, whereas the Community edition is *eventually consistent.*

NoSQL and Neo4j

Graph databases are not the only alternative or complementary solutions to the shortcomings of relational databases. Although the first use of the term *NoSQL* dates from the late 1990s, it was only toward the end of the 2000s that NoSQL options became more focused and could be set into one of four different sectors or families: *key-value, column-family, document,* and *graph* databases.[3] Another group is the multimodel category, which includes combinations of concepts and features from at least two of the four main groups.

■ **Note** Contrary to the assumption in some quarters, *NoSQL* does not stand for "No to SQL." The proper sense of the acronym is "Not only SQL"—referring to alternatives to the relational database.

Key-value stores represent data by storing large sets of values, with each value based on a key. This simple data structure allows related applications to store its data in a schema-less way. The column-family database, modeled after Google's BigTable, can be described simply as rows of objects that contain columns of related data. As with key-value stores, column-family databases also have key values pairs that represent a row. Document databases represent a collection of "documents"; each one has its own collection of keys and values. In some ways, documents contained within a document database are like rows in relational database. In addition, querying against a unique id or key is a typical method used to retrieve a document.

The first big difference between graph databases and other NoSQL categories is the data model. Each type of node can have any number of properties. In addition, those properties can be changed over time, which provides a model that does not require a schema. This schema-less nature is certainly not unique in the NoSQL world, but when you consider that nodes can have arbitrary relationships that do not need to be determined ahead of time or carefully modeled in after an initial release, the difference between graphs and other NoSQL options begins to take shape. When you couple that with the fact that arbitrary relationships can also have any number of their own configurable properties, the difference is even clearer. Finally, because graphs can be quickly adapted to changes in business needs, especially in making connections between data, organizations are enabled to ask the right questions from the data as the needs arise, and those questions do not have to be precisely identified prior to data capture.

---

[3]`http://blog.monitis.com/index.php/2011/05/22/picking-the-right-Nosql-database-tool/`

Summary

This chapter provided a brief overview of graph theory as well as a look at the main elements of a graph database. Graph databases were compared to relational databases as well as to other NoSQL options, together with some use cases for graph databases. The next chapter covers how to install Neo4j quickly and how to test out its querying capability with its web-based UI and console tools.

CHAPTER 2

Up and Running with Neo4j

This chapter covers the requirements for running Neo4j as well as the steps for installing an instance of the Neo4j database on your computer. To set you on the path to mastering data management with Neo4j, I introduce the Neo4j Browser tool and walk you through the basics of the Neo4j query language, Cypher.

Neo4j

Neo4j began its life in 2000, when Emil Eifrem, Johan Svensson, and Peter Naubauer—the creators of Neo4j—began to notice a significant amount of overhead in both the performance and work required in one of their applications. The first and most significant aspect of the overhead could be traced to the mismatch of their content management system's model with the relational database. While the properties of the model could be stored in and retrieved from tables with relative ease, they observed that connections between the data imposed significant processing time for queries. Moreover, the performance of the queries grew worse as the connections among the data became more complex. Finally, the time and effort that was required to manage those relationships placed even more overhead on the application's development lifecycle.

After seeking out alternatives and performing a few rounds of research, they began to build out Project Neo. Neo aimed to introduce a database that offered a better way to model, store, and retrieve data while keeping all of the core concepts—such as ACIDity, transactions, and so forth—that made relational databases into a proven commodity.

Subsequent research and development has propelled the Neo4j to the top spot in popularity, justifying the tagline associated with the Neo4j logo on promotional materials, "The World's Leading Graph Database."[1] As you will come to see after working with Neo4j on your own, it fits extremely well with many different use cases, domains, and industries.

Requirements and Installation

The installation of Neo4j is straightforward and, regardless of whether you prefer Windows, Linux, or Mac, it should take very little time to get running once it has been downloaded. If you are ready to get started with the quick install, then browse to neo4j.com/download for a 30-day trial of the enterprise version. Click the download link and then choose the version for your operating system. If you run into problems downloading from the neo4j site, you can also visit `http://www.graphstory.com/practicalneo4j` and go to the download section to get the specific version as it applies to the remainder of this book.

[1] `http://db-engines.com/en/ranking/graph+dbms`

■ **Note** In addition to installing a version of Neo4j on your local machine, you can visit `http://www.graphstory.com/practicalneo4j` to setup a free, fully configured Neo4j instance of the enterprise version for personal use. You will be provided with your own free trial, a knowledge base, and email support from Graph Story.

Requirements

The requirements in Table 2-1 apply to a single instance of Neo4j. In terms of capability and performance for a single instance, memory and disk capability are the primary performance constraints. The amount of memory impacts the graph size that can fit in memory and disk I/O capability affects read/write performance.

Table 2-1. *Requirements for Running Neo4j*

	Minimum	Recommended
CPU	Intel Core i3	Intel Core i7
Memory	2GB	16-32GB
Disk	10GB SATA	SSD with SATA
Filesystem	ext4	ext4, ZFS

Versions

As of this writing, Neo Technology, the commercial entity that supports the ongoing development of Neo4j, offers a community license as well as enterprise subscriptions. This book uses the enterprise version, which includes the most critical features for exploring Neo4j. With the enterprise edition, the pricing and feature set has been set to match the current operational stage of a business. For example, the personal edition of Neo4j is in line with an early-stage or bootstrap company.

■ **Note** The types of licenses can be found in Table 2-2, which display only some of the more pertinent differences in capability and support with Neo4j. The license types are those available at time of writing publishing and are likely to evolve.

Table 2-2. *Neo4j License and Feature List*

	Community	Personal	Startup	Enterprise
Primary Features				
Property Graph Model	X	X	X	X
Native Graph Processing	X	X	X	X
Native Graph Storage	X	X	X	X
ACID	X	X	X	X
Cypher	X	X	X	X
Language Drivers	X	X	X	X
REST API	X	X	X	X
Memory	X	X	X	X
Disk	X	X	X	X
Filesystem	X	X	X	X
Performance and Scalability				
High-Performance Cache		X	X	X
Clustering		X	X	X
Online Backup		X	X	X
Advanced Monitoring		X	X	X
Support				
Commercial Email Support			X	X
Commercial Phone Support				X
Support Hours			10 x 5	Up to 24 x 7
License				
Production instances		3	3	3+
Test instances		3	3	3+
Developer Support		Up to 2	2	3+

Java

The "j" in Neo4j stands for *Java*, and the Java Development Kit (JDK) is required to run it. So before unpacking the download archive, make sure you have Oracle's JDK installed on your computer. If you already have the JDK installed, make sure it is at least version 7. If you need to install it, then be sure to use the latest stable version of JDK7. After you have installed JDK7 or verified that it has already been installed, you can proceed to the next section depending on your preferred operating system

■ **Note** To get you up and running as quickly as possible, this chapter uses the console to run Neo4j.

Installation

After downloading the version of Neo4j that is compatible with your operating system, follow the appropriate set of steps below.

■ **Note** Throughout this book, {NEO4J_ROOT} refers to the top-level installation directory for Neo4j.

Windows

Neo4j provides an installer version for Windows, but for the exercise in this chapter we will use the console:

1. Ensure that you have Java version 7 or higher running on your computer.
2. Extract the zip into a preferred directory on your computer.
3. Double-click on `{NEO4J_ROOT}\bin\Neo4j.bat`.
4. Open a browser and go to `http://localhost:7474`.
5. Stop the server by executing "Ctrl-C" in the corresponding open console window.

Linux/Unix

1. Ensure that you have Java version 7 or higher running on your computer.
2. Extract the archive into a preferred directory on your computer.
3. Open a command prompt and change directory to `{NEO4J_ROOT}\bin`.
4. Run the command `./neo4j start`.
5. Open a browser and go to `http://localhost:7474`.
6. Stop the server by executing `./neo4j stop` in the console.

Mac OSX

Ensure that you have Java version 7 or higher running on your computer. While it is possible to follow the Linux/Unix install instructions for Mac OS, users familiar with using Homebrew can install the latest stable version of Neo4j with the command, `brew install neo4j && neo4j start`.

This will provide a Neo4j instance running on `http://localhost:7474`. The installation files will reside in `/usr/local/Cellar/neo4j/community-{NEO4J_ROOT}/libexec/`—available to tweak settings and symlink the database directory if desired. After the installation has completed, you can run Neo4j from the terminal.

The server can be started in the background from the terminal with the command `neo4j start` and then stopped again with `neo4j stop`. The server can also be started in the foreground with the neo4j console, and it can send the log output to the terminal.

The Neo4j Browser

One of the most useful tools included with the database is the Neo4j Browser, a web-based shell (Figure 2-1). Version 2.x of Neo4j contains significant enhancements to the features, speed, and visualization tools over the previous incarnations of the web-based tool.

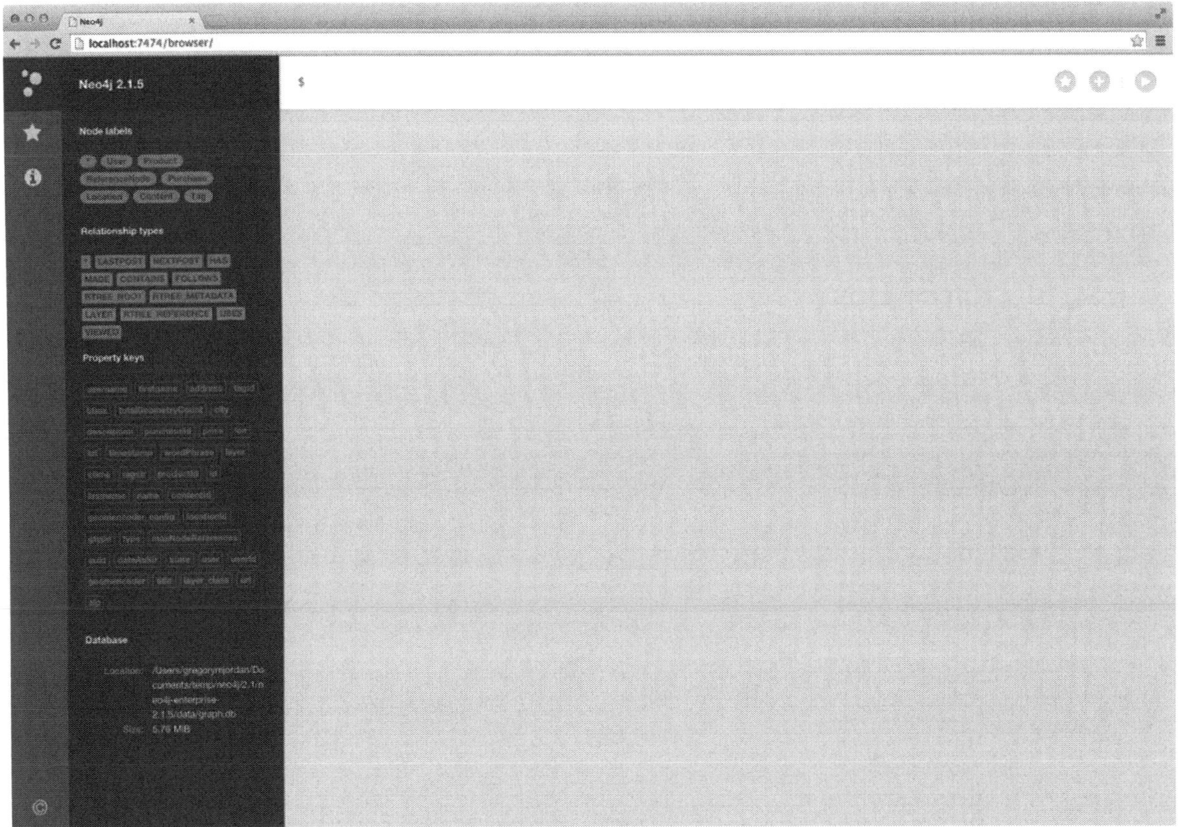

Figure 2-1. *The Neo4j Browser*

In addition to execution of the commands to perform CRUD (Create, Read, Update, and Delete) operations against the Neo4j database, the web interface provides helpful features to inspect the connected database instance as well as the system configuration settings. As in Figure 2-1, the Neo4j Browser shows labels, relationship types, and property keys that are contained within the data.

■ **Tip** The web-based shell uses a default value and can be accessed using the port number 7474. However, you can change the port address by updating the server configuration located in the `{NEO4J_ROOT}/conf/neo4j-server.properties` file using the setting for `org.neo4j.server.webserver.port`. Changing this setting might be necessary if there are restrictions on your network for port ranges.

When a populated database is accessed through the Browser, many of the top-level properties of Neo4j are displayed. For example, by clicking on one of the relationship types in Figure 2-2, a query is executed and displays sets of related nodes that contain the node ID of both the “start” node and “end” node.

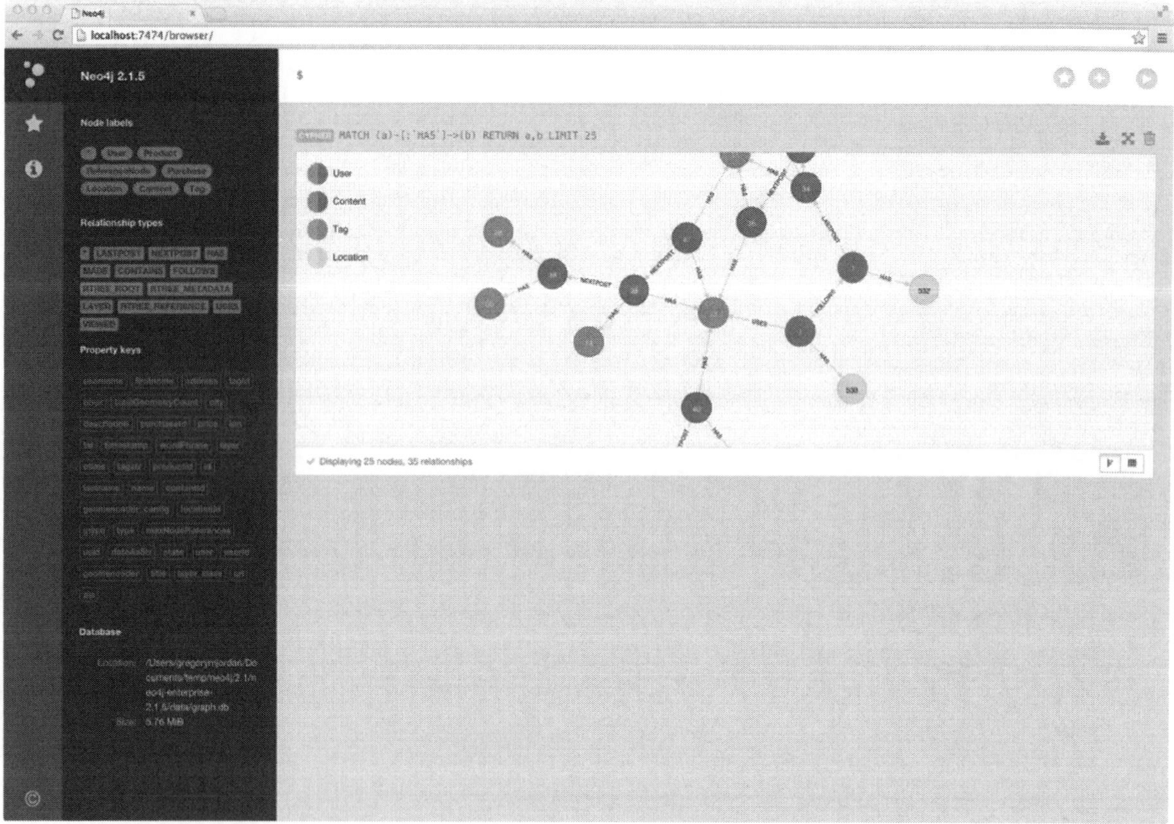

***Figure 2-2.** The Neo4j Browser showing a visual graph result after executing a Cypher command*

Figure 2-3 displays new tools in 2.x that offer shortcuts to perform common tasks. For example, one the new features available is the ability to save and archive Cypher queries for later use. In addition, some shortcuts provide a stubbed-out version of Cypher statements, such as the “Create a node” option under the *General* section.

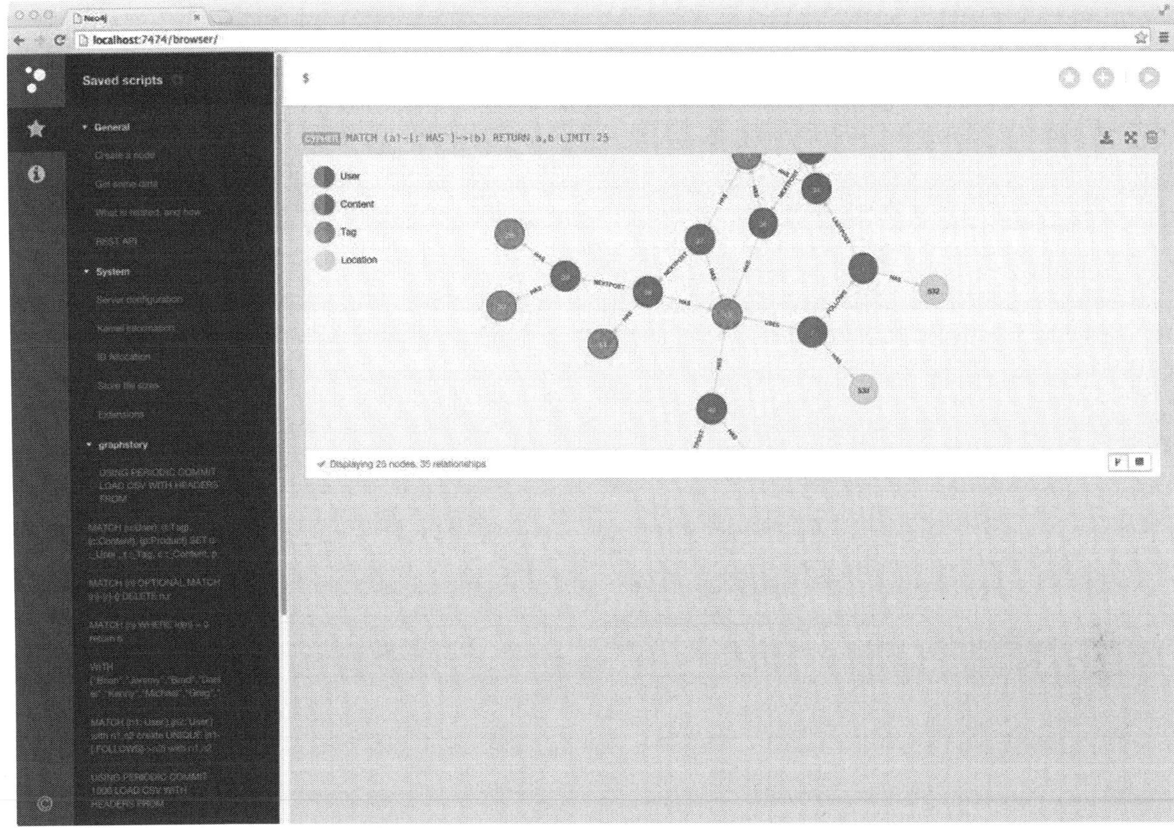

Figure 2-3. *The Neo4j Browser showing quick commands and saved scripts*

Introducing Cypher

Cypher is the declarative query language used for data manipulation in Neo4j. It is similar in many ways to how a relational database depends on Structured Query Language (SQL) to perform data operations. However, Cypher is not yet a standard graph database language that can interact with other graph database platforms. If you have some familiarity with SQL, you will probably be able grasp Cypher quickly. In addition, the expressive and relatively simple nature of Cypher allows it to be a tool that can be used beyond the confines of an organization's technology-centered groups, similarly to the way SQL is used in an ad hoc way outside many IT departments.

■ **Note** A *declarative language* is a high-level type of language in which the purpose is to instruct the application on what needs to be done or what you want from the application, as opposed to how to do it. A *procedural language*, by contrast, instructs the application what to do, step by step.

While there are a number of language drivers as well as a native API to execute CRUD operations, Cypher is the primary access tool for Neo4j.

Cypher will be covered in much greater detail in Chapter 4, but it is apposite at this point to get a feel for this centerpiece of the Neo4j world from the following simple examples of Cypher queries.

Create

CREATE is analogous to an INSERT statement in SQL. Listing 2-1 is a very basic example of a CREATE operation.

Listing 2-1. Example CREATE query statement

```
CREATE (n:Business { name : 'GraphStory', description : 'Graph as a Service' })
```

Start

In the latest version of Neo4j, the START clause has become an optional part of a read operation. The counterparts in SQL are portions of the FROM and WHERE clauses. In Listing 2-2, the lowercase business represents the variable being returned, which is closer to the SELECT clause in SQL, but in this case the business variable also returns all of the properties (or *columns*, as they are referred to in a relational database). The Business index is equivalent to a table in the relational database world, and the name='GraphStory' portion is similar to a WHERE clause.

Listing 2-2. Example START query statement on the index Business

```
START business=node:Business (name = 'GraphStory')
RETURN business
```

Match

A MATCH clause represents a similar operation as a JOIN would in SQL. The Cypher statement in Listing 2-3 displays how to return a collection of people who like GraphStory.

Listing 2-3. Sample MATCH query statement in earlier versions of Neo4j

```
START business=node:Business (name = 'GraphStory')
MATCH people-[:LIKE]->business
RETURN people
```

A shorter way to represent the same result is to use Label, which excludes the START clause. The example shown in Listing 2-4 is the current recommended way of executing a MATCH result.

Listing 2-4. The recommended way to execute a MATCH query statement

```
MATCH person-[:LIKE]->(b:Business { name: "Graph Story"})
RETURN person
```

Set

The SET statement is analogous to an UPDATE statement in SQL. Listing 2-5 is a basic example of a SET operation.

Listing 2-5. Example MATCH query statement

```
MATCH (b:Business { name: 'GraphStory' })
SET b.description = 'The Leading Graph Database as a Service Provider'
RETURN b
```

Summary

This chapter provided a quick overview of Neo4j, including the requirements for running the server in your local environment, as well as the steps to install for Windows, Linux/Unix, and Mac OSX. It also introduced the Cypher query language. The next chapter will discuss modeling for Neo4j and will begin to explore the Cypher language a bit more.

PART 2

Managing Your Data with Neo4j

CHAPTER 3

Modeling

This chapter reviews the elements that make up Neo4j and the proper way to view relationships within the model. This chapter recurs to some of the concepts first addressed in earlier chapters from the perspective of how modeling is handled within Neo4j. It also explores a little more of the Cypher language, but only as it applies to our modeling effort. Chapter 4 will deal with Cypher in greater depth. Finally, this chapter goes over some common models found in various domains and looks at some of the common issues that data architects and developers face when modeling for a graph. The chapter will begin with an overview of data modeling and why it can help ensure your application starts on a solid foundation.

Data Modeling

If you are comfortable with the concepts of modeling, feel free to skip ahead to the next section. If, however, you are still fairly new to data modeling or just need a refresher, this section will provide a quick conceptual overview and cover the basics for proper modeling.

Data Modeling Overview

Data models serve as visual representations of the specific data that will reside within database and almost exclusively in support of an external application. The models represent objects, such as a User or Shopping Cart, the connections between the objects, and the rules that determine how the objects are stored within the database. The model typically concentrates on what data will be stored and how it will be organized. The specific functions or how the application will operate on the model should be considered separate from the modeling tasks. One common analogy of the model are the blueprints of a house, where there is direction as to how the spaces are defined but the exact contents remain to be determined after the main construction is completed.

In addition, for the some areas the data model is independent from the constraints of the database platform. As you will see in the later sections of this chapter, there is a divergence that takes place when modeling relationships within a relational database versus modeling within Neo4j. In either event, the model still serves as the high-level, conceptual representation for all of the data points.

Why Is Data Modeling Important?

Regardless of whether you are using a graph database like Neo4j or a relational database, modeling is a critical part in helping to ensure your application's data can be stored and retrieved as efficiently as possible. In the case where there is a dedicated *database administrator* (DBA), the model is provided as a diagram—almost like a set of "blueprints"—to use as a guide while creating the actual database. In most cases, the model represents the basics of the tables, the primary and foreign keys, and the meta-information on properties, such as their type. The model might also contain constraint information, such as whether a value of field is required or can be null or empty.

Although the model can and likely will evolve over time, maintaining it in a diagram format or similar way is important to ensure an efficient and cohesive design. It could be argued that for some applications either the domain is limited enough or the objects representing the model are so well defined and documented that a model diagram is unnecessary. In addition, it has been suggested that the time involved to create a model diagram can slow down the development process.

However, most applications that start small will grow over time and the object code will—at some point—probably be passed from the initial developers to a new set of developers. Without a diagram to quickly demonstrate all of the data points represented within an application, the time and effort involved to explain the model will likely grow as well as make it much more difficult to most efficiently add, update, or remove specific pieces of the model.

Data Model Components

The data model is developed in the first stage of the project and will evolve over time. Even as relational databases have changed over the past forty years, they have retained certain design limitations, which, in turn, makes the initial data modeling task a critical path within the scope of an application development project. Although NoSQL options have helped the outcome of projects by lowering the risk of modifications to the model, the task of modeling is still critical to successful application development.

In the data modeling stage, whether with an agile focus or otherwise, the project team, specifically analysts and developers, will usually begin by having discussions with the application owners to understand the requirements of the model. These discussions should yield at least one important result, which is an *entity-relationship* (ER) diagram. The ER diagram is an important resource for an application project team because it provides a common understanding of how the application's data will be represented.

Entity-Relationship Model

Although many variants of the theme existed prior to it, the entity-relationship model is credited to Peter Chen in his 1976 paper, "The Entity-Relationship Model: Toward a Unified View of Data."[1] Chen's original description and design was adapted to more common usage today for data analysts and administrators. The ER model is specifically useful because of how well it maps to the structure of a relational model.

In addition, the ER model is fairly simple to create and can be understood by all members of the team and wider organization with minimal instruction as well as act as the instructions to one or more team members on how to specifically construct the database as it applies to the platform in use. Perhaps the most important aspect of the ER model is that it acts as a universal way to communicate. Without its ubiquity, the method and manner of describing and visualizing data models could vary from project to project.

Entities

Entities are characteristically viewed as the central objects within the ER model. Most often data modelers will strive to use terms that are easily recognizable to each member of the project team in order to describe the entity. Conversely, you should stay away from terminology that is not commonly used or not the default within the domain or industry. For example, when modeling applications that deal with constructing residential areas, it would be more common to use the word "house" rather than "abode"—even though they are synonyms.

We can see in Figure 3-1 that the model diagram employs the use of a box—a standard shape to symbolize entities. In some model diagrams, the entities—as well as the relationships and attributes—will be shown in specific colors to further visually distinguish each part of the model.

---

[1]Peter Chen, "The Entity-Relationship Model: Toward a Unified View of Data," September 22–24, 1975, ACM Transactions on Database Systems, Vol. 1, No. 1 (March 1976), pp. 9–36.

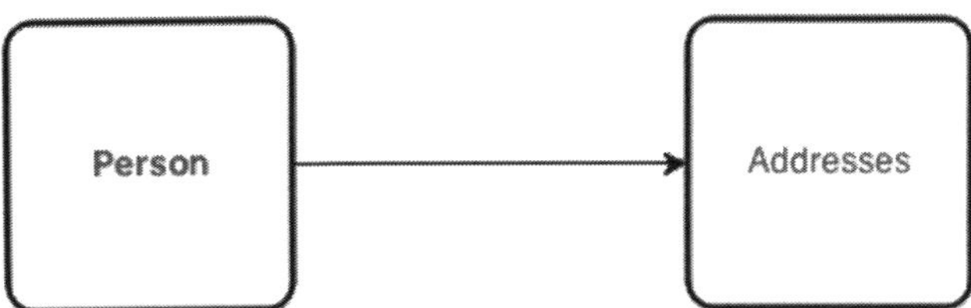

Figure 3-1. *A simple ER model*

Relationships

As you might surmise from Figure 3-1, relationships represent the connections or associations between entities. In most cases, the relationship can be expressed using a verb. For example, if you were going to connect people who use your application with where they live, you would typically express it as "a user has addresses." In addition, you would normally want to address cardinality, which measures how many times one entity type might be connected to another distinct entity type. To express that a user has many addresses, the cardinality would be denoted as "1:M" (one-to-many).

The relationship objects within the ER diagram usually address the optionality and direction of the association between entities as well. Addressing the optionality of the relationship can be handled conveniently through its cardinality. For example, you can express an optional relationship by showing its cardinality as "0:1". The direction of the relationship—often referred to as the *parent-child*—is shown by using an arrow pointing from the parent entity to the child entity, e.g. Person ➤ Address. In addition to arrows and lines with numeric representations, cardinality, direction, and optionality can be expressed graphically. Figure 3-2 displays the special symbols that are often used in ER diagrams to express relationships between entities: in this case, a relationship of one to many as one person could have many addresses.

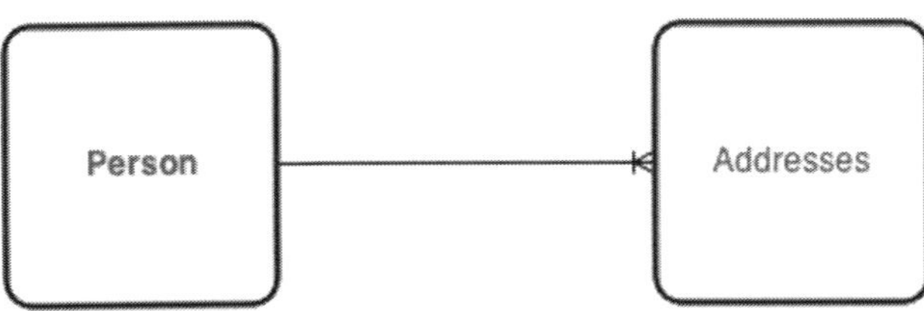

Figure 3-2. *A simple ER model*

Attributes

Attributes act as an identity, characteristic, or descriptor for an entity. For example, a User entity might use an identity attribute (also known as a *key*) which is named "Person ID". The "Person ID" attribute can be used to identify a specific instance of that entity type. In the case of descriptor attribute, the User entity might include "Person Name" or "Person Email."

In some entities, a single attribute might contain one or more of its sibling attributes, which is referred to as a composite attribute. For example, the Address entity could have the attributes number, street, city, state, and ZIP code, which together form the composite attribute called "Address", shown in Figure 3-3.

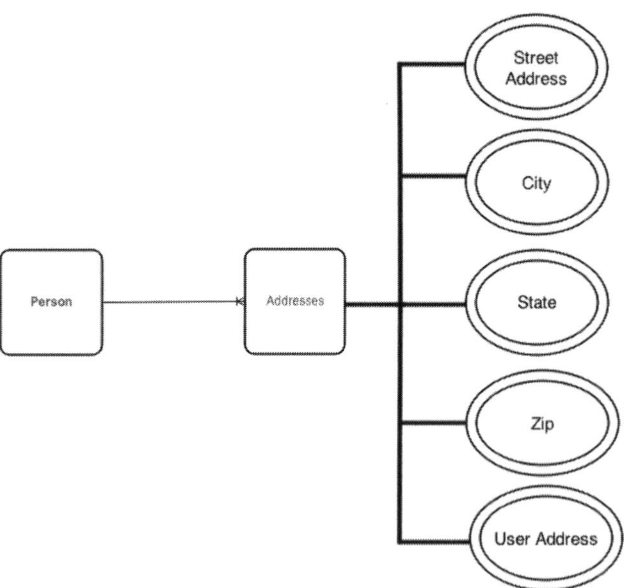

Figure 3-3. *A ER model with attributes*

Challenges in Using Entity-Relationship Modeling with Neo4j

Traditional entity-relationship models accept information and content that can be freely and easily contained within a relational database and are typically only a good match for a relational structure. In fact, they are insufficient for models in which the data cannot be suitably represented in relational form, as is the case with frequently changing, semi-structured data. One of the biggest challenges for many applications is the possible frequency and scope of change to the way model is structured. As detailed in Chapter 1, these types of modifications for relational systems are nontrivial, involve at least moderate risk, and are often significant causes for changes from one database platform to another.

Modeling with Neo4j

This section begins to build out the model for the application to be discussed in the later chapters of the book. The model contains some likely familiar themes in terms of its structure and includes five areas that have been identified as the most significant portions of both consumer and business data: *social, intent, consumption, interest,* and *location* graphs. These five graph types are certainly not the only use cases that make sense for Neo4j, but they are in wide use and intrinsically shaped.

As part of our examination of the graph model for these areas, we will examine the companion model structure as designed for a relational database. As noted in the data model overview section, a divergence takes place when modeling relationships within a relational database versus modeling within Neo4j. The divergence is not significant in terms of the data being captured, but, as Table 3-1 shows, the main components of an entity-relationship model in Neo4j may be known by different names and take vastly different shapes.

Table 3-1. *The Main Components of the ER Model Compared to Neo4j*

Entity—Relationship	Neo4j
Entity	Node
Relationship	Relationship
Attribute	Property

In either event, the model still serves as the high-level, conceptual representation for all of the data points. The companion model will also allow us to see the transformation that would occur when moving from the relational setting to the graph setting. Again, we will explore a bit more of the Cypher language in this chapter but only as it applies to our modeling aim. In addition, your preferred programming language is important to how you might consider some aspects of your model, but it is not critical to understanding the essential concepts for modeling with Neo4j.

Modeling Relationships

As you will likely find in working more frequently with graphs, the node types can seem more natural than tables, especially when creating and managing relationships. However, there are some common pitfalls or issues that can surface during the first exercises in modeling.

Directed relationships are an important aspect of graph databases and understanding how they should be modeled is necessary to improving the design, efficiency and manageability of your Neo4j database. The example in Figure 3-4 clearly denotes the direction to infer that "Greg works at GraphStory." In turn, this relationship implies that "GraphStory is an employer of Greg."

Figure 3-4. *Directed relationship type*

It is not necessary to explicitly add both relationship types, as shown in Figure 3-5, because one directed connection, by definition, suffices for the other direction. In fact, the speed of traversing the graph is not dependent on the direction.

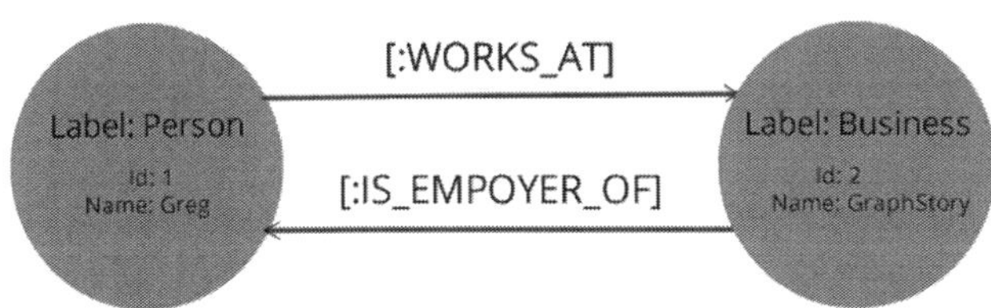

Figure 3-5. *Two relationship connections are unneccesary as the first implies the other*

While some connections between nodes naturally suggest how the direction should be set, others have a mutual or bidirectional relationship. Consider Figure 3-6, in which "GraphStory is a partner with NeoTechnology." In these bidirectional relationships, a second relationship connection, as with directed relationship, is unnecessary. Again, as is the case with directed relationships, it is faster to have a single relationship with an arbitrary direction.

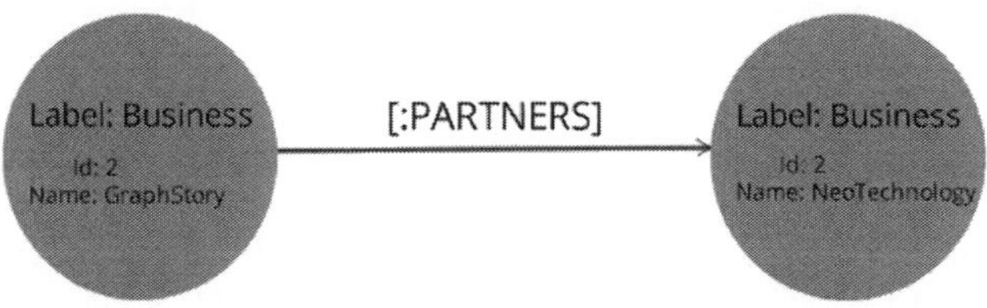

Figure 3-6. *Bidirectional relationship with an arbitrary direction*

Modeling Constraints

Ensuring that specific properties within the model remain unique is an important feature of any database and Neo4j is no different. With Neo4j 2.0, the concept of adding unique constraints based on labels was added. You can use unique constraints, as shown in Listing 3-1, to ensure that property values are unique for all nodes with a specific label. If you are creating the constraint after nodes have been created, then be aware that the new constraint could take some time to become enforced as any existing data must be scanned beforehand.

Listing 3-1. Creating a Unique Constraint

```
CREATE CONSTRAINT ON (business:Business) ASSERT business.businessname IS UNIQUE
```

When adding a unique constraint on a node's property, please note that this process will also create an index on the specific property and, therefore, you will not be able to add a separate index for the property. The index can be used to perform lookups for specific nodes. If you need for some reason to remove the constraint, as shown in Listing 3-2, and require an index on that property, then you will need to create a new index to support lookups.

Listing 3-2. Dropping a Unique Constraint

```
DROP CONSTRAINT ON (business:Business) ASSERT business.businessname IS UNIQUE
```

Modeling Use Cases

To begin building out the model for the application to be developed in the later chapters of the book, the following sections examine in turn the five areas identified as the most significant portions of consumer and business data—namely, social, interest, consumption, location, and intent graphs.

Social Graph

The social graph is the most widely discussed type of graph in the list of graph use cases. In its more well-known incarnation, the social graph represents the degree of connection between users on a particular application, such as Twitter. Facebook's social graph is the largest social graph in the world, developed on a mostly proprietary technology stack.

In Neo4j, the social graph is typically defined in one of two manners. The first is a direct connection that implies a mutual connection, which is similar to the approach user connections are made on Facebook. The second approach is where one user follows another user, similar to the connections created on Twitter. In Figure 3-7 and 3-8, we can see how both of these connections methods might be modeled within a relational database.

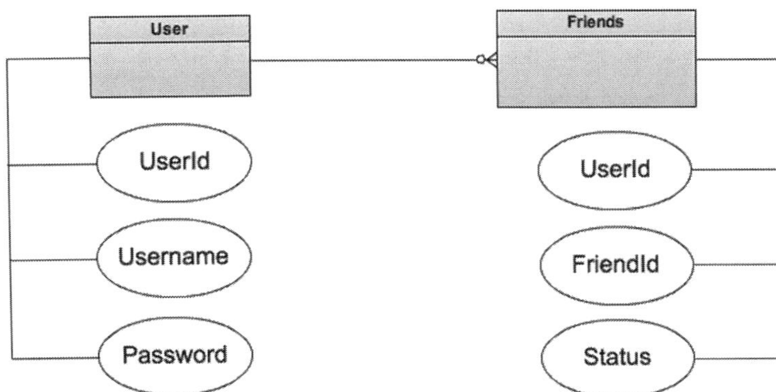

Figure 3-7. *Entity-relationship diagram with mutual connections*

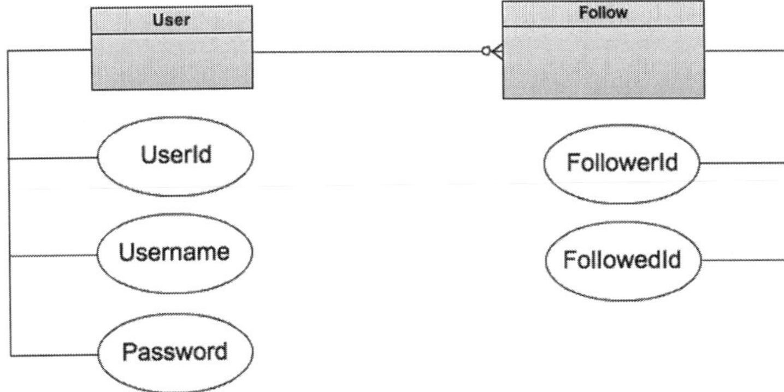

Figure 3-8. *Entity-relationship diagram with a one-way connection*

Figures 3-9 and 3-10 show how the same relationships would be modeled for Neo4j. In Figure 3-9, the direction is shown as a single relationship between two nodes. As mentioned earlier in this chapter, you should avoid duplicating a typed relationship between two nodes. However, this is one exception to the directionality of relationship modeling, as it is necessary to define whether the relationship is mutual and, indirectly, allows for certain features to be enabled.

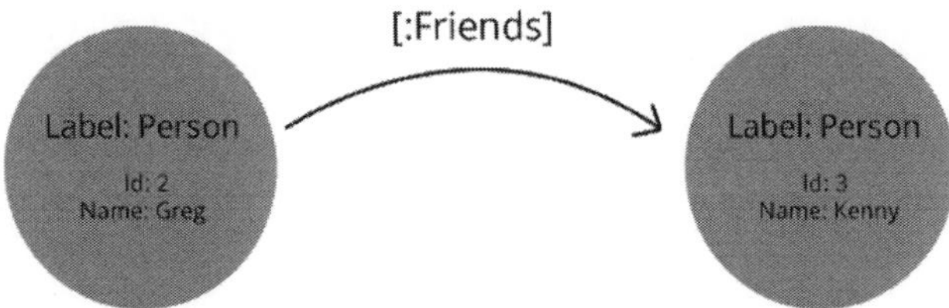

Figure 3-9. *Graph diagram with mutual connection. The direction implies who made the request*

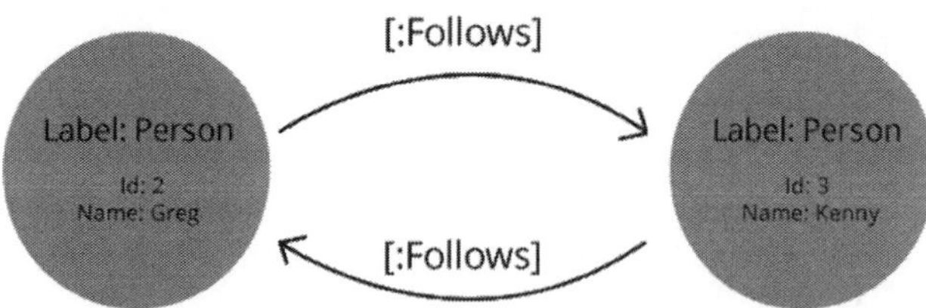

Figure 3-10. *Graph diagram with specific directed connections*

While deciding the manner in which your social model should be established, it is important to consider that there is more than just a technology decision at stake, but, potentially, a business decision as well. While both models allow for exploring connections in either direction from a technical standpoint, the bidirectional relationship implies that only one user action needs to occur in order to establish a mutual connection.

In addition, using the bidirectional or mutual option, by definition, will reduce the number of relationships comparatively by 50 percent. The problem of dense nodes—think of any celebrity who might have millions of followers but only follows a few other users—is less a factor in performance in the latest version of Neo4j. However, directional relationships can sometimes have an impact and need to be considered carefully. For the purposes of the book's example application, we will consider the directional relationship for the social aspect, such as the connection method found in applications such as Twitter.

Interest Graph

The interest graph is closely connected to the intent graph. However, the interest graph is principally concerned with the connecting a person with her specific interests. In that sense, the interest graph would allow for an application to make recommendations regarding related items of interest much in the same way a thesaurus can offer synonyms of a specific word. When combining the interest graph with a person's demographic or social graph, an application can make recommendations that typically have a higher degree of connectedness and relevance. Figure 3-11 demonstrates how an interest graph could be created within a relational model.

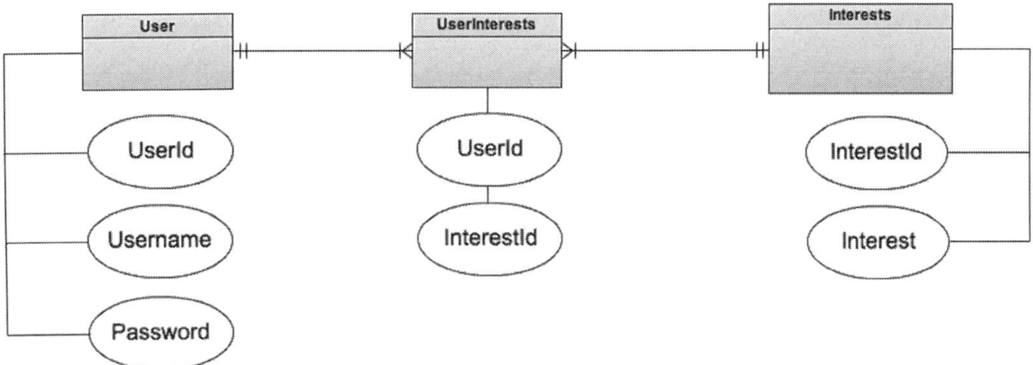

***Figure 3-11.** Entity relationship diagram with a user's interests*

Figure 3-12 shows the interest graph as it could be modeled for Neo4j. The interesting aspect in this graph type is how the named relationship in this model, "UserInterests", could be quickly modified to show a degree of interest and the date and time when the interest was established.

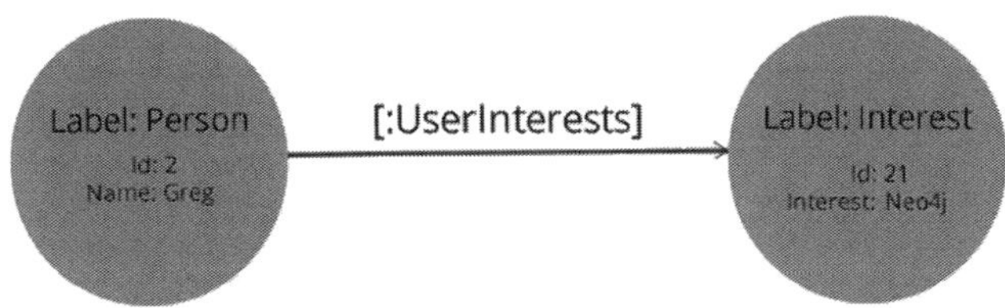

***Figure 3-12.** Graph diagram with a user's interests*

As you can see in Figure 3-13, adding a simple measurement for frequency is fairly trivial. Although adding the same measurement in the relational model is possible, the change would probably not happen as easily. More importantly, connecting people with those who have similar interests will be even easier and much faster as the degrees of connection begin to increase.

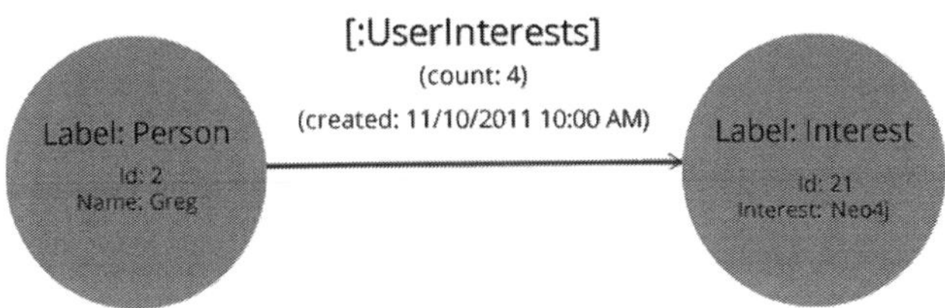

***Figure 3-13.** Graph diagram with a user's interests, including properties for the named relationship*

Consumption Graph

While the consumption graph is primarily focused on the items that one might purchase – whether it is a good or service – it also can be viewed from perspectives outside of pure commerce, such as the consumption of video content or other digital content. In that sense, it is related somewhat to the Interest graph.

Figure 3-14 displays how consumption might be modeled within a relational database. In this case, the model could have taken the form of an e-commerce product catalog.

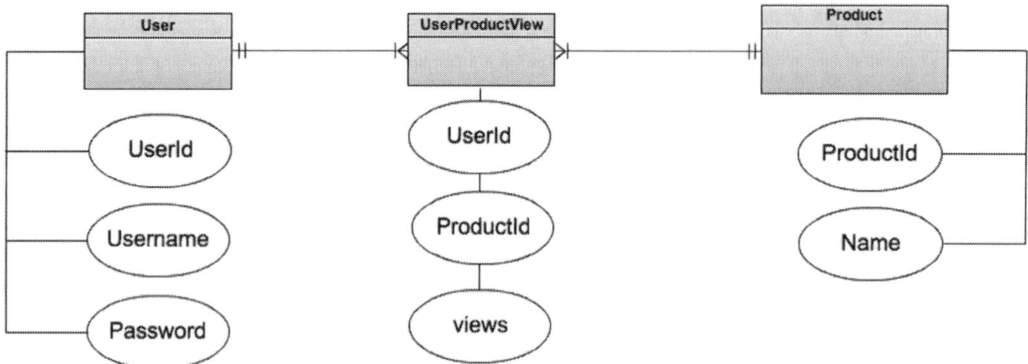

Figure 3-14. *Entity relationship diagram with a user's product views*

To gain a wider view of consumption, we are more interested in viewing consumption as a whole and not just in terms of retail items. Therefore, the model needs to be expanded to account for other forms of consumption, as shown in the relational model in Figure 3-15. In expanding this beyond the simple commerce system, one method to accomplish this feature is to modify the join table to ensure that it provides a type. As you might surmise, expanding the scope of the consumption view can get unmanageable very quickly.

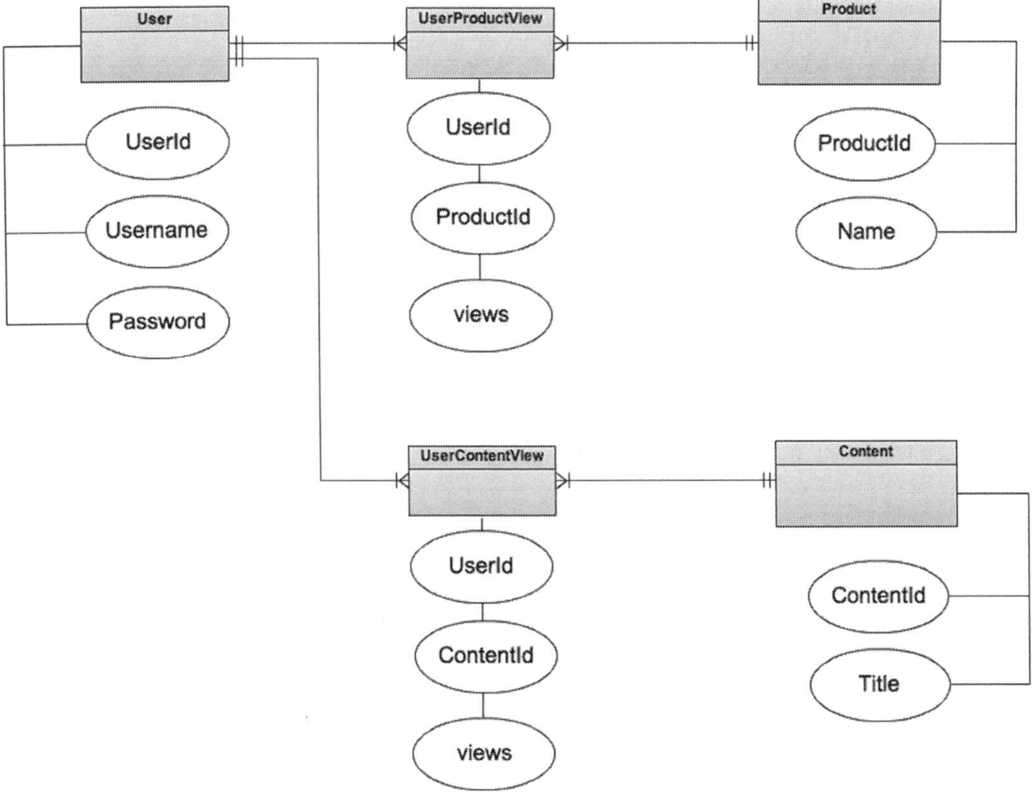

***Figure 3-15.** Entity relationship diagram with a user's product views and content views*

However, we can see in Figure 3-16 that creating relationships between different node types in Neo4j is fairly clear and can be quickly expanded beyond its initial scope.

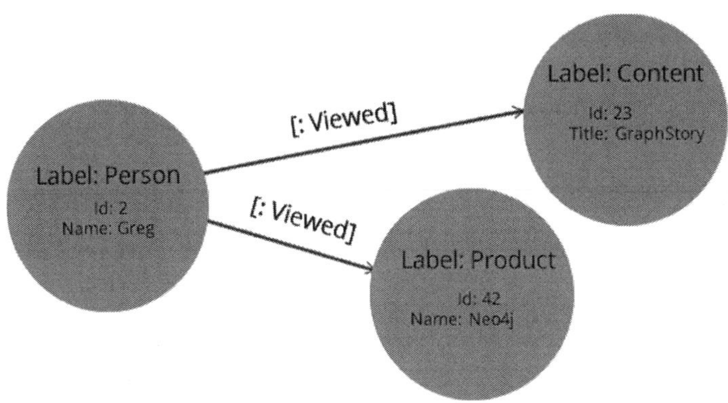

***Figure 3-16.** Graph diagram with a user's product views and content views*

Location Graph

A Gartner study referred to this graph use case as the *mobile graph*, but a better name would be the *location graph*. The name *mobile graph* carries an implication that it is applied to devices within a specific network, such as a cellular provider. However, that specific scope would likely limit the effectiveness of its practical use because it would be confined to a specific network or mobile devices.

The location graph would be better applied to a broad scope of any object that has been connected to a specific location. The relational model design for that scope is shown in Figure 3-17, which displays a user connected to addresses that could have multiple types, such as mailing address or billing address.

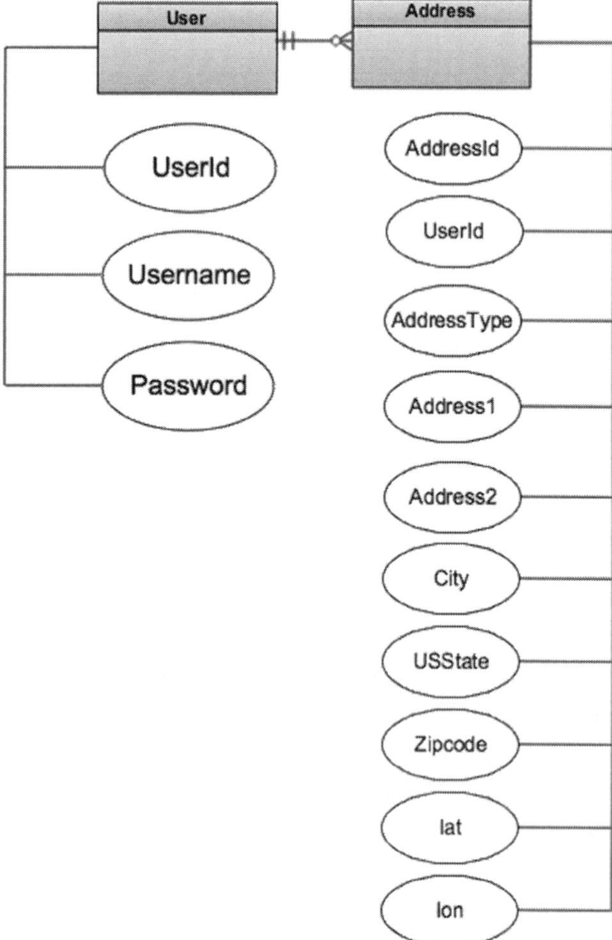

Figure 3-17. *Entity-relationship diagram of locations*

To address the domain in a graph, the location model can be created using a node type called location, but use one of at least to ways to manage the type of location as demonstrated in Figures 3-18 and 3-19. In Figure 3-18, we use labels to represent address types. Using this approach, new types of locations can be added to application design more easily.

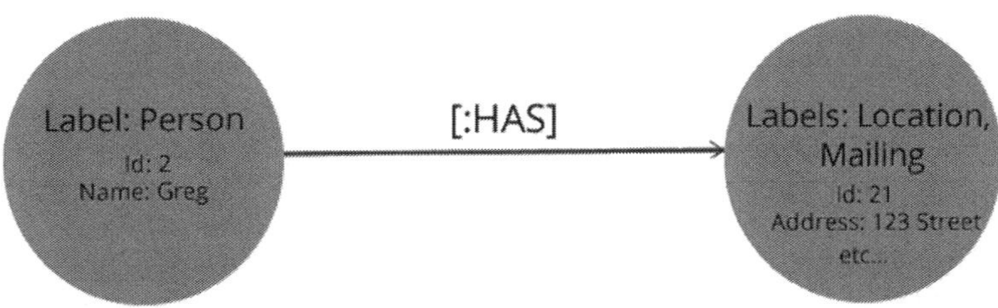

Figure 3-18. *Using labels to represent location or address types*

Figure 3-19 uses relationships to represent address types. Using this approach, new types of locations can also be added to application design more easily. In addition, we can add properties to the relationship, such as "Greg's Mailing Address".

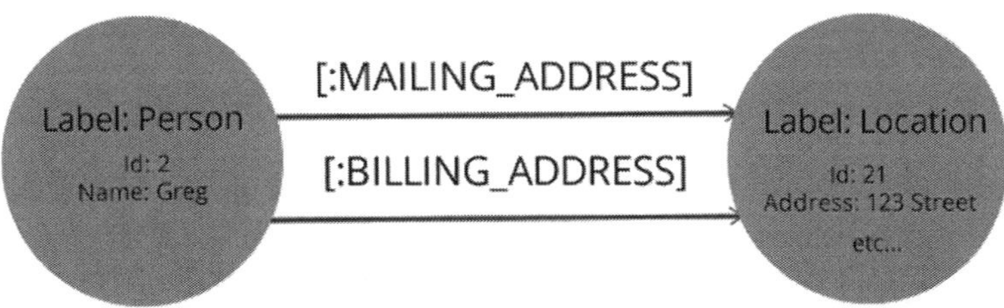

Figure 3-19. *Using relationships to connect location or address types to a user*

In addition to handling the model more elegantly, we could more easily connect other node types to these locations if the scope of the application changes. Finally, we can use the Neo4j spatial plugin to handle geo searches such as locations within a boundary.

Intent Graph

The intent graph seeks to map out a motivation or reasoning using a combination of other subgraphs from social, consumption, interest, mobile and location. The intent graph might also be defined as the predictive graph in that it uses those subgraphs to make predictions based on formulized intent. Based on those subgraphs, applications can make suggestions or provide options that are in line with the calculated user intent and as such the value and complexity of the intent graph is high.

For example, it would extremely valuable for Amazon—as well as other retailers—to understand how to ensure adequate inventory and minimal time-to-delivery for any product they offer. While Amazon can factor in certain events, such as popularity of a product, those factors provide a limited view as compared to coupling them with connections, interest and location. To complete such a task with relational databases, the model would take a form similar to the one shown in Figure 3-20.

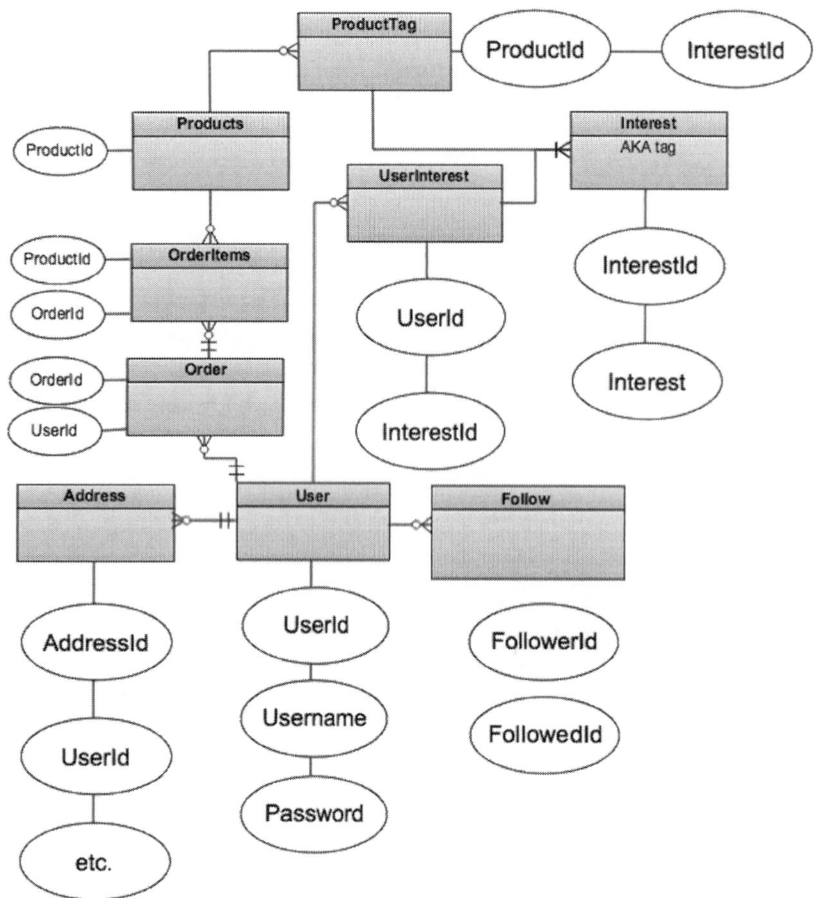

Figure 3-20. *Tables to show user purchase intent, aka recommendations*

The relational model could simply provide User's friends that purchased certain Products, but to go deeper in the recommendation it would be helpful to connect the users to friends who are nearby, share the same interests as well as only show products that have the same interests, AKA "tags". Although doing this in a relational model is certainly achievable, the number of joins could impact performance as the network of users, products, locations and interests begins to grow. In addition, the query plan would need to be known ahead of time or dynamically generated.

We can see that in the graph model, shown in Figure 3-21, the has simpler way to display the interconnectedness of each of the other four graph types as well as the ability to quickly connect intent with location. In addition to creating an easy way to view, the query plan would not need to be precisely known ahead of time.

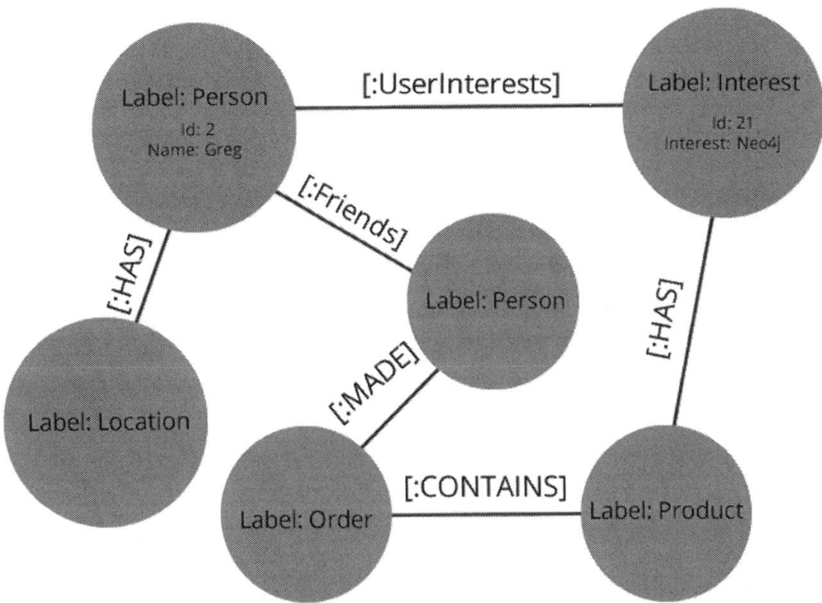

Figure 3-21. *Getting products ordered by friends who live nearby and use the same tags*

The intent graph has obvious and practical use for retailers, but there are number of other areas to which it could be applied. For example, hospitals and clinics could use the same combination of graphs to understand how to more effectively prepare for short-term seasonal staffing needs or even get a better understanding of the day-to-day change that could impact long-term treatment options.

Summary

This chapter provided an overview of data modeling and why it is important, and it contrasted the concepts when modeling from a relational database perspective and a graph perspective. We took a tour through five model types, exploring the differences when modeling for a relational database and modeling for Neo4j. The next chapter will examine importing data into a Neo4j graph database.

CHAPTER 4

Querying

Neo4j includes a powerful and expressive query language called *Cypher*. Cypher is a declarative query language that provides for very efficient reading and writing of data within Neo4j. This chapter starts with some background on Cypher and then moves to an overview of some basic Cypher operations.

If you are familiar with Structured Query Language (SQL), then you will notice some similarities between it and the Cypher language. The section "SQL to Cypher" describes some of those similarities and compares statements in SQL and Cypher.

This chapter goes on to discuss read statements, more advanced statements that exploit the benefits of various functions within Cypher, some elementary write statements, and some more advanced write operations. The chapter closes with a look at proper removal clauses and functions.

Cypher Basics

Cypher was created to be optimally accessible and simple to use for the widest possible array of users: software developers, business analysts, and technical architects. The most common query operations in Cypher are meant to focus on *what* needs to be retrieved and not on *how* it is retrieved. This section covers concepts that are important to understand as you begin to use Cypher—whether through REST, within the web UI, or embedded within your applications.

Note To get started with the Cypher and follow along with the examples in this chapter, you will need to have a running instance of Neo4j. To quickly setup a Neo4j server instance, go to `http://www.graphstory.com/practicalneo4j`. You will be provided with your own trial instance, a knowledge base, and email support from Graph Story.

Cypher shares some traits with SQL and uses similar keyword statements to run operations inside the Neo4j database. In many cases, a query is made up of several clauses to achieve an end result. As an example of Cypher's ability to focus on what is retrieved rather than on how the data is retrieved, a query may start by retrieving a large set of nodes from the graph and then ultimately return a subcollection of the large set—sometimes referred to as *subgraph*.

Transactions

Beyond its superior speed and scaling abilities, another significant advantage of using Neo4j for data operations is its transactional capability. Any Cypher query that modifies the graph will run in a transaction and will always either fully succeed on each query or not succeed at all.

When a data modification begins, it will either start with a new transaction or run within a transaction that already exists. If a transaction does not exist in the current operation, Cypher will create one and commit it once the query finishes. When a transaction is available within the current operation, the query will run inside that transaction and the success of entire transaction determines whether any data will be committed. Of course, it is sometimes necessary to add multiple queries within a single transaction, as follows:

1. Start a new transaction
2. Add the Cypher queries
3. Commit the transaction

A query will hold the changes in memory until the whole query has finished executing. A large query will consequently need a JVM with lots of heap space.

Compatibility

Neo4j is a stable, proven database option and supports mission-critical applications for companies big and small, but new features will be blended in over time. As Neo4j evolves, the Cypher language will evolve as well. The development team working on Neo4j, specifically on Cypher, is mindful of adding new syntax or modifying existing syntax to ensure minimal disruption in the application lifecycle. To that end, configuration options enable support of different Cypher versions.

■ **Note** Throughout this book, {NEO4J_ROOT} refers to the top-level installation directory for Neo4j.

To configure a specific Cypher version for use throughout an entire Neo4j system, you can modify a line within the {NEO4J_ROOT}/conf/neo4j.properties configuration file and specify the version you prefer as shown in Listing 4-1.

Listing 4-1. Explicitly Setting the Cypher Version in the Neo4j Configuration Properties

```
# Enable this to specify a parser other than the default one.
# cypher_parser_version=2.0
```

To enable a specific version on a case-by-case basis or to override a specific parser version, you can add the version number to your Cypher query, as shown in Listing 4-2.

Listing 4-2. Specifying the Cypher Version in a Cypher Query

```
CYPHER 1.9 START person=node(0)
WHERE person.name="Greg"
RETURN person
```

SQL to Cypher

If you understand and use SQL, moving into Cypher requires only a small conceptual adjustment. Using a CRUD (Create, Read, Update, Delete) comparison of some common SQL commands with how they would be written in Cypher, this section introduces the basics of Cypher through a prior knowledge of SQL. Later sections in this chapter cover Cypher in greater depth.

INSERT and CREATE

We start with a simple SQL command to add a User to a relational database and its counterpart in Cypher, as shown in Listings 4-3 and 4-4. In both examples, we employ the User part of the "schema", but the CREATE command in the Cypher example implies that values are going to be added and does not need an explicit VALUES command.

Listing 4-3. SQL Query to INSERT a User

```
INSERT INTO User (username) VALUES ("greg")
```

Listing 4-4. Cypher Query to CREATE a User

```
CREATE (u:User {username:"greg"})
```

Two unique and amazingly powerful advantages of Neo4j that can be realized through Cypher are adding additional schema descriptors to Node entities through labels and adding new properties without having to use an equivalent to the SQL ALTER TABLE command. In a relational database, if you needed another column, then you would need to run a SQL similar to that shown in Listing 4-5.

Listing 4-5. ALTER TABLE Statement in SQL

```
ALTER TABLE table_name
ADD my_new_column_name datatype
```

In Neo4j, if you wanted to add a new property to a node, then you would just add the property as a part of executing the cypher, as shown in Listing 4-6.

Listing 4-6. Add a New Property to a Node

```
CREATE (u:User {username:"greg",  business: "Graph Story"})
```

SELECT and START / MATCH

Listing 4-7 is the simple command to retrieve a User from a relational database; Listing 4-8 is its counterpart in Cypher. Some additional SELECT-style operations will be covered later in this chapter.

Listing 4-7. SQL Query to SELECT a User

```
SELECT *
FROM User
WHERE username = "greg"
```

Listing 4-8. Cypher Query to START with a Node of Type User

```
START user=node:User(username="greg")
RETURN user
```

Specifying the User part of the "schema" and identifying the property on which to search are common to both listings. However, the Cypher query uses START to locate a specific node with a specific value on a specific property. The necessary values to be returned are specified at the end of the statement.

Note In the latest release of Neo4j, you should use `MATCH` as opposed to `START` when performing reading operations.

In Listings 4-9 and 4-10, respectively, the SQL SELECT statement is modified slightly to return specific values, and the Cypher MATCH statement is used to perform a similar operation.

Listing 4-9. SQL Query to SELECT a User

```
SELECT fullname, email, username
FROM User
WHERE username = "greg"
```

Listing 4-10. Cypher Query to MATCH on a LABEL of Type User

```
MATCH (u:User {username: "greg"} )
RETURN u.fullname, u.email, u.username
```

Both listings again specify the User part of the "schema" and use a specific property upon which to search. However, the Cypher example now uses a MATCH statement to begin the query, then specifies the property and value, and, finally, specifies at the end of the statement the values to be returned.

UPDATE and SET

To modify existing records within a table, SQL provides an UPDATE command to alter existing values. In Cypher, the same principle is applied through the SET command, analogous to the SET command in SQL. Listings 4-11 and 4-12 contrast the two usages.

Listing 4-11. SQL Query to UPDATE a User

```
UPDATE User
SET fullname="Greg Jordan"
WHERE username="greg"
```

Listing 4-12. Cypher Query to UPDATE a User

```
MATCH (u:User {username: "greg"} )
SET u.fullname = 'Greg Jordan'
RETURN u
```

DELETE

Deleting a record in a relational database and in Neo4j are nearly identical in terms of syntax, the one exception being that the record search is performed before the DELETE command in Cypher, as shown in Listings 4-13 and 4-14.

Listing 4-13. SQL Query to DELETE a User

```
DELETE FROM User
WHERE username="greg"
```

Listing 4-14. Cypher Query to DELETE a User

```
MATCH (u:User {username: "greg"} )
DELETE u
```

If you delete a node that has relationships, you need to be sure to remove the relationships as well. The good news is that all of those steps can be done in the same command, as shown in Listing 4-15. A demonstration of how to remove specific relationships from nodes will be given later in this chapter.

Listing 4-15. Cypher Query to DELETE a User and Its Relationships

```
MATCH (u:User {username: "greg"} )-[r]-()
DELETE u
```

Cypher Clauses

Beyond the basics of Cypher covered through a CRUD comparison with SQL in the preceding section are many more commands and functions at your disposal. This section starts out with a look at some useful Cypher clauses.

Return

The RETURN clause simply returns the parts of the graph that are necessary for display or further analysis within your application. The RETURN is similar to the SELECT statement found in SQL. Typically, applications concerned with domains such as social networks want to analyze the relationships but only return properties for display. However, you can include nodes as well as relationships in your operations when necessary. Listings 4-16, 4-17, and 4-18 show various combinations available when using the RETURN clause.

Listing 4-16. RETURN the Nodes Found in the MATCH

```
MATCH (u:User {username: "greg"} )
RETURN u
```

Listing 4-17. RETURN a Property Using an Alias

```
MATCH (u:User {username: "greg"} )
RETURN u.username AS uname
```

Listing 4-18. RETURN All Elements Found in the MATCH

```
MATCH (u:User {username: "greg"} ) -[r]-()
RETURN u,r
```

WITH, ORDER BY, SKIP, and LIMIT

The clauses covered in this section are often used together to structure what is returned at different points in the query. The WITH clause allows you to pass a subquery result on to the next part of the query and to manipulate the data in some way before proceeding. In Listing 4-19, the WITH statement is used in conjunction with DISTINCT, which removes duplicates from the values.

In many applications, it is impractical and inefficient to return the entire result set for a specific query. For example, in a social graph application that contains status updates, it is likely that the users will only want to see the latest updates and have a way to periodically retrieve previous ones. In addition, it is more performant to request a specific result set and only later to retrieve subsequent subsets. Using the SKIP and LIMIT clauses allows for this to happen quite easily.

Many applications require data to be ordered based on a specific property that exists on an entity, such as alphabetical ordering of a list of users or second level of ordering on a linked list of status updates. Listing 4-19 shows the clauses used together to retrieve updates in a specific user's status update feed.

Listing 4-19. Using WITH, ORDER BY, SKIP and LIMIT to Retrieve Status Updates

```
MATCH (u:User {username: {u} })-[:FOLLOWS*0..1]->f
WITH DISTINCT f,u
MATCH f-[:CURRENT]-lp-[:NEXT*0..]-su
RETURN  su, f.username as username, f=u as owner
ORDER BY su.timestamp desc
SKIP {s}
LIMIT 4
```

Listing 4-20 shows the clauses used together to retrieve status updates in a specific user's status update feed, adding an ORDER BY to the WITH clause.

Listing 4-20. Retreiving Status Udpates of a User and the Users Being Followed

```
MATCH (u:User {username: {u} })-[:FOLLOWS*0..1]->f
WITH DISTINCT f,u
ORDER BY u.username
MATCH f-[:CURRENT]-lp-[:NEXT*0..]-su
RETURN  su, f.username as username, f=u as owner
ORDER BY su.timestamp desc
SKIP {s}
LIMIT 4
```

Using

When setting up a MATCH statement or WHERE clause with a Cypher query, Neo4j can use the property information supplied in the query to determine an index that should be used to perform the look up. However, the index selected by Neo4j might not be the best choice from a performance perspective because Cypher might begin the search in an index that is not applicable to the search. As shown in Listings 4-21 and 4-22, the USING clause allows you to specify an index that should be used (sometimes referred to as an *index hint*).

Listing 4-21. A Query with USING INDEX to Explicitly Specify an Index to Be Searched

```
MATCH (u:User)
USING INDEX u:USER(username)
WHERE u.username = 'greg'
RETURN u
```

If your query could achieve better performance by scanning all the nodes via a LABEL, use USING SCAN, as shown in Listing 4-22.

Listing 4-22. A Query with USING SCAN to Explicitly Specify an LABEL Type and the Filtering on a Property

```
MATCH (u:User)
USING SCAN u:USER
WHERE u.username = 'greg'
RETURN u
```

Reading

The preceding sections have covered a number of Cypher queries that read from the graph. This section digs a little deeper into a few of the reading clauses that will likely make up the majority of the read statements in your Neo4j applications.

Match

The MATCH clause is the primary clause for retrieving data from your graphs and specifying the starting points in your queries. Listings 4-23 through 4-26 exemplify ways that MATCH is used in combination with other clauses to return data.

Listing 4-23. MATCH Using a Label, Returning All Nodes of Type User

```
MATCH (u:User )
RETURN u
```

Listing 4-24. MATCH Using a Label and Property and Specifying a Relationship Type or Direction

```
MATCH (a:User {username:"greg"})--(b)
RETURN a,b
```

Listing 4-25. MATCH Using a Label and Property and a Label on the Other Node but No Specific Relationship Type or Direction

```
MATCH (u1:User {username: "greg"} )--(u2:User)
RETURN u1, u2
```

Listing 4-26. MATCH Using a Label and Property and Two Relationship Types

```
MATCH (u:User {userId:1} )-[:CURRENT|FAVORITE]-(s)
RETURN u,s
```

Optional Match

The OPTIONAL MATCH (Listing 4-27), which is a new clause in Neo4j 2.0, allows Cypher to match patterns against your graph database, but the primary difference is that if no matches are found, NULLs will be returned for any missing parts of the pattern. It is analogous to an outer join in SQL. In prior releases of Neo4j, a question mark was supplied next to the relationship type.

Listing 4-27. OPTIONAL MATCH

```
MATCH (u1:User {username: "greg"} )
OPTIONAL MATCH (u1)-[f:FOLLOWS]->(u2)
RETURN f
```

Where

WHERE is always used in conjunction with another clause, such as MATCH, WITH and/or START. Listings 4-28 through 4-32 exemplify the use of WHERE to filter on results with MATCH.

Listing 4-28. MATCH Where a Property Has a Certain Value

```
MATCH (u:User)
WHERE u.active = true
RETURN u
```

Listing 4-29. MATCH Where a Property Has a regex Match

```
MATCH (u:User)
WHERE u.username = "gre.*"
RETURN u
```

Listing 4-30. MATCH Using a Property regex Case-Insensitive Match

```
MATCH (u:User)
WHERE u. username = "(?i)GRE.*"
RETURN u
```

Listing 4-31. MATCH Where a Property Matches a Value in a Collection

```
MATCH (u:User)
WHERE u. username  IN ["greg","jeremy"]
RETURN u
```

Listing 4-32. MATCH Using a Property regex Case-Insensitive Match

```
MATCH (u:User {username: "greg"} )
WHERE NOT (f)-[:FOLLOWS]-(u)
RETURN f
```

Start

In certain instances, your application can provide a starting point with the query to begin at a certain point within the graph. Nonetheless, the START clause is optional and Cypher can infer a starting point based on other clauses within the query, as shown in Listings 4-33 and 4-34. Again, you should use `MATCH` in most read operations when specifying a beginning point in your statement. `START` should be used when working with legacy indexes.

Listing 4-33. START Using a Node id

```
START n=node (1)
RETURN n
```

Listing 4-34. START Using a Property in a Lucene Index

```
START n=node:nodes("username:greg")
RETURN n
```

Writing

The preceding sections covered a number of clauses that allow writing to occur within the graph. This section shows some clauses for writing to the graph.

SET

The "SQL to Cypher" section covered some common SET operations. Listings 4-35, 4-36, and 4-37 are further examples of using SET in Cypher.

Listing 4-35. Set Properties from a Map

```
MATCH (user { username: "greg" })
SET user += { active: TRUE , business: 'Graph Story' }
```

Listing 4-36. Set Multiple Properties in a SET

```
MATCH (user { username: "greg" })
SET user.business: 'Graph Story', user.lastname: 'Jordan'
```

Listing 4-37. Set Multiple Labels on a Node in a SET

```
MATCH (user { username: "greg" })
SET user :WRITER:DEVELOPER
```

REMOVE

DELETE allows you to remove nodes and relationships. To remove a property, however, you need to use the REMOVE clause. Listings 4-38 and 4-39 show how to remove properties from nodes and relationships.

Listing 4-38. Remove a Property from a Node

```
MATCH  (u1:User {username: "greg"} )
REMOVE u1.email
RETURN u1
```

Listing 4-39. Remove a Label from a Node

```
MATCH  (u1  {username: "greg"} )
REMOVE u1:User
RETURN u1
```

Summary

In this chapter, you learned about Cypher, Neo4j's declarative query language. It provides for very efficient reading and writing of data within Neo4j, and it shares similarities to SQL in the relational database world. You also learned that, although there are many different ways to find starting points within a Cypher query, most often a MATCH should be used to filter on a beginning node or set of nodes. Finally, you reviewed the Cypher commands and clauses that will most often be used within your applications. The next chapter discusses importing and managing data from outside data sources.

CHAPTER 5

Importing from Another Data Source

One of the most common tasks you need to perform when working with a new database technology is importing and syncing data from another data source. This chapter explores what you should consider before beginning that process. It discusses the processes and tools for importing data into Neo4j and how to select the best process or tool for a specific situation.

In selecting from among the many ways for importing or synchronizing from another data source, give careful consideration to your goal. To avoid wasting time on a process or tool that does match the scope of your work, start from the goal of the data import and work back from that point. Each new version of Neo4j makes the process of importing data easier, but the tools and processes form only part of the import equation.

Import Considerations

To work backward from your goal, you need to be able to answer the question, "What's the purpose of the data import?" If your goal is to have only enough representative data to test your application, some of the processes and tools described in this chapter would be overkill and may be ruled out.

On the other hand, if your application will import existing data from a production data source or if you need to consider options such as near real-time syncing of data, then you will probably need to consider a mix of tools to complete the work. Moreover, directly importing data might not always make sense, such that incorporating data-as-a-service might be a better fit for the goal. Table 5-1 tabulates a number of scenarios that you are apt to encounter, together with appropriate tools. This chapter presents some guidelines about which tools to use and when.

Table 5-1. *Considerations for Importing Data*

Task	Stage	Frequency	Data Size	Tool(s)
Import	Development/Test	One time	>5M	Built-in tools
Migrate	Production	One time	<10M	Built-in tools, programmatic
Import	Production	Scheduled	Varied	Built-in tools, programmatic Third-party datasource tools
Sync (to Neo4j)	Production	Scheduled	Varied	Built-in tools, programmatic, messaging queue system

The next section offers some examples of using specific tools for specific jobs in importing or syncing data.

Examples

The types of tools you use for your imports or synchronizations should be based on your goals. The following scenarios commonly occur in development:

- A new application without legacy data
- An existing application that is switching to a graph database
- An existing application that will use a graph and another data store

---

■ **Note** To get the working examples for this chapter, go to `www.graphstory.com/practicalneo4j` and download Chapter 5.

Test Data with Cypher

If you are building out a new application that has no any legacy data, your best bet is to use Cypher in one form or another to import data. For example, creating a spreadsheet with sample data and saving it as a CSV file can be done fairly easily and quickly. Next, you could use the newly available `LOAD CSV` to take a few generated files and run a quick import.

However, there is an alternative that might be acceptable during the development and testing stages, depending on your application's or organization's demands. By using a few Cypher statements, you can build out a small, representative graph for your application and do so within just a few minutes.

In this example, we will create a very small graph that represents users in a social network. We will use the Twitter method of user relationships, which is a bidirectional relationship called `FOLLOWS`. We will start by first creating a list of users by using a Cypher statement. Again, we are just aiming for some test data to use in our fledgling application, so the variation on the size of the user set will be limited but still representative of what the application requires and will take only a few minutes to run. Listing 5-1 shows the Cypher command that will create the users.

Listing 5-1. Cypher Command to Create the Users

```
WITH
["Brian","Jeremy","Brad","Daniel","Kenny","Michael","Greg","Leonard"] AS fname,
["Seesharp","Phpish","Pychamp","Rubyster","Relman","Writesalot","Goodguy","Graphman"] AS lname
FOREACH (r IN range(0,7) |
        CREATE (:User {id:r, username : lower(fname[r % size(fname)]+""+r), firstname : fname[r %
size(fname)], lastname : lname[r % size(lname)]  }
));
```

■ **Note** Adding a large number of nodes or relationships to your local graph or remote graph will take some time. In addition, you should have—at a minimum—4 GB to spare for the Neo4j server for the best performance.

Listing 5-1 creates eight users in the graph with a distinct ID and username but keeps the first name and last name as set in the Array. By running `MATCH (n:`User`) RETURN n LIMIT 25`, you can verify the users were added. Next, we will associate the users to each other by adding the `FOLLOWS` relationship, as shown in Listing 5-2.

Listing 5-2. Cypher Command for All Users to Follow All Other Users

```
MATCH (n1:`User`),(n2:`User`)
WITH n1,n2
CREATE UNIQUE (n1-[:FOLLOWS]->n2)
WITH n1,n2
WHERE n1<> n2
RETURN n1,n2
```

When you run the Cypher statement in the web UI from Listing 5-2, the result—when separated a bit for readability—should look like the image in Figure 5-1 and show all users following all other users.

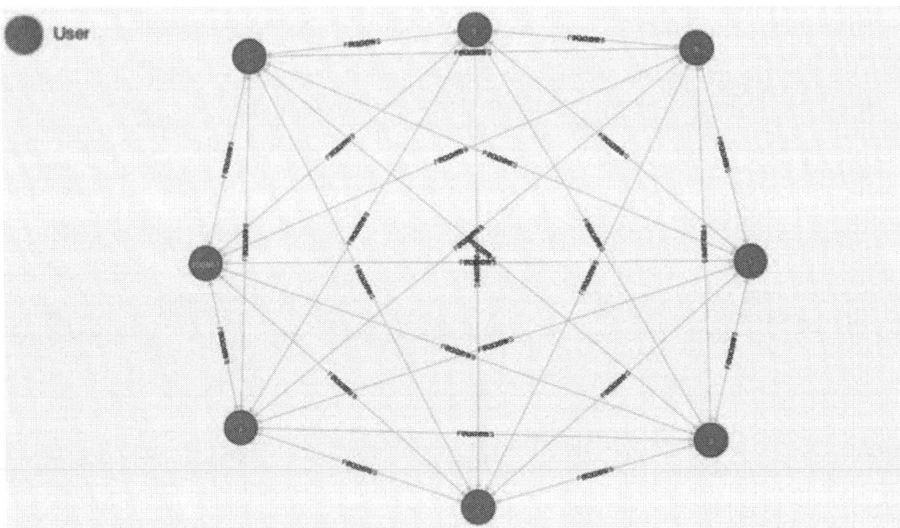

Figure 5-1. *Graph of all users following all other users*

Test Data with Load CSV

When you are building an application and the data needs to be representative and as close to production-ready as possible, using the LOAD CSV option is the next step. In this example, we are going to stick with the social application example and use CSV files to generate users, relationships between users, posts, and posts that users have selected as their favorites.

■ **Note** Before running a LOAD CSV command in a live environment, it would be prudent to test the CSV file before creating any new nodes or relationships. One way to test would be to execute a LOAD CSV command and simply RETURN the contents, as shown in Listing 5-3.

Listing 5-3. Cypher Command to Test CSV File

```
LOAD CSV WITH HEADERS FROM "http://site.com/THEFILE.csv" AS csvLine
RETURN csvLine.header1, csvLine.header2, csvLine.headerX
```

The first CSV file we will import is going to create the User nodes. In this example, the users have a `userId` (which we can reference later to create relationships), a username, and a first name. The Cypher statement also includes a PERIODIC COMMIT statement to ensure that the query data does not stack up.

Creating a Unique Index

Before you run the LOAD CSV comment in Listing 5-3, you need to create an index for later lookups in the import process. Because you know ahead of time that the `userId` value will be unique, you can add a unique constraint that creates a unique index, which is faster than a standard index. In your web UI, you can run the code in Listing 5-4 to create the unique index on the User node.

Listing 5-4. Cypher Command for All Users to Follow All Other Users

```
CREATE CONSTRAINT ON (u:User) ASSERT u.userId IS UNIQUE
```

Next, by running the Cypher statement in Listing 5-5, you add the Users to the graph. You can verify the results by running `MATCH (n:`User`) RETURN n LIMIT 25`.

Listing 5-5. Cypher Command for All Users to Follow All Other Users

```
USING PERIODIC COMMIT 1000
LOAD CSV WITH HEADERS FROM "http://www.graphstory.com/practicalneo4j-book/code/chapter5/csv/list_of_
users.csv" AS csvLine
CREATE (u:User { userId: toInt(csvLine.userId), username: csvLine.username, firstname: csvLine.
firstname })
```

Creating Relationships

The second CSV file we import will create the relationships between the nodes. There are number of methods to create the CSV for this purpose. In this case, I just created a simple PHP script to generate a CSV file, as shown in Listing 5-6. This script creates a way for each user to randomly follow ten other users in the graph.

Listing 5-6. PHP Script to Create Followers for Users

```
$fp = fopen('followers.csv', 'w');
fputcsv($fp, array('userId', 'followerid'));
//total number of userIds in the user list
$totalusers = 5492;
for ($i = 1; $i <= $totalusers; $i++) {
        $rn = rand(1, $totalusers);
        $c = 1;
        for ($j = $rn; $j <= $totalusers; $j++) {
                $c++;
                if($j! = $i) {
                        fputcsv($fp, array($i, $j));
                }

                if($c == 10){
                        break;
                }
        }
}
fclose($fp);
echo 'Data saved to csvfile.csv';
```

Loading the Relationships

Next, you can use the LOAD CSV command, as shown in Listing 5-7, to match the userId via the unique index and to create a relationship of FOLLOWS between the nodes.

Listing 5-7. Cypher Command for All Users to Follow All Other Users

```
USING PERIODIC COMMIT
LOAD CSV WITH HEADERS FROM "http://www.graphstory.com/practicalneo4j-book/code/chapter5/csv/
followers.csv" AS csvLine
MATCH (u1:User { userId: toInt(csvLine.userId)} ) ,(u2:User { userId: toInt(csvLine.followerid)} )
CREATE (u1)-[:FOLLOWS]->(u2)
```

By running the command shown in Listing 5-8, you can output a sample of the new relationships created with the LOAD CSV command, which should look similar to the output shown in Figure 5-2.

Listing 5-8. Cypher Command for All Users to Follow All Other Users

```
MATCH (a)-[:`FOLLOWS`]->(b) RETURN a,b LIMIT 25
```

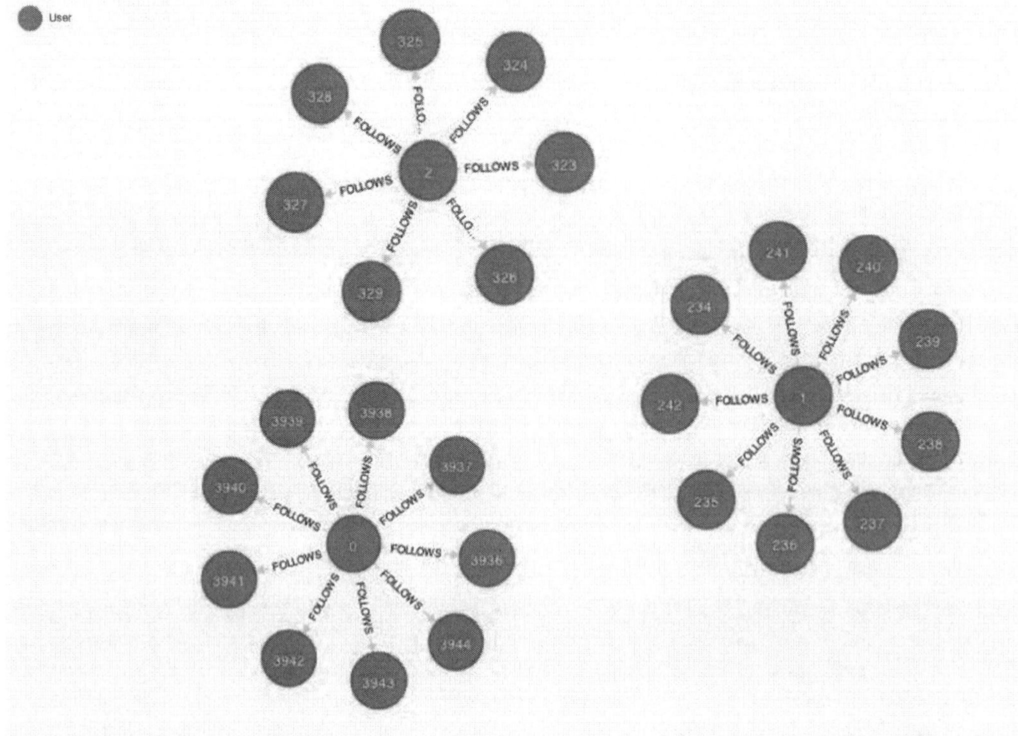

Figure 5-2. *Graph of all users following all other users*

Adding the Content Using a Linked List

The next step in the process is loading content and relating them to Users. For the purposes of this example, I generated three separate CSV files that we are using to create a linked list of status updates, rather than relating each specific status update directly to a User. Although the number of status updates is limited to three in this example, in a real-world application the expectation is that the number of status updates will grow.

Indeed, some users may add thousands of status updates, so the number of direct relationships could grow into a densely connected Node. The latest release of Neo4j helps with the dense node problem by splitting relationships by type and direction, which will help as Users take on more followers and follow other Users.

However, it also makes sense to address this from a graph perspective to improve performance and design. In most cases, the status updates will be returned in pages of a specific value—say, 15 per page—and the application will not require immediate access to each connected status update other than through an identifier to show a single status. In addition, the retrieval and filter of nodes can happen with the sequence of nodes already in their desired order.

Loading the "Current" Status

The first file contains the "current" status update made by a user. The current status refers to the most recent status update for a specific user. I will connect them to the user by taking the userId and matching it to a User, and then by creating a relationship type called CURRENT. First, I execute a LOAD CSV command (Listing 5-9) to ensure that the data has the necessary properties.

Listing 5-9. Loading the Current Status to Review before Importing

```
LOAD CSV WITH HEADERS FROM "http://www.graphstory.com/practicalneo4j-book/code/chapter5/csv/
currentstatus.csv" AS csvLine
return csvLine.statusId, csvLine.userId, csvLine.status
limit 5
```

Listing 5-10 provides the LOAD CSV command that you will need to execute to load the status updates into the graph. As an added bonus, this will also create the relationship between the User and its current Status.

Listing 5-10. Importing the CURRENT Status Updates

```
USING PERIODIC COMMIT
LOAD CSV WITH HEADERS FROM "http://www.graphstory.com/practicalneo4j-book/code/chapter5/csv/
currentstatus.csv" AS csvLine
MATCH (u1:User { userId: toInt(csvLine.userId)} )
CREATE (u1)-[:CURRENT]->(s:Status { statusId: toInt(csvLine.statusId), userId: csvLine.userId,
status: csvLine.status })
```

■ **Important** Before you run the LOAD CSV for the CURRENTSTATUS import, be sure to create another unique index by running `CREATE CONSTRAINT ON (s:Status) ASSERT s.statusId IS UNIQUE.`

Once the command is run, you can run the following command `MATCH (u:User {userId:1} )-[:CURRENT]->(s) RETURN u,s` and you should see a result like the one shown in Figure 5-3.

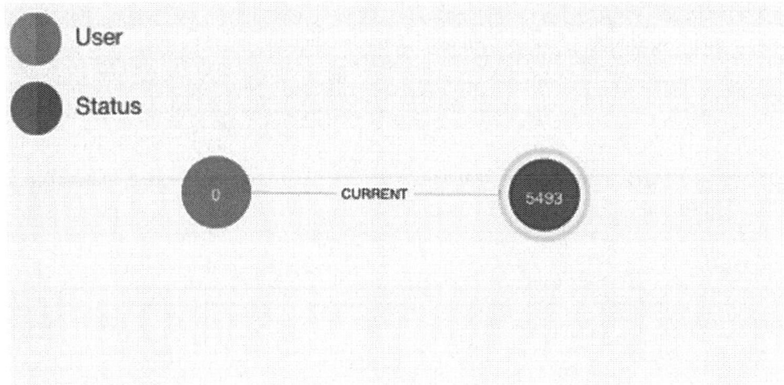

Figure 5-3. *Testing the results of the CURRENT status import*

Loading the "NEXT" Status

As the last step for loading status updates, you can import the final set and associate them through a LOAD CSV using the NEXT relationship type for each one, shown in Listings 5-11 and 5-12. You can use the statusId as a key because it is unique.

Listing 5-11. First Set of "NEXT" Status Updates with LOAD CSV

```
USING PERIODIC COMMIT
LOAD CSV WITH HEADERS FROM "http://www.graphstory.com/practicalneo4j-book/code/chapter5/
csv/nextstatus1.csv" AS csvLine
MATCH (s1:Status { statusId: toInt(csvLine.lastStatusId)} )
CREATE (s1)-[:NEXT]->(s:Status { statusId: toInt(csvLine.statusId), userId: csvLine.userId, status:
csvLine.status })
```

Listing 5-12. Second Set of "NEXT" Status Updates with LOAD CSV

```
USING PERIODIC COMMIT
LOAD CSV WITH HEADERS FROM "http://www.graphstory.com/practicalneo4j-book/code/chapter5/
csv/nextstatus2.csv" AS csvLine
MATCH (s1:Status { statusId: toInt(csvLine.nextToLastStatusId)} )
CREATE (s1)-[: NEXT]->(s:Status { statusId: toInt(csvLine.statusId), userId: csvLine.userId, status:
csvLine.status })
```

Once the first "NEXT" status command is run, you can run the command `MATCH (u:User {userId:1} )-[:CURRENT]->(s) -[:NEXT]-(n) return u,s,n` and you should see a result like the one shown in Figure 5-4. Finally, run the second "NEXT" status command and then run the command `MATCH (u:User {userId:1} )-[:CURRENT]->(s)-[:NEXT*0..2]-(n) return u,s,n` and you should see a result like the one shown in Figure 5-5.

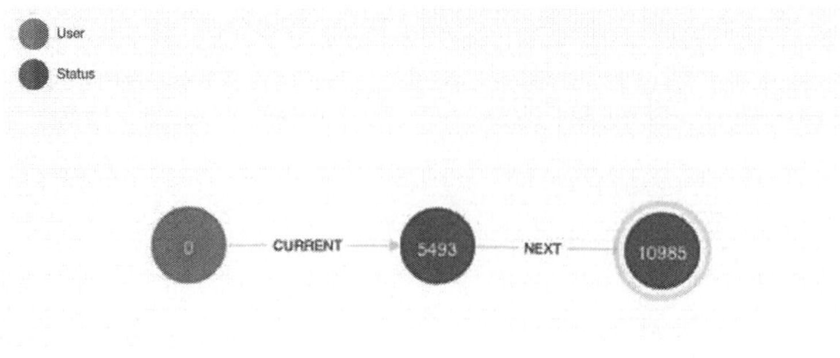

Figure 5-4. *Displaying the user, current status, and next status*

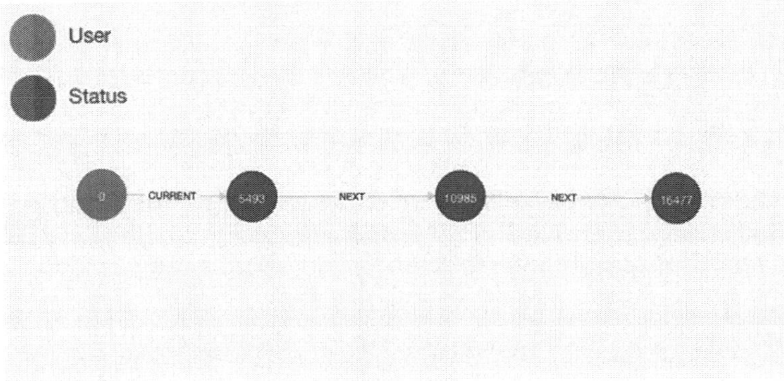

Figure 5-5. Final set of NEXT status updates

■ **Tip** If any of the unique constraints were necessary only for the purposes of the import, then you could run a command such as `DROP CONSTRAINT ON (s:Status) ASSERT s.statusId IS UNIQUE` to remove the constraint. Finally, you could also run `MATCH (s) WHERE s:Status REMOVE s.statusId` to remove the property from the Node. In this application, we'd likely keep them, because they could be used for quick lookups.

Adding User Favorites

The last step in the process is loading a CSV that contains a list of the userIds and statusIds that denote a "favorite" status update. In the concept application being created, the "favorite" feature allows users to favorite their own status updates as well as others within the network. Listing 5-13 shows the LOAD CSV command that will create the favorites per User.

Listing 5-13. Adding Favorite Status Updates

```
USING PERIODIC COMMIT
LOAD CSV WITH HEADERS FROM "http://www.graphstory.com/practicalneo4j-book/code/chapter5/csv/
favorite.csv" AS csvLine
MATCH (u1:User { userId: toInt(csvLine.userId)} ),(s1:Status { statusId: toInt(csvLine.statusId)} )
CREATE (u1)-[:FAVORITE]->(s1)
```

After running the LOAD CSV command for favorites, run `` MATCH (a)-[:`FAVORITE`]->(b) RETURN a,b LIMIT 5 `` to see a small sample. The result should look like the one in Figure 5-6.

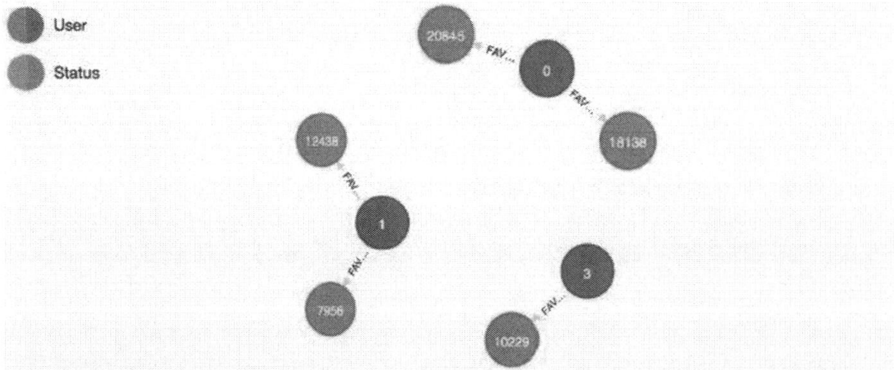

Figure 5-6. *"Favorite" status updates by user*

Summary

This chapter presented some of the processes for creating or moving data into Neo4j for application development and for migration of application data for an existing application. You are now familiar with using Cypher statements directly, employing the LOAD CSV command, and setting up a programmatic method to import data based on your application's needs. Before selecting the best way to import or synchronize from another data source, always give careful consideration to your goal.

The next chapter will explore extending Neo4j through the use of plugins and unmanaged extensions.

CHAPTER 6

Extending Neo4j

One of the benefits of using Neo4j is being able to extend the database through the use of Java-based plugins and extensions. Neo4j plugins are the quickest and most reliable way to add or create additional capability for the REST API and to add new functionality to your graph-based applications. Plugins can extend the functionality that already exists within nodes and relationships and can do so while ensuring the integrity of upgrades to the database.

This chapter examines the process for creating a plugin development environment. It shows you how to create your first plugin and how to build a security-based plugin using the Neo4j framework. Finally, it considers unmanaged extensions, which can provide you finer-grained control, albeit at a cost to the performance of your Neo4j server unless properly managed.

Plugin Development Environment for Neo4j

This section covers the basics of configuring a development environment to build out your first Neo4j plugin. If you did not work through the installation steps in Chapter 2, please take a few minutes to review and walk through the installation.

Note To get started with the Cypher and follow along with the examples in this chapter, you will need to have a running instance of Neo4j. To quickly setup a Neo4j server instance, go to `http://www.graphstory.com/practicalneo4j`. You will be provided with your own trial instance, a knowledge base, and email support from Graph Story.

IDE

Although it is possible to work through this chapter using another Java IDE, I recommend that you install Eclipse to follow along with the specific examples.

Readme If you already configured Eclipse while working through another chapter, you can skip ahead to the "Maven Plugin" section. If you do not have Eclipse, download the Version 3.7 Indigo package "Eclipse IDE for Java EE Developers" from `http://www.eclipse.org/downloads/`.

Once Eclipse has been installed, you can open it and select a workspace for your application. A *workspace* in Eclipse is simply an arbitrary directory on your computer where you choose to keep your code projects. When you first open Eclipse, the program will ask you to specify which workspace you want to use (Figure 6-1). Choose a path that works for you. If you are working through all the language chapters, then you could use the same workspace for each project.

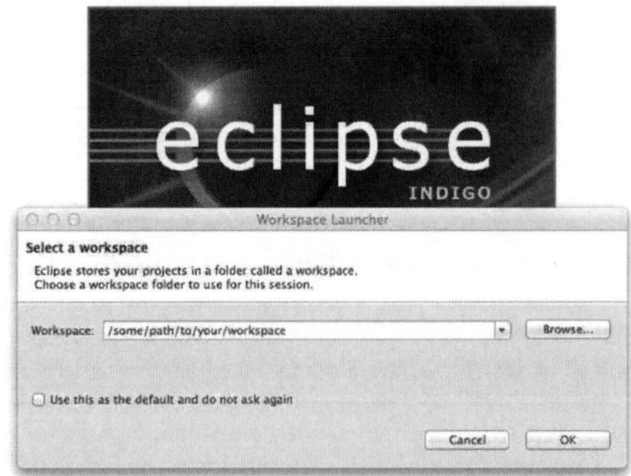

Figure 6-1. *Opening Eclipse and choosing a workspace*

Maven Plugin

The Eclipse IDE offers a convenient way to add new tools through their plugin platform. This section walks you through the process for adding new plugins to Eclipse, which is straightforward and usually involves only a few steps.

■ **Readme** To use the examples in this chapter, you will need to have installed and configured Maven. The files and installation instructions for Maven are available at `http://maven.apache.org/download.cgi`.

A specific plugin called m2e provides support for managing code dependencies with Apache Maven. Maven helps to provide a standard way to build projects, which in turn can set a clear definition of the following:

- What should be included within the project
- An easy way to publish project information
- A way to share JARs across several projects
- Management of library dependencies

The goal of the m2e project is to provide Maven support in the Eclipse IDE, making it easier to edit Maven's main pom.xml, run a build from the IDE, and much more. For many Java developers, the level of integration significantly eases the consumption of Java artifacts either being hosted on open source repositories such as Maven Central or another trusted Maven repository.

■ **Readme** If you have already configured Eclipse with Maven, you can skip ahead to the "Neo4j Server Plugin" section.

Installing the SLF4J Plugin

To install the Maven Plugin, you will need to install the slf4j-api, which is responsible for logging. If you have Eclipse installed and open, proceed through these steps:

1. From the Help menu, select "Install New Software" to open the dialog, which will look like the one shown in Figure 6-2.

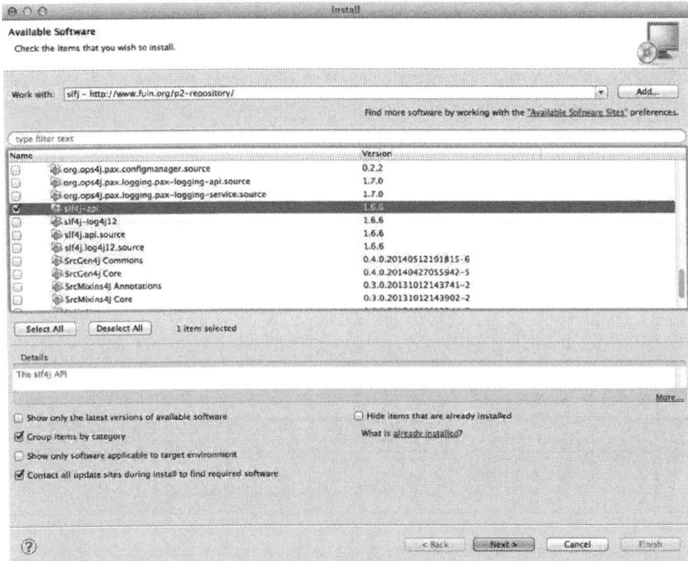

Figure 6-2. *Installing the SLF4J plugin into Eclipse*

2. Paste the URL `http://www.fuin.org/p2-repository/` for the update site into the "Work With" text box, and hit the Enter (or Return) key.
3. Expand "Maven osgi-bundles" and select "slf4j-api".
4. Click the Next button to go to the license page.
5. Choose the option to accept the terms of the license agreement, and click the Finish button.
6. You may need to restart Eclipse to continue.

Installing the Maven Plugin

Now that the SLF4J plugin is installed, you can proceed through the steps below to add the Maven plugin to Eclipse:

1. Again, from the Help menu, select "Install New Software" to open the dialog, which will appear similar to the one shown in Figure 6-2.
2. Paste the following URL—`http://download.eclipse.org/technology/m2e/releases-for` the update site into the "Work With" text box, and hit the Enter (or Return) key.
3. In the populated table like the one in Figure 6-3, check the box next to the name of the plug-in, and then click the Next button.

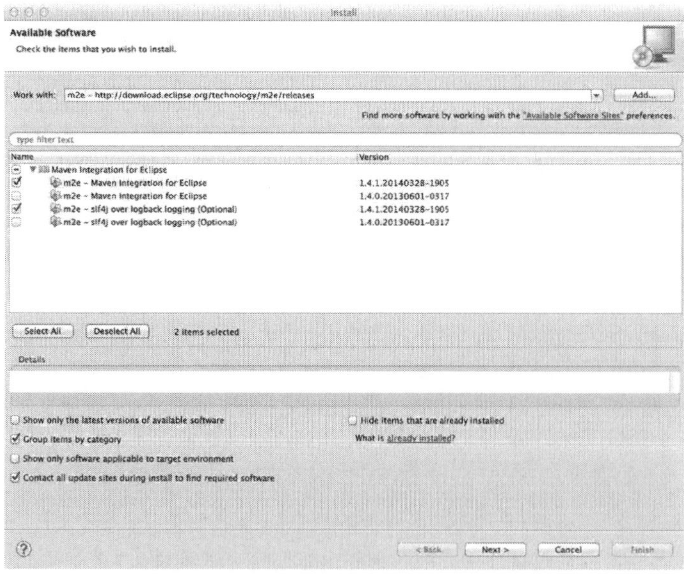

Figure 6-3. *Installing the Maven plugin into Eclipse*

4. Click the Next button to go to the license page.

5. Choose the option to accept the terms of the license agreement, and click the Finish button.

6. You may need to restart Eclipse to continue.

Setting Up Maven Projects

After installing Eclipse and setting up the Maven plugin, you have the minimum requirements to work with your project in the workspace. Next, import the project into your workspace following these steps:

1. Go to `www.graphstory.com/practicalneo4j` and download the archive file for "Practical Neo4j for Plugins". Unzip the archive file on to your computer.

2. In Eclipse, select File ➤ Import and type project in the "Select an import source".

3. Under the "Maven" heading, select "Existing Maven Projects". You should now see a window similar to Figure 6-4.

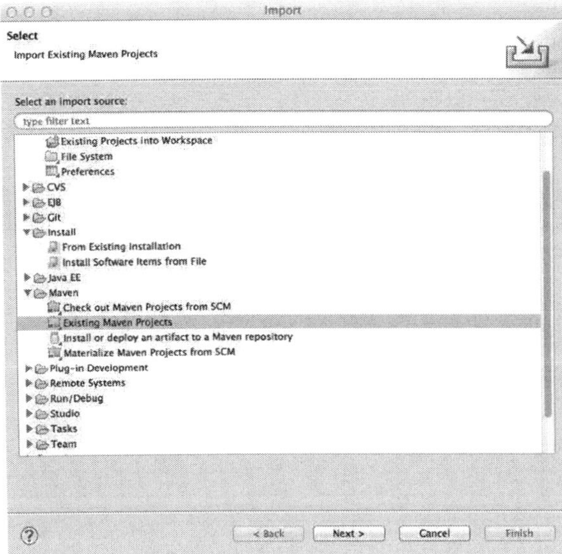

Figure 6-4. *Importing an existing Maven project*

4. Now that you have selected "Existing Maven Projects", click the "Next ➤" button. The dialogue should now show an option to "Select root directory". Click the "Browse" button and find the root path of the "practicalneo4j-extending-neo4j" archive.

5. Next, check the option for "Copy project into workspace" and click the "Finish" button, as shown in Figure 6-5.

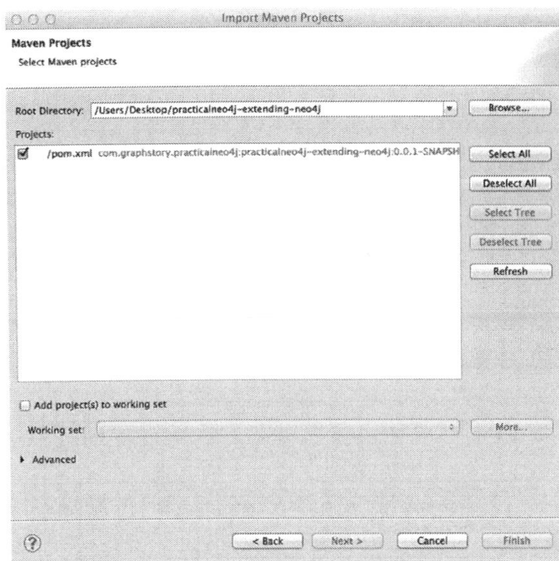

Figure 6-5. *Importing Maven project into Eclipse*

6. Once the project is finished importing into your workspace, you should have a directory structure that looks similar to the one shown in Figure 6-6.

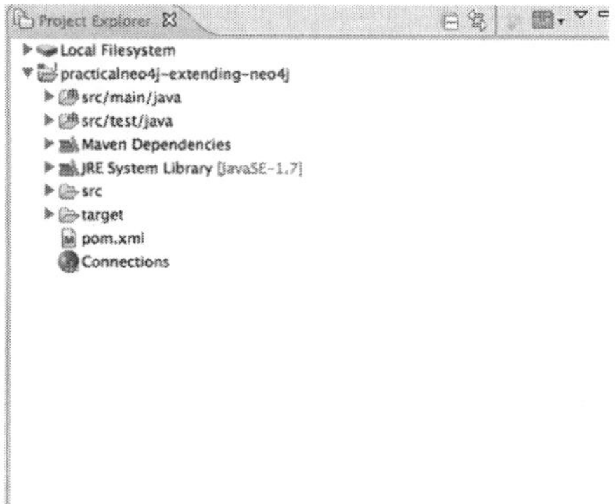

Figure 6-6. *The local project for the Neo4j plugins*

Neo4j Server Plugins

To create a plugin, your code must extend the `org.neo4j.server.plugins.ServerPlugin` class. Your plugin should also ensure that it will produce one the following items:

- An iterable of node, relationship, or path
- Any Java primitive or string
- An instance of a `org.neo4j.server.rest.repr.Representation`

The plugin could include parameters, a point of extension, and any necessary application logic. Listing 6-1 exemplifies how, when creating the plugin, to be sure that the discovery point type in the `@PluginTarget` and the `@Source` parameter are of the same type.

Listing 6-1. Example of a Neo4j Plugin That Returns All Relationships from a Node

```
package com.graphstory.practicalneo4j.plugin;

import java.util.ArrayList;

import org.neo4j.graphdb.Direction;
import org.neo4j.graphdb.Node;
import org.neo4j.graphdb.Relationship;
import org.neo4j.graphdb.Transaction;
import org.neo4j.server.plugins.Description;
import org.neo4j.server.plugins.PluginTarget;
import org.neo4j.server.plugins.ServerPlugin;
import org.neo4j.server.plugins.Source;

@Description("An extension to the Neo4j Server for getting all nodes or relationships")
public class GraphStoryPlugin extends ServerPlugin {
```

```
        @Description("Get all nodes related to this node")
        @PluginTarget(Node.class)
        public Iterable<Relationship> getRelatedNodes(@Source Node node)
        {
                ArrayList<Relationship> relationships = new ArrayList<>();

                try (Transaction tx = node.getGraphDatabase().beginTx())
                {
                        for (Relationship relationship : node.getRelationships(Direction.BOTH))
                        {
                                relationships.add(relationship);
                        }
                        tx.success();
                }
                return relationships;
        }
}
```

■ **Important** Make sure to include a file in the META-INF/services directory called `org.neo4j.server.plugins.ServerPlugin` that includes the path to your plugin. This must be included in your .jar file. An example in the chapter code can be reused in your own project.

Adding and Accessing the Plugin

To deploy the code to your Neo4j server instance, simply compile it into a .jar file and place it in the server classpath (which is typically the "plugins" directory under the Neo4j server home directory). You will need to restart the server in order for the plugin to be accessible.

Once the server has been restarted, you can call the Listing 6-2 from the command line or some other tool, such as the Chrome extension POSTMAN.

Listing 6-2. Executing the Plugin Endpoint via Command Line and Curl

```
curl -X POST http://localhost:7474/db/data/ext/GraphStoryPlugin/node/7/getRelatedNodes -H "Content-
Type: application/json"
```

Security Plugins

You may also use the plugin methodology to introduce a finer level of security control for your applications. In such cases, instead of extending the `org.neo4j.server.plugins.ServerPlugin` class, your code would need to implement the `org.neo4j.server.rest.security.SecurityRule`. Listing 6-3 exemplifies how to verify a list of IPs before allowing access.

Listing 6-3. Implementing a Security Rule

```
package com.graphstory.practicalneo4j;

import java.util.Arrays;

import javax.servlet.http.HttpServletRequest;

import org.apache.log4j.Logger;
import org.neo4j.server.rest.security.SecurityFilter;
import org.neo4j.server.rest.security.SecurityRule;

public class GraphStoryIPCheck implements SecurityRule {

        static Logger log = Logger.getLogger(GraphStoryIPCheck.class);

        public static final String REALM = "GraphStory";

        @Override
        public boolean isAuthorized(HttpServletRequest request)
        {
                String IPs[] = { "128.0.0.1", "173.193.188.115" };

                if (Arrays.asList(IPs).contains(request.getRemoteAddr())) {
                        System.out.println("passed");
                        return true;
                }
                else {
                        System.out.println("did not pass");
                        return false;
                }
        }

        @Override
        public String forUriPath()
        {
                return "/*";
        }

        @Override
        public String wwwAuthenticateHeader()
        {
                return SecurityFilter.basicAuthenticationResponse(REALM);
        }
}
```

In this example, the security rule is registered by adding the rules class to the neo4j-server.properties config file, as shown in Listing 6-4. When you restart Neo4j and attempt to access Neo4jBrowser, you should notice—unless your IP matches one of those listed—that you are unable to access the browser.

Listing 6-4. Adding the Security Rule to neo4j-server.properties

```
org.neo4j.server.rest.security_rules= com.graphstory.practicalneo4j.GraphStoryIPCheck
```

Unmanaged Extensions

In some applications you create, you might require fine-grained control over server-side operations within the database. To make this possible, Neo4j includes an unmanaged extension API. Listing 6-5 contains an example of returning the db availability.

Listing 6-5. An Unmanaged Extension to Show if the Database Is Available

```
package com.graphstory.practicalneo4j.unmanaged;

import java.io.IOException;

import javax.ws.rs.GET;
import javax.ws.rs.Path;
import javax.ws.rs.Produces;
import javax.ws.rs.core.Context;
import javax.ws.rs.core.MediaType;
import javax.ws.rs.core.Response;
import javax.ws.rs.core.Response.Status;

import org.codehaus.jackson.JsonGenerationException;
import org.codehaus.jackson.map.JsonMappingException;
import org.codehaus.jackson.map.ObjectMapper;
import org.neo4j.graphdb.GraphDatabaseService;

@Path("/graphstory")
public class GraphStoryResource
{
        private final GraphDatabaseService database;

        public GraphStoryResource(@Context GraphDatabaseService database)
        {
                this.database = database;
        }

        @GET
        @Produces(MediaType.TEXT_PLAIN)
        @Path("/dbname")
        public Response dbAvailable() throws JsonGenerationException, JsonMappingException, IOException
        {
                // Do stuff with the database
                ObjectMapper objectMapper = new ObjectMapper();

                return Response.status(Status.OK).entity(objectMapper.writeValueAsString(database.
                isAvailable(5000))).build();
        }
}
```

■ **Warning** Neo4j unmanaged extensions allow you to deploy arbitrary JAX-RS classes to the server, which if not managed properly can consume significant heap space on the server and degrade Performance.

As shown in Listing 6-6, the extension is registered by using a comma-separated list of JAXRS packages containing JAXRS Resource with one package name for each mountpoint in the neo4j-server.properties config file. You can then access the extension results by going to `http://localhost:7474/unmanaged/graphstory/dbname` in your browser.

Listing 6-6. Adding the Unmanaged Extension to neo4j-server.properties by Package Name

```
org.neo4j.server.thirdparty_jaxrs_classes=com.graphstory.practicalneo4j.unmanaged=/unmanaged
```

Summary

This chapter showed you, largely through examples, the processes for creating a plugin development environment and for building and adding plugins that best fit the needs of your application, such as security-based plugins using the Neo4j framework. You also learned how unmanaged extensions enable finer-grained control but need to be managed to avoid degrading the performance of your Neo4j server.

In the final part of this book, "Developing with Neo4j," you will explore the sample application in the context of Neo4j drivers in tandem with various programming languages—C#, PHP, Python, Ruby, Spring Data, and Java Rest Binding—each covered in an independent chapter.

PART 3

Developing with Neo4j

CHAPTER 7

Neo4j + .NET

This chapter focuses on using .NET and Neo4j and reviewing the code for a working application that integrates the five graph model types covered in Chapter 3. As with other languages that offer drivers for Neo4j, the integration takes place using a Neo4j server instance with the Neo4j REST API. The chapter is divided into the following topics:

- Neo4j and .NET Development Environment
- Neo4jClient API
- Developing a .NET and Neo4j web application

Tip In each chapter that explores a particular language paired with Neo4j, I recommend that you start a free trial on `www.graphstory.com` or have installed a local Neo4j server instance, as shown in Chapter 2.

For this chapter, I assume that you have a good understanding of HTML, JavaScript, and CSS, as well as .NET web application development. I also assume that you have a basic understanding of the *model-view-controller* (MVC) pattern SMF and some knowledge of ASP.NET MVC5 framework. Although an understanding of a previous release of the ASP.NET MVC framework should suffice, I recommend that you have an understanding of the key differences in MVC5 to follow the code examples and sample applications provided in the book.

.NET and Neo4j Development Environment

Preliminary to this chapter's discussion of the .NET Neo4j web application, this section covers the basics of configuring a development environment.

Installing Visual Studio Express for Web

In this chapter, you will be using Visual Studio Express 2013 for Web. You can get the installer by visiting `http://www.asp.net/vwd` and following the installations instructions provided by Microsoft.

Adding the Project to Visual Studio

Once you have installed Visual Studio for the Web, you have the minimum requirements to work with the .NET project. To import the project, follow these steps:

1. Go to `http://www.graphstory.com/practicalneo4j` and download the zip/archive file for "Practical Neo4j for .NET".
2. Unzip the archive file on to your computer to your preferred location. The project dependencies are included as part of the project.
3. Open Visual Studio, then select File ➤ Open Project. Next, select the main project file in the project folder from the unzipped archived, as shown in Figure 7-1.

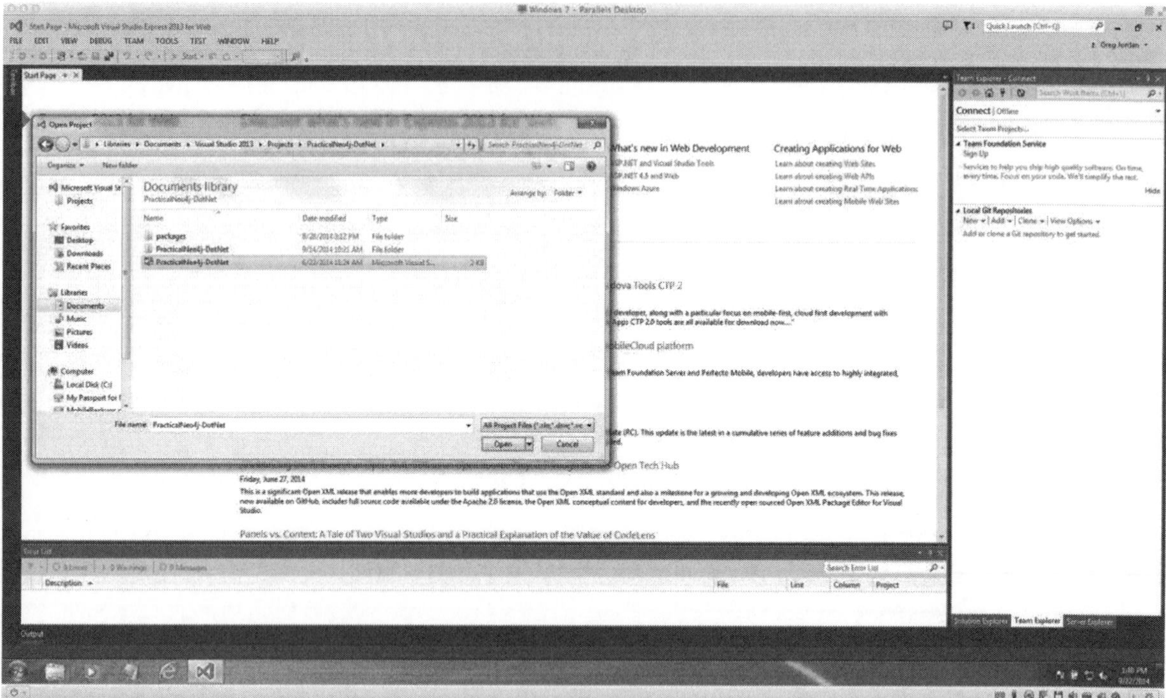

Figure 7-1. *Opening the sample project in Visual Studio for the Web*

Neo4jClient

This section covers basic operations and usage of the Neo4jClient with the goal of reviewing the specific code examples before implementing it within an application. The next section of this chapter will walk you through a sample application with specific graph goals and models.

Like most of the language drivers and libraries available for Neo4j, the purpose of Neo4jClient is to provide a degree of abstraction over the Neo4j REST API. In addition, the Neo4jClient provides some additional enhancements that might otherwise be required at some other stage in the development of your .Net application.

■ **Note** Neo4jClient is maintained by the super-awesome Tatham Oddie and supported by a number of great .NET Neo4j developers. If you would like to get involved with Neo4jClient, go to `https://github.com/Readify/Neo4jClient`.

Each of the following brief sections covers concepts that tie either directly or indirectly to features of Neo4jClient. If you choose to go through each language chapter, you should notice how each library covers those features and functionality in similar ways but takes advantage of the language-specific capabilities to ensure the language-specific API is flexible and performant.

Managing Nodes and Relationships

Chapters 1 and 2 covered the elements of a graph database, including the most basic of graph concepts, the node. Managing nodes and their properties will probably account for the bulk of your application's graph-related code.

Creating a Node

The maintenance of nodes is set in motion with the creation process, as shown in Listing 7-1. Creating a node begins with setting up a connection to the database and making the node instance. Next, the node properties are set, and then the node can be saved to the database.

Listing 7-1. Creating a Node

```
var _graphClient = new GraphClient(new Uri("http://localhost:7474/db/data"));

User user = new User { username = "Greg"};

// use ExecuteWithoutResults if you do not need to return a result node.
_graphClient.Cypher
              .Create(" (user:User {user}) ")
        .WithParam("user",user)
        .ExecuteWithoutResults();

// or use results with single to return the first node returned in the collection.

User resultUser = _graphClient.Cypher
              .Create(" (user:User {user}) ")
        .WithParam("user",user)
        .Return(u => u.As<User>())
        .Results.Single();
```

■ **Warning** Although it is possible to manually construct and execute Cypher queries with the Neo4jClient, it is highly discouraged because it could introduce security issues through Cypher injections.

Retrieving and Updating a Node

Once nodes have been added to the database, you will need a way to retrieve and modify them. Listing 7-2 shows the process for finding a node by its node id value and for retrieving a node and updating it in the same query execution.

Listing 7-2. Retrieving and Updating a Node

```
var _graphClient = new GraphClient(new Uri("http://localhost:7474/db/data"));

// retrieve a user by their user.userId
User u = _graphClient.Cypher
              .Match("(user:User)")
        .Where<User>(user => user.userId == "10")
        .Return(user => user.As<User>())
        .Results.Single();

// update the user by their user.id

        _graphClient.Cypher
        .Match("(user:User)")
        .Where<User>(user => user.userId == "10")
        .Set("user.Business = { business }")
        .WithParam("business ", "Graph Story")
        .ExecuteWithoutResults();
```

Removing a Node

Once a node's graph id has been set and saved into the database, it becomes eligible to be removed when necessary. In order to remove a node, a match can be made on a node object instance and then the node can be deleted in the same query execution (Listing 7-3).

■ **Note** You cannot delete any node that is currently set as the start point or end point of any relationship. You must remove the relationship before you can delete the node.

Listing 7-3. Deleting a Node

```
var _graphClient = new GraphClient(new Uri("http://localhost:7474/db/data"));

// delete a user
_graphClient.Cypher
    .Match("(user:User)")
    .Where<User>(user => user.userId == "10")
    .Delete("user")
    .ExecuteWithoutResults();

// delete a user and its relationships
_graphClient.Cypher
    .OptionalMatch("(user:User)<-[r]-()")
    .Where<User>(user => user.userId == "10")
    .Delete("r, user")
    .ExecuteWithoutResults();
```

Creating a Relationship

Creating a relationship between two nodes with Neo4jClient can be handled in a few different ways, but the most efficient is to retrieve the nodes and create the relationship in the same cypher statement. As shown in Listing 7-4, the query sets up a relationship between two users by using the FOLLOWS relationship type.

■ **Note** Both the start and end nodes used to create a relationship must already be saved within the database before the relationship can be saved.

Listing 7-4. Finding Two Nodes and Creating a Relationship between Them

```
var _graphClient = new GraphClient(new Uri("http://localhost:7474/db/data"));

_graphClient.Cypher
    .Match("(user1:User)", "(user2:User)")
    .Where<User>(user1 => user1.userId == "10")
    .AndWhere<User>(user2 => user2.userId == "1")
    .Create("user1-[:FOLLOWS]->user2")
    .ExecuteWithoutResults();
```

Retrieving Relationships

Once a relationship has been created between two or more nodes, then the relationship can be retrieved based on one of the nodes within the relationship (Listing 7-5).

Listing 7-5. Retrieving Relationships

```
var _graphClient = new GraphClient(new Uri("http://localhost:7474/db/data"));

_graphClient.Cypher
        . Match("(user1:User)-[f:FOLLOWS]-(user2:User)")
        .Where<User>(user1 => user1.userId == "10")
        .AndWhere<User>(user2 => user2.userId == "1")
        .Return((f) => new {
                Relationship = f.As< Relationship >()
        })
        .Results.Single();
```

Deleting a Relationship

Once a relationship's graph id has been set and saved into the database, it becomes eligible to be removed when necessary. In order to remove a relationship, it must be set as a relationship object instance and then the delete method for the relationship (Listing 7-6) can be called.

Listing 7-6. Deleting a Relationship

```
var _graphClient = new GraphClient(new Uri("http://localhost:7474/db/data"));

// removing a relationship using a WHERE clause
_graphClient.Cypher
    .Match("(user1:User)-[f:FOLLOWS]-(user2:User)")
    .Where<User>(user1 => user1.userId == "10")
    .AndWhere(user2 => user2.userId == "1")
    .Delete("f")
    .ExecuteWithoutResults();

// removing a relationship using a MATCH clause
_graphClient.Cypher
    .Match(" (u1:User {username:{u1}} )-[f:FOLLOWS]->(u2:User {username:{u2}} ) ")
    .WithParams( new {u1 = "user1", u2 = "user2"} )
    .Delete("f")
    .ExecuteWithoutResults();
```

Using Labels

Labels function as specific meta-descriptions that can be applied to nodes. Labels were introduced in Neo4j 2.0 to help in querying, but they can also function as a way to quickly create a subgraph.

Adding a Label to Nodes

In Neo4jClient, you can add one more labels to a node. As Listing 7-7 shows, the SET is used to add a label to an existing node.

■ **Caution** A label will not exist on the database server until it has been added to at least one node.

Listing 7-7. Adding a Label to a Node

```
var _graphClient = new GraphClient(new Uri("http://localhost:7474/db/data"));

_graphClient.Cypher
            .Match("(user:User)")
.Where<User>(user => user.userId == "10")
.Set(" user :Developer")
.ExecuteWithoutResults();
```

Removing a Label

Removing a label uses similar syntax as adding a label to a node. After the given label has been removed from the node (Listing 7-8), the return value is a list of labels still on the node.

Listing 7-8. Removing a Label from a Node

```
var _graphClient = new GraphClient(new Uri("http://localhost:7474/db/data"));

_graphClient.Cypher
              .Match("(user:User)")
.Where<User>(user => user.userId == "10")
.Remove(" user :Developer")
.ExecuteWithoutResults();
```

Debugging

As part of developing Cypher queries, you will from time to time need to view the actual query that's being executed for debugging purposes. To that end, each query can be set to a variable as well as access the QueryText and QueryParameters output through the Query object, as shown in Listing 7-9.

Listing 7-9. Removing a Label from a Node

```
var query =_graphClient.Cypher
              .Match("(user:User)")
.Where<User>(user => user.userId == "10")
.Remove(" user :Developer")
.ExecuteWithoutResults();
```

Developing a .NET Neo4j Application

Preliminary to building out your first .NET Neo4j application, this section covers the basics of configuring a development environment.

Preparing the Graph

To spend more time highlighting code examples for each of the more common graph models, you will use a preloaded instance of Neo4j including necessary plugins, such as the spatial plugin.

■ **Tip** To quickly setup a server instance with the sample data and plugins for this chapter, go to `graphstory.com/practicalneo4j`. You will be provided with your own free trial instance, a knowledge base, and email support from Graph Story. Alternatively, you may run a local Neo4j database instance with the sample data by going to `graphstory.com/practicalneo4j`, downloading the zip file containing the sample database and plugins, and adding them to your local instance.

Using the Sample Application

If you have already downloaded the sample application from `graphstory.com/practicalneo4j` for .NET and configured it with your local application environment, you can skip ahead to the section ".NET Application Configuration." Otherwise, you will need to go back to the ".NET and Neo4j Development Environment" section in this chapter and set up your local environment in order to follow along with examples in the sample application.

.NET Application Configuration

Before diving into the code examples, you need to update the configuration for the .Net application. In Visual Studio, open the file Web.config and edit the GraphStory connection string information. If you are using a free account from `graphstory.com`, you will change the username, password, and URL in Listing 7-10 with the one provided in your graph console on `graphstory.com`.

Listing 7-10. Database Connection Setting in Web.config

```
<connectionStrings>
  <add name="graphStory" connectionString="https://username:password@theURL:7473/db/data" />
</connectionStrings>
```

If you have installed a local Neo4j server instance, you can modify the configuration to use the local address and port that you specified during the installation, as in Listing 7-11.

Listing 7-11. Database Connection Setting in Web.config for a Local Instance of Neo4j

```
<connectionStrings>
  <add name="graphStory" connectionString="http://localhost:7474/db/data" />
</connectionStrings>
```

Once the environment is properly configured and started, you can open and run the application by hitting F5, and then you should see a page like the one shown in Figure 7-2.

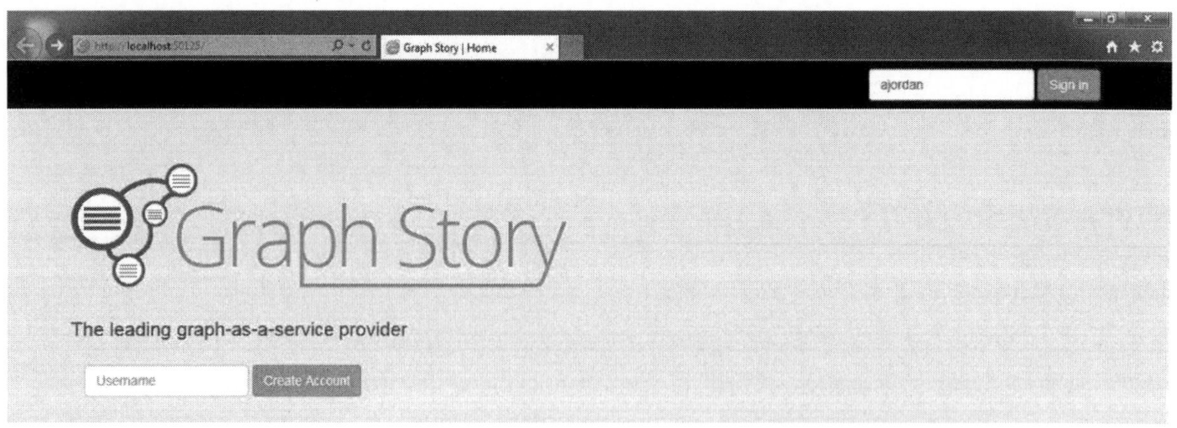

Figure 7-2. *The .NET sample application home page*

Neo4jModule and Ninject

To avoid repeating the connection information through out the application, the application makes use of the open source dependency injector, Ninject.

■ **Note** Ninject is included as part of the application configuration, so you shouldn't need to do anything to make it work during the review of the application.

Ninject works by binding the Neo4jClient to the application using the Neo4jModule located in the App_Start/ Modules folder, a snippet of which is shown in Listing 7-12.

Listing 7-12. Neo4jModule.cs

```
public class Neo4jModule : NinjectModule
{
        /// <summary>Loads the module into the kernel.</summary>
        public override void Load()
        {
            Bind<IGraphClient>().ToMethod(InitNeo4JClient).InSingletonScope();
        }

        private static IGraphClient InitNeo4JClient(IContext context)
        {
            var neo4JUri = new Uri(ConfigurationManager.ConnectionStrings["graphStory"].
            ConnectionString);
            var graphClient = new GraphClient(neo4JUri);
            graphClient.Connect();

            return graphClient;
        }
}
```

Once the Neo4jModule is added, it can be registered with the application in the NinjectWebCommon file, which is located in the App_Start folder. The module is registered in the `RegisterServices` method as shown in Listing 7-13. Once the Module is registered, an `IGraphClient` instance can be called within the application, such as within the service layer, to perform operations on your database.

Listing 7-13. The RegisterServices method in NinjectWebCommon.cs

```
namespace PracticalNeo4j_DotNet.App_Start
{
        public static class NinjectWebCommon
        {

                ...
                //other methods
                ...

                private static void RegisterServices(IKernel kernel)
                {
                                kernel.Load <Neo4jModule>();
                }
        }
}
```

Controller and Service Layers

All of the controllers in the sample application extend a parent controller called `GraphStoryController`. The `GraphStoryController` provides access to the `GraphStory` class and the `GraphStoryInterface` service. The SecurityController provides a login check on the application as well as providing the string value of the username that is currently logged into the application via the cookie called `graphstoryUserAuthKey`.

The `GraphStory` object encapsulates the domain objects for the sample application and is primarily used for convenience. This object allows domain objects to be sent to the service layer and returned, in some cases, with additional objects and properties.

The `GraphStoryInterface` service provides access to each of the individual service interfaces that support persistence and other service-level operations on each of the domain objects. For example, if an exception is raised in the service layer, such as when attempting to create a User that matches an existing User's username, then the `GraphStory` object can be returned with message information, such as an error message, which can then be used to determine the next part of the application flow as well as return messages to the view.

Social Graph Model

This section explores the social graph model and a few of the operations that typically accompany the use of that type of model. In particular, this section looks at the following:

- The User Entity
- Sign-up and Login
- Updating a user
- Creating a relationship type through a user by following other users
- Managing user content, such as displaying, adding, updating, and removing status updates

■ **Note** The sample graph database used for these examples is loaded with data so that you can immediately begin working with representative data in each of the graph models. In the case of the social graph—and for other graph models, as well—you will login with the user **ajordan**. Going forward, please login with **ajordan** to see each of the working examples.

User Node Entity

I approach the social graph model by reviewing the code for creating a `User` node in the graph via the sign-up process. Later in this section, you will briefly review the code to validate a user attempting to login. In each case, the code contains brief validation routines to demonstrate the basics of running checks against data. In the case of sign-up, the code will check to see if a `User` already exists with the same username.

Node Entities

To begin, open the `User` class located in the `Models` package. Like the other classes in the application, the User entity has properties that are commonly found in similar applications, such as firstname and lastname (Listing 7-14). One significant difference is that the `NodeReference` class is included. The `NodeReference` is added to the object when called from the database and is especially helpful when doing Cypher queries that require the `START` clause to complete the function or operation.

Listing 7-14. The User Object

```
using System;
using System.Collections.Generic;
using System.Linq;
using System.Web;
using Neo4jClient;

namespace PracticalNeo4j_DotNet.Models
{
    public class User
    {
        public long nodeId { get; set; }
        public NodeReference noderef { get; set; }
        public string userId { get; set; }
        public string username { get; set; }
        public string firstname { get; set; }
        public string lastname { get; set; }
    }}
```

Sign-Up

The HTML required for the user sign-up form is shown in Listing 7-15 and can be found in the `{PROJECTROOT}/Views/Home/index.cshtml` file. The important item to note in the HTML form is that the **graphStory** object and then **class name** and then **property** are used to specify what is passed to the controller and, subsequently, to the service layer for saving to the database.

Listing 7-15. HTML Snippet of Sign-Up in Views/Home/Index.cshtml

```
<form class="navbar-form navbar-left" action="/signup/add"
        role="form" id="createaccountform" method="post">
            <div class="form-group">
                <input type="text" placeholder="Username"
                name="graphStory.user.username" class="form-control">
            </div>
            <button type="submit" class="btn btn-success">Create Account</button>
</form>
```

■ **Note** While the sample application creates a user without a password, I am certainly not suggesting or advocating this approach for a production application. Excluding the password property was done in order to create a simple sign-up and login that helps keep the focus on the more salient aspects of the Neo4jClient library.

Sign-Up Controller

In the SignupController class, use a method called Add to control the flow of the sign-up process, shown in Listing 7-16. This particular controller does not extend the GraphStoryController class or the SecurityController class because it does not need to check the user login status or have access to the accompanying values. It does include access to the GraphStoryInterface, which will access the save method of the UserInterface and return a GraphStory object.

If no errors were returned during the save attempt, the request is redirected via RedirectToRoute to a message view in the HomeController to thank the user for signing up. Otherwise, a ViewBag is set with an error variable and output the error message back to the specified view.

Listing 7-16. The SignupController

```
public class SignupController : Controller
{
        private GraphStoryInterface graphStoryService;

        public SignupController(GraphStoryInterface graphStoryService) {
            this.graphStoryService = graphStoryService;
        }

        public ActionResult Add(GraphStory graphStory)
        {
            graphStory = graphStoryService.userInterface.save(graphStory);

            if (graphStory.haserror==false)
            {
                return RedirectToRoute(new { controller = "Home", action = "msg",
                msg = "Thank you," + graphStory.user.username });
            }
```

```
            else
            {
                ViewBag.error = graphStory.error;
                return View("~/Views/Home/Index.cshtml");
            }

        }
}
```

Adding a User

Each domain object must have a corresponding interface and implementation in order to manage the respective domain object. As a part of the architecture, each interface is part of the main service layer created with the GraphStoryService class, which implements the GraphStoryInterface. In addition, each of the implementation classes adds the IGraphClient in order to have access to the injected GraphClient via the Neo4jModule.

In this case, the UserService class implements the methods found in UserInterface, both of which are located in the Service folder. The UserInterface is shown in Listing 7-17.

Listing 7-17. The UserInterface Class

```
public interface UserInterface
{
    User getByUserName(string username);
    GraphStory login(GraphStory graphStory);
    GraphStory save(GraphStory graphStory);
    User update(User user);
    List<User> following(string username);
    MappedUserLocation getUserLocation(String currentusername);
    List<User> searchNotFollowing(String currentusername, String username);
    List<User> follow(String currentusername, String username);
    List<User> unfollow(String currentusername, String username);
}
```

■ **Note** Although the chapter does not dive into the details of the GraphStoryService and GraphStoryInterface classes, they will be reused throughout the application. As noted previously, the GraphStoryService class is used for convenience in order to have access to each specific interface by using a single top-level service interface.

In the UserService class, you will notice several implemented methods to manage the User object. To add the User object to the database, use the save method, which will first check to see if a username has already been added to the database. If no user exists, then the user will be saved to the database, as shown in Listing 7-18.

Listing 7-18. UserService Class

```
public class UserService : UserInterface
{
        private readonly IGraphClient _graphClient;
        private User tempuser;

        public UserService(IGraphClient graphClient)
        {
        _graphClient = graphClient;
        }

        public GraphStory save(GraphStory graphStory)
                {
                        graphStory.user.username = graphStory.user.username.ToLower();
                        // if userexists is false, save the user
                        if (userExists(graphStory.user.username)==false)
                        {
                                graphStory.user.userId = Guid.NewGuid().ToString();

                                User u=   _graphClient.Cypher
                            .Create(" (user:User {user}) ")
                            .WithParam("user", graphStory.user)
                            .Return(user => user.As<User>())
                            .Results.Single();

                        graphStory.user = u;
                        } // otherwise, return an error msg
                        else
                        {
                            graphStory.haserror = true;
                            graphStory.error = "The username you entered already exists.";
                        }

                        return graphStory;
                }

         private bool userExists(string username)
                {
                        bool userFound = false;

                        if (getByUserName(username) != null) {
                                userFound = true;
                }

                return userFound;
                }
```

```
            public User getByUserName(string username)
            {
                    User u = null;
                            Node<User> n = _graphClient.Cypher
                            .Match(" (user:User {username:{user}} ) ")
                            .WithParam("user", username.ToLower())
                            .Return(user => user.As<Node<User>>())
                            .Results.Single();

                            // set user
                            u = n.Data;
                            // set node id
                            u.noderef = n.Reference;

            return u;
        }
}}
```

Login

This section reviews the login process for the sample application. To execute the login process, use the `LoginController` as well as the `User` and `UserService` classes. Before reviewing the controller and service layer, take a quick look at the front-end code for the login.

Login Form

The HTML required for the user login form is shown in Listing 7-19 and can be found in the `{PROJECTROOT}/Views/_Home.cshtml` layout file. Again, one important item to note in the HTML form is that the **graphStory** object then **class name** then **property** are used to specify what is passed to controller and, subsequently, to the service layer for querying the database.

Listing 7-19. The `login` Form

```
<form class="navbar-form navbar-right" action="/login" role="form" method="post">
        <div class="form-group">
        <input type="text" placeholder="Username" name="graphStory.user.username" class="form-control">
        </div>
        <button type="submit" class="btn btn-success">Sign in</button>
</form>
```

Login Controller

In the LoginController class, you will use the method named Index to control the flow of the login process, as shown in Listing 7-20. Inside the Index controller method, the GraphStoryInterface will pass the login method of the UserInterface the GraphStory object from the HTML form shown in Listing 7-20 and then return a GraphStory object back to the controller.

Listing 7-20. The login Controller

```
public ActionResult Index(GraphStory graphStory)
{
            graphStory = this.graphStoryService.userInterface.login(graphStory);

            if (graphStory.haserror == false)
            {
                HttpCookie userCookie = new HttpCookie(graphstoryUserAuthKey);
                userCookie.Value = graphStory.user.username;
                userCookie.Expires = DateTime.Now.AddDays(20);
                Response.Cookies.Add(userCookie);

                return RedirectToRoute(new { controller = "Social", action = "Index" });
            }
            else
            {
                ViewBag.error = graphStory.error;
                return View("~/Views/Home/Index.cshtml");
            }
  }
```

If no errors were return during the login attempt, a cookie is added to the response and the request is redirected via RedirectToRoute to the social home page, shown in Figure 7-3. Otherwise, the View will specify the HTML page to return as well as use the ViewBag object to add the error messages that need to be displayed back to the View.

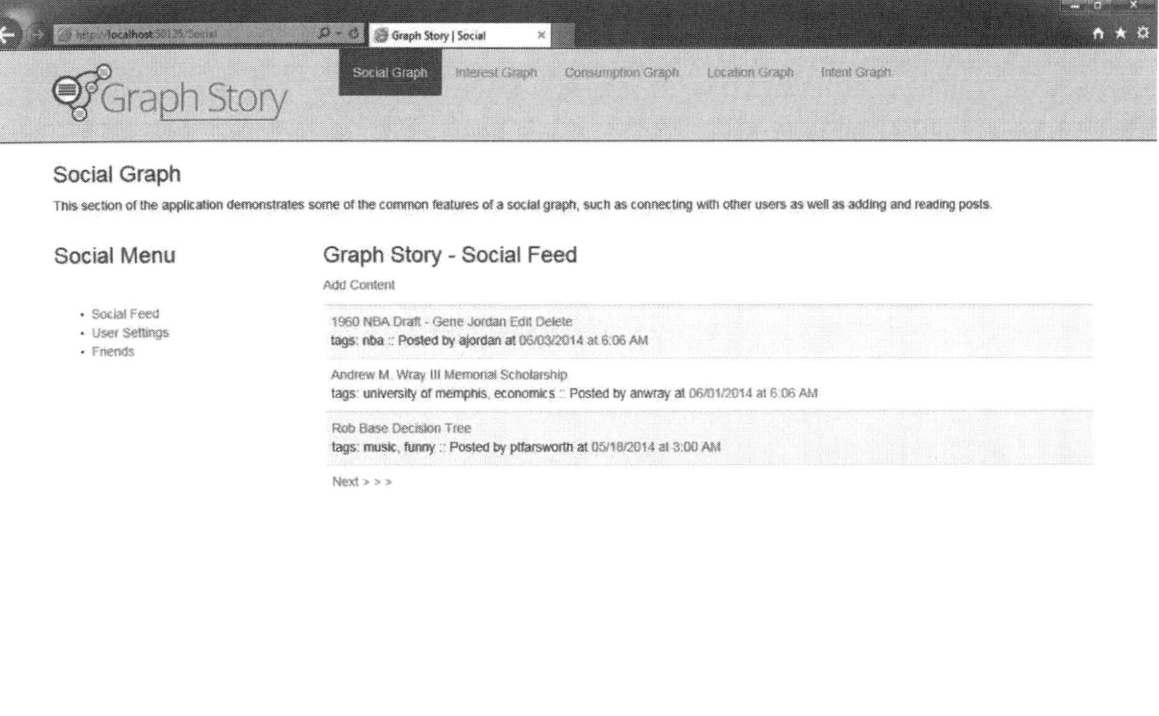

Figure 7-3. *The Social Graph home page*

Login Service

To check to see if the user values being passed through are connected to a valid user combination in the database, the application uses the `login` method in `UserService`. As shown in the `UserService` code in Listing 7-21, the result of the `getByUsername` method is assigned to the `tempUser` variable.

If the result is not null, the result is set on the `User` object of the `GraphStory` service object. Otherwise, a message is added to the `GraphStory` error property and returned to the controller along with the original `User` object.

Listing 7-21. `UserService` Class with the `login` Method

```
public class UserService : UserInterface
{
        private readonly IGraphClient _graphClient;

        private User tempuser;
```

```
        public UserService(IGraphClient graphClient)
        {
            _graphClient = graphClient;
        }

                public GraphStory login(GraphStory graphStory)
                {
                        tempuser = getByUserName(graphStory.user.username.ToLower());

                if (tempuser!=null)
                        {
                        // set the graphStory.user to the tempuser var
                        graphStory.user = tempuser;
                        }
                // or if not found, then return error.
                        else{
                                graphStory.haserror = true;
                                graphStory.error = "The username you entered does not exist.";
                        }

                        return graphStory;
         }

                public User getByUserName(string username)
                {
                        User u = null;
                                Node<User> n = _graphClient.Cypher
                                .Match(" (user:User {username:{user}} ) ")
                                .WithParam("user", username.ToLower())
                                .Return(user => user.As<Node<User>>())
                                .Results.Single();

                        // set user
                        u = n.Data;
                        // set node id
                        u.noderef = n.Reference;

                return u;
        }
}
```

Updating a User

To access the page for updating a user, click on the "User Settings" link in the social graph section, as shown in Figure 7-4. In this example, the front-end code uses an AJAX request via PUT and inserts—or, in the case of the **ajordan** user, updates—the first and last name.

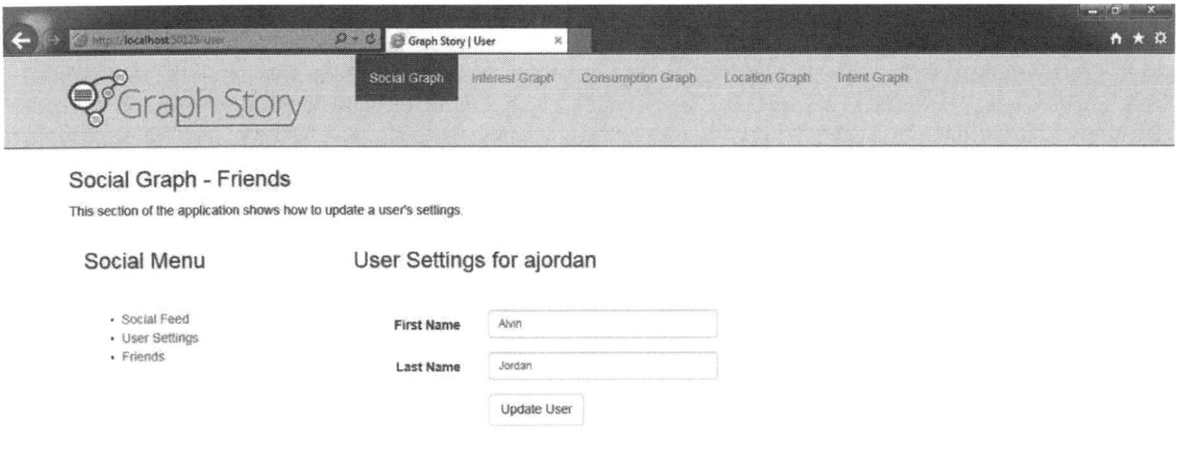

Figure 7-4. The User Settings page

User Update Form

The user settings form is located in {PROJECTROOT}/Views/User/Index.cshtml and is similar in structure to the other forms presented in the Sign Up and Login sections. One difference is that you have added the value property to the input element as well as the variables for displaying the respective stored values. If none exist, the form fields will be empty. (See Listing 7-22).

Listing 7-22. User Update Form MOVED

```
<form class="form-horizontal" id="userform">
            <div class="form-group">
                <label for="firstname" class="col-sm-2 control-label">First Name</label>
                <div class="col-sm-10">
                    <input type="text" class="form-control input-sm" id="firstname" name="user.
                    firstname" value="@Html.DisplayFor(model => model.firstname)" />
                </div>
            </div>
            <div class="form-group">
                <label for="lastname" class="col-sm-2 control-label">Last Name</label>
                <div class="col-sm-10">
                    <input type="text" class="form-control input-sm" id="lastname" name="user.
                    lastname" value="@Html.DisplayFor(model => model.lastname)" />
                </div>
            </div>
            <div class="form-group">
                <div class="col-sm-offset-2 col-sm-10">
                    <button type="submit" id="updateUser" class="btn btn-default">Update
                    User</button>
                </div>
            </div>
        </form>
```

User Controller

The UserController class contains a method called Edit, which takes the User object argument. The "Sign-Up" and "Login" examples use the GraphStory object to pass through values. This example demonstrates another way to pass values into the back-end code (Listing 7-23).

Notice that the User object is converted from a JSON string and returns a User object as Json. The response could be used to update the form elements, but because the values are already set within the form there is no need to update the values. In this case, the application uses the JSON response to let the user know if the update succeeded or not via a standard JavaScript alert message.

Listing 7-23. UserController Edit Method

```
public JsonResult Edit(User user)
{
            user.username = graphstoryUserAuthValue;
            graphStoryService.userInterface.update(user);
            return Json(User);
}
```

User Update Method

To complete the update, the Edit method calls the update method in UserService layer. Because the object being passed into the update method did nothing more than modify the first and last name of an existing entity, you can use the SET clause via Cypher to update the properties in the graph, as shown in Listing 7-24. This Cypher statement also uses the WithParams clause, which requires an array of parameter objects as its argument, to pass the updated values to the SET clause.

Listing 7-24. Update Method for a User

```
public User update(User user)
{
            _graphClient.Cypher
                .Match(" (user:User {username:{user}} ) ")
                .WithParam("user", user.username.ToLower())
                .Set("user.firstname = {fn}, user.lastname = {ln} ")
                .WithParams(new {fn=user.firstname,ln=user.lastname })
                .ExecuteWithoutResults();

            return user;
}
```

■ **Note** Each of the controllers and the front-end code make use of similar syntax. The next and subsequent sections will therefore not feature the controller and front-end code and instead focus on the Neo4jClient aspects of the application. The controllers and front-end code will be referenced, but not listed directly in the following sections.

Connecting Users

A common feature in social media applications is to allow users to connect to each other through an explicit relationship. The following sample application uses the directed relationship type called `FOLLOWS`. By going to the "Friends" page within the social graph section, you can see the list of the users the current user is following, search for new friends to follow, add them, and remove friends the current user is following. The `UserController` contains each of the methods to control the flow for these features, including `friends`, `searchbyusername`, `follow`, and `unfollow`.

To display the list of the users the current user is following, the `friends` method in the `UserController` calls the `following` method in `UserService`. The `following` method in `UserService`, shown in Listing 7-25, creates a list of users by matching the current user's `username` with directed relationship `FOLLOWS` on the variable `user`. If the list contains users, it will be returned to the controller and displayed in the right-hand part of the page, as shown in Figure 7-5. The display code for showing the list of users can be found in `{PROJECTROOT}/Views/User/Friends.cshtml`.

Listing 7-25. `UserService`—`following` Method

```
// UserService

public List<User> following(string username)
{
            List<User> following = _graphClient.Cypher
                .Match(" (user { username:{u}})-[:FOLLOWS]->(users)  ")
                .WithParam("u", username.ToLower())
                .Return(users => users.As<User>())
                .OrderBy("users.username")
                .Results.ToList<User>();

            return following;
}
```

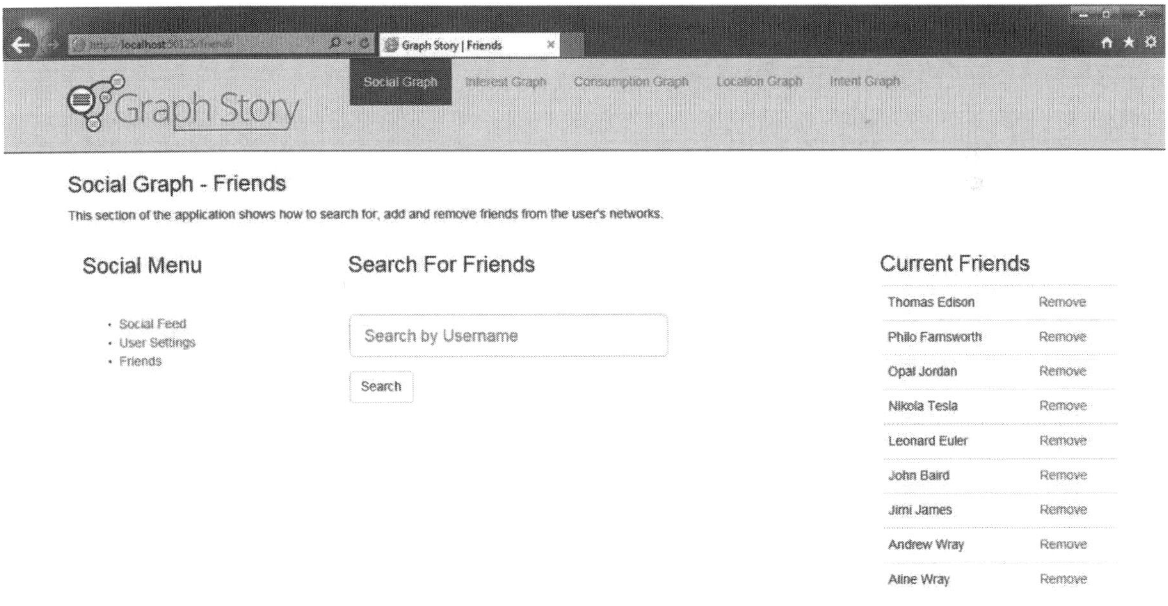

Figure 7-5. *The Friends page*

To search for users to follow, the UserController uses the Searchbyusername method, which calls the searchNotFollowing in UserService. The first part of the WHERE clause in searchNotFollowing returns users whose username matches on a wildcard String value (Listing 7-26). The second part of the WHERE clause in searchNotFollowing checks to make sure the users in the MATCH clause are not already being followed by the current user.

Listing 7-26. searchNotFollowing Method in the UserService

```
// UserService

public List<User> searchNotFollowing(String currentusername, String username)
{
            username = username.ToLower() + ".*";

            List<User> following = _graphClient.Cypher
                .Match(" (n:User), (user { username:{c}})   ")
                .WithParam("c", currentusername.ToLower())
                .Where(" (n.username =~ {u} AND n <> user) ")
                .AndWhere("(NOT (user)-[:FOLLOWS]->(n)) ")
                .WithParam("u", username)
                .Return(n => n.As<User>())
                .OrderBy("n.username")
                .Results.ToList<User>();

            return following;
}
```

The searchByUsername in {PROJECTROOT}/Content//js/graphstory.js uses an AJAX request and formats the response in renderSearchByUsername. If the list contains users, it will be displayed in the center of the page under the search form, as shown in Figure 7-5. Otherwise, the response will display "No Users Found".

Once the search returns results, the next action would be to click on the "Add as Friend" link, which will call the addfriend method in graphstory.js. This will perform an AJAX request to the follow method in the UserController and call follow in UserService. The follow method in UserService, shown in Listing 7-27, will create the relationship between the two users by first finding each entity via the MATCH clause and then use the CreateUnique clause to create the directed FOLLOWS relationship. Once the operation is completed, the next part of the query then runs a MATCH on the users being followed to return the full list of followers ordered by the username.

Listing 7-27. The follow Method

```
// UserService

// follows a user and also returns the list of users being followed
public List<User> follow(String currentusername, String username)
{
    List<User> following = _graphClient.Cypher
        .Match(" (user1:User {username:{cu}} ), (user2:User {username:{u}} ) ")
        .WithParams(new { cu = currentusername.ToLower(), u = username.ToLower() })
        .CreateUnique("user1-[:FOLLOWS]->user2")
        .With(" user1 ")
        .Match("  (user1)-[f:FOLLOWS]->(users) ")
```

```
        .Return(users => users.As<User>())
        .OrderBy("users.username")
        .Results.ToList<User>();

    return following;
}
```

The unfollow feature for the FOLLOWS relationships uses a nearly identical application flow as follows feature. In the unfollow method, shown in Listing 7-28, the controller passes in two arguments: the current username and username to be unfollowed. As with the follow method, once the operation is completed, the next part of the query then runs a MATCH on the users being followed to return the full list of followers ordered by the username.

Listing 7-28. The unfollow Method

```
// UserService
// unfollows a user and also returns the list of users being followed
public List<User> unfollow(String currentusername, String username)
{
        List<User> following = _graphClient.Cypher
        .Match(" (user1:User {username:{cu}} )-[f:FOLLOWS]->(user2:User {username:{u}} ) ")
        .WithParams( new {cu = currentusername.ToLower(), u = username.ToLower()} )
        .Delete("f")
        .With(" user1 ")
        .Match("  (user1)-[f:FOLLOWS]->(users) ")
        .Return(users => users.As<User>())
        .OrderBy("users.username")
        .Results.ToList<User>();
        return following;
}
```

User-Generated Content

Another important feature in social media applications is being able to have users view, add, edit, and remove content—sometimes referred to as *user-generated content*. In the case of this content, you will not be creating connections between the content and its owner but creating a linked list of status updates. In other words, you are connecting a User to their most recent status update and then connecting each subsequent status to the next update through the CURRENTPOST and NEXTPOST directed relationship types, respectively.

This approach is used for two reasons. First, the sample application displays a given number of posts at a time, and using a limited linked list is more efficient than getting all status updates connected directly to a user and then sorting and limiting the number of items to return. Second, it also helps to limit the number of relationships that are placed on the User and Content entities. Therefore, the overall graph operations should be made more efficient by using the linked list approach. Listing 7-29 shows the properties that are included in a CONTENT object.

Listing 7-29. The Content Object

```
public class Content
{
        public long nodeId { get; set; }
        public NodeReference noderef { get; set; }
        public string contentId { get; set; }
        public string title { get; set; }
        public string url { get; set; }
```

```
        public string tagstr { get; set; }
        public long timestamp { get; set; }
        public string userNameForPost { get; set; }
        private string TimestampAsStr;
        public string timestampAsStr
        {
            get
            {
                System.DateTime datetime = new DateTime(1970, 1, 1, 0, 0, 0, 0,
                System.DateTimeKind.Utc);
                datetime = datetime.AddSeconds(this.timestamp).ToLocalTime();

                this.timestampAsStr = datetime.ToString("MM/dd/yyyy") + " at " + datetime.
                ToString("h:mm tt");
                return TimestampAsStr;
            }
            set
            {
                TimestampAsStr = value;
            }
        }
        public List<Tag> tags { get; set; }
        public User user { get; set; }
        public Content next { get; set; }
}
```

Getting Status Updates

To display the first set of status updates, start with the Index method inside of the SocialController. This method accesses the getContent method within ContentService, which takes an argument of the GraphStory object, the current user's username, the page being request and the number of items to be returned. The page refers to set number of objects within a collection. In this instance the paging is zero-based, so you will request page 0 and limit the page size to 3 in order to return the first page.

The getContent method in ContentService, shown in the first part of Listing 7-30, first determines whom the user is following and then matches that set of users with the status updates, starting with the CURRENTPOST. The CURRENTPOST is then matched on the next three status updates via the [:NEXTPOST*0..3] section of the query. Finally, the query uses a ViewModel to return only the properties that are necessary to display back to the View in the application.

Listing 7-30. The getContent Method in ContentService

```
public GraphStory getContent(GraphStory graphStory, string username, int page, int pagesize)
{

            graphStory.content = _graphClient.Cypher.Match(" (u:User {username: {u} }) ")
                .WithParam("u", username)
                .With("u")
                .Match(" (u)-[:FOLLOWS*0..1]->f  ")
                .With(" DISTINCT f,u ")
                .Match(" f-[:CURRENTPOST]-lp-[:NEXTPOST*0..3]-p")
                .Return(() => Return.As<MappedContent>("{contentId: p.contentId, title: p.title,
                url: p.url," +
```

```
                " tagstr: p.tagstr, timestamp: p.timestamp, userNameForPost: f.username,
                owner: f=u}"))
            .OrderByDescending("p.timestamp")
            .Skip(page)
            .Limit(pagesize)
            .Results.ToList();

        return graphStory;
}
```

Using View Models

For many applications, it is necessary to return only certain elements of the model to complete the parts of the view. In addition, the view sometimes requires display elements that are not provided within the core model objects. In the case of .NET applications, the solution to this challenge is to add classes known as ViewModels.

For example, the MappedContent shown in Listing 7-31 allows the application to return properties from both the Content and User classes as well as properties, such as the TimestampAsStr, that are modifications of an existing property. As you walk through the remainder of the graph examples, you will review a number of the ViewModel classes that were created to satisfy the needs within the View sections of the application.

Listing 7-31. The View Model Object: Mapped Content

```
public class MappedContent
{
        public string contentId { get; set; }
        public string title { get; set; }
        public string url { get; set; }
        public string tagstr { get; set; }
        public long timestamp { get; set; }
        public string userNameForPost { get; set; }
        private string TimestampAsStr;
        public string timestampAsStr
        {
            get
            {
                System.DateTime datetime = new DateTime(1970, 1, 1, 0, 0, 0, 0,
                System.DateTimeKind.Utc);
                datetime = datetime.AddSeconds(this.timestamp).ToLocalTime();

                this.timestampAsStr = datetime.ToString("MM/dd/yyyy") + " at " + datetime.
                ToString("h:mm tt");
                return TimestampAsStr;
            }
            set
            {
                TimestampAsStr = value;
            }
        }

        public bool owner { get; set; }
 }
```

Adding a Status Update

The page shown in Figure 7-6 shows the form to add a status update for the current user, which is displayed when clicking on the "Add Content" link just under the "Graph Story - Social Feed" header. The HTML for the form can be found in `{PROJECTROOT}/Views/Social/Posts.cshtml`. The form uses the `addContent` function in `graphstory.js` to `POST` a new status update as well as return the response and add it to the top of the status update stream. In the `SocialController`, use the add method to pass the content to the service layer, as shown in Listing 7-32.

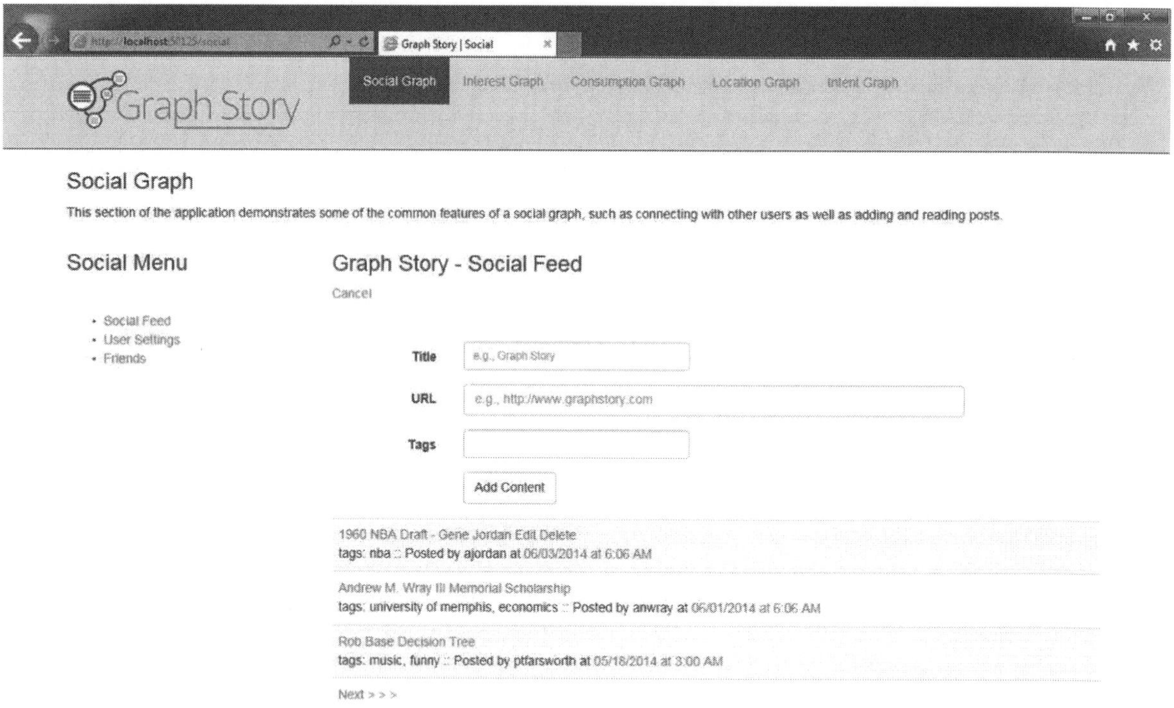

Figure 7-6. *Adding a status update*

Listing 7-32. The add Method in the Social Controller

```
// add content
[HttpPost]
public JsonResult add(Content jsonObj) {
    MappedContent mappedContent = graphStoryService.contentInterface.add(jsonObj,graphstoryUserAuth
    Value);
    mappedContent.userNameForPost = graphstoryUserAuthValue;
    return  Json(jsonObj,JsonRequestBehavior.AllowGet);
}
```

The add method for `ContentService` is shown in Listing 7-32. When a new status update is created, in addition to its graph id, the add method also generates a contentId, which is performed using the `Guid.NewGuid` method.

The add method makes the status the CURRENTPOST but also determines whether a previous CURRENTPOST exists and, if one does, changes its relationship type to NEXTPOST. In addition, the tags connected to the status update will be merged into the graph and connected to the status update via the HAS relationship type.

Listing 7-33. The add Method in ContentService

```
public MappedContent add(Content content, string username)
{
    content.contentId = Guid.NewGuid().ToString();
    content.timestamp = (long)(DateTime.UtcNow.Subtract(new DateTime(1970, 1, 1))).TotalSeconds;

    content.tagstr = removeTrailingComma(content.tagstr);

    // splits up the comma separated string into arrays and removes any empties.
    // each tag uses MERGE and connected to the the content node thru the HAS,
    e.g content-[:HAS]->tag
    // remember that MERGE will create if it doesn't exist otherwise based on the
    properties provided
    String[] tags = content.tagstr.Split(",".ToCharArray(), StringSplitOptions.RemoveEmptyEntries);

    MappedContent contentItem = _graphClient.Cypher
    .Match(" (user { username: {u}}) ")
    .WithParam("u", username)
    .CreateUnique(" (user)-[:CURRENTPOST]->(newLP:Content { title:{title}, url:{url}, " +
    " tagstr:{tagstr}, timestamp:{timestamp}, contentId:{contentId} }) ")
    .WithParams(new { title = content.title, url = content.url,
        tagstr = content.tagstr, timestamp=content.timestamp, contentId=content.contentId})
    .With("user, newLP")
    .ForEach(" (tagName in {tags} | " +
    "MERGE (t:Tag {wordPhrase:tagName})" +
    " MERGE (newLP)-[:HAS]->(t) " +
    " )")
    .WithParam("tags",tags)
    .With("user, newLP")
    .OptionalMatch(" (newLP)<-[:CURRENTPOST]-(user)-[oldRel:CURRENTPOST]->(oldLP)")
    .Delete(" oldRel ")
    .Create(" (newLP)-[:NEXTPOST]->(oldLP) ")
    .With("user, newLP")
    .Return(() => Return.As<MappedContent>(" { contentId: newLP.contentId, title: newLP.title,
    url: newLP.url," +
    " tagstr: newLP.tagstr, timestamp: newLP.timestamp, userNameForPost: {u}, owner: true } "))
    .Results.Single();

    return contentItem;
}
```

Editing a Status Update

When status updates are displayed, the current user's status updates will contain a link to "Edit" the status. Once clicked, it will open the form, similar to the "Add Content" link, but it will populate the form with the status update values and modify the form button to read "Edit Content", as shown in Figure 7-7. Notice that clicking "Cancel" under the heading removes the values and returns the form to its ready state.

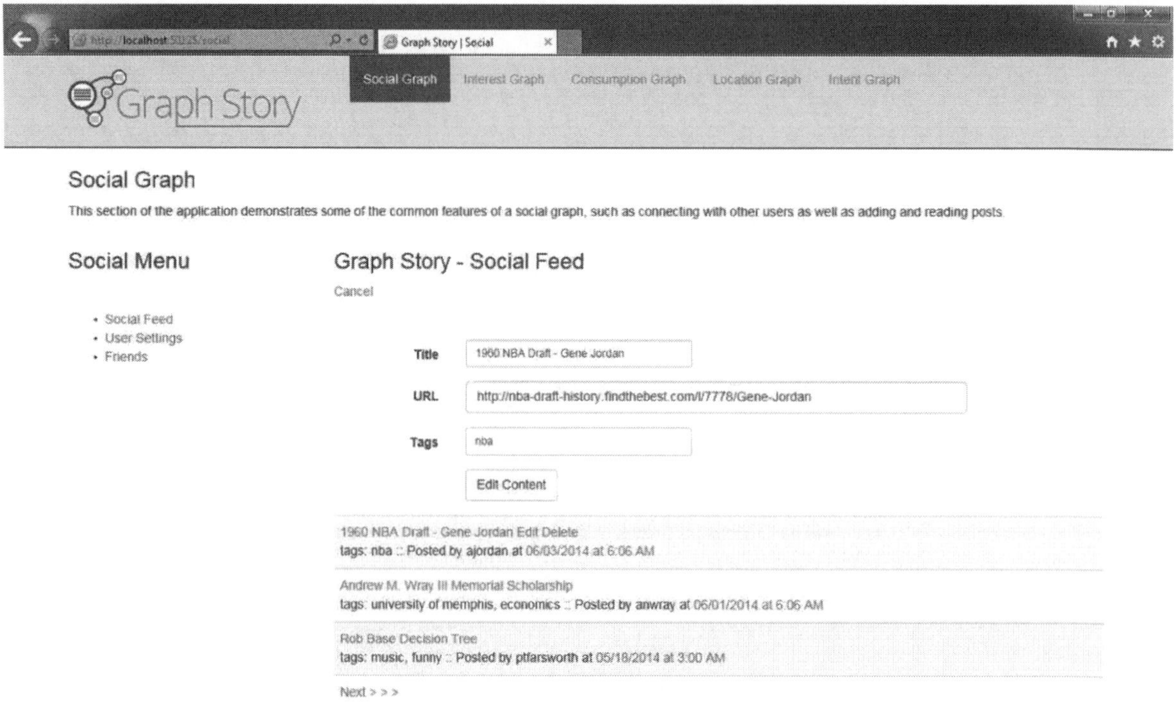

Figure 7-7. *Editing a status update*

The edit feature, like the add feature, uses a method in the `SocialController` and a function in `graphstory.js`, which are edit and updateContent, respectively. The `edit` method passes in the content object, with its content id, and then calls the edit method in `ContentService`, as shown in Listing 7-34.

In the case of the edit feature, you do not need to update relationships. Instead, simply retrieve the existing node by its generated String Id (not its graph id), update its properties where necessary, and save it back to the graph.

Listing 7-34. The `edit` Method in `ContentService`

```
public MappedContent edit(Content content, string username)
{
    content.tagstr = removeTrailingComma(content.tagstr);

    // splits up the comma separated string into arrays and removes any empties.
    // each tag uses MERGE and connected to the the content node thru the HAS,
    e.g content-[:HAS]->tag
    // remember that MERGE will create if it doesn't exist otherwise based on the
    properties provided
    String[] tags = content.tagstr.Split(",".ToCharArray(), StringSplitOptions.RemoveEmptyEntries);

    MappedContent mappedContent = _graphClient.Cypher
        .Match(" (c:Content {contentId:{contentId}})-[:NEXTPOST*0..]-()-[:CURRENTPOST]-(user {
        username: {u}}) ")
        .WithParams(new { u = username, contentId = content.contentId})
        .Set(" c.title = {title}, c.url = {url}, c.tagstr = {tagstr} ")
```

```
        .WithParams(new {title=content.title, url=content.url, tagstr=content.tagstr })
        .ForEach(" (tagName in {tags} | " +
        "MERGE (t:Tag {wordPhrase:tagName})" +
        " MERGE (c)-[:HAS]->(t) " +
        " )")
        .WithParam("tags", tags)
        .With("user, c")
        .Return(() => Return.As<MappedContent>(" { contentId: c.contentId, title: c.title,
        url: c.url," +
    " tagstr: c.tagstr, timestamp: c.timestamp, userNameForPost: user.username, owner: true } "))
    .Results.Single();

    return mappedContent;
}
```

Deleting a Status Update

As with the "edit" option, when status updates are displayed, the current user's status updates contain a link to "Delete" the status. Once clicked, it asks if you want it deleted (no regrets!) and, if accepted, generates an AJAX GET request to call the delete method in the SocialController. This method then calls the delete method in ContentService, shown in Listing 7-35.

The Cypher in the delete method begins by finding the user and content that will be used in the rest of the query. In the first MATCH, you can determine if this status update is the CURRENTPOST by checking to see if it is related to a NEXTPOST. If this relationship pattern matches, make the NEXTPOST into the CURRENTPOST with CREATE UNIQUE.

Next, the query will ask if the status update is somewhere the middle of the list, which is performed by determining if the status update has incoming and outgoing NEXTPOST relationships. If the pattern is matched, then connect the before and after status updates via NEXTPOST.

Regardless of the status update's location in the linked list, retrieve it and its relationships and then delete the node along with all of its relationships.

To recap, if one of the relationship patterns matches, replace that pattern with the nodes on either side of the status update in question. Once that has been performed, then the node and its relationships can be removed from the graph.

Listing 7-35. The delete Method for ContentService

```
public void delete(string contentId, string username)
{
    _graphClient.Cypher
        .Match("(u:User { username: {u} }), (c:Content { contentId: {contentId} })")
        .WithParams(new { u = username, contentId = contentId})
        .With("u,c")
        .Match(" (u)-[:CURRENTPOST]->(c)-[:NEXTPOST]->(nextPost) ")
        .Where("nextPost is not null ")
        .CreateUnique(" (u)-[:CURRENTPOST]->(nextPost) ")
        .With(" count(nextPost) as cnt ")
        .Match(" (before)-[:NEXTPOST]->(c:Content { contentId: {contentId}})-[:NEXTPOST]->(after) ")
        .Where(" before is not null AND after is not null ")
        .CreateUnique(" (before)-[:NEXTPOST]->(after) ")
        .With(" count(before) as cnt ")
        .Match(" (c:Content { contentId: {contentId} })-[r]-() ")
        .Delete("c,r")
        .ExecuteWithoutResults();
}
```

Interest Graph Model

This section looks at the interest graph and examines some basic ways it can used to explicitly define a degree of interest. The following topics are covered:

- Adding filters for owned content
- Adding filters for connected content
- Analyzing connected content (count tags)

Tag Entity

Listing 7-36 displays the Tag entity, which will be used determine a user's interest and network of interest based on user she follows. The tag entity also has incoming relationships with Users and Products, but the relationship is defined using the other entities. To that point, it is not necessary to explicitly annotate the relationships on both entities because one implies the other.

Listing 7-36. The Tag Object

```
public class Tag
{
    public long nodeId { get; set; }
    public NodeReference noderef { get; set; }
    public string wordPhrase { get; set; }
}
```

Interest in Aggregate

Inside the view method of the `InterestController`, we retrieve all of the user's tags and their friends' tags by calling, respectively, the `userTags` and `tagsInNetwork` methods found in the `TagService` class (Listing 7-37).

Listing 7-37. `tagsInMyNetwork` Located in the `TagService` Class

```
public GraphStory tagsInMyNetwork(GraphStory graphStory)
{
            graphStory.tagsInNetwork = _graphClient.Cypher
                .Start(new { u = graphStory.user.noderef })
                .Match("u-[:FOLLOWS]->f")
                .With("distinct f")
                .Match(" f-[:CURRENTPOST]-lp-[:NEXTPOST*0..]-c")
                .With("distinct c")
                .Match(" c-[ct:HAS]->(t)")
                .With("distinct ct, t")
                .Return(() => Return.As<MappedContentTag>("{name: t.wordPhrase,
                label: t.wordPhrase, " +
                    " id: count(*) }"))
                .OrderByDescending("count(*) ")
                .Results.ToList();
```

```
        graphStory.userTags = _graphClient.Cypher
            .Start(new { u = graphStory.user.noderef })
            .Match("u-[:CURRENTPOST]-lp-[:NEXTPOST*0..]-c")
                        .With("distinct c")
            .Match(" c-[ct:HAS]->(t)")
            .With("distinct ct, t")
            .Return(() => Return.As<MappedContentTag>(" {name: t.wordPhrase, label:
            t.wordPhrase, " +
                " id: count(*) }" ))
            .OrderByDescending("count(*) ")
            .Results.ToList();

        return graphStory;
}
```

This is displayed Figure 7-8 in the left-hand column. The display code is located in `{PROJECTROOT}/Views/Interest/Index.cshtml`.

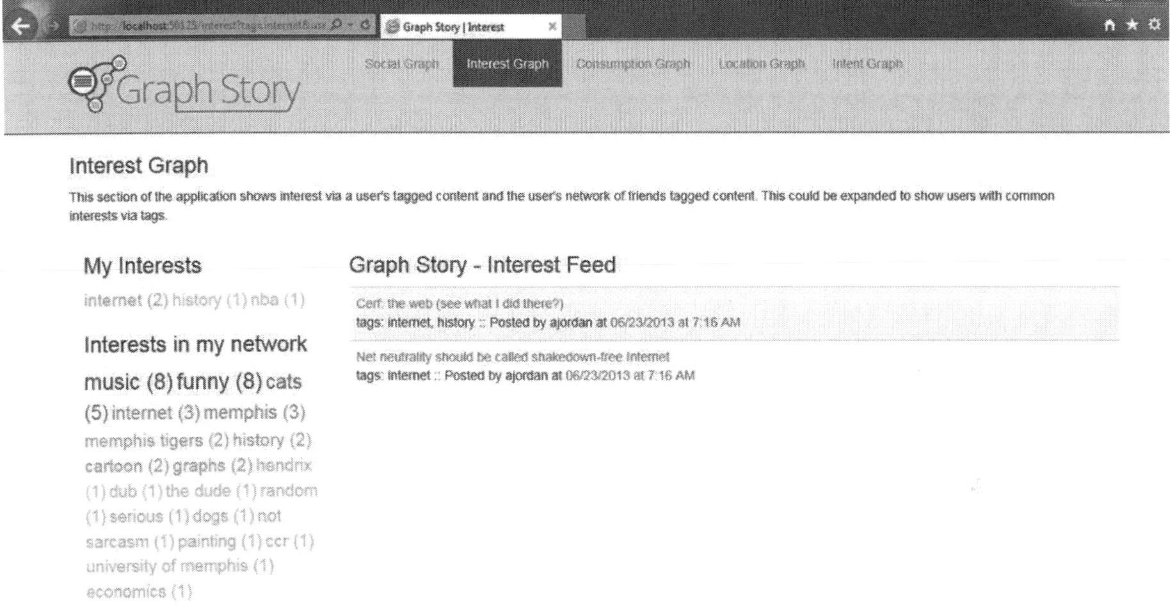

Figure 7-8. *Filtering the current user's content*

The `tagsInMyNetwork` method uses two queries, which are shown in Listing 7-38. The `tagsInNetwork` finds users being followed, accesses all of their content, and finds connected tags through the `HAS` relationship type. Finally, the method returns an `iterable` of `MappedContentTag`.

The `userTags` method is similar but is concerned only with content and, subsequently, tags connected to the current user. Both methods limit the results to 30 items. The methods return `MappedContentTag`, which supports an autosuggest plugin in the view and requires both a label and name to be provided in order to execute. This autosuggest feature is used in the status update form as well as some search forms found later in this chapter.

Listing 7-38. The MappedContentTag

```
public class MappedContentTag
{
        public string id {get; set;}
        public string label {get; set;}
        public string name {get; set;}
}
```

Filtering Managed Content

Once the list of tags for the user and for the group that she follows has been provided, the content can be filtered based of the generated tag links, which is shown in Figure 7-8. If a tag is clicked on the inside of the "My Interests" section, then the `getContentByTag` method, displayed in Listing 7-39, will called be with the `isCurrentUser` value set to true.

Listing 7-39. getContentByTag in ContentService

```
public List<MappedContent> getContentByTag(string username, string tag, bool isCurrentUser)
{
            List<MappedContent> mappedContent = null;

            if (isCurrentUser == true)
            {
                mappedContent = _graphClient.Cypher.Match(" (u:User {username: {u} }) ")
                .WithParam("u", username)
                .With("u")
                .Match(" u-[:CURRENTPOST]-lp-[:NEXTPOST*0..]-p ")
                .With(" DISTINCT u,p ")
                .Match(" p-[:HAS]-(t:Tag {wordPhrase : {wp} } )")
                .WithParam("wp",tag)
                .Return(() => Return.As<MappedContent>(" { contentId: p.contentId, title: p.title,
                url: p.url," +
                    " tagstr: p.tagstr, timestamp: p.timestamp, userNameForPost: u.username, owner:
                      true } "))
                .OrderByDescending("p.timestamp")
                .Results.ToList();
            }
            else
            {
                mappedContent = _graphClient.Cypher.Match(" (u:User {username: {u} }) ")
                .WithParam("u", username)
                .With("u")
                .Match(" (u)-[:FOLLOWS]->f ")
                .With(" DISTINCT f ")
                .Match(" f-[:CURRENTPOST]-lp-[:NEXTPOST*0..]-p ")
                .With(" DISTINCT f,p ")
                .Match(" p-[:HAS]-(t:Tag {wordPhrase : {wp} } )")
                .WithParam("wp", tag)
                .Return(() => Return.As<MappedContent>(" { contentId: p.contentId, title: p.title,
                url: p.url, " +
```

```
                "tagstr: p.tagstr, timestamp: p.timestamp, userNameForPost: f.username, owner:
                false } "))
            .OrderByDescending("p.timestamp")
            .Results.ToList();

        }

        return mappedContent;
}
```

As with a query for the `getContent` method in `ContentService`, the first query in `getContentByTag` returns a collection of `MappedContent` items based on the matching tag, placing no limit on the number of status updates to be returned. In addition, it marks the `owner` property as true, because you've determined ahead of time that you are returning only the current user's content.

Filtering Connected Content

If a tag is clicked on the inside of the "Interests in my Network" section, then the `getContentByTag` method will be called with the `isCurrentUser` value set to false, as shown in Listing 7-39.

The second query is nearly identical to the first query found in `getContentByTag`, except that it will factor in the users being followed and exclude the current user. The method also returns a collection of `MappedContent` items and matches resulting content to a provide tag, placing no limit on the number of status updates to be returned. In addition, it marks the owner property as false. The results of calling this method are shown in Figure 7-9.

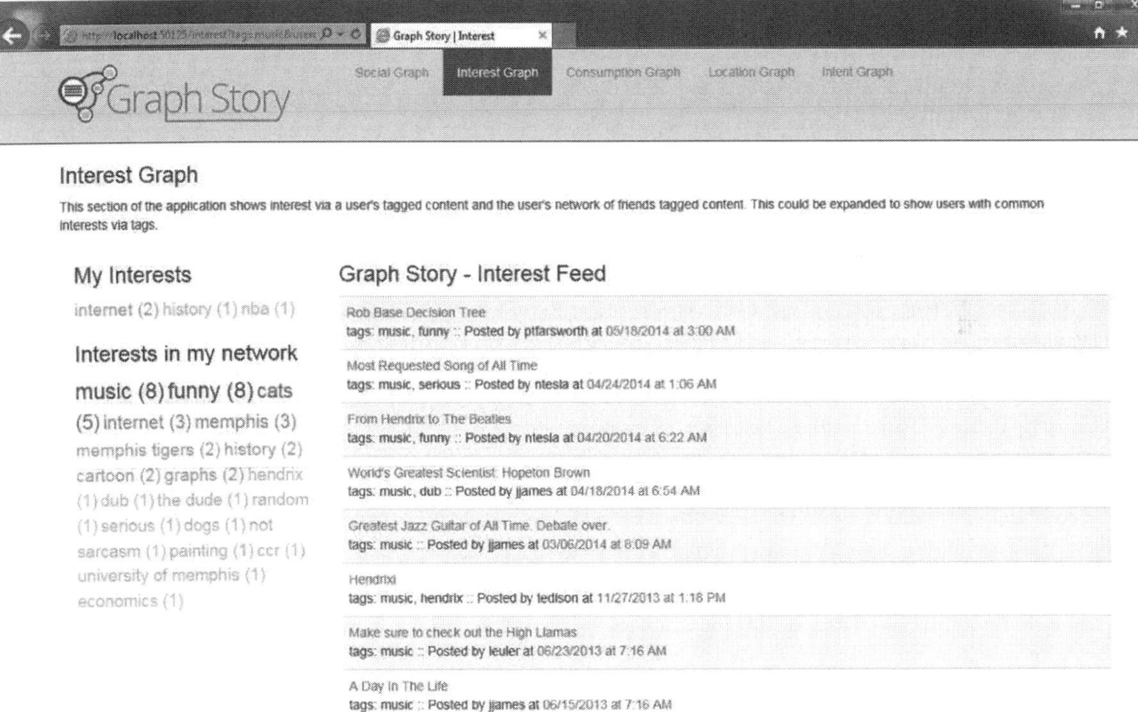

Figure 7-9. *Filtering the content of current user's friends*

Consumption Graph Model

This section examines a few techniques to capture and use patterns of consumption generated implicitly by a user or users. For the purposes of your application, you will use the prepopulated set of products provided in the sample graph. The code required for the console will reinforce the standard persistence operations, this section focuses on the operations that take advantage of this model type, including:

- Capturing consumption
- Filtering consumption for users
- Filtering consumption for messaging

Product Entity

The Product entity will be used to demonstrate the consumption graph— specifically how a user's product trail can be provided. As shown in Listing 7-40, this entity is similar to the other entities that have been outlined for this chapter.

Listing 7-40. The `Product` Object

```
public class Product
{
        public long nodeId { get; set; }
        public NodeReference noderef { get; set; }
        public string productId { get; set; }
        public string title { get; set; }
        public string description { get; set; }
        public string tagstr { get; set; }
        public string content { get; set; }
        public string price { get; set; }
}
```

Capturing Consumption

The process above for creating code that directly captures consumption for a user could also be done by creating a graph-backed service to consume the webserver logs in real time, or by creating another data store to create the relationships. The result would be the same in any event: a process that connects nodes to reveal a pattern of consumption.

The sample application used the `createUserViewAndReturnViews` method in `ProductService` first to find the Product entity being viewed and then to create an explicit relationship type called `VIEWED`. As you may have noticed, this is the first relationship type in the application that also contains properties. In this case, you are creating a timestamp with a `Date` object and String value of the timestamp. The query, provided in Listing 7-41, checks to see if a `VIEWED` relationship already exists between the user and the product using `MERGE`.

In the `MERGE` section of the query, if the result of the `MERGE` is zero matches, then a relationship is created with key value pairs on the new relationship—specifically, `dateAsStr` and `timestamp`. Finally, the query uses `MATCH` to return the existing product views.

Listing 7-41. The createUserViewAndReturnViews Method in ProductService

```
// capture view and return all views
public List<MappedProductUserViews> createUserViewAndReturnViews(string username, long
productNodeId)
{
    DateTime datetime = DateTime.UtcNow;
    string timestampAsStr = datetime.ToString("MM/dd/yyyy") + " at " +
        datetime.ToString("h:mm tt");
    long timestampAsLong = (long)(datetime.Subtract(new DateTime(1970, 1, 1))).TotalSeconds;

    List<MappedProductUserViews> mappedProductUserViews =  _graphClient.Cypher
        .Match(" (p:Product), (u:User { username:{u} }) ")
        .WithParam("u",username)
        .Where("id(p) = {productNodeId}")
        .WithParam("productNodeId",productNodeId)
        .With(" u,p")
        .Merge(" (u)-[r:VIEWED]->(p)")
        .Set(" r.dateAsStr={d}, r.timestamp={t} ")
        .WithParams(new { d = timestampAsStr, t = timestampAsLong })
        .With(" u ")
        .Match("  (u)-[r:VIEWED]->(p) ")
        .Return(() => Return.As<MappedProductUserViews>("{ title: p.title, "+
            "dateAsStr: r.dateAsStr }"))
        .OrderByDescending("r.timestamp")
        .Results.ToList();
     return mappedProductUserViews;
}
```

Filtering Consumption for Users

One practical use of the consumption model would be to create a content trail for users, as shown in Figure 7-10. As a user clicks on items in the scrolling product stream, the interaction is captured using createUserViewAndReturnViews, which ultimately returns a List of relationship objects of the VIEWED type, which are displayed using the ViewModel object called MappedProductUserViews.

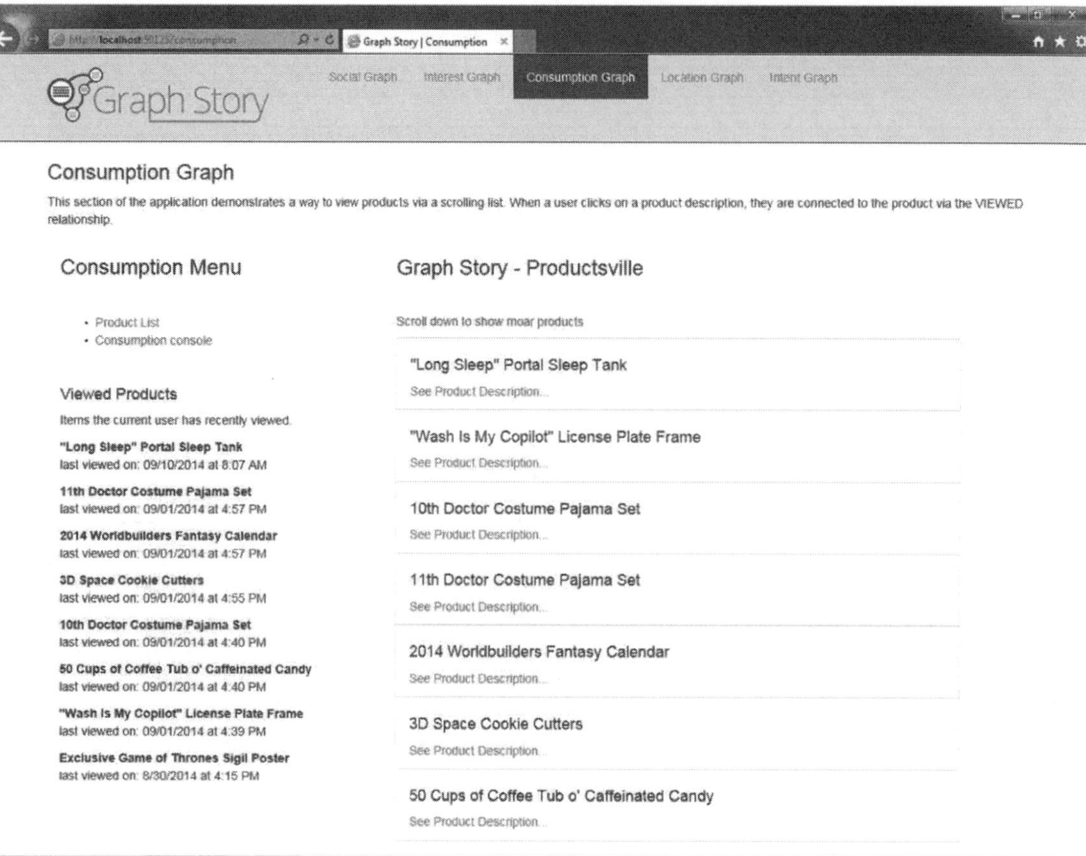

Figure 7-10. *The scrolling Product and Product Trail page*

In the `ConsumptionController`, you will take a look at the `CreateUserProductViewRel` method to see how the process begins inside the controller. The controller method first saves the view and then returns the complete history of views using the `getProductTrail`, which can be found in the ProductService class (Listing 7-42). The process is started when the `createUserProductViewRel` function is called, which is located in `graphstory.js`.

Listing 7-42. `getProductTrail` in the `ProductService`

```
public List<MappedProductUserViews> getProductTrail(string username)
{

            List<MappedProductUserViews> mappedProductUserViews =  _graphClient.Cypher
                .Match("(u:User { username: {username} })-[r:VIEWED]->(p)")
                .WithParam("username", username)
                .Return(() => Return.As<MappedProductUserViews>("{ title: p.title, "+
                    "dateAsStr: r.dateAsStr }"))
                .OrderByDescending("r.timestamp")
                .Results.ToList();

            return mappedProductUserViews;
}
```

Filtering Consumption for Messaging

Another practical use of the consumption model is to create a personalized message for users, as displayed in Figure 7-11. In this case, a filter allows the "Consumption Console" to narrow down to a very specific group of users who visited a product that was also tagged with a keyword or phrase each user had explicitly used.

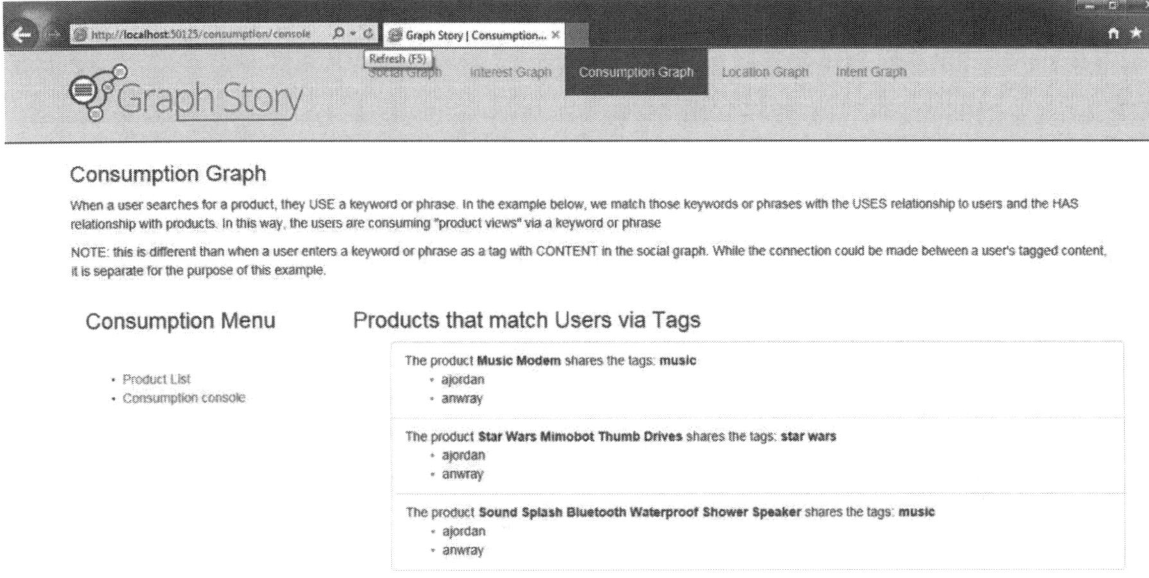

Figure 7-11. *The consumption console*

Using `usersWithMatchingTags` found in the ProductService class and shown in Listing 7-43, the application optionally provides a tag as a string and simply returns the product title and the user and tags that are a match.

Listing 7-43. The `usersWithMatchingTags` Method in `ProductService`

```
// getProductsHasATagAndUserUsesAMatchingTag
public List<MappedProductUserTag> usersWithMatchingTags(string tag)
{
            List<MappedProductUserTag> mappedProductUserTags = null;
            if(!String.IsNullOrEmpty(tag)){
                mappedProductUserTags = _graphClient.Cypher
               .Match("(t:Tag { wordPhrase: {wp} })")
               .WithParam("wp", tag)
               .Match(" (p:Product)-[:HAS]->(t)<-[:USES]-(u:User) ")
```

```
            .Return(() => Return.As<MappedProductUserTag>("{ title: p.title , " +
               "users: collect(u.username), tags: collect(distinct t.wordPhrase) }"))
            .Results.ToList();
        }else{
            mappedProductUserTags = _graphClient.Cypher
            .Match(" (p:Product)-[:HAS]->(t)<-[:USES]-(u:User) ")
            .Return(() => Return.As<MappedProductUserTag>("{ title: p.title ,  " +
            "users: collect(u.username), tags: collect(distinct t.wordPhrase) }"))
            .Results.ToList();
        }

        return mappedProductUserTags;
}
```

Either query will return a list of MappedProductUserTag ViewModel objects, as shown in Listing 7-44.

Listing 7-44. The View Mode Object—MappedProductUserTag

```
public class MappedProductUserTag
{
        public string title {get; set;}
        public List<string> users { get; set; }
        public List<string> tags { get; set; }
}
```

Location Graph Model

This section explores the location graph model and a few of the operations that typically accompany it. In particular, it looks at the following:

- The spatial plugin
- Filtering on location
- Products based on location

The example will demonstrate how to add a console to enable you to connect products to locations in an ad hoc manner.

Location Entity

The Location entity provides a way to store geopoints for stores and each of the stores have various products in stock (Listing 7-45). Because the Location entity does not require any START-based queries, the NodeReference is excluded as a property.

Listing 7-45. The Location Object

```
public class Location
{
        public long nodeId { get; set; }
        public string locationId {get;set;}
        public string name { get; set; }
        public string address { get; set; }
```

```
        public string city { get; set; }
        public string state { get; set; }
        public string zip { get; set; }
        public double lat { get; set; }
        public double lon { get; set; }
}
```

The User object also contains a relationship to Location via the HAS relationship type. User locations are retrieved through the getUserLocation method, shown in Listing 7-46, which is located in the UserService class. Listing 7-46 also provides the ViewModel object named MappedUserLocation, which returns the necessary properties for the Location view layer.

Listing 7-46. getUserLocation in UserService

```
public MappedUserLocation getUserLocation(string currentusername)
{
            MappedUserLocation mappedUserLocation = _graphClient.Cypher
               .Match(" (u:User { username : {u} } )-[:HAS]-(l:Location) ")
               .WithParam("u", currentusername)
               .Return(() => Return.As<MappedUserLocation>("{ username: u.username, address:
               l.address," +
                  " city:l.city, state: l.state, zip: l.zip, lat: l.lat, lon: l.lon} "))
               .Results.First();

            return mappedUserLocation;

}

public class MappedUserLocation
{
        public string username { get; set; }
        public string address { get; set; }
        public string city { get; set; }
        public string state { get; set; }
        public string zip { get; set; }
        public double lat { get; set; }
        public double lon { get; set; }
}
```

Search for Nearby Locations

To search for nearby locations, as shown in Figure 7-12, use the current user's location, obtained with getUserLocation, and then the returnLocationsWithinDistance (Listing 7-47) to provide the location information and the type of location being requested. The returnLocationsWithinDistance method in LocationService also uses a method called addDistanceTo to place a string value of the distance between the starting point and the respective location.

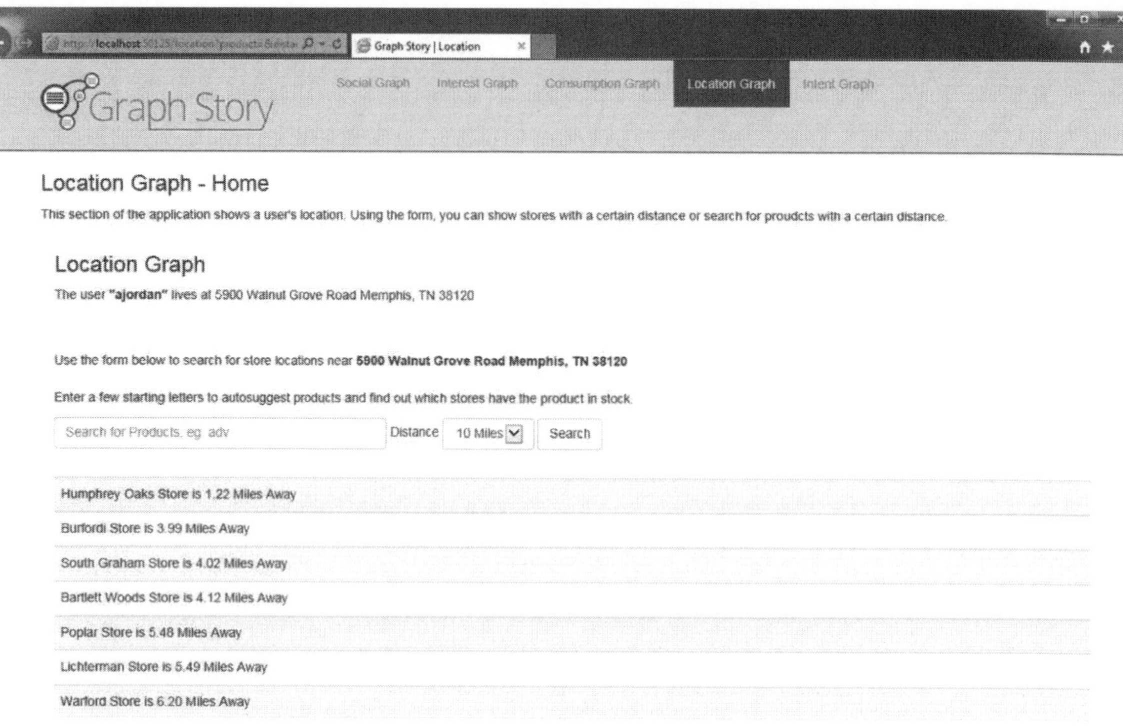

Figure 7-12. *Searching for Locations within a certain distance of the User location*

Listing 7-47. `returnLocationsWithinDistance` in the `LocationService`

```
public List<MappedLocation> returnLocationsWithinDistance(double lat, double lon, double distance,
string locationType)
{
    var q = string.Format(distanceQueryAsString(lat, lon, distance));

    List<MappedLocation> mappedLocations = _graphClient.Cypher
        .Start(new { n = Node.ByIndexQuery("geom", q) })
        .Where(" n.type = {locationType} ")
        .WithParam("locationType", locationType)
        .Return(() => Return.As<MappedLocation>("{locationId: n.locationId, address: n.address , " +
                " city: n.city , state: n.state, zip: n.zip , name: n.name, lat: n.lat , lon: n.lon}"))
        .Results.ToList();
    addDistanceTo(mappedLocations, lat, lon);

    return mappedLocations;
}
```

Locations with Product

To search for products nearby, as shown in Figure 7-13, the application makes use of an autosuggest AJAX request, which ultimately calls the search method in the `ProductService` class. The method, shown in Listing 7-48, returns an array of `MappedProductSearch` objects to the product field in the search form and applies the selected product's `productNodeId` to the subsequent location search (Listing 7-49).

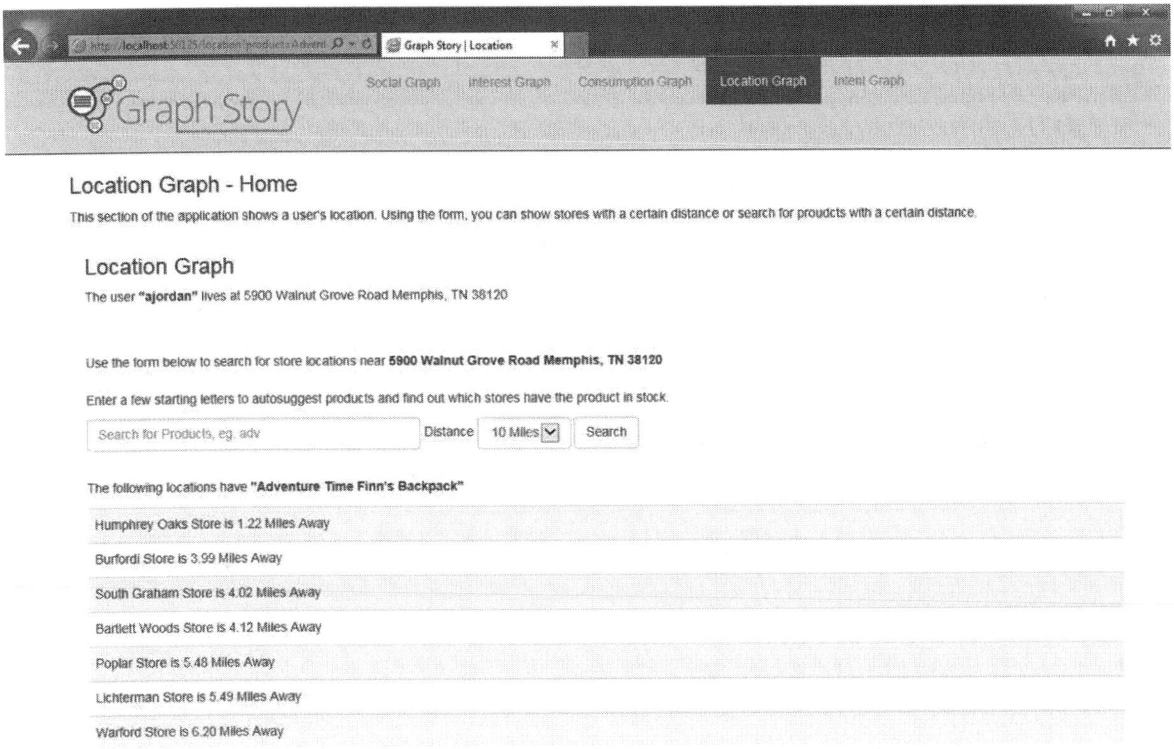

Figure 7-13. *Searching for Products in stock at Locations within a certain distance of the User location*

For almost all cases, it is recommended not to use the graphId because it can be recycled when its node is deleted. In this case, the productNodeId should be consider safe to use, because products would not be in danger of being deleted but only removed from a Location relationship.

Listing 7-48. Search Method in `ProductService`

```
public MappedProductSearch[] search(String q)
{

            q = q.Trim().ToLower() + ".*";

            MappedProductSearch[] mappedProductSearch=_graphClient.Cypher
                .Match("(p:Product)")
                .Where("lower(p.title) =~ {q}")
```

```
                .WithParam("q", q)
                .Return(() => Return.As<MappedProductSearch>(" { name: count(*), " +
                " id: TOSTRING(ID(p)), label: p.title  }"))
                .OrderBy("p.title")
                .Limit(5)
                .Results.ToArray();

            return mappedProductSearch;
}
```

Listing 7-49. The View Model Object—`MappedProductSearch`

```
public class MappedProductSearch
{
        public string id { get; set; }
        public string label { get; set; }
        public string name { get; set; }
}
```

Once the product and distance have been set and the search is executed, the LocationController tests to see if a prouctNodeId property has been set. If so, the controller calls `returnLocationsWithinDistanceAndHasProduct` in the LocationService, as shown in Listing 7-50.

Listing 7-50. The `returnLocationsWithinDistanceAndHasProduct` in the `LocationService`

```
public GraphStory returnLocationsWithinDistanceAndHasProduct(GraphStory graphStory, double lat,
double lon, double distance)
{

            string q = distanceQueryAsString(lat, lon, distance);
            List<MappedLocation> mappedLocations= _graphClient.Cypher
                .Start(new { n = Node.ByIndexQuery("geom", q), p = graphStory.product.noderef})
                .Match(" n-[:HAS]->p ")
                .Return(() => Return.As<MappedLocation>(" { locationId: n.locationId, address:
                n.address , " +
                    " city: n.city , state: n.state, zip: n.zip , name: n.name, lat: n.lat , lon:
                    n.lon} "))
                 .Results.ToList();

            addDistanceTo(mappedLocations, lat, lon);
            graphStory.mappedLocations = mappedLocations;

            return graphStory;
}
```

Intent Graph Model

The last part of the graph model exploration considers all the other graphs in order to suggest products based on the `Purchase` entity, shown in Listing 7-51. The intent graph also considers the products, users, locations, and tags that are connected based upon the `Purchase` entity.

Listing 7-51. The Purchase Object

```
public class Purchase
{
        public long nodeId { get; set; }
        public string purhcaseId { get; set; }
}
```

In addition, each one of the following examples makes use of the `MappedProductUserPurchase` ViewModel found in Listing 7-52.

Listing 7-52. The View Model Object - MappedProductUserPurchase

```
public class MappedProductUserPurchase
{
        public string productId { get; set; }
        public string title { get; set; }
        public List<string> fullname { get; set; }
        public string wordPhrase { get; set; }
        public int cfriends { get; set; }
}
```

Products Purchased by Friends

To get all of the products that have been purchase by friends, the `friendsPurchase` method is called from `PurchaseService`, as shown in Listing 7-53.

The query, shown in Listing 7-53, finds the users being followed by the current user and then matches those users to a purchase that has been `MADE` which `CONTAINS` a product. The return value is a set of properties that identify the product title, the name of the friend or friends, and the number of friends who have bought the product. The result is ordered by the number of friends who have purchased the product and then by product title, as shown in Figure 7-14.

Listing 7-53. The `friendsPurchase` Method in `PurchaseService`

```
public List<MappedProductUserPurchase> friendsPurchase(string userId)
{
          return _graphClient.Cypher
              .Match("(u:User { userId : {userId} } )-[:FOLLOWS]-(f)-[:MADE]->()-[:CONTAINS]->p")
              .WithParam("userId", userId)
              .Return(() => Return.As<MappedProductUserPurchase>("{ productId:p.productId,title:p.
              title," +
               "fullname:collect(f.firstname + ' ' + f.lastname),wordPhrase:null,cfriends:
               count(f) } "))
              .OrderByDescending("count(f)")

              .Results.ToList();
}
```

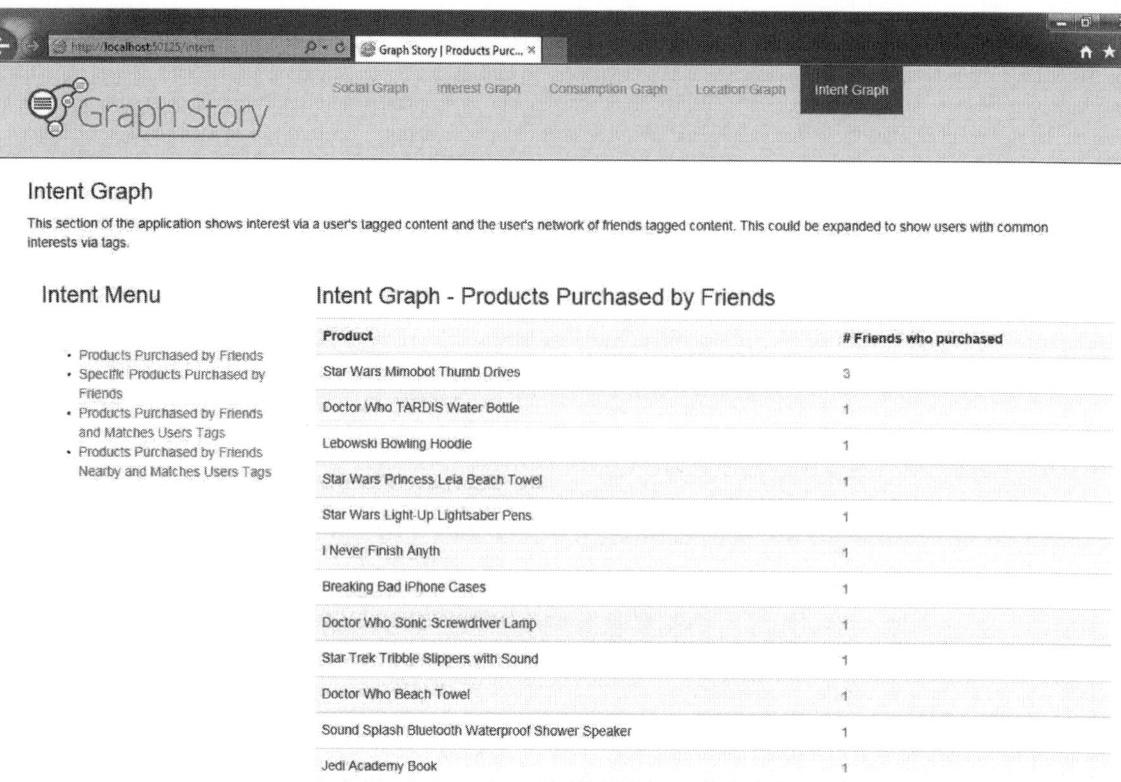

Figure 7-14. *Products purchased by friends*

Specific Products Purchased by Friends

If you click on the "Specific Products Purchased By Friends" link, you can specify a product, in this case "Star Wars Mimbot Thumb Drives", and then search for friends who have purchased this product, as shown in Figure 7-15. This is done via the `friendsPurchaseByProduct` method in `PurchaseService`, which is shown in Listing 7-54.

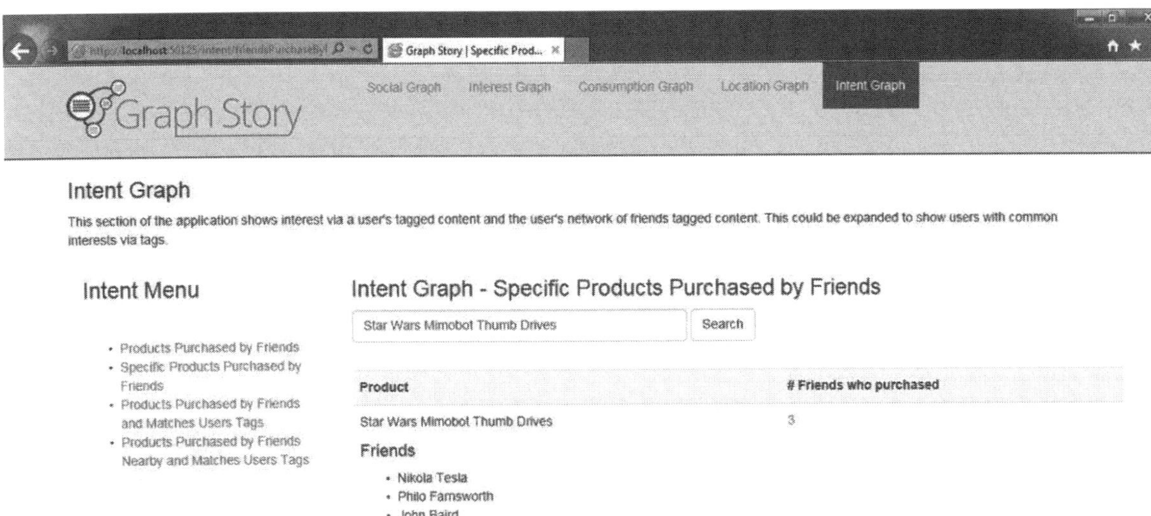

Figure 7-15. *Specific Products Purchased by Friends*

Listing 7-54. The `friendsPurchaseByProduct` Method in `PurchaseService`

```
public List<MappedProductUserPurchase> friendsPurchaseByProduct(string userId, string title)
{
            return _graphClient.Cypher
                .Match("(p:Product)")
                .Where("lower(p.title) =lower({title})")
                .WithParam("title", title)
                .With("p")
                .Match("(u:User { userId : {userId} } )-[:FOLLOWS]-(f)-[:MADE]->()-[:CONTAINS]->(p) ")
                .WithParam("userId", userId)
                .Return(() => Return.As<MappedProductUserPurchase>("{productId:p.productId,title:p.
                title," +
                "fullname:collect(f.firstname + ' ' + f.lastname),wordPhrase:null,cfriends:
                count(f) }"))
                .OrderByDescending("count(f)")
                .Results.ToList();
}
```

Products Purchased by Friends and Matches User's Tags

In this next instance, we want to determine products that have been purchased by friends but also have tags that are used by the current user. The result of the query is shown in Figure 7-16.

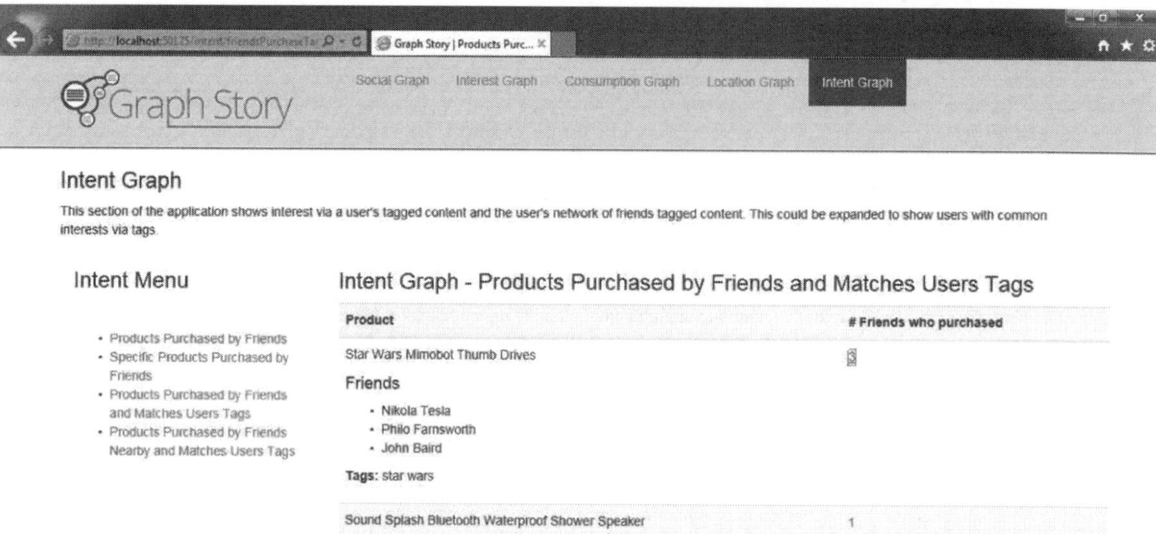

Figure 7-16. *Products Purchased by Friends and Matches User's Tags*

Using `friendsPurchaseTagSimilarity` in `PurchaseService`, shown in Listing 7-55, the application provides the userId to the query and uses the `FOLLOWS`, `MADE`, and `CONTAINS` relationships to return products purchases by users being followed. The subsequent MATCH statement takes the USES and HAS directed relationship types to determine the TAG connections the resulting products and the current user have in common.

Listing 7-55. The `friendsPurchaseTagSimilarity` Method in `PurchaseService`

```
public List<MappedProductUserPurchase> friendsPurchaseTagSimilarity(string userId)
{
            return _graphClient.Cypher
                .Match("(u:User { userId : {userId} } )-[:FOLLOWS]-(f)-[:MADE]->()-[:CONTAINS]->p")
                .WithParam("userId", userId)
                .With("u,p,f")
                .Match("u-[:USES]->(t)<-[:HAS]-p")
                .Return(() => Return.As<MappedProductUserPurchase>("{productId:p.productId,title:p.
                title," +
                "fullname:collect(f.firstname + ' ' + f.lastname),wordPhrase:t.wordPhrase,cfriends:
                count(f)}"))
                .OrderByDescending("count(f)")
                .Results.ToList();
}
```

Products Purchased by Friends Nearby and Matches User's Tags

To find products that match with a specific user's tags and have been purchased by friends who live within a set distance of the user, use the `friendsPurchaseTagSimilarityAndProximityToLocation` method, which is easily world's longest method name and is located in `PurchaseService` class. The method uses the MappedProductUserPurchase `ViewModel`, as shown in Listing 7-56.

Listing 7-56. The `friendsPurchaseTagSimilarityAndProximityToLocation` method in `PurchaseService`

```
public List<MappedProductUserPurchase> friendsPurchaseTagSimilarityAndProximityToLocation(double
lat, double lon, double distance, string userId)
{
            var q = string.Format(distanceQueryAsString(lat, lon, distance));

            return  _graphClient.Cypher
                .Start(new { n = Node.ByIndexQuery("geom", q) })
                .With("n")
                .Match("(u:User { userId : {userId} } )-[:USES]->(t)<-[:HAS]-p")
                .WithParam("userId", userId)
                .With("n,u,p,t")
                .Match("u-[:FOLLOWS]->(f)-[:HAS]->(n) ")
                .With("p,f,t")
                .Match("f-[:MADE]->()-[:CONTAINS]->(p)")
                .Return(() => Return.As<MappedProductUserPurchase>("{productId:p.productId,title:p.
                title," +
                "fullname:collect(f.firstname + ' ' + f.lastname),wordPhrase:t.wordPhrase,cfriends:
                count(f)}"))
                .OrderByDescending("count(f)")
                .Results.ToList();

}
```

The query begins starts with a location search within a certain distance, then matching the current user's tags to products. Next, the query matches friends based the location search. The resulting friends are matched against products that are in the set of user tag matches. The result of the query is shown in Figure 7-17.

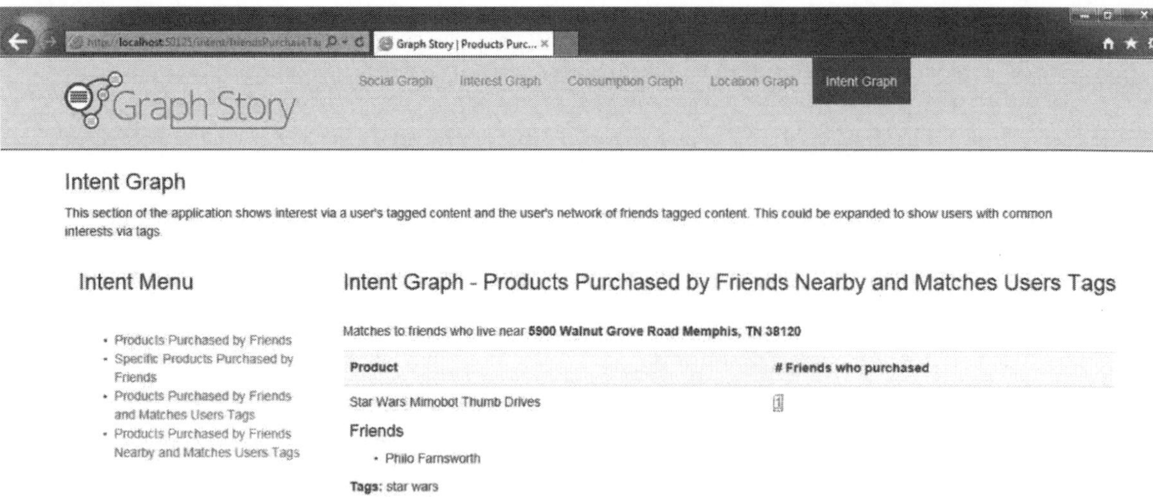

Figure 7-17. *Products Purchased by Friends Nearby and Matches User's Tags*

Summary

This chapter presented the setup for .NET and Neo4j and sample code for using the Neo4Client driver. It proceeded to look at sample code for setting up a social network and examining interest within the network. It then looked at the sample code for capturing and viewing consumption—in this case, product views— and the queries for understanding the relationship between consumption and a user's interest. Finally, it looked at using geospatial matching for locations and examples of methods for understanding user intent within the context of user location, social network, and interests.

The next chapter will review using PHP in tandem with Neo4j, covering the same concepts presented in this chapter but in the context of a PHP driver for Neo4j.

CHAPTER 8

Neo4j + PHP

This chapter focuses on using PHP with Neo4j and creating a working application that integrates the five graph model types covered in Chapter 3. As with other languages that offer drivers for Neo4j, the integration takes place using a Neo4j server instance with the Neo4j REST API. This chapter is divided into the following topics:

- PHP and Neo4j Development Environment
- Neo4jPHP
- Developing a PHP and Neo4j application

In each chapter that explores a particular language paired with Neo4j, I recommend that you start a free trial on `www.graphstory.com` or have installed a local Neo4j server instance as shown in Chapter 2.

Tip To quickly set up a server instance with the sample data and plugins for this chapter, go to `graphstory.com/practicalneo4j`. You will be provided with your own free trial instance, a knowledge base, and email support from Graph Story.

For this chapter, I assume that you have at least a beginning knowledge of PHP and a basic understanding of how to configure PHP for your preferred operating system. To proceed with the examples in this chapter, you will need to have installed and configured PHP 5.3.28 or greater. In addition, the sample application uses the Apache HTTP server and php5_module.

Do This If you do not have Apache HTTP installed, it is highly recommended that you follow the instructions at `http://httpd.apache.org/` based on your operating system. Configuring PHP with a local instance of Apache HTTP is beyond the scope of this book, but the basic steps can be found at `http://www.php.net/manual/en/refs.utilspec.server.php`.

I also assume that you have a basic understanding of the model-view-controller (MVC) pattern and some knowledge of PHP frameworks that provide an MVC pattern. There are, of course, a number of excellent PHP frameworks from which to choose, but I had to pick one for the illustrative purposes of the application in this chapter. I chose the Slim PHP framework because it is limited in its scope and allows the focus to remain on the application to the greatest extent possible. This chapter is focused on integrating Neo4j into your PHP skill set and projects and does not dive deeply into the best practices of developing with PHP or PHP frameworks.

PHP and Neo4j Development Environment

Preliminary to this chapter's discussion of the PHP and Neo4j application, this section covers the basics of configuring a development environment. Again, if you have not worked through the installation steps in Chapter 2, please take a few minutes to review and walk through the installation.

■ **Readme** Although each language chapter walks through the process of configuring the development environment based on the particular language, certain steps are covered repeatedly in multiple chapters. While the initial development environment setup in each chapter is somewhat redundant, it allows each language chapter to stand on its own. Bearing this in mind, if you have already configured Eclipse with the necessary plugins while working through another chapter, you can skip ahead to the section "Adding the Propse."

IDE

The reasons behind the choice of an IDE vary from developer to developer and are often tied to the choice of programming language. I chose the Eclipse IDE for a number of reasons but mainly because it is freely available and versatile enough to work with all the programming languages featured in this book.

Although you are welcome to choose a different IDE or other programming tool for building your application, I recommend that you install and use Eclipse to be able to follow the PHP and Neo4j examples and the related examples found throughout the book and online.

■ **Tip** If you do not have Eclipse, please visit `http://www.eclipse.org/downloads/` and download the Indigo package, titled "Eclipse IDE for Java EE Developers." The Indigo package is also labeled "Version 3.7."

Once you have installed Eclipse, open it and select a *workspace* for your application. A *workspace* in Eclipse is simply an arbitrary directory on your computer. As shown in Figure 8-1, when you first open Eclipse, the program will ask you to specify which workspace you want to use. Choose the path that works best for you. If you are working through all of the language chapters, you can use the same workspace for each project.

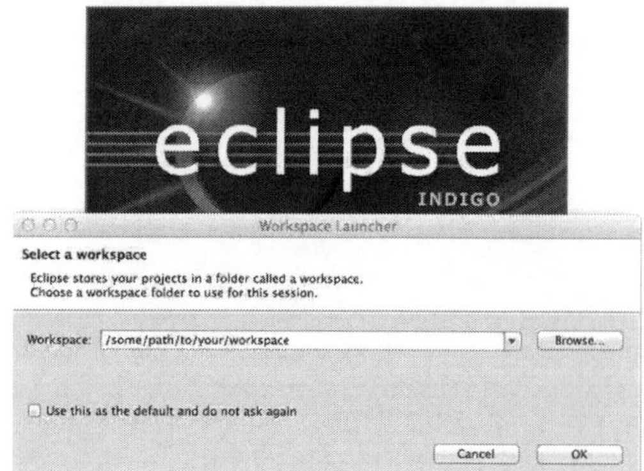

Figure 8-1. *Opening Eclipse and choosing a workspace*

Aptana Plugin

The Eclipse IDE offers a convenient way to add new tools through their plugin platform. The process for adding new plugins to Eclipse is straightforward and usually involves only a few steps to install a new plugin—as you will see in this section.

A specific web-tool plugin called Aptana provides support of server-side languages like Python as well as client languages such as CSS and JavaScript. This chapter and the other programming language chapters use the plugin to edit both server- and client-side languages. A benefit of using a plugin such as Aptana is that it can provide code-assist tools and code suggestions based on the type of file you are editing, such as CSS, JS, or HTML. The time saved with code-assist tools is usually significant enough to warrant their use. Again, if you feel comfortable exploring within your preferred IDE or other program, please do so.

To install the Aptana plugin, you need to have Eclipse installed and opened. Then proceed through the following steps:

1. From the Help menu, select "Install New Software" to open the dialog, which will look like the one in Figure 8-2.

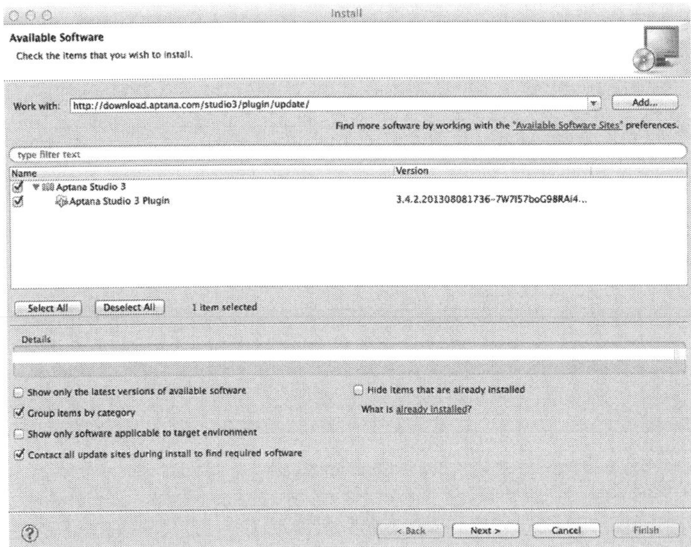

Figure 8-2. *Installing the Aptana plugin*

2. Paste the URL for the update site, `http://download.aptana.com/studio3/plugin/install`, into the "Work with" text box, and hit the Enter (or Return) key.

3. In the populated table below, check the box next to the name of the plugin, and then click the Next button.

4. Click the Next button to go to the license page.

5. Choose the option to accept the terms of the license agreement, and click the Finish button.

6. You may need to restart Eclipse to continue.

Adding the Project to Eclipse

After installing Eclipse plugin, you have the minimum requirements to work with your project in the workspace. To keep the workflow as fluid as possible for each of the language example application, use the project import tool with Eclipse. To import the project into your workspace, follow these steps:

1. Go to `www.graphstory.com/practicalneo4j` and download the archive file for "Practical Neo4j for PHP." Unzip the archive file on to your computer.
2. In Eclipse, select File ➤ Import and type "project" in the "Select an import source."
3. Under the "General" heading, select "Existing Projects into Workspace". You should now see a window similar to Figure 8-3.

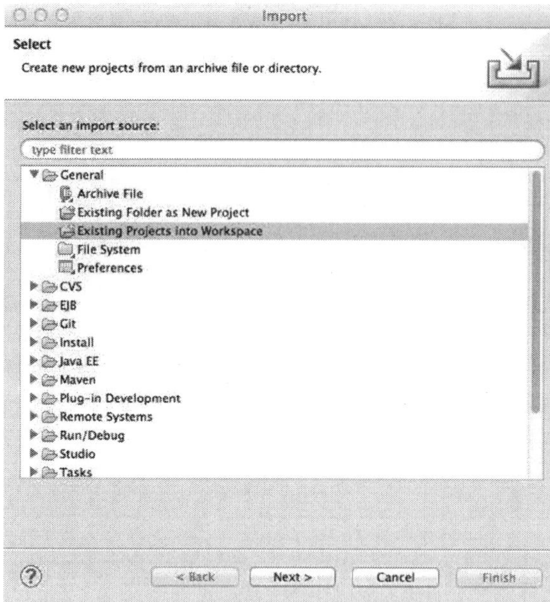

***Figure 8-3.** Importing the project into Eclipse*

4. Now that you have selected "Existing Projects into Workspace", click the "Next >" button. The dialogue should now show an option to "Select root directory." Click the "Browse" button and find the root path of the "practicalneo4j-php" archive.
5. Next, check the option for "Copy project into workspace" and click the "Finish" button, as shown in Figure 8-4.

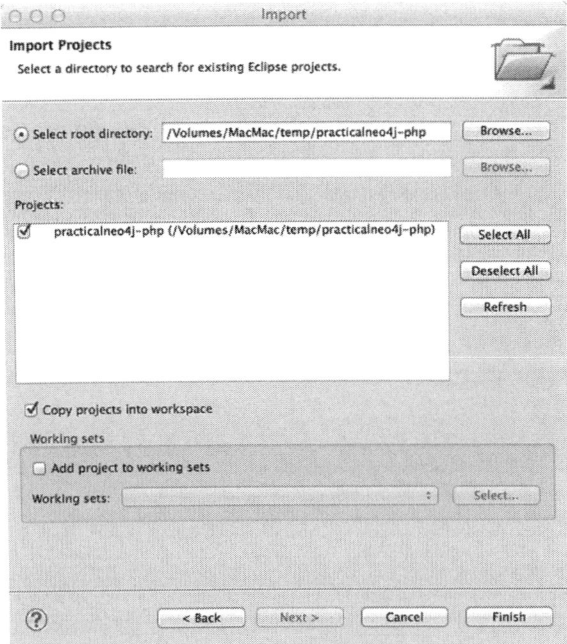

Figure 8-4. *Selecting the project location*

6. Once the project is finished importing into your workspace, you should have a directory structure that looks similar to the one shown in Figure 8-5.

Figure 8-5. *Snapshot of the imported project*

Composer

The project in this chapter also makes use of Composer, which is a tool for dependency management in PHP. Composer allows you to explicitly declare any of the PHP libraries your project needs and then installs them in your project for you. This is a huge benefit when your application depends upon one or more PHP libraries, which is the case with the sample application in this chapter and will probably be the case with most of your PHP projects.

■ **Tip** To download Composer and get information about installing it, go to `https://getcomposer.org/`.

Even though the sample project in this chapter has all of the dependencies already set, you should take some time and become familiar with Composer and how to use it in your projects. The example in Listing 8-1 shows the contents of the Composer file that is included within this project.

Listing 8-1. `composer.json` file for the sample project

```
{
    "name": "slim/slim-skeleton",
    "description": "A Slim Framework skeleton application for rapid development",
    "keywords": ["microframework","rest","router"],
    "homepage": "http://github.com/codeguy/Slim-Skeleton",
    "license": "MIT",
    "authors": [
        {
            "name": "Josh Lockhart",
            "email": "info@joshlockhart.com",
            "homepage": "http://www.joshlockhart.com/"
        }
    ],
    "require": {
        "php": ">=5.3.0",
        "monolog/monolog": "1.*",
        "slim/slim": "2.*",
        "slim/views": "0.1.*",
        "twig/twig": "1.*",
        "everyman/neo4jphp": "dev-master"
    }
}
```

The first section contains meta-information about the project, but the most important section is the *require* key/value section. The require section shows the specific dependencies for the project. Once Composer is installed and you have added a `composer.json` file to the root of your project, you can execute the command in Listing 8-2. The example in Listing 8-2 assumes that you have installed Composer using the global installation method.

Listing 8-2. Creating a project with Composer

```
// Replace [my-neo4j-app] with the desired directory name or path for your new application.
composer create-project slim/slim-skeleton [my-neo4j-app]
```

Slim PHP

Slim is a PHP implementation of what is often called a *micro framework*. The aim of a micro framework is to help you quickly build out powerful web applications and APIs using only what is absolutely necessary to get the job done.

■ **Note** Slim is maintained by the outstanding PHP dev Josh Lockhart and supported by a number of equally outstanding committers, including our technical reviewer Jeremy Kendall. If you would like to get involved with Slim, please visit `http://www.slimframework.com/`.

Listing 8-3. SlimPHP Example of GET Route

```
<?php
... include file code omitted for brevity...

//setup app
$app = new \Slim\Slim(array(
    'log.enabled' =>    true,
    'log.level' =>      \Slim\Log::DEBUG,
    'log.writer' => $logWriter,
    'view' => new \Slim\Views\Twig()
));

...code omitted for brevity...

// new GET route to /somepath
$app->get('/somepath', function() use ($app){
        //render this html file
   $app->render('graphs/social/posts.html');
});
```

Local Apache Configuration

To follow the sample application found later in this chapter, you will need to properly configure your local Apache webserver to use the workspace project in Eclipse as the document root. One way to accomplish this is adding a virtual host to Apache. Listing 8-4 covers the basic configuration for adding a virtual host to the `httpd-vhosts.conf file`.

■ **Important** If you do not have Apache HTTP installed, go to `http://httpd.apache.org/` and follow the instructions based on your operating system. Configuring PHP with a local instance of Apache HTTP is out of scope for this book, but you can find the basic configuration steps at `http://www.php.net/manual/en/refs.utilspec.server.php`.

Listing 8-4. Minimum Configuration for `httpd-vhosts.conf`

```
NameVirtualHost *:80
<VirtualHost *:80>
        # add practicalneo4j-php to your hosts file OR substiute your
        ServerName practicalneo4j-php
        DocumentRoot /path/to/your/workspace/practicalneo4j-php/app/public
```

```
        <Directory /path/to/your/workspace/practicalneo4j-php/app/public>
                RewriteEngine On
                RewriteCond %{REQUEST_FILENAME} !-f
                RewriteRule ^(.*)$ index.php [QSA,L]
                Options Indexes FollowSymLinks MultiViews
                AllowOverride All
                Order allow,deny
                Allow from all
        </Directory>
</VirtualHost>
```

In addition the configuration changes for your local Apache webserver, complete the following two items to finalize your development environment:

1. Point your virtual host document root to your new application's public/ directory.
2. Ensure logs/ and templates/cache are web writeable.

Neo4jPHP

This section covers basic operations and usage of the Neo4jPHP library with the goal of understanding the library before implementing it within an application. The next section of this chapter will walk you through a sample application with specific graph goals and models.

Like most of the language drivers and libraries available for Neo4j, the purpose of Neo4jPHP is to provide a degree of abstraction over the Neo4j REST API. In addition, the Neo4jPHP API provides some additional enhancements that might otherwise be required at some other stage in the development of your PHP application, such as caching.

■ **Note** Neo4jPHP is maintained by the super-awesome Josh Adell and supported by a number of great PHP graphistas. If you would like to get involved with Neo4jPHP, go to `https://github.com/jadell/neo4jphp`.

Each of the following brief sections covers concepts that tie either directly or indirectly to features and functionality found within the Neo4j Server and REST API. If you choose to go through each language chapter, you will notice how each library covers those features and functionality in similar ways but takes advantage of the language-specific capabilities to ensure that the API is flexible and performant.

Managing Nodes and Relationships

Chapters 1 and 2 covered the elements of a graph database, which includes the most basic of graph concepts: the node. Managing nodes and their properties and relationships will probably account for the bulk of your application's graph-related code.

Creating a Node

The maintenance of nodes is set in motion with the creation process, as shown in Listing 8-5. Creating a node begins with setting up a connection to the database and making the node instance. The node properties are set next, and then the node can be saved to the database.

Listing 8-5. Creating a Node

```
<?php
require_once '../vendor/autoload.php';
// Neo4jClient class
require_once '../neo4j/Neo4jClient.php';

// Create Neo4j client
$neo4jClient = new Everyman\Neo4j\Client('localhost', 7474);
Neo4Client::setClient($neo4jClient);

// setup the node
$user = $neo4jClient->makeNode();

// populate & save the node
$ user->setProperty('name', 'Greg')->setProperty('business', 'Graph Story')->save();
```

Retrieving and Updating a Node

Once nodes have been added to the database, you will need a way to retrieve and modify them. Listing 8-6 shows the process for finding a node by its node id value and updating it.

Listing 8-6. Retrieving and Updating a Node

```
<?php
// Neo4jClient class
// ...omitted...

// Create Neo4j client
// ...omitted...

// retrieve the node by its node id value, in this case 10
$user = $neo4jClient->getNode(10);

// update & save the node
$user->setProperty('name', 'Greg')->setProperty('business', 'Crowdplace')->save();
```

Removing a Node

Once a node's graph id has been set and saved into the database, it becomes eligible to be removed when necessary. In order to remove a node, set a variable as a node object instance and then call the delete method for the node (Listing 8-7).

■ **Note** You cannot delete any node that is currently set as the start point or end point of any relationship. You must remove the relationship before you can delete the node.

Listing 8-7. Deleting a Node

```
<?php
// Neo4jClient class
// ...omitted...

// Create Neo4j client
// ...omitted...

// retrieve the node by its node id value, in this case 10
$user = $neo4jClient->getNode(10);

// delete the node
$user->delete();
```

Creating a Relationship

Neo4jPHP offers two different methods for creating relationships: one using the *relateTo* method; the other using the *makeRelationship* method. The example in Listing 8-8 sets up the relationship using the *relateTo* method, which is the less verbose of the two options.

■ **Note** Both the start and end nodes of a relationship must already be established within the database before the relationship can be saved.

Listing 8-8. Relating Two Nodes

```
<?php
// Neo4jClient class
// ...omitted...

// Create Neo4j client
// ...omitted...

// retrieve the node by its node id value, in this case 10
$greg = $neo4jClient->getNode(10);

// retrieve the node by its node id value, in this case 1
$jeremy = $neo4jClient->getNode(1);

// populate & save the relationship ($greg follows $jeremy)
$greg->relateTo($jeremy,'FOLLOWS')->save();
```

Retrieving Relationships

Once a relationship has been created between one or more nodes, the relationship can be retrieved based on a node.

Listing 8-9. Retrieving Relationships

```
<?php
// Neo4jClient class
// ...omitted...

// Create Neo4j client
// ...omitted...

// retrieve the node by its node id value, in this case 10
$greg = $neo4jClient->getNode(10);

// get all relationships
$gregRels = $greg->getRelationships();

// get relationships based on relationship named 'FOLLOWS'
$ gregKNOWSRels = $greg->getRelationships(array('FOLLOWS'));
```

Deleting a Relationship

Once a relationship's graph id has been set and saved into the database, it becomes eligible to be removed when necessary. In order to remove a relationship, it must be set as a relationship object instance and then the delete method for the relationship can be called.

Listing 8-10. Deleting a Relationship

```
<?php
// Neo4jClient class
// ...omitted...

// Create Neo4j client
// ...omitted...

// retrieve the Relationshipby its Relationship id value, in this case 20
$rel = $client->getRelationship(20);

// delete the relationship
$rel->delete();
```

Using Labels

Labels function as specific meta-descriptions that can be applied to nodes. Labels were introduced in Neo4j 2.0 to help in querying, and they can also function as a way to quickly create a sub-graph.

Adding a Label to Nodes

In Neo4jPHP, you can add one more labels to a node. As Listing 8-10 shows, the *addLabels* function takes one or more labels as argument. You can return each of the labels on a node by calling its *getLabels* function. The value used for the label should be any nonempty string or numeric value.

■ **Caution** A label will not exist on the database server until it has been added to at least one node.

Listing 8-10. Creating a Label and Adding It to a Node

```
<?php
// Neo4jClient class
// ...omitted...

// Create Neo4j client
// ...omitted...

// retrieve the node by its node id value, in this case 10
$greg = $neo4jClient->getNode(10);

// create three labels
$userLabel = $client->makeLabel('User');
$devLabel = $client->makeLabel('Developer');
$memeLabel = $client->makeLabel('GoodGuyGreg');

// add the labels to $greg
$labels = $greg->addLabels(array($userLabel, $devLabel, $memeLabel));

// get the labels for $greg
$labels = $greg->getLabels();
```

Removing a Label

Removing a label uses similar syntax as adding a label to a node. After the given label has been removed from the node (Listing 8-12), the return value is a list of labels still on the node.

Listing 8-12. Removing a Label from a Node

```
<?php
// Neo4jClient class
// ...omitted...

// Create Neo4j client
// ...omitted...

// retrieve the node by its node id value, in this case 10
$greg = $neo4jClient->getNode(10);

// delete the relationship
$remainingLabels = $node->removeLabels(array($memeLabel));
```

Querying with a Label

To get nodes that use a specific label, use the function called *getNodes*. This function returns value as a result Row object, which can be iterated over like an array.

Listing 8-13. Querying with a Label

```
<?php
// Neo4jClient class
// ...omitted...

// Create Neo4j client
// ...omitted...

// get the label
$devLabel = $client->makeLabel('Developer');

// return the nodes
$devNodes = $devLabel->getNodes();

// Only return nodes that have whose name property value is "Greg"
$nodes = $devLabel->getNodes("name", "Greg");
```

Developing a PHP and Neo4j Application

Preliminary to building out your first PHP and Neo4j application, this section covers the basics of configuring a development environment.

Again, if you have not worked through the installation steps in Chapter 2, please take a few minutes to install it.

Preparing the Graph

In order to spend more time highlighting code examples for each of the more common graph models, we will use a preloaded instance of Neo4j including necessary plugins, such as the spatial plugin.

■ **Tip** To quickly set up a server instance with the sample data and plugins for this chapter, go to `graphstory.com/practicalneo4j`. You will be provided with your own free trial instance, a knowledge base, and email support from Graph Story. Alternatively, you may run a local Neo4j database instance with the sample data by going to graphstory.com/practicalneo4j, downloading the zip file containing the sample database and plugins, and adding them to your local instance.

Using the Sample Application

If you have already downloaded the sample application from `graphstory.com/practicalneo4j` for PHP and configured it with your local application environment, you can proceed to the "Slim Application Configuration" section. Otherwise, you will need to go back to the "PHP and Neo4j Development Environment" section and set up your local environment in order to follow the examples in the sample application.

Slim Application Configuration

Before diving into the code examples, you need to update the configuration for the Slim application. In Eclipse (or the IDE you are using), open the file `{PROJECTROOT}/app/service/AppConfig.php` and edit the GraphStory connection string information. If you are using a free account from graphstory.com, you will change the username, password and URL in Listing 8-14 with the one provided in your graph console on graphstory.com.

Listing 8-14. Database Connection Settings for a Remote Service such as Graph Story

```
$neo4jClient = new Everyman\Neo4j\Client('someurl.graphstory.com', 7473);
$neo4jClient->getTransport()->useHttps()->setAuth('username', 'password');
```

If you have installed a local Neo4j server instance, you can modify the configuration to use the local address and port that you specified during the installation, similar to the example shown in Listing 8-15.

Listing 8-15. Database Connection Settings for Local Enviroment

```
$neo4jClient = new Everyman\Neo4j\Client('localhost', 7474);
```

Once the environment is properly configured and started, you can open a browser to the url, `http://practicalneo4j-PHP`, and you should see a page like the one shown in Figure 8-6.

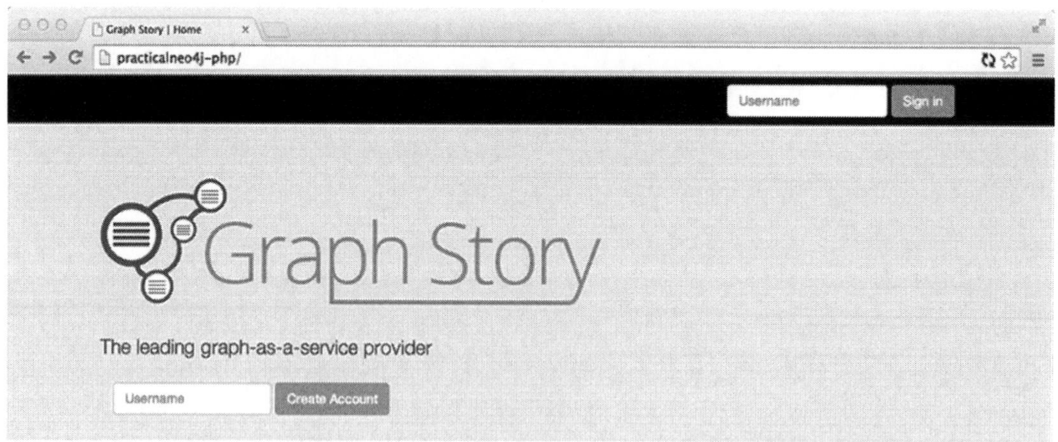

Figure 8-6. *The PHP sample application home page*

Social Graph Model

This section explores the social graph model and a few of the operations that typically accompany the use of that type of model. In particular, this section looks at the following:

- Sign-up and Login
- Updating a user
- Creating a relationship type through a user by following other users
- Managing user content, such as displaying, adding, updating, and removing status updates

---

■ **Note** The sample graph database used for these examples is loaded with data, so you can immediately begin working with representative data in each of the graph models. In the case of the social graph—and for other graph models, as well—you will login with the user **ajordan**. Going forward, please login with **ajordan** to see each of the working examples.

Sign Up

The HTML required for the user sign-up form is shown in Listing 8-16 and can be found in the `{PROJECTROOT}/app/templates/home/index.mustache` file.

Listing 8-16. HTML Snippet of the Sign-Up Form

```
<form class="navbar-form navbar-left" action="/signup/add" role="form"
id="createaccountform" method="post">
                    <div class="form-group">
                            <input type="text" placeholder="Username" name="username"
                            class="form-control">
                    </div>
<button type="submit" class="btn btn-success">Create Account</button>   
</form>
```

■ **Note** While the sample application creates a user without a password, I am certainly not suggesting or advocating this approach for a production application. Excluding the password property was done in order to create a simple sign-up and login that helps keep the focus on the more salient aspects of the Neo4jPHP library.

Sign-Up Route

In the sign-up route, start by doing a look up on the `username` passed in the request and see if it already exists in the database using the `getByUsername` method found in the `User` service layer, as provided in Listing 8-17. If no match is found, then the username is passed on to the `saveUser` method.

If no errors were returned during the save attempt, the request is redirected and a message is passed to thank the user for signing up. Otherwise, the error message back to the home view informs the user of the problem.

Listing 8-17. The Signup Controller Route

```
// create new user & redirect
$app->post('/signup/add', function() use ($app){
    $params = $app->request()->post();
        // make sure the user name was passed.
        $username = trim($params['username']);

        //FYI - this is one way to log with SLIM
        // $app->log->debug('some message then a variable: ' . $username);

    if (!empty($username)) {
            // lower case the username.
                $username=strtolower($username);

            // see if there's already a User node with this username
        $checkuser = User::getByUsername($username);

                //No? then save it
        if(is_null($checkuser)){
                // setup the object
            $user = new User();
            $user->username = $username;
                        // save it
            User::saveUser($user);
                        // redirect to thank you page
            $app->redirect('/thankyou?u='.$username);
        }
                // show the "try again" message.
        else {
            $app->view()->setData(array('error' =>
               'The username "'.$username.'" already exists. Please try again.'));
            $app->render('home/index.mustache');
        }
        // username field was empty
    } else {
        $app->view()->setData(array('error' => 'Please enter a username.'));
        $app->render('home/index.mustache');
    }
});
```

Adding a User

In each part of the five graph areas covered in the chapter, the domain object will have a corresponding service to manage the persistence operations within the database. In this case, the User class covers the management of the application's user nodes using a mix of Neo4jPHP convenience methods and executing Cypher queries.

To save a node and label it as a User, the saveUser method, shown in Listing 8-18, makes use of the Neo4jPHP save method by passing in the username param and value. Once the node is created, the Neo4jPHP addLabels method applies the User label.

Listing 8-18. The saveUser Method in the User Class

```
public static function saveUser(User $user){
        if(!$user->node){
                $user->node = new Node(Neo4Client::client());
        }
        $userlabel = Neo4Client::client()->makeLabel('User');
        // set properties
        $user->node->setProperty('username', $user->username);
        $user->node->setProperty('firstname', $user->firstname);
        $user->node->setProperty('lastname', $user->lastname);
        // save the node
        $user->node->save()->addLabels(array($userlabel));
        //set the id on the user object
        $user->id = $user->node->getId();
}
```

Login

This section reviews the login process for the sample application. To execute the login process, we also use the login route as well as User class. Before reviewing the controller and service layer, take a quick look at the front-end code for the login.

Login Form

The HTML required for the user login form is shown in Listing 8-19 and can be found in the {PROJECTROOT}/app/templates/global/homeheader.mustache layout file.

Listing 8-19. The Login Form

```
<form class="navbar-form navbar-right" action="/login" role="form" method="post">
<div class="form-group">
<input type="text" placeholder="Username" name="username" class="form-control">
                    </div>
<button type="submit" class="btn btn-success">Sign in</button>
</form>
```

Login Route

In the {PROJECTROOT}/app/public/index.php file, use the login route to control the flow of the login process, as shown in Listing 8-20. Inside the login route, we used the getByUsername method to check if the user exists in the database.

Listing 8-20. The Login Route

```
// login
$app->post('/login', function() use ($app){
    $params = $app->request()->post();

        // make sure the user name was passed.
        $username = trim($params['username']);

        if (!empty($username)) {
                // lower case the username.
                $username=strtolower($username);
                $app->log->debug($username);
                $checkuser = User::getByUsername($username);

                // match
                if(!is_null($checkuser)){

                        $_SESSION['username'] = $username;

                        $app->redirect('/intent');
                }else{
                $app->view()->setData(array('msg' => 'The username you entered was not found.'));
                        $app->render('home/message.mustache');
                }
        }
        else{
            $app->view()->setData(array('msg' => 'Please enter a username.'));
                $app->render('home/message.mustache');
        }

})->name('login');
```

If the user is found during the login attempt, a cookie is added to the response and the request is redirected via `redirect` to the social home page, shown in Figure 8-7. Otherwise, the route will specify the HTML page to return as well as add the error messages that need to be displayed back to the view.

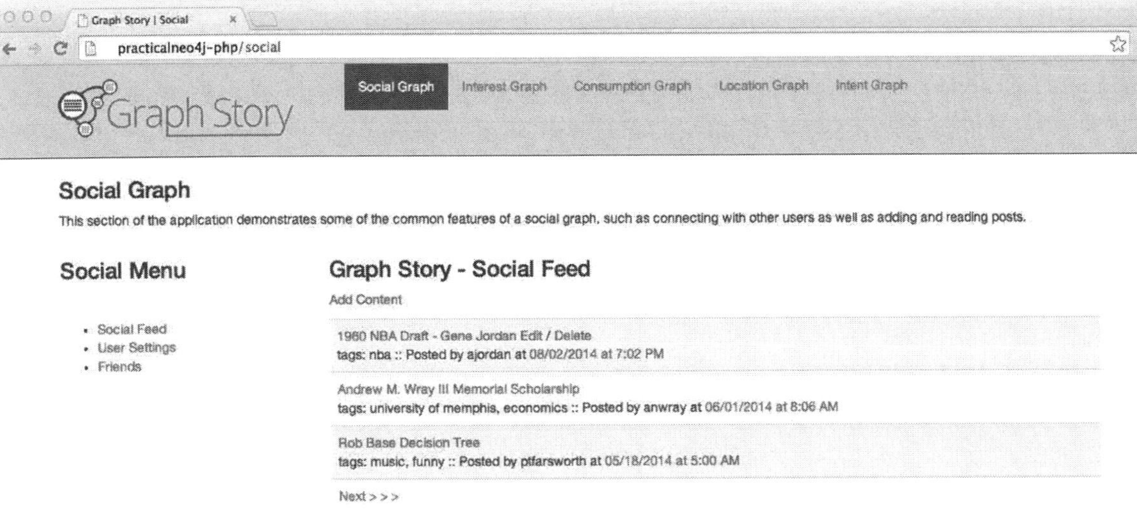

Figure 8-7. *The social graph home page*

Login Service

To check to see if the user values being passed through are connected to a valid user combination in the database, the application uses the getByUsername method in the User class. As shown in the Listing 8-21, the result of the g getByUsername method is assigned to the user variable.

If the result is not null or empty, the result is set on the User object and returned to the controller layer of the application.

Listing 8-21. The getByUsername Method in the User Class

```
public static function getByUsername($username)
{
        $userlabel = Neo4Client::client()->makeLabel('User');
        $nodes= $userlabel->getNodes('username', $username);

        if (empty($nodes) || count($nodes)==0) {
                return null;
        }else{
                return self::fromArray($nodes[0]);
        }
}
```

Now that the user is logged in, he can edit his settings, create relationships with other users in the graph, and create his own content.

Updating a User

To access the page for updating a user, click on the "User Settings" link in the social graph section, as shown in Figure 8-8. In this example, the front-end code uses an AJAX request via PUT and inserts—or, in the case of the **ajordan** user, updates—the first and last name of the user.

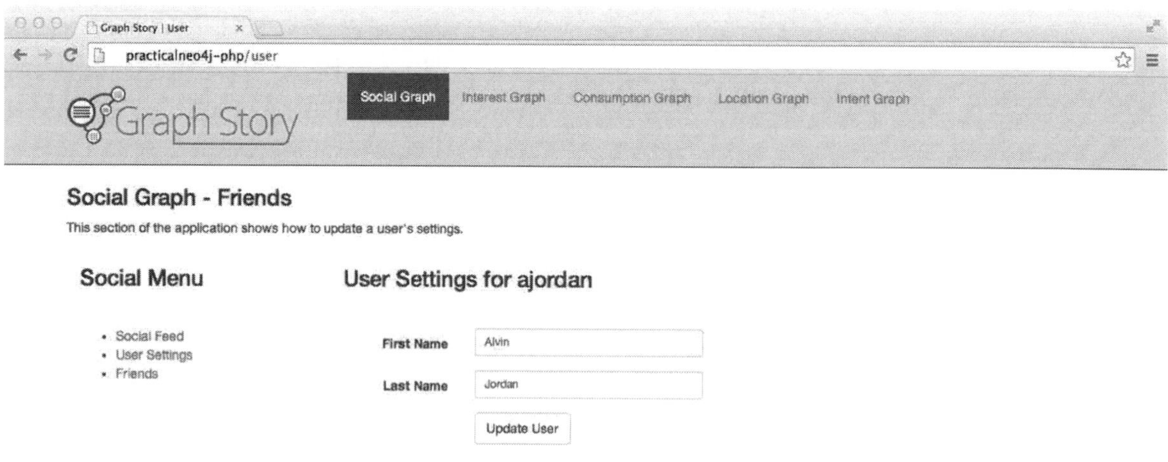

Figure 8-8. *The User Settings page*

User Update Form

The user settings form is located in `{PROJECTROOT}/app/templates/graphs/social/user.mustache` and is similar in structure to the other forms presented in the Sign Up and Login sections. One difference is that we have added the `value` property to the input element as well as the variables for displaying the respective stored values. If none exist, the form fields will be empty (Listing 8-22).

Listing 8-22. User Settings Form

```
<form class="form-horizontal" id="userform">
  <div class="form-group">
    <label for="firstname" class="col-sm-2 control-label">First Name</label>
    <div class="col-sm-10">
      <input type="text" class="form-control input-sm" id="firstname" name="user.firstname"
value="{{user.firstname}}" />
    </div>
  </div>
  <div class="form-group">
    <label for="lastname" class="col-sm-2 control-label">Last Name</label>
    <div class="col-sm-10">
      <input type="text" class="form-control input-sm" id="lastname" name="user.lastname"
value="{{user.lastname}}" />
    </div>
  </div>
```

```
  <div class="form-group">
    <div class="col-sm-offset-2 col-sm-10">
      <button type="submit" id="updateUser" class="btn btn-default">Update User</button>
    </div>
  </div>
</form>
```

User Edit Route

The application contains a route with the path /user/edit, which takes the JSON object argument. The User object is converted from a JSON string and returns a User object as JSON. The response could be used to update the form elements, but because the values are already set within the form there is no need to update the values. In this case, the application uses the JSON response to let the user know if the update succeeded or not via a standard JavaScript alert message (Listing 8-23).

Listing 8-23. User edit Route

```
// edit a user
$app->put('/user/edit', function() use ($app){
        $params = json_decode($app->request()->getBody());
        $user=User::updateUser($_SESSION['username'],$params->firstname,$params->lastname);
        echo json_encode($user);
});
```

User Update Method

To complete the update, the controller layer calls the updateUser method in User class. Because the object being passed into the update method did nothing more than modify the first and last name of an existing entity, you can use the SET clause via Cypher to update the properties in the graph, as shown in Listing 8-24. This Cypher statement also makes use of the MATCH clause to retrieve the User node.

Listing 8-24. The updateUser Method in the User Class

```
public static function updateUser($username,$firstname,$lastname){

        $queryString="MATCH (user:User {username:{u}} )  " .
        "SET user.firstname = {fn}, user.lastname = {ln}".
        "RETURN user";

        $query = new Everyman\Neo4j\Cypher\Query(Neo4Client::client(), $queryString, array(
                        'u' => $username,
                        'fn' => $firstname,
                        'ln' => $lastname));

        $result = $query->getResultSet();

        return self::returnAsUsers($result);
}
```

Connecting Users

A common feature in social media applications is to allow users to connect to each other through an explicit relationship. In the sample application, we use the directed relationship type called FOLLOWS. By going to the "Friends" page within the social graph section, you can see the list of the users the current user is following, search for new friends to follow, add them and remove friends the current user is following. The user management section of the App class contains each of the routes to control the flow for these features, specifically the routes that cover friends, search_by_user_name, follow and unfollow.

To display the list of the users the current user is following, the /friends route, showing in Listing 8-26, calls the following method in User class. The following method in User, also shown in Listing 8-25, creates a list of users by matching the current user's username with directed relationship FOLLOWS on the variable user.

Listing 8-25. The /friends Route and the following Method

```
// friends route that shows connected users via FOLLOW relationship
$app->get('/friends', $isLoggedIn, function() use ($app){
        $user = User::getByUsername($_SESSION['username']);
        $following =  User::following($_SESSION['username']);
        $app->view()->setData(array('user' => $user,
                        'following' => $following,
                        'title'=>'User Settings'));
        $app->render('graphs/social/friends.mustache');
});

// the following method in the User class
public static function following($username)
{
        $queryString = "MATCH (user { username:{u}})-[:FOLLOWS]->(users) ".
        " RETURN users ORDER BY users.username";
        $query = new Everyman\Neo4j\Cypher\Query(Neo4Client::client(), $queryString,
                        array('u' => $username));
        $result = $query->getResultSet();
        return self::returnAsUsers($result);
}
```

If the list contains users, it will be returned to the controller and displayed in the right-hand part of the page, as shown in Figure 8-9. The display code for showing the list of users can be found in {PROJECTROOT}/ app/templates/graphs/social/friends.mustache and is shown in the code snippet in Listing 8-26.

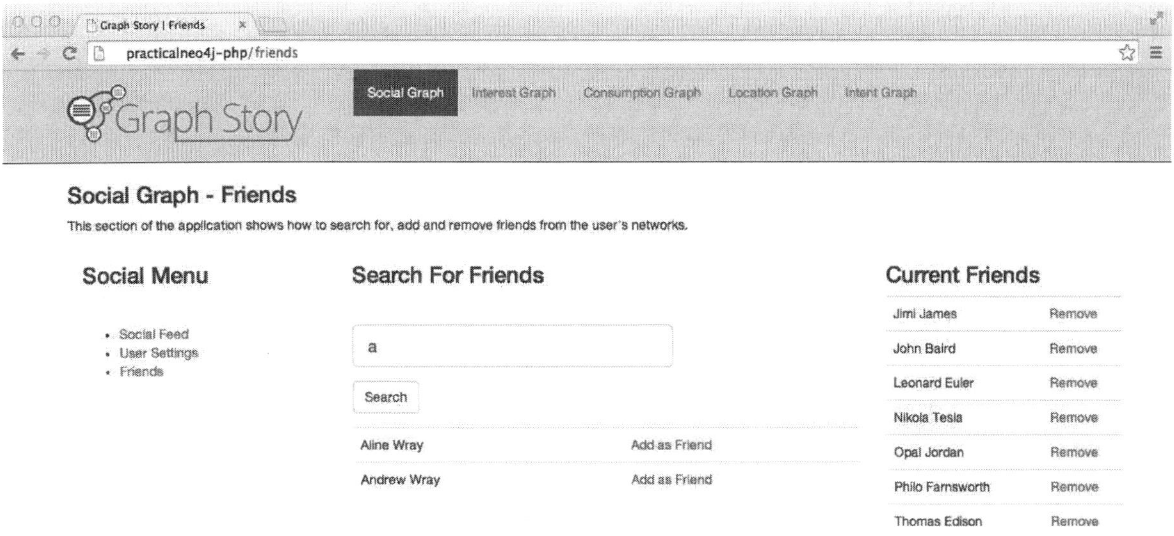

Figure 8-9. The Friends page

Listing 8-26. The HTML Code Snippet for Displaying the List of Friends

```
<div class="col-md-3">
        <h3>Current Friends</h3>
        <table class="table" id="following">
                {{#following}}
                        <tr><td>{{firstname}} {{lastname}}</td><td><a href="#" id="{{username}}"
                        class="removefriend">Remove</a></td></tr>
                {{/following}}
                {{^following}}
                        No friends :(
                    {{/following}}
                </table>
</div>
```

To search for users to follow, the user section contains a GET route /searchbyusername and passes in a username value as part of the path. This route executes the searchByUsername method found in User class, showing the second part of Listing 8-27. The first part of the WHERE clause in the method returns users whose username matches on a wildcard String value. The second part of the WHERE clause in the method checks to make sure the users in the MATCH clause are not already being followed by the current user.

Listing 8-27. The searchbyusername Route and searchByUsername Service Method

```
//search users by name
$app->get('/searchbyusername/:u', function($u) use ($app){
        $users = User::searchByUsername($u,$_SESSION['username']);
        echo '{"users": ' . json_encode($users) . '}';
});
```

```
// search by user returns users in the network that aren't already being followed
public static function searchByUsername($username, $currentusername)
{
        // wild card search on $username - which is just a string passed
        // in from the request, e.g. the letter 'a'
        $username=$username.'.*';
        $queryString = "MATCH (n:User), (user { username:{c}}) " .
        "WHERE (n.username =~ {u} AND n <> user) AND (NOT (user)-[:FOLLOWS]->(n)) ".
        " RETURN n";
        $query = new Everyman\Neo4j\Cypher\Query(Neo4Client::client(), $queryString, array(
                        'u' => $username,
                        'c' => $currentusername));
        $result = $query->getResultSet();
        return self::returnAsUsers($result);
}
```

The searchByUsername in {PROJECTROOT}/app/public/js/graphstory.js uses an AJAX request and formats the response in render SearchByUsername. If the list contains users, it will be displayed in the center of the page under the search form, as shown in Figure 8-9. Otherwise, the response will display "No Users Found."

Once the search returns results, the next action would be to click on the "Add as Friend" link, which will call the addfriend method in graphstory.js. This will perform an AJAX request to the follow route, which will then call the follow method in the User class. The follow method in User, shown in Listing 8-28, will create the relationship between the two users by first finding each entity via the MATCH clause and then use the CreateUnique clause to create the directed FOLLOWS relationship. Once the operation is completed, the next part of the query then runs a MATCH on the users being followed to return the full list of followers ordered by the username.

Listing 8-28. The follow Route and follow Service Method

```
// takes current user session and will follow :username, e.g. one way follow
$app->get('/follow/:username', function ($username) use ($app) {
        $following = User::follow($_SESSION['username'], $username);
        echo '{"following": ' . json_encode($following) . '}';
});

// the follow method in the User class
public static function follow($username, $userTofollow)
{

        $queryString = " MATCH (user1:User {username:{cu}} ), ".
                        " (user2:User {username:{u}} ) " .
                        " CREATE UNIQUE user1-[:FOLLOWS]->user2 " .
                        " WITH user1" .
                        " MATCH (user1)-[f:FOLLOWS]->(users)" .
                        " RETURN users " .
                        " ORDER BY users.username";

        $query = new Everyman\Neo4j\Cypher\Query(Neo4Client::client(), $queryString, array(
                        'cu' => $username,
                        'u' => $userTofollow
        ));
        $result = $query->getResultSet();

        return self::returnAsUsers($result);
}
```

The unfollow feature for the FOLLOWS relationships uses a nearly identical application flow as follows feature. In the unfollow method, shown in Listing 8-29, the controller passes in two arguments—the current username and username to be unfollowed. As with the follows method, once the operation is completed, the next part of the query then runs a MATCH on the users being followed to return the full list of followers ordered by the username.

Listing 8-29. The unfollow Route and unfollow Service Method

```
// takes current user session and will unfollow :username
$app->get('/unfollow/:username', function ($username) use ($app) {
        $following = User::unfollow($_SESSION['username'], $username);
        echo '{"following": ' . json_encode($following) . '}';
});

// the unfollow method in the User class
public static function unfollow($username, $userToUnfollow)
{
        $queryString = "MATCH (user1:User {username:{cu}} )-[f:FOLLOWS]->".
                        " (user2:User {username:{u}} ) " .
                        " DELETE f " .
                        " WITH user1" .
                        " MATCH (user1)-[f:FOLLOWS]->(users)" .
                        " RETURN users " .
                        " ORDER BY users.username";

        $query = new Everyman\Neo4j\Cypher\Query(Neo4Client::client(), $queryString, array(
                        'cu' => $username,
                        'u' => $userToUnfollow
        ));
        $result = $query->getResultSet();

        return self::returnAsUsers($result);
}
```

User-Generated Content

Another important feature in social media applications is being able to have users view, add, edit, and remove content—sometimes referred to as *user-generated content*. In the case of this content, we will not be creating connections between the content and its owner, but creating a linked list of status updates. In other words, you are connecting a User to their most recent status update and then connecting each subsequent status to the next update through the CURRENTPOST and NEXTPOST directed relationship types, respectively.

This approach is used for two reasons. First, the sample application displays a given number of posts at a time, and using a limited linked list is more efficient than getting all status updates connected directly to a user and then sorting and limiting the number of items to return. Second, it helps to limit the number of relationships that are placed on the User and Content entities. Therefore, the overall graph operations should be more efficient using the linked list approach.

Getting the Status Updates

To display the first set of status updates, start with the social route of the social section of the sample PHP application. This method accesses the get_content method within Content service class, which takes an argument of the current user's username and the page being requested. The page refers to set number of objects within a collection. In this instance the paging is zero-based, so will request page 0 and limit the page size to 4 in order to return the first page.

The getContent method in Content class, shown in Listing 8-30, will first determine whom the user is following and then match that set of user with the status updates starting with the CURRENTPOST. The CURRENTPOST is then matched on the next three status updates via the [:NEXTPOST*0..3] section of the query. Finally, the method uses a loop to add a readable date and time string property—based on the timestamp—on the results returned to the controller and view.

Listing 8-30. The getContent Method in the Content Class

```
public static function getContent($username, $s) {
       // we're doing LIMIT 4.  at present were' only displaying 3. the extra item
        // is to ensure there's more to view, so the next skip will be 3, then 6, then 12
        $queryString = " MATCH (u:User {username: {u} })-[:FOLLOWS*0..1]->f  " .
                        " WITH DISTINCT f,u " .
                        " MATCH f-[:CURRENTPOST]-lp-[:NEXTPOST*0..3]-p   " .
                        " RETURN  p, f.username as username, f=u as owner  " .
                        " ORDER BY p.timestamp desc SKIP {s} LIMIT 4 ";
        $query = new Everyman\Neo4j\Cypher\Query(Neo4Client::client(), $queryString, array(
                        'u' => $username,
                        's' => $s
        ));
        $result = $query->getResultSet();
        return self::returnMappedContent($result);
}
```

Adding a Status Update

Figure 8-10 shows the form to add a status update for the current user, which is displayed when clicking on the "Add Content" link just under the "Graph Story - Social Feed" header. The HTML for the form can be found in {PROJECTROOT}/app/templates/graphs/social/posts.mustache. The form uses the add_content function in graphstory.js to POST a new status update as well as return the response and add it to the top of the status update stream.

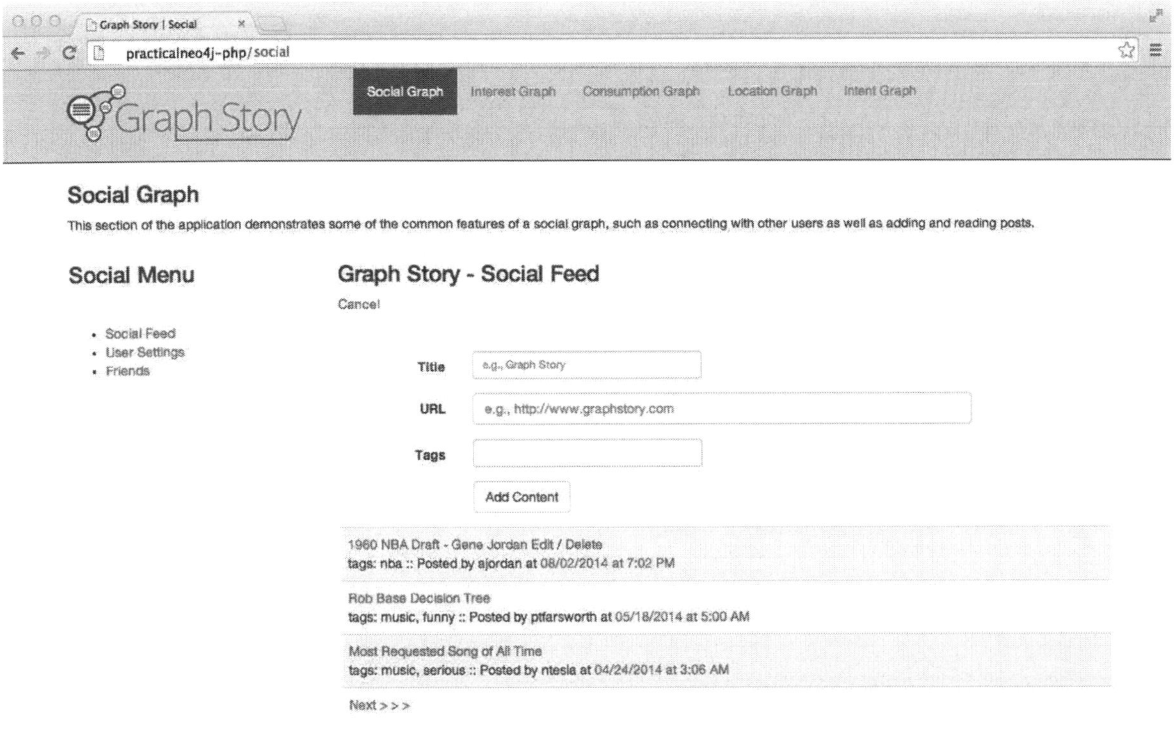

Figure 8-10. *Adding a status update*

The post content route and `addContent` method are shown in Listing 8-31. When a new status update is created, in addition to its graph id, the `addContent` method also generates a contentId, which performs using the `uniqid` method.

The `addContent` method also makes the status the `CURRENTPOST`. Determine whether a previous `CURRENTPOST` exists and, if one does, change its relationship type to `NEXTPOST`. In addition, the tags connected to the status update will be merged into the graph and connected to the status update via the `HAS` relationship type.

Listing 8-31. `addContent` Route and `addContent` Method for a Status Update

```
// add a status update - route
$app->post('/posts/add', function() use ($app){
        $request = $app->request();
    $contentParams = json_decode($request->getBody());

        $content = new Content();
        $content->title=$contentParams->title;
        $content->url=$contentParams->url;

        // are tags set?
        if(isset($contentParams->tagstr)){
                $content->tagstr=$contentParams->tagstr;
        }
        $content =  Content::addContent($_SESSION['username'], $content);
```

```
        $app->response->headers->set('Content-Type', 'application/json');

        echo json_encode($content);

})->name('add-content');

// add a status update
public static function addContent($username, Content $content) {

        $tagstr=self::trimContentTags($content->tagstr);
        $tags=explode(',', $tagstr);

        $queryString = " MATCH (user { username: {u}}) " .
                " CREATE UNIQUE (user)-[:CURRENTPOST]->(p:Content { title:{title}, url:{url}, " .
                " tagstr:{tagstr}, timestamp:{timestamp}, contentId:{contentId} }) " .
                " WITH user, p" .
                " FOREACH (tagName in {tags} |  " .
                " MERGE (t:Tag {wordPhrase:tagName}) " .
                " MERGE (p)-[:HAS]->(t) " .
                " )" .
                " WITH user, p " .
        " OPTIONAL MATCH  (p)<-[:CURRENTPOST]-(user)-[oldRel:CURRENTPOST]->(oldLP)" .
        " DELETE oldRel " .
        " CREATE (p)-[:NEXTPOST]->(oldLP) " .
        " RETURN p, {u} as username, true as owner  ";

        $query = new Everyman\Neo4j\Cypher\Query(Neo4Client::client(), $queryString, array(
                        'u' => $username,
                        'title' => $content->title,
                        'url' => $content->url,
                        'tagstr' =>  $tagstr,
                        'tags' => $tags,
                        'timestamp' => time(),
                        'contentId' => uniqid()
        ));
        $result = $query->getResultSet();
        return self::returnMappedContent($result);
}
```

Editing a Status Update

When status updates are displayed, the current user's status updates will contain a link to "Edit" the status. Once clicked, it will open the form, similar to the "Add Content" link, but will populate the form with the status update values as well as modify the form button to read "Edit Content", as shown in Figure 8-11. As with many similar UI features, clicking "Cancel" under the heading will remove the values and return the form to its ready state.

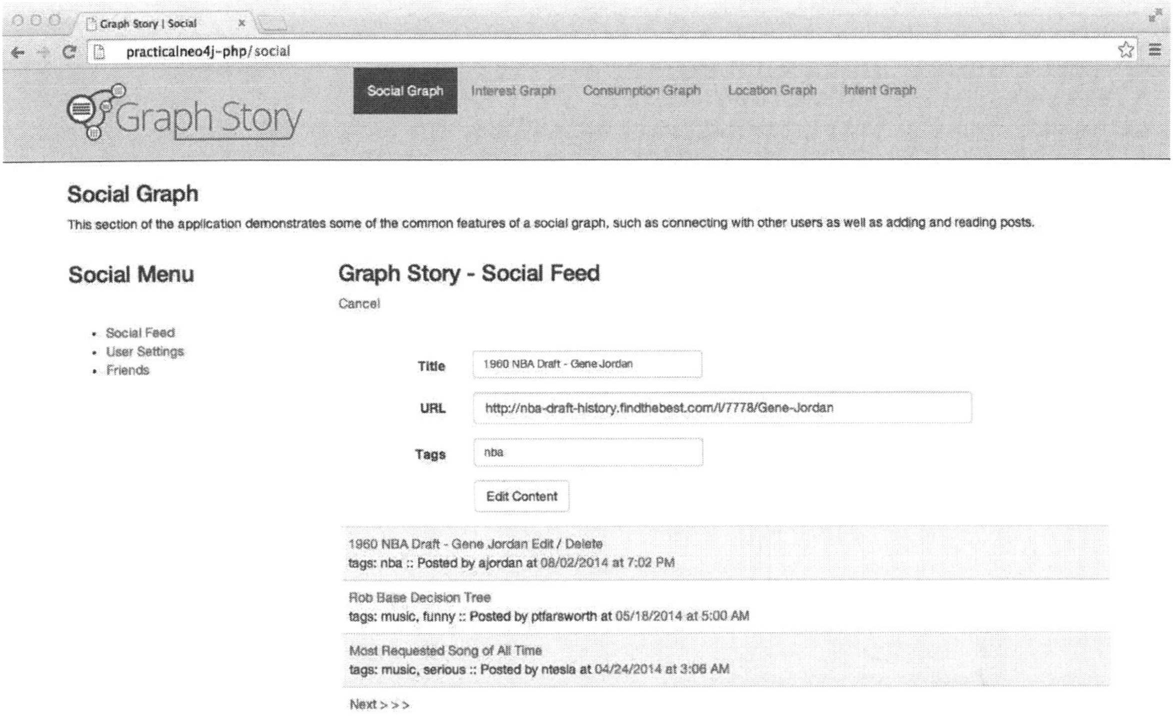

Figure 8-11. Editing a status update

As with the add feature, the edit feature will use a route as well as a function in `graphstory.js`, which are `edit` and `editContent`, respectively. The edit content route passes in the content object, with its content id, and then calls the `editContent` method in Content class, as shown in Listing 8-32.

In the case of the edit feature, we will not need to update relationships. Instead, simply retrieve the existing node by its generated String Id (not its graph id), update its properties where necessary, and save it back to the graph.

Listing 8-32. Edit Route and Method for a Status Update

```
// edit a status update - route
$app->put('/posts/edit', function() use ($app){
        $request = $app->request();
    $contentParams = json_decode($request->getBody());
    $content = Content::getStatusUpdate(
                $contentParams->contentId,
                $_SESSION['username']


    );
    $content = $content[0];

    $content->title=$contentParams->title;
        $content->url=$contentParams->url;
```

```
        // are tags set?
        if (isset($contentParams->tagstr)) {
                $content->tagstr = $contentParams->tagstr;
        }

        $content =  Content::editContent($_SESSION['username'], $content);

        $app->response->headers->set('Content-Type', 'application/json');

        echo json_encode($content);
})->name('edit-content');

// edit a status update
public static function editContent($username, Content $content) {

        $tagstr=self::trimContentTags($content->tagstr);
        $tags=explode(',', $tagstr);

        $queryString =  " MATCH (p:Content { contentId: {contentId} } )-[:NEXTPOST*0..]".
                "-()-[:CURRENTPOST]-(user { username: {u} } ) " .
                " SET p.title = {title}, p.url = {url}, p.tagstr = {tagstr}" .
                " FOREACH (tagName in {tags} |  " .
                " MERGE (t:Tag {wordPhrase:tagName}) " .
                " MERGE (p)-[:HAS]->(t) " .
                " )" .
                " RETURN p, {u} as username, true as owner " ;
        $query = new Everyman\Neo4j\Cypher\Query(Neo4Client::client(), $queryString, array(
                        'contentId' => $content->contentId,
                        'u' => $username,
                        'title' => $content->title,
                        'url' => $content->url,
                        'tagstr' =>  $tagstr,
                        'tags' => $tags
        ));
        $result = $query->getResultSet();
        return self::returnMappedContent($result);
}
```

Deleting a Status Update

As with the "edit" option, when status updates are displayed, the current user's status updates contain a link to "Delete" the status. Once clicked, it will ask if you want it deleted (no regrets!) and, if accepted, generate an AJAX GET request to call the delete route and corresponding method in the `Content` class, shown in Listing 8-33.

The Cypher in the delete method begins by finding the user and content that will be used in the rest of the query. In the first `MATCH`, you can determine if this status update is the `CURRENTPOST` by checking to see if it is related to a `NEXTPOST`. If this relationship pattern matches, make the `NEXTPOST` into the `CURRENTPOST` with `CREATE UNIQUE`.

Next, the query will ask if the status update is somewhere the middle of the list, which is performed by determining if the status update has incoming and outgoing NEXTPOST relationships. If the pattern is matched, then connect the before and after status updates via NEXTPOST.

Regardless of the status update's location in the linked list, retrieve it and its relationships and then delete the node along with all of its relationships.

To recap, if one of the relationship patterns matches, replace that pattern with the nodes on either side of the status update in question. Once that has been performed, the node and its relationships can be removed from the graph.

Listing 8-33. Deleting a Status Update

```
// remove a status update
public static function deleteContent($username, $contentId) {

        $queryString = " MATCH (u:User { username: {u} }), (c:Content { contentId: {contentId} }) " .
        " WITH u,c " .
        " MATCH (u)-[:CURRENTPOST]->(c)-[:NEXTPOST]->(nextPost) " .
        " WHERE nextPost is not null " .
        " CREATE UNIQUE (u)-[:CURRENTPOST]->(nextPost) " .
        " WITH count(nextPost) as cnt " .
        " MATCH (before)-[:NEXTPOST]->(c:Content { contentId: {contentId}})-[:NEXTPOST]->(after) " .
        " WHERE before is not null AND after is not null " .
        " CREATE UNIQUE (before)-[:NEXTPOST]->(after) " .
        " WITH count(before) as cnt " .
        " MATCH (c:Content { contentId: {contentId} })-[r]-() " .
        " DELETE c, r";
        $query = new Everyman\Neo4j\Cypher\Query(Neo4Client::client(), $queryString, array(
                'u' => $username,
                'contentId' => $contentId
        ));
        $query->getResultSet();

}
```

Interest Graph Model

This section looks at the interest graph and examines some basic ways it can be used to explicitly define a degree of interest. The following topics are covered:

- Adding filters for owned content
- Adding filters for connected content
- Analyzing connected content (count tags)

Interest in Aggregate

Inside the /interest route, we retrieve all of the user's tags and their friends tags by calling, respectively, the userTags and tagsInNetwork methods found in the Tag class. This is displayed in the left-hand column ikn Figure 8-12.

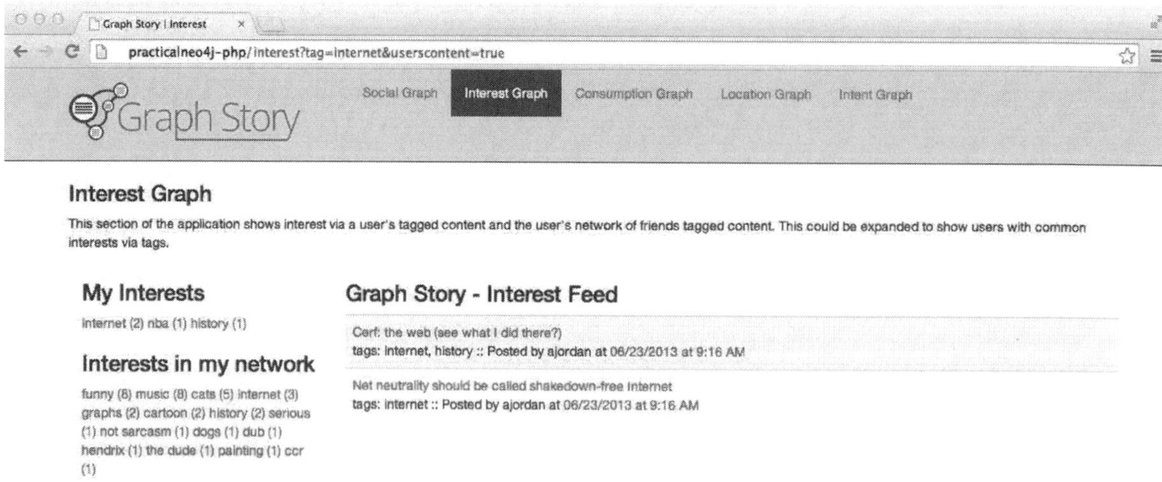

Figure 8-12. *Filtering the current user's content*

The display code is located in {PROJECTROOT}/ app/templates/graphs/interest/index.mustache. The interest route uses two queries, which are shown in Listing 8-35 and 8-36. The getFollowingContentWithTag finds users being followed, accesses all of their content, and finds connected tags through the HAS relationship type.

The getUserContentWithTag method is similar, but is concerned only with content and, subsequently, tags connected to the current user. Both methods limit the results to 30 items. As mentioned earlier, the methods return an array of content and tags, which supports an autosuggest plugin in the view and requires both a label and name to be provided in order to execute. This autosuggest feature is used in the status update form as well as some search forms found later in this chapter.

Listing 8-34. The interest Route

```
# show tags within the user's network (theirs and those being followed)
$app->get('/interest', $isLoggedIn,  function () use ($app) {

        # get the user's tags
        $userTags = Tag::userTags($_SESSION['username']);

        # get the tags of user's friends
        $tagsInNetwork=Tag::tagsInNetwork($_SESSION['username']);

        $contents = null;

        $userscontent = $app->request()->get('userscontent');
```

```
        if(!empty($userscontent)){

                $tag = $app->request()->get('tag');

                # if the user's content was requested
                if($userscontent === "true"){
                        $contents = Content::getUserContentWithTag($_SESSION['username'],$tag);
                # if the user's friends' content was requested
                }else{
                        $contents = Content::getFollowingContentWithTag(
                                        $_SESSION['username'],$tag);
                }
        }

        $app->view()->setData(array('contents'=>$contents,
                        'userTags'=>$userTags,
                        'tagsInNetwork'=>$tagsInNetwork,
                        'title'=>'Interest'));
        $app->render('graphs/interest/index.mustache');
})->name('interest');
```

Filtering Managed Content

Once the list of tags for the user and for the group she follows has been provided, the content can be filtered based of the generated tag links, as shown in Figure 8-12. If a tag is clicked on the inside of the "My Interests" section, then the `getUserContentWithTag` method, displayed in Listing 8-35, will be called.

Listing 8-35. Get the Content of the Current User Based on a Tag

```
public static function getUserContentWithTag($username,$wp){
        $queryString = " MATCH (u:User {username: {u} })-[:CURRENTPOST]-lp-[:NEXTPOST*0..]-p " .
        " WITH DISTINCT u,p" .
        " MATCH p-[:HAS]-(t:Tag {wordPhrase : {wp} } )" .
        " RETURN  p.contentId as contentId, p.title as title, p.tagstr as tagstr, " .
        " p.timestamp as timestamp, p.url as url, u.username as username, true as owner" .
        " ORDER BY p.timestamp DESC";

        $query = new Everyman\Neo4j\Cypher\Query(Neo4Client::client(), $queryString, array(
                   'u' => $username,
                   'wp' => $wp
        ));
        $result = $query->getResultSet();

        foreach($result as $row){
                   $row->timestampAsStr = date('n/d/Y',$row['timestamp']) .
                      ' at ' . date('g:i A',$row['timestamp']);
        }

        return $result;
 }
```

Filtering Connected Content

If a tag is clicked on the inside of the "Interests in my Network" section, then `getFollowingContentWithTag` method will be called, as shown in Listing 8-36. The second query is nearly identical the first query found in the `interest` route, except it will factor in the users being followed and exclude the current user.

The method also returns a collection of status updates based on the matching tag, placing no limit on the number of status updates to be returned. In addition, it marks the owner property as true, because you've determined ahead of time you are returning only the current user's content. The results of calling this method are shown in Figure 8-13.

Listing 8-36. Get the Content of the Users Being Followed Based on a Tag

```
public static function getFollowingContentWithTag($username,$wp){
        $queryString = " MATCH (u:User {username: {u} })-[:FOLLOWS]->f" .
        " WITH DISTINCT f" .
        " MATCH f-[:CURRENTPOST]-lp-[:NEXTPOST*0..]-p" .
        " WITH DISTINCT f,p" .
        " MATCH p-[:HAS]-(t:Tag {wordPhrase : {wp} } )" .
        " RETURN  p.contentId as contentId, p.title as title, p.tagstr as tagstr, " .
        " p.timestamp as timestamp, p.url as url, f.username as username, false as owner" .
        " ORDER BY p.timestamp DESC";

        $query = new Everyman\Neo4j\Cypher\Query(Neo4Client::client(), $queryString, array(
                  'u' => $username,
                  'wp' => $wp
        ));
        $result = $query->getResultSet();

        foreach($result as $row){
                 $row->timestampAsStr = date('n/d/Y',$row['timestamp']) .
                         ' at ' . date('g:i A',$row['timestamp']);
        }

        return $result;
}
```

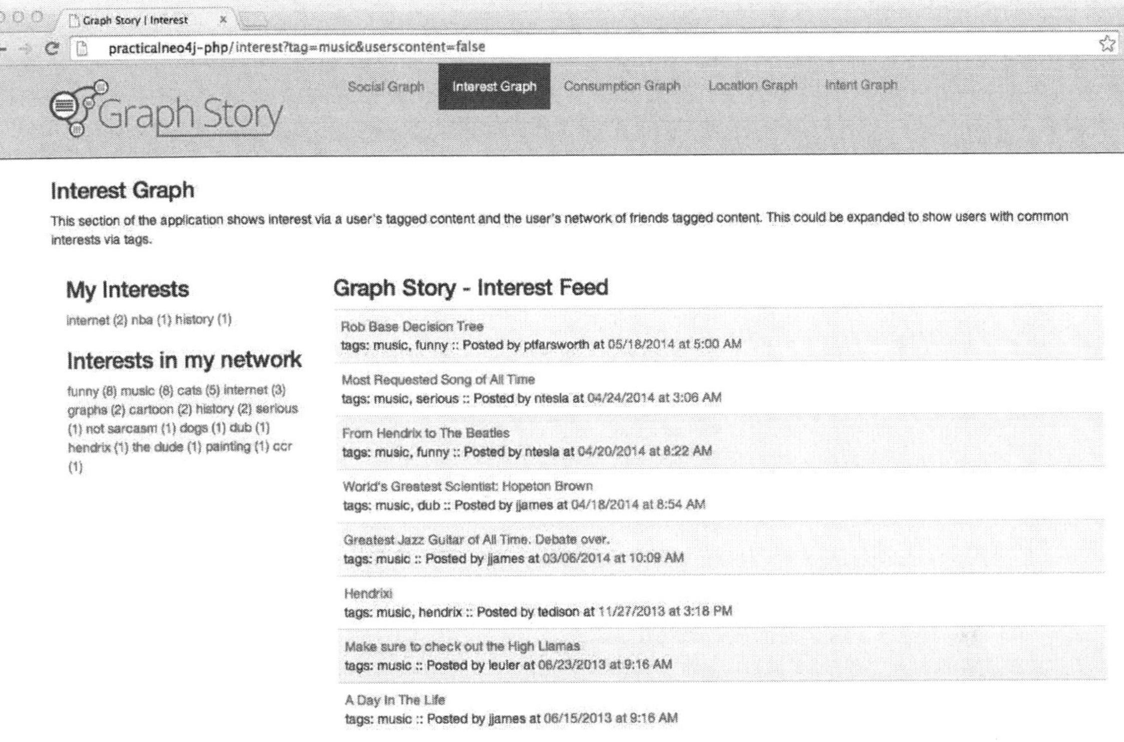

Figure 8-13. *Filtering content of the current user's friends*

Consumption Graph Model

This section examines a few techniques to capture and use patterns of consumption generated implicitly by a user or users. For the purposes of your application, you will use the prepopulated set of products provided in the sample graph. The code required for the console will reinforce the standard persistence operations, but this section focuses on the operations that take advantage of this model type, including:

- Capturing consumption
- Filtering consumption for users
- Filtering consumption for messaging

Capturing Consumption

The process above for creating code that directly captures consumption for a user could also be done by creating a graph-backed service to consume the webserver logs in real time, or by creating another data store to create the relationships. The result would be the same in any event: a process that connects nodes to reveal a pattern of consumption (Listing 8-37).

Listing 8-37. Consumption Route to Show a List of Products and the Product Trail of the Current User

```
# show products and products VIEWED by user
$app->get('/consumption', $isLoggedIn,  function() use ($app){
        # get products by page
        $products = Product::getProducts(0);

        $next = true;

        $nextPageUrl = "/consumption/10";

        $productTrail = Product::getProductTrail($_SESSION['username']);

        $app->view()->setData(array('products'=>$products,
                        'next'=>$next,
                        'nextPageUrl'=>$nextPageUrl,
                        'productTrail'=>$productTrail,
                        'title'=>'Consumption'));
        $app->render('graphs/consumption/index.mustache');
})->name('consumption');
```

The sample application used the createUserViewAndReturnViews method in the Product class to first find the product being viewed and then create an explicit relationship type called VIEWED. As you might have noticed, this is the first relationship type in the application that also contains properties. In this case, we are creating a timestamp with a date and string value of the timestamp. The query, provided in Listing 8-38, checks to see if a VIEWED relationship already exists between the user and the product using MERGE.

In the MERGE section of the query, if the result of the MERGE is zero matches, then a relationship is created with key value pairs on the new relationship, specifically dateAsStr and timestamp. Finally, the query uses MATCH to return the existing product views.

Listing 8-38. Add consumption_add Route and create_user_view_and_return_views Method

```
// add a product via VIEWED relationship and return VIEWED products
$app->get('/consumption/add/:productNodeId', function($productNodeId) use ($app){

        #save the view and return the full list of views
        $productTrail=Product::createUserViewAndReturnViews(
               $_SESSION['username'],$productNodeId);

        $app->response->headers->set('Content-Type', 'application/json');

        echo '{"productTrail": ' . json_encode($productTrail) . '}';

})->name('consumption-add');

// the method to add a user view of a product and return all views
public static function createUserViewAndReturnViews($username,$productNodeId){

        $productNodeId = intval($productNodeId);
        # create timestamp and string display
        $ts = time();
        $timestampAsStr = date('n/d/Y',$ts) . ' at ' . date('g:i A',$ts);
```

```
        $queryString = " MATCH (p:Product), (u:User { username:{u} })" .
                                " WHERE id(p) = {productNodeId}" .
                                " WITH u,p" .
                                " MERGE (u)-[r:VIEWED]->(p)" .
                                " SET r.dateAsStr={timestampAsStr}, r.timestamp={ts}" .
                                " WITH u " .
                                " MATCH (u)-[r:VIEWED]->(p)" .
                                " RETURN p.title as title,  r.dateAsStr as dateAsStr" .
                                " ORDER BY r.timestamp desc";

        $query = new Everyman\Neo4j\Cypher\Query(Neo4Client::client(), $queryString, array(
                    'u' => $username,
                    'productNodeId' => $productNodeId,
                    'timestampAsStr' => $timestampAsStr,
                    'ts' => $ts,
        ));
        $result = $query->getResultSet();

        return  self::returnMappedProductUserView($result);
}
```

Filtering Consumption for Users

One practical use of the consumption model is to create a content trail for users, as shown in Figure 8-14. As a user clicks on items in the scrolling product stream, the interaction is captured using `createUserViewAndReturnViews`, which ultimately returns a `List` of relationship objects of the `VIEWED` type.

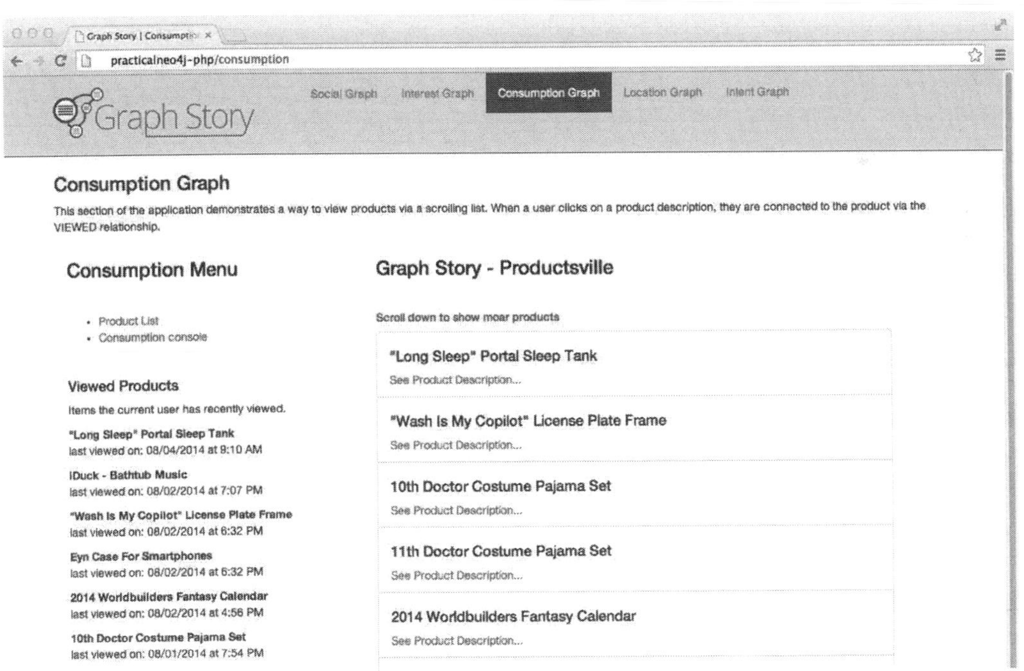

***Figure 8-14.** The Scrolling Product and Product Trail page*

In the consumption graph section, we take a look at the `consumption` route to see how the process begins inside the controller. The controller method first saves the view and then returns the complete history of views using the `getProductTrail`, which can be found in the `Product` class. The process is started when the `createUserProductViewRel` function is called, which is located in `graphstory.js`.

Filtering Consumption for Messaging

Another practical use of the consumption model is to create a personalized message for users, as displayed in Figure 8-15. In this case, we have a filter that allows the "Consumption Console" to narrow down to a very specific group of users who visited a product that was also tagged with a keyword or phrase each user had explicitly used (Listing 8-39).

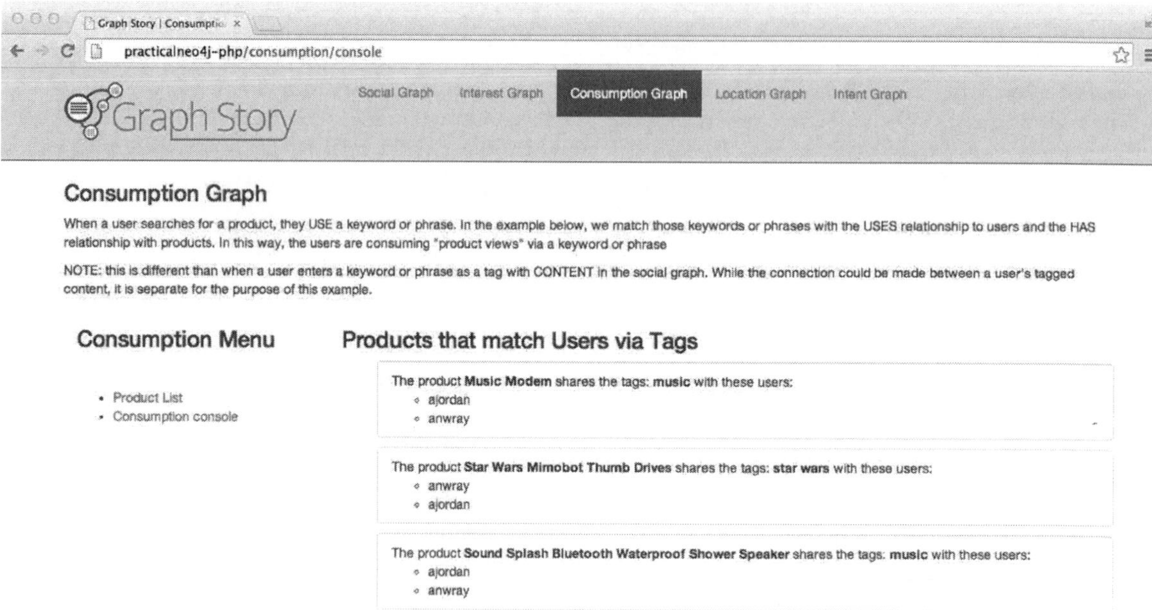

Figure 8-15. *The consumption console*

Listing 8-39. The Consumption Console Route and Methods to Get Connected Products and Users via Tags

```
// displays products that are connected to users via a tag relationship
$app->get('/consumption/console', $isLoggedIn,  function() use ($app){

        $usersWithMatchingTags = null;

        $tag = $app->request()->get('tag');

        # was tag supplied, then get product matches based on specific tag
        if(!empty($tag)){
                $usersWithMatchingTags =
                        Product::getProductsHasSpecificTagAndUserUsesSpecificTag($tag);
        }else{
                $usersWithMatchingTags = Product::getProductsHasATagAndUserUsesAMatchingTag();
        }
```

```
        $app->view()->setData(array('usersWithMatchingTags'=>$usersWithMatchingTags,
                         'title'=>'Consumption Console'));
        $app->render('graphs/consumption/console.mustache');
})->name('consumption-console');

// products that share any tag with a user
public static function getProductsHasATagAndUserUsesAMatchingTag(){

        $queryString = " MATCH (p:Product)-[:HAS]->(t)<-[:USES]-(u:User) " .
                " RETURN p.title as title , collect(u.username) as users, " .
                " collect(distinct t.wordPhrase) as tags ";

        $query = new Everyman\Neo4j\Cypher\Query(Neo4Client::client(), $queryString, null);
        $result = $query->getResultSet();

        return $result;
}

// products that share a specific tag with a user
public static function getProductsHasSpecificTagAndUserUsesSpecificTag($tag){

        $queryString = " MATCH (t:Tag { wordPhrase: {wp} }) " .
                         " WITH t " .
                         " MATCH (p:Product)-[:HAS]->(t)<-[:USES]-(u:User) " .
                         " RETURN p.title as title,collect(u) as u, collect(distinct t) as t ";

        $query = new Everyman\Neo4j\Cypher\Query(Neo4Client::client(), $queryString, array(
                    'wp' => $tag
        ));
        $result = $query->getResultSet();

        return $result;
}
```

Location Graph Model

This section explores the location graph model and a few of the operations that typically accompany it. In particular, it looks at the following:

- The spatial plugin
- Filtering on locationProducts based on location

The example demonstrates how to add a console to enable you to connect products to locations in an ad hoc manner (Listing 8-40).

Listing 8-40. Location Route for Showing Locations or Locations with Specific Product

```
// show locations nearby or locations that have a specific product
$app->get('/location', $isLoggedIn,  function() use ($app){

    // get the user's locations
    $userlocations = UserLocation::getUserLocation($_SESSION['username']);
```

```
    #was distances provided
    $distance = $app->request()->get('distance');

    if (!empty($distance)) {
        # use first location
        $ul = $userlocations[0];

        $productNodeId = $app->request()->get('productNodeId');

        $lq = UserLocation::getLQ($ul,$distance);

        $app->log->debug($lq);

        if (!empty($productNodeId)) {

            $locations = Location::locationsWithinDistanceWithProduct($lq,$ul,$productNodeId);
            $app->view()->setData(array('locations' => $locations,
                'mappedUserLocation'=>$userlocations));
        }
        else{
            $locations = Location::locationsWithinDistance($lq, $ul,"business");
            $app->view()->setData(array('locations' => $locations,
                'mappedUserLocation'=>$userlocations));
        }

    }
    else{
        $app->view()->setData(array('mappedUserLocation'=>$userlocations));
    }
    $app->view()->setData(array('title'=>'Location'));
    $app->render('graphs/location/index.mustache');

})->name('location');
```

Search for Nearby Locations

To search for nearby locations, as shown in Figure 8-16, use the current user's location, obtained with `getUserLocation`, and then use the `locationsWithinDistance`. The `locationsWithinDistance` method in `Location` service class uses a method called `distance` to return a string value of the distance between the starting point and the respective location (Listing 8-41).

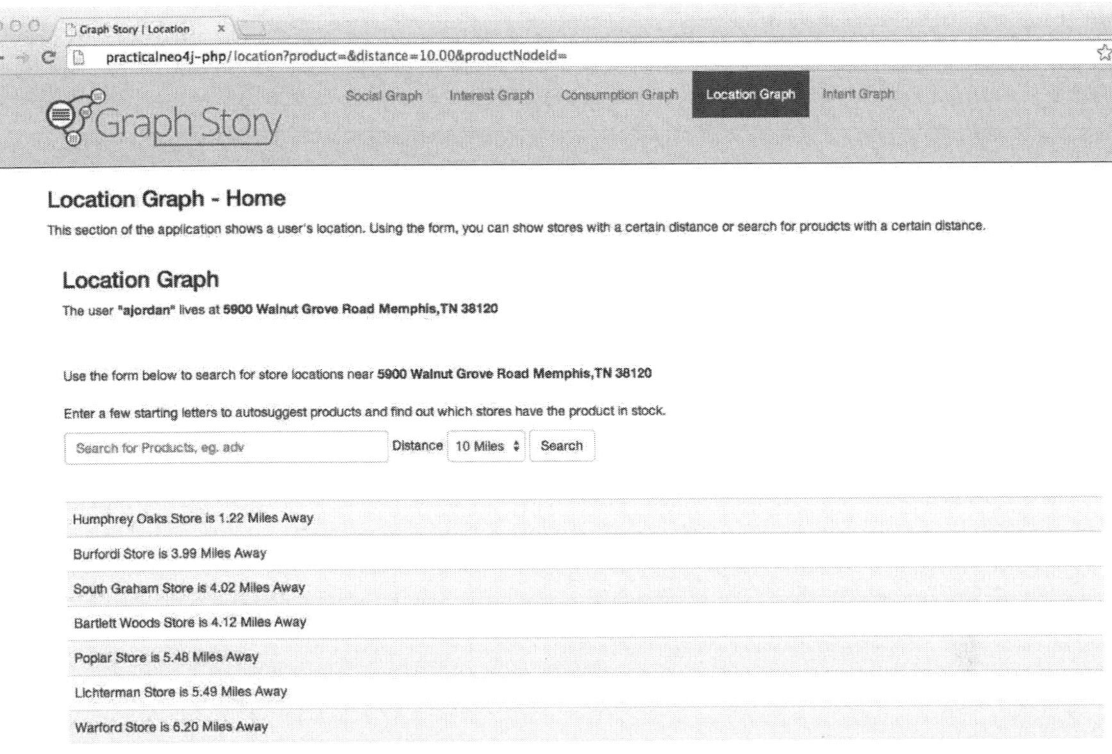

Figure 8-16. *Searching for Locations within a certain distance of User location*

Listing 8-41. The `locations_within_distance` Method in the Location Class

```
public static function locationsWithinDistance($lq,$mappedUserLocation,$locationType){
        $queryString = " START n = node:geom({lq}) WHERE n.type = {locationType}  " .
        " RETURN n.locationId as locationId, n.address as address, n.city as city, " .
        " n.state as state, n.zip as zip, n.name as name, n.lat as lat, n.lon as lon";

        $query = new Everyman\Neo4j\Cypher\Query(Neo4Client::client(), $queryString, array(
                'lq' => $lq,
                'locationType' => $locationType
        ));
        $result = $query->getResultSet();

        foreach($result as $row){
```

```
            $row->distanceToLocation =
                    self::distance(floatval($mappedUserLocation["lat"]),
                                   floatval($mappedUserLocation["lon"]),
                                   floatval($row["lat"]),
                                   floatval($row["lon"]),
                                   "M") . " Miles away";

        }

        return $result;
}
```

Locations with Product

To search for products nearby, as shown in Figure 8-17, the application makes use of an autosuggest AJAX request, which ultimately calls the search method in the Product service class. The method, shown in Listing 8-42, returns an array of objects to the product field in the search form and applies the selected product's `productNodeId` to the subsequent location search.

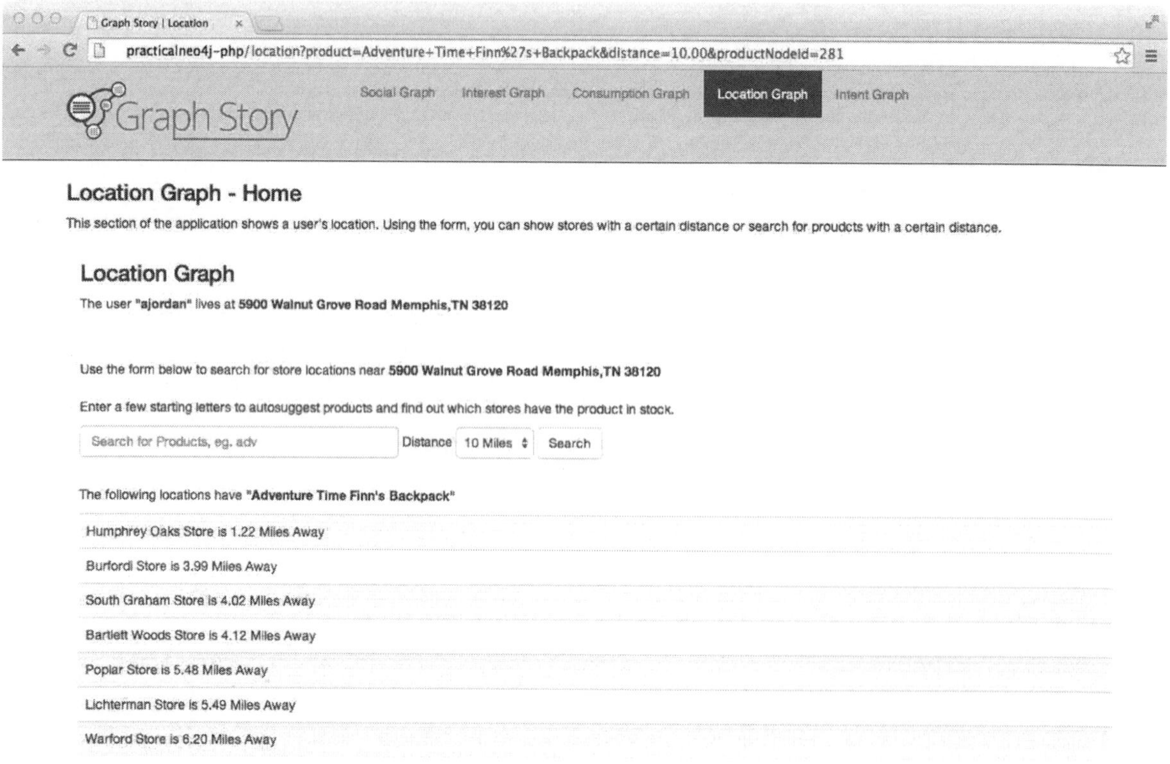

Figure 8-17. *Searching for Products in stock at Locations within a certain distance of the User location*

Listing 8-42. The product_search Route and product_search Methods

```
// return product array as json
$app->get('/productsearch/:q', function($q) use ($app){
    # get matches
    $productsFound = Product::productSearch($q);

    $app->response->headers->set('Content-Type', 'application/json');

    echo json_encode($productsFound);

})->name('productsearch');

// product_search method - located in the Product service class.
public static function productSearch($q){

        $q = trim($q) . ".*";

        $queryString = " MATCH (p:Product) WHERE lower(p.title) =~ {q} ".
        " RETURN count(*) as name, TOSTRING(ID(p)) as id, p.title as label " .
        " ORDER BY p.title " .
        " LIMIT 5 ";

        $query = new Everyman\Neo4j\Cypher\Query(Neo4Client::client(), $queryString, array(
                    'q' => $q
        ));
        $result = $query->getResultSet();

        return self::returnMappedProductSearch($result);
}
```

For almost all cases, it is recommended not to use the graphId because it can be recycled when its node is deleted. In this case, the productNodeId should be consider safe to use, because products would not be in danger of being deleted but only removed from a Location relationship.

Once the product and distance have been set and the search is executed, the Location route tests to see if a productNodeId property has been set. If so, the locationsWithinDistanceWithProduct method is called from the Location class, which is shown in Listing 8-43.

Listing 8-43. The locationsWithinDistanceWithProduct Method in the Location Class

```
public static function locationsWithinDistanceWithProduct($lq,$mappedUserLocation,$productNodeId){
        $queryString = " START n = node:geom({lq}),  p=node({productNodeId}) " .
                " MATCH n-[:HAS]->p " .
                " RETURN n.locationId as locationId, n.address as address, " .
                " n.city as city,  n.state as state, n.zip as zip, n.name as name, " .
                " n.lat as lat, n.lon as lon";

        $query = new Everyman\Neo4j\Cypher\Query(Neo4Client::client(), $queryString, array(
                'lq' => $lq,
                'productNodeId' => intval($productNodeId)
        ));
```

```
        $result = $query->getResultSet();

        foreach($result as $row){
                $row->distanceToLocation =
                        self::distance(floatval($mappedUserLocation["lat"]),
                                floatval($mappedUserLocation["lon"]),
                                floatval($row["lat"]),
                                floatval($row["lon"]),
                                "M") . " Miles away";
        }

        return $result;
}
```

Intent Graph Model

The last part of the graph model exploration considers all the other graphs in order to suggest products based on the Purchase node type. The intent graph also considers the products, users, locations, and tags that are connected based on a Purchase.

Products Purchased by Friends

To get all of the products that have been purchase by friends, the friendsPurchase method is called from Purchase class, which is shown in Listing 8-45. The corresponding route is shown in Listing 8-44.

Listing 8-44. Intent Route to Show Purchases Made by Friends

```
// purchases by friends
$app->get('/intent', $isLoggedIn,  function() use ($app){
    $mappedProductUserPurchaseList = Purchase::friendsPurchase($_SESSION['username']);
    $app->view()->setData(array(
            'mappedProductUserPurchaseList' => $mappedProductUserPurchaseList,
        'title' =>"Products Purchased by Friends"));
    $app->render('graphs/intent/index.mustache');
})->name('intent');
```

The query shown in Listing 8-45 finds the users being followed by the current user and then matches those users to a purchase that has been MADE which CONTAINS a product. The return value is a set of properties that identify the product title, the name of the friend or friends, as well the number of friends who have bought the product. The result is ordered by the number of friends who have purchased the product and then by product title, as shown in Figure 8-18.

Listing 8-45. The friendsPurchase method in the Purchase Class

```
// products purchased by friends
public static function friendsPurchase($username){
       $queryString =
               " MATCH (u:User {username: {u} } )-[:FOLLOWS]-(f)-[:MADE]->()-[:CONTAINS]->p" .
                " RETURN p.productId as productId,  " .
                " p.title as title, " .
                " collect(f.firstname + ' ' + f.lastname) as fullname, " .
                " null as wordPhrase, count(f) as cfriends " .
```

```
            " ORDER BY cfriends desc, p.title ";
        $query = new Everyman\Neo4j\Cypher\Query(Neo4Client::client(), $queryString, array(
            'u' => $username
        ));
        $result = $query->getResultSet();
        return $result;
}
```

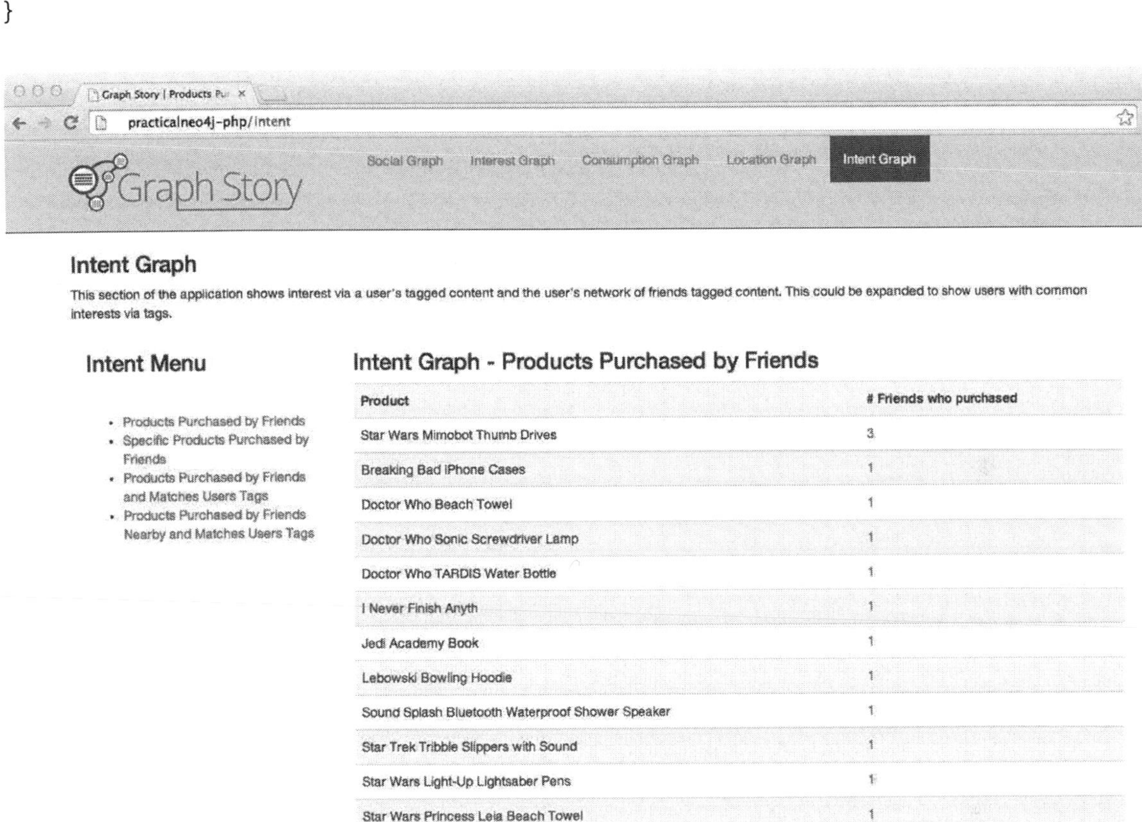

Figure 8-18. *Products Purchased By Friends*

Specific Products Purchased by Friends

If you click on the "Specific Products Purchased By Friends" link, you can specify a product, in this case "Star Wars Mimobot Thumb Drives", and then search for friends who have purchased this product, as shown in Figure 8-19. This is done via the `friendsPurchaseByProduct` route and method of the same name in `Purchase` service class, both of which are shown in Listing 8-46.

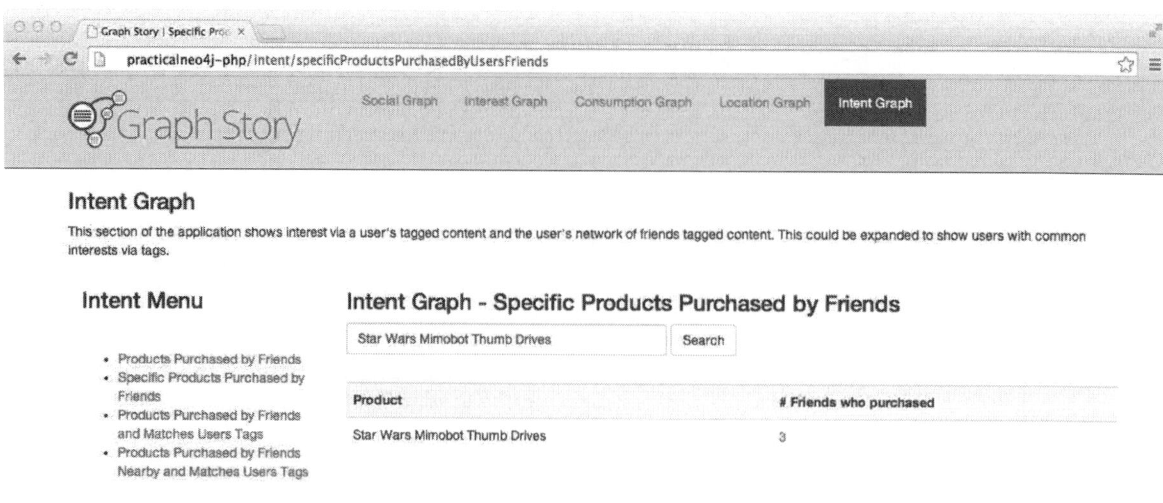

Figure 8-19. *Specific Products Purchased by Friends*

Listing 8-46. The friends_purchase_by_product Route and Method

```
// specific product purchases by friends
$app->get('/intent/friendsPurchaseByProduct', $isLoggedIn,  function() use ($app){
    $mappedProductUserPurchaseList = Purchase::friendsPurchaseByProduct(
                    $_SESSION['username'],
                    "Star Wars Mimobot Thumb Drives");
    $app->view()->setData(array(
            'mappedProductUserPurchaseList' => $mappedProductUserPurchaseList,
            'title' =>"Specific Products Purchased by Friends"));
    $app->render('graphs/intent/index.mustache');
})->name('friendsPurchaseByProduct');

// a specific product purchased by friends
public static function friendsPurchaseByProduct($username,$title){
        $queryString = " MATCH (p:Product) " .
                " WHERE lower(p.title) =lower({title}) " .
                " WITH p " .
                " MATCH (u:User {username: {u} } )-[:FOLLOWS]-(f)-[:MADE]->()-[:CONTAINS]->(p) " .
                " RETURN p.productId as productId,  " .
                " p.title as title, " .
                " collect(f.firstname + ' ' + f.lastname) as fullname, " .
                " null as wordPhrase, count(f) as cfriends " .
                " ORDER BY cfriends desc, p.title ";
                $query = new Everyman\Neo4j\Cypher\Query(Neo4Client::client(), $queryString, array(
                        'u' => $username,
                        'title' => $title
                ));
         $result = $query->getResultSet();
        return $result;
}
```

Products Purchased by Friends and Matches User's Tags

In this next instance, we want to determine products that have been purchased by friends but also have tags that are used by the current user (Listing 8-47). The result of the query is shown in Figure 8-20.

Listing 8-47. Product and Tag Similarity of the Current Users's Friends

```
// friends bought specific products. match these products to tags of the current user
$app->get('/intent/friendsPurchaseTagSimilarity', $isLoggedIn,  function() use ($app){
    $mappedProductUserPurchaseList = Purchase::friendsPurchaseTagSimilarity(
                    $_SESSION['username']);
    $app->view()->setData(array(
                    'mappedProductUserPurchaseList' => $mappedProductUserPurchaseList,
        'title' =>"Products Purchased by Friends and Matches User's Tags"));
    $app->render('graphs/intent/index.mustache');
})->name('friendsPurchaseTagSimilarity');
```

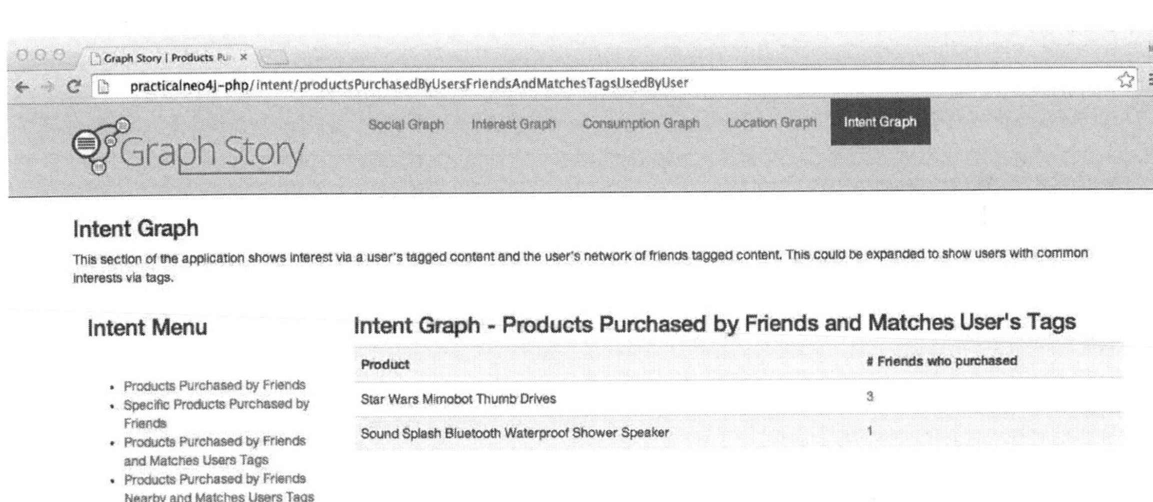

Figure 8-20. *Products Purchased by Friends and Matches User's Tags*

Using `friendsPurchaseTagSimilarity` in Purchase service class, shown in Listing 8-48, the application provides the userId to the query and uses the `FOLLOWS`, `MADE`, and `CONTAINS` relationships to return product purchases by users being followed. The subsequent `MATCH` statement takes the `USES` and `HAS` directed relationship types to determine the tag relationships the resulting products and the current user have in common.

Listing 8-48. The Method to Find Products Purchased by Friends and Matches Current User's Tags

```
// products purchased by friends that match the user's tags
public static function friendsPurchaseTagSimilarity($username){
        $queryString =
                " MATCH (u:User {username: {u} } )-[:FOLLOWS]-(f)-[:MADE]->()-[:CONTAINS]->p " .
                " WITH u,p,f " .
                " MATCH u-[:USES]->(t)<-[:HAS]-p " .
                " RETURN p.productId as productId,  " .
                " p.title as title, " .
```

```
                " collect(f.firstname + ' ' + f.lastname) as fullname, " .
                " t.wordPhrase as wordPhrase, " .
                " count(f) as cfriends " .
                " ORDER BY cfriends desc, p.title ";
                $query = new Everyman\Neo4j\Cypher\Query(Neo4Client::client(), $queryString, array(
                        'u' => $username
                ));
        $result = $query->getResultSet();
        return $result;
}
```

Products Purchased by Friends Nearby and Matches User's Tags

To find products that match with a specific user's tags and have been purchased by friends who live within a set distance of the user is performed by the `friendsPurchaseTagSimilarityAndProximityToLocation` method, easily the world's longest method name, and is located in the Purchase class (Listing 8-49).

Listing 8-49. The `friendsPurchaseTagSimilarityAndProximityToLocation` Route

```
// friends that are nearby bought this product. the product should also matches tags of the current
user
$app->get('/intent/friendsPurchaseTagSimilarityAndProximityToLocation',
                $isLoggedIn, function() use ($app){
    // get the user's locations
    $userlocations = UserLocation::getUserLocation($_SESSION['username']);

    // create the location query using first location
    $lq = UserLocation::getLQ($userlocations[0],"10.00");

    # get result set
    $mappedProductUserPurchaseList =
    Purchase::friendsPurchaseTagSimilarityAndProximityToLocation($_SESSION['username'],$lq);

    $app->view()->setData(array(
        'mappedProductUserPurchaseList' => $mappedProductUserPurchaseList,
        'mappedUserLocation'=>$userlocations,
        'title' =>"Products Purchased by Friends Nearby and Matches User's Tags"));
    $app->render('graphs/intent/index.mustache');
})->name('friendsPurchaseTagSimilarityAndProximityToLocation');
```

The `friendsPurchaseTagSimilarityAndProximityToLocation` route calls the `friendsPurchaseTagSimilarityAndProximityToLocation` method shown in Listing 8-50.

Listing 8-50. The `friendsPurchaseTagSimilarityAndProximityToLocation` Method in the Purchase Class

```
// user's friends' purchases who are nearby and the products match the user's tags
public static function friendsPurchaseTagSimilarityAndProximityToLocation($username,$lq){
        $queryString = " START n = node:geom({lq}) " .
                        " WITH n " .
                        " MATCH (u:User {username: {u} } )-[:USES]->(t)<-[:HAS]-p " .
                        " WITH n,u,p,t " .
```

```
                " MATCH u-[:FOLLOWS]->(f)-[:HAS]->(n) " .
                " WITH p,f,t " .
                " MATCH f-[:MADE]->()-[:CONTAINS]->(p) " .
                " RETURN p.productId as productId, " .
                " p.title as title, " .
                " collect(f.firstname + ' ' + f.lastname) as fullname, " .
                " t.wordPhrase as wordPhrase, " .
                " count(f) as cfriends " .
                " ORDER BY cfriends desc, p.title ";
        $query = new Everyman\Neo4j\Cypher\Query(Neo4Client::client(), $queryString, array(
                'u' => $username,
                'lq' => $lq
        ));
    $result = $query->getResultSet();
    return $result;
}
```

The query begins starts with a location search within a certain distance, then matches the current user's tags to products. Next, the query matches friends based the location search. The resulting friends are matched against products that are in the set of user tag matches. The result of the query is shown in Figure 8-21.

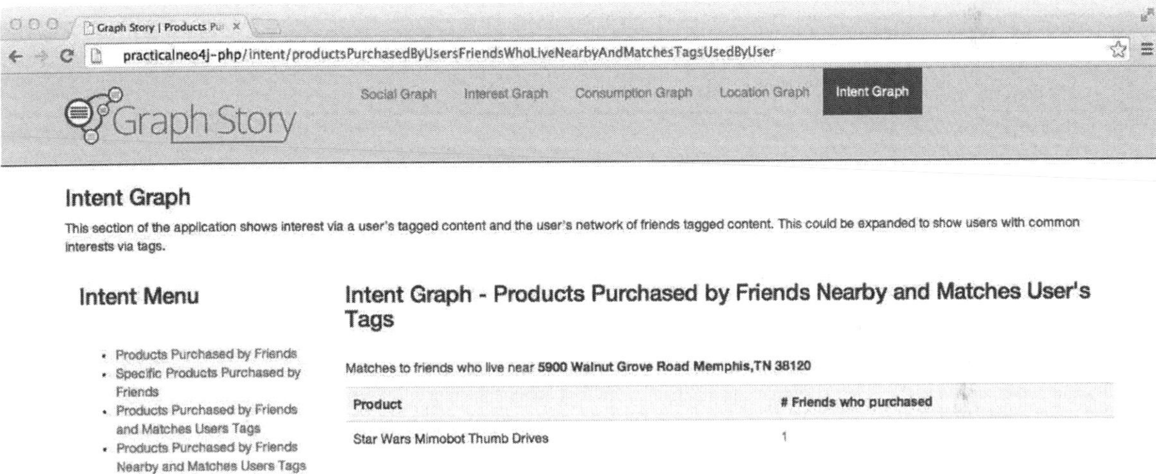

Figure 8-21. *Products Purchased by Friends Nearby and Matches User's Tags*

Summary

This chapter presented the setup for a development environment for PHP and Neo4j and sample code using the Neo4jPHP driver. It proceeded to look at sample code for setting up a social network and examining interest within the network. It then looked at the sample code for capturing and viewing consumption—in this case, product views—and the queries for understanding the relationship between consumption and a user's interest. Finally, it looked at using geospatial matching for locations and examples for understanding user intent within the context of their location, social network, and interests.

The next chapter will review using Python and Neo4j, covering the same concepts presented in this chapter but in the context of a Python driver for Neo4j.

CHAPTER 9

Neo4j + Python

This chapter focuses on using Python with Neo4j and reviewing the code for a working application that integrates the five graph model types covered in Chapter 3. As with other languages that offer a driver for Neo4j, the integration takes place using a Neo4j server instance with the Neo4j REST API. This chapter is divided into the following topics:

- Python and Neo4j Development Environment
- Py2neo
- Developing a Python and Neo4j application

In each chapter that explores a particular language paired with Neo4j, I recommend that you start a free trial on `www.graphstory.com` or have installed a local Neo4j server instance as shown in Chapter 2.

Tip To quickly set up a server instance with the sample data and plugins for this chapter, go to `graphstory.com/practicalneo4j`. You will be provided with your own free trial instance, a knowledge base, and email support from Graph Story.

For this chapter, I assume that you have a good understanding of HTML, JavaScript, and CSS, at least a beginning knowledge of Python, and a basic understanding of how to configure Python for your preferred operating system. To proceed with the examples in this chapter, I recommend you install and configure Python 2.7. While the examples should work with later versions of Python with some modifications, Python 2.7 is the version used in this chapter. In addition, the sample application uses the Apache HTTP server and wsgi_module.

Do This If you do not have Apache HTTP installed, it is highly recommended that you follow the instructions at `http://httpd.apache.org/` based on your operating system. Configuring Python and the wsgi_module with a local instance of Apache HTTP is beyond the scope of this book, but the basic configuration steps can be found at `https://code.google.com/p/modwsgi/`.

I also assume that you have a basic understanding of the model-view-controller (MVC) pattern and some knowledge of Python frameworks that provide an MVC pattern. There are, of course, a number of excellent Python frameworks from which to choose, but I had to pick one for the illustrative purposes of the application in this chapter. I chose the Bottle framework because it is limited in its scope and allows the focus to remain on the application to the greatest extent possible. This chapter is focused on integrating Neo4j into your Python skill set and projects and does not dive deeply into the best practices of developing with Python or Python frameworks.

Python and Neo4j Development Environment

Preliminary to this chapter's discussion of the Python and Neo4j application, this section covers the basics of configuring a development environment.

■ **Readme** Although each language chapter walks through the process of configuring the development environment based on the particular language, certain steps are covered repeatedly in multiple chapters. While the initial development environment setup in each chapter is somewhat redundant, it allows each language chapter to stand on its own. Bearing this in mind, if you have already configured Eclipse with the necessary plugins while working through another chapter, you can skip ahead to the section "Adding the Project to Eclipse."

IDE

The reasons behind the choice of an IDE vary from developer to developer and are often tied to the choice of programming language. I chose the Eclipse IDE for a number of reasons but mainly because it is freely available and versatile enough to work with most of the programming languages featured in this book.

Although you are welcome to choose a different IDE or other programming tool for building your application, I recommend that you install and use Eclipse to be able to follow the Python examples and the related examples found throughout the book and online.

■ **Tip** If you do not have Eclipse, please visit `http://www.eclipse.org/downloads/` and download the Indigo package that is titled "Eclipse IDE for Java EE Developers." The Indigo package is also labeled "Version 3.7."

Once you have installed Eclipse, open it and select a *workspace* for your application. A *workspace* in Eclipse is simply an arbitrary directory on your computer. As shown in Figure 9-1, when you first open Eclipse, the program will ask you to specify which workspace you want to use. Choose the path that works best for you. If you are working through all of the language chapters, you can use the same workspace for each project.

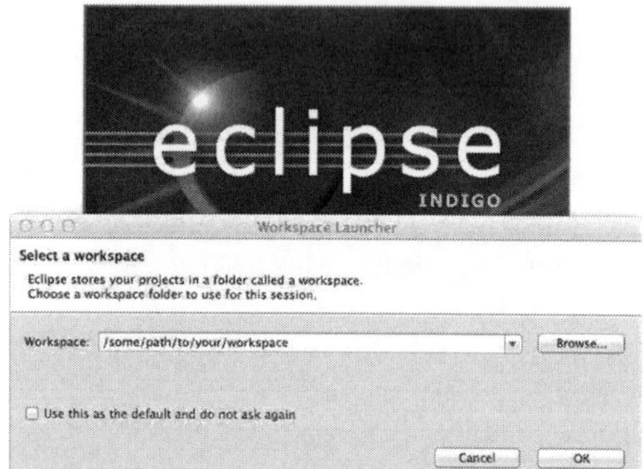

Figure 9-1. *Opening Eclipse and choosing a workspace*

Aptana Plugin

The Eclipse IDE offers a convenient way to add new tools through their plugin platform. The process for adding new plugins to Eclipse is straightforward and usually involves only a few steps to install a new plugin—as you will see in this section.

A specific web-tool plugin called Aptana provides support of server-side languages like Python as well as client languages such as CSS and JavaScript. This chapter and the other programming language chapters use the plugin to edit both server- and client-side languages. A benefit of using a plugin such as Aptana is that it can provide code-assist tools and code suggestions based on the type of file you are editing, such as CSS, JS, or HTML. The time saved with code-assist tools is usually significant enough to warrant their use. Again, if you feel comfortable exploring within your preferred IDE or other program, please do so.

To install the Aptana plugin, you need to have Eclipse installed and opened. Then proceed through the following steps:

1. From the Help menu, select "Install New Software" to open the dialog, which will look like the one in Figure 9-2.

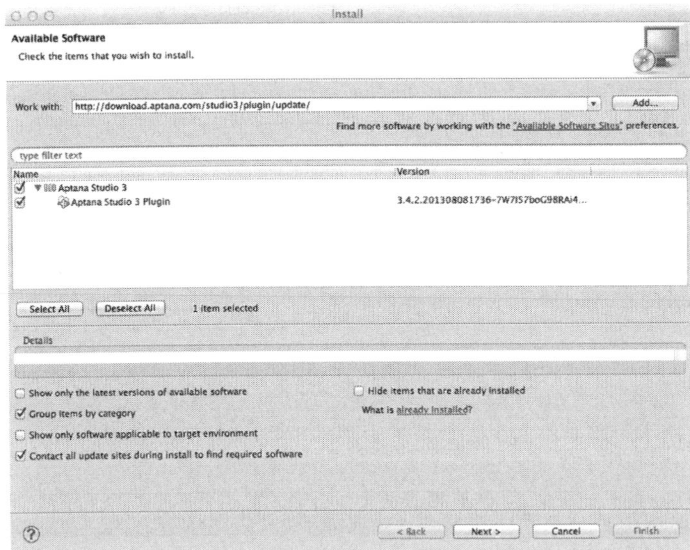

Figure 9-2. *Installing the Aptana plugin*

2. Paste the URL for the update site, `http://download.aptana.com/studio3/plugin/install`, into the "Work With" text box, and hit the Enter (or Return) key.
3. In the populated table below, check the box next to the name of the plugin, and then click the Next button.
4. Click the Next button to go to the license page.
5. Choose the option to accept the terms of the license agreement, and click the Finish button.
6. You may need to restart Eclipse to continue.

Log Watcher

When working with applications, it is often helpful to have a way to view application output through server logs. There are a few plugins available for Eclipse for this purpose, such as LogWatcher. With LogWatcher, you can watch output for multiple files inside or outside of Eclipse as well as filters to highlight or skip over specific patterns. At time of writing, the LogWatcher does not have an update URL for quick installation. To manually install LogWatcher, visit `http://graysky.sourceforge.net/` and follow the quick installation steps and set up the view to suit your development environment.

Adding the Project to Eclipse

After installing Eclipse plugin, you will have the minimum requirements to work with your project in the workspace. To keep the workflow as fluid as possible for each of the language sample applications, use the project import tool with Eclipse. To import the project into your workspace, follow these steps:

1. Go to `www.graphstory.com/practicalneo4j` and download the archive file for "Practical Neo4j for Python." Unzip the archive file on to your computer.
2. In Eclipse, select File ➤ Import and type project in the "Select an import source."
3. Under the "General" heading, select "Existing Projects into Workspace". You should now see a window similar to Figure 9-3.

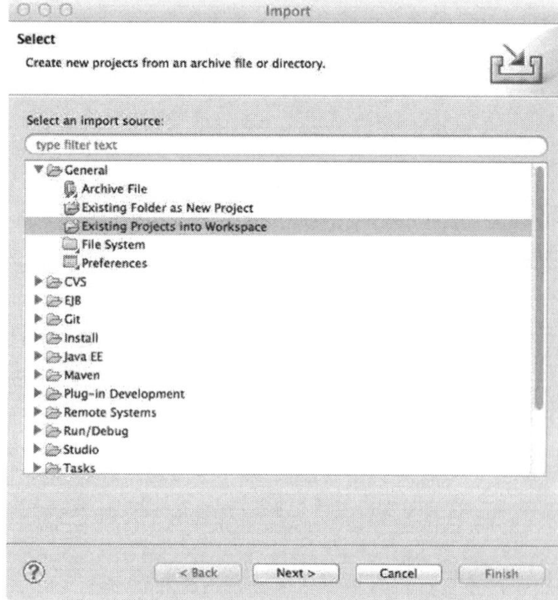

Figure 9-3. *Importing the project into Eclipse*

4. Now that you have selected "Existing Projects into Workspace", click the "Next >" button. The dialogue should now show an option to "Select root directory." Click the "Browse" button and find the root path of the "practicalneo4j-python" archive.
5. Next, check the option for "Copy project into workspace" and click the "Finish" button, as shown in Figure 9-4.

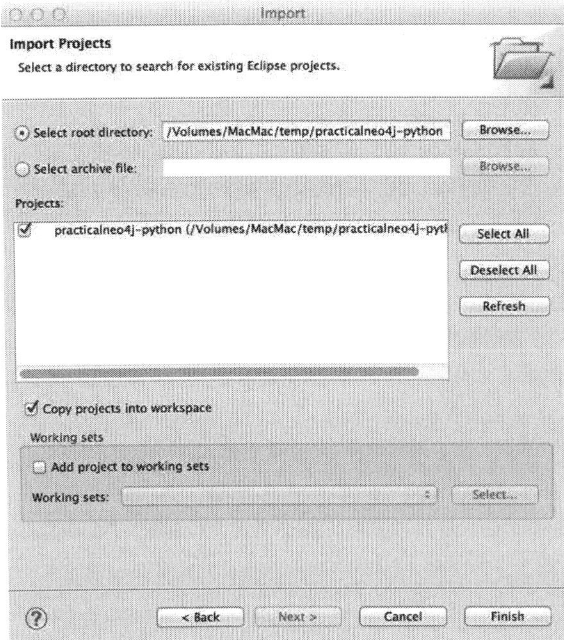

Figure 9-4. *Selecting the project location*

6. Once the project is finished importing into your workspace, you should have a directory structure that looks like the one shown in Figure 9-5.

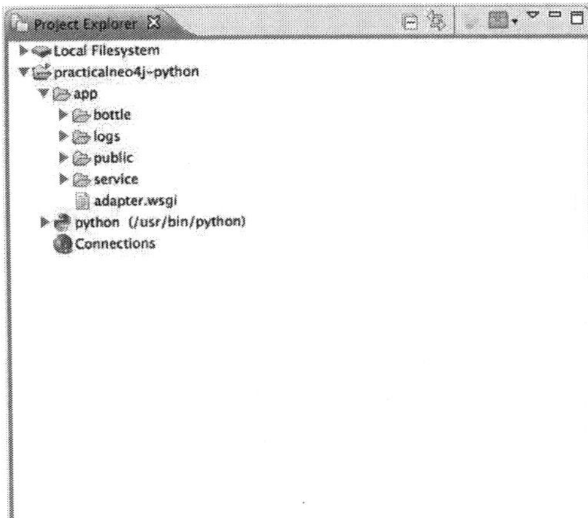

Figure 9-5. *Snapshot of the imported project*

Bottle Web Framework for Python

Bottle is a Python implementation of what is often called a *micro framework*. The aim of a micro framework is to help you quickly build out powerful web applications and APIs only using what is absolutely necessary to get the job done.

Bottle is fast, simple, and lightweight and uses the Python specification known as the *Web Server Gateway Interface*. It is distributed as a single file module and has no dependencies other than the Python Standard Library. As you can see in Listing 9-1, the code required for processing a request and providing a response is fairly limited.

■ **Note** Bottle is maintained by the Python dev Marcel Hellkamp and supported by a number of equally outstanding committers. If you would like to get involved with Bottle, please visit `http://bottlepy.org/`.

Listing 9-1. Bottle Example of GET Route

```
from bottle import route, template

# home page
@route('/')
def index():
    return template("public/templates/home/index.html", title="Home")
```

Local Apache Configuration

To follow the sample application found later in this chapter, you will need to properly configure your local Apache webserver to use the workspace project in Eclipse as the document root. One way to accomplish this is adding a virtual host to Apache. Listing 9-2 covers the basic configuration for adding a virtual host to the httpd-vhosts.conf file.

■ **Important** If you do not have Apache HTTP installed, go to `http://httpd.apache.org/` and follow the instructions based on your operating system. Configuring Python with a local instance of Apache HTTP is out of the scope of this book, but you can find the basic configuration steps at `https://code.google.com/p/modwsgi/`.

Listing 9-2. Minimum Configuration for `httpd-vhosts.conf`

```
NameVirtualHost *:80
<VirtualHost *:80>
        ServerName practicalneo4j-python
        DocumentRoot /path/to/your/workspace/practicalneo4j-python/app/public

        <Directory /path/to/your/workspace/practicalneo4j-python/app/public>
                Options None
                AllowOverride None
                Order allow,deny
                allow from all
        </Directory>

        WSGIDaemonProcess graphstory user=_www group=_www processes=1 threads=15
        WSGIProcessGroup graphstory
```

```
    WSGIApplicationGroup %{GLOBAL}
    WSGIScriptAlias / /path/to/your/workspace/practicalneo4j-python/app/adapter.wsgi

    Alias /css/ /path/to/your/workspace/practicalneo4j-python/app/public/css/
    Alias /fonts/ /path/to/your/workspace/practicalneo4j-python/app/public/fonts/
    Alias /img/ /path/to/your/workspace/practicalneo4j-python/app/public/img/
    Alias /js/ /path/to/your/workspace/practicalneo4j-python/app/public/js/

    <Directory /path/to/your/workspace/practicalneo4j-python/app/bottle>
            Options None
            AllowOverride None
            Order allow,deny
            allow from all
    </Directory>

    ErrorLog /path/to/your/workspace/practicalneo4j-python/app/logs/error.log
    LogLevel warn
</VirtualHost>
```

Py2neo

This section covers basic operations and usage of the Py2neo library with the goal of understanding the library before implementing it within an application. The next section of this chapter will walk you through a sample application with specific graph goals and models.

Like most of the language drivers and libraries available for Neo4j, the purpose of Py2neo is to provide a degree of abstraction over the Neo4j REST API. In addition, the Py2neo API provides some additional enhancements that might otherwise be required at some other stage in the development of your Python application, such as caching.

■ **Note** Py2neo is maintained by the super-awesome Nigel Small and supported by a number of great Python graphistas. If you would like to get involved with Py2neo, go to `https://github.com/nigelsmall/py2neo`.

Each of the following brief sections covers concepts that tie either directly or indirectly to features and functionality found within the Neo4j Server and REST API. If you choose to go through each language chapter, then you should notice how each library covers those features and functionality in similar ways but takes advantage of the language-specific capabilities to ensure the API is flexible and performant.

Managing Nodes and Relationships

Chapters 1 and 2 covered the elements of a graph database, which includes the most basic of graph concepts: the node. Managing nodes and their properties and relationships will probably account for the bulk of your application's graph-related code.

Creating a Node

The maintenance of nodes is set in motion with the creation process, as shown in Listing 9-3. Creating a node begins with setting up a connection to the database and making the node instance. The node properties are set next, and then the node can be saved to the database.

Listing 9-3. Creating a Node

```
from py2neo import neo4j, ogm, node, rel

# set connection information (defaults to: http://localhost:7474/db/data/)
graph_db = neo4j.GraphDatabaseService("https://user:password@graphstory.com:7473/db/data/")

# simple method to create node.
user, = graph_db.create({"name": "Greg", 'business': 'Graph Story'})
```

■ **Warning** The `create` method will always return a list, even when only creating a single node or relationship. Add a trailing comma to automatically unpack a list containing a single node, as shown in the example.

Retrieving and Updating a Node

Once nodes have been added to the database, you will need a way to retrieve and modify them. Listing 9-4 shows the process for finding a node by its node id value and updating it.

Listing 9-4. Retrieving and Updating a Node

```
from py2neo import neo4j, ogm, node, rel

# set connection information (defaults to: http://localhost:7474/db/data/)
graph_db = neo4j.GraphDatabaseService()

# find the user node by it's node id. In this example, nodeId of 1
userNode = graph_db.node(1)

# update a property - this replaces all existing properties with properties provided.
userNode.set_properties({"business " : "Graph Story" })
```

Removing a Node

Once a node's graph id has been set and saved into the database, it becomes eligible to be removed when necessary. To remove a node, set a variable as a node object instance and then call the delete method for the node (Listing 9-5).

■ **Note** You cannot delete any node that is currently set as the start point or end point of any relationship. You must remove the relationship before you can delete the node.

Listing 9-5. Deleting a Node

```
from py2neo import neo4j, ogm, node, rel

# set connection information (defaults to: http://localhost:7474/db/data/)
graph_db = neo4j.GraphDatabaseService()

# find the user node by it's node id
userNode = graph_db.node(1)

# delete the node
userNode.delete()

# in some cases you might want to delete the node AND related notes and relationships
userNode.detele_related()
```

Creating a Relationship

Py2neo offers different methods to create relationships. The example in Listing 9-6 sets up the relationship using a simple create method.

■ **Note** Both the start and end nodes of a relationship must already be established within the database before the relationship can be saved.

Listing 9-6. Relating Two Nodes

```
from py2neo import neo4j, ogm, node, rel

# set connection information (defaults to: http://localhost:7474/db/data/)
graph_db = neo4j.GraphDatabaseService()

# create two nodes
greg, = graph_db.create({"name": "Greg"})
brad, = graph_db.create({"name": "Brad"})

# create the relationship between the two nodes
graph_db.create(rel(greg, "FOLLOWS", brad))
```

Retrieving Relationships

Once a relationship has been created between one or more nodes, then the relationship can be retrieved based on a node (Listing 9-7).

Listing 9-7. Retrieving Relationships

```
from py2neo import neo4j, ogm, node, rel

# set connection information (defaults to: http://localhost:7474/db/data/)
graph_db = neo4j.GraphDatabaseService()

greg = graph_db.node(1)
brad = graph_db.node(10)

# find relationship via outgoing relationship
rels = greg.match_outgoing(rel_type="FOLLOWS", end_node= brad)

# find relationship ignoring the direction of the relationship
rels = greg.match(rel_type="FOLLOWS", other_node= brad)
```

Deleting a Relationship

Once a relationship's graph id has been set and saved into the database, it becomes eligible to be removed when necessary. To remove a relationship, set it as a relationship object instance and then call the delete method for the relationship (Listing 9-8).

Listing 9-8. Deleting a Relationship

```
from py2neo import neo4j, ogm, node, rel

# set connection information (defaults to: http://localhost:7474/db/data/)
graph_db = neo4j.GraphDatabaseService()

greg = graph_db.node(1)
brad = graph_db.node(10)

# find single relationship
rel = graph_db.match_one(start_node=greg, rel_type="FOLLOWS", end_node= brad)

# you could also set bidirectional to True if reversed relatioships should be matched
rel = graph_db.match_one(start_node=greg, rel_type="FOLLOWS", end_node= brad, bidirectional=True)

# delete relationship
rel.delete()
```

Using Labels

Labels function as specific meta-descriptions that can be applied to nodes. Labels were introduced in Neo4j 2.0 in order to help in querying and can also function as a way to quickly create a subgraph.

Adding a Label to Nodes

In Py2neo, you can add one more labels to a node. As Listing 9-9 shows, the *add_labels* function takes one or more labels as argument. You can return each of the labels on a node by calling its *get_labels* function. The value used for the label should be any nonempty string or numeric value.

■ **Caution** A label will not exist on the database server until it has been added to at least one node.

Listing 9-9. Retrieving a Node and Adding a Label to It

```
from py2neo import neo4j, ogm, node, rel

# set connection information (defaults to: http://localhost:7474/db/data/)
graph_db = neo4j.GraphDatabaseService()

# find the user node by its node id
userNode = graph_db.node(1)

# add the label
userNode.add_labels("User")
```

Removing a Label

Removing a label uses similar syntax as adding a label to a node. After the given label has been removed from the node (Listing 9-10), the return value is a list of labels still on the node.

Listing 9-10. Removing a Label from a Node

```
from py2neo import neo4j, ogm, node, rel

# set connection information (defaults to: http://localhost:7474/db/data/)
graph_db = neo4j.GraphDatabaseService()

# find the user node by it's node id
userNode = graph_db.node(1)

# remove the label
userNode.remove_labels("Developer")
```

Querying with a Label

To get nodes that use a specific la bel, use the function called *getNodes*. This function returns value is a result Row object, which can be iterated over like an array (Listing 9-11).

Listing 9-11. Querying with a Label

```
from py2neo import neo4j, ogm, node, rel

# set connection information (defaults to: http://localhost:7474/db/data/)
graph_db = neo4j.GraphDatabaseService()

# property_key and property_value default to None
users = list(graph_db.find('User', property_key='name', property_value='Brad'))
```

Developing a Python and Neo4j Application

Preliminary to building out your first Python and Neo4j application, this section covers the basics of configuring a development environment.

Again, if you have not worked through the installation steps in Chapter 2, please take a few minutes to install it.

Preparing the Graph

In order to spend more time highlighting code examples for each of the more common graph models, you will use a preloaded instance of Neo4j including necessary plugins, such as the spatial plugin.

■ **Tip** To quickly set up a server instance with the sample data and plugins for this chapter, go to `graphstory.com/practicalneo4j`. You will be provided with your own free trial instance, a knowledge base, and email support from Graph Story. Alternatively, you may run a local Neo4j database instance with the sample data by going to `graphstory.com/practicalneo4j`, downloading the zip file containing the sample database and plugins, and adding them to your local instance.

Using the Sample Application

If you have already downloaded the sample application from `graphstory.com/practicalneo4j` for Python and configured it with your local application environment, you can skip ahead to the next section, "Bottle Application Configuration". Otherwise, you will need to go back to the section in this chapter titled "`Python and Neo4j Development Environment`" section and set up your local environment in order to follow the examples in the sample application.

Bottle Application Configuration

Before diving into the code examples, you need to update the configuration for the Bottle application. In Eclipse (or the IDE you are using), open the file `{PROJECTROOT}/app/bottle/graphstory.py` and edit the GraphStory connection string information. If you are using a free account from `graphstory.com`, you will change the username, password, and URL in Listing 9-12 with the one provided in your graph console on `graphstory.com`.

Listing 9-12. Database Connection Settings

```
graph_db = neo4j.GraphDatabaseService("https://username:password@theURL:7473/db/data/")
```

If you have installed a local Neo4j server instance, you can modify the configuration to use the local address and port that you specified during the installation, as in the example shown in Listing 9-13.

Listing 9-13. Database Connection Settings for Local Enviroment

```
graph_db = neo4j.GraphDatabaseService("http://localhost:7474/db/data/")
```

Once the environment is properly configured, you can open a browser to the URL, `http://practicalneo4j-python`, and you should see a page like the one shown in Figure 9-6.

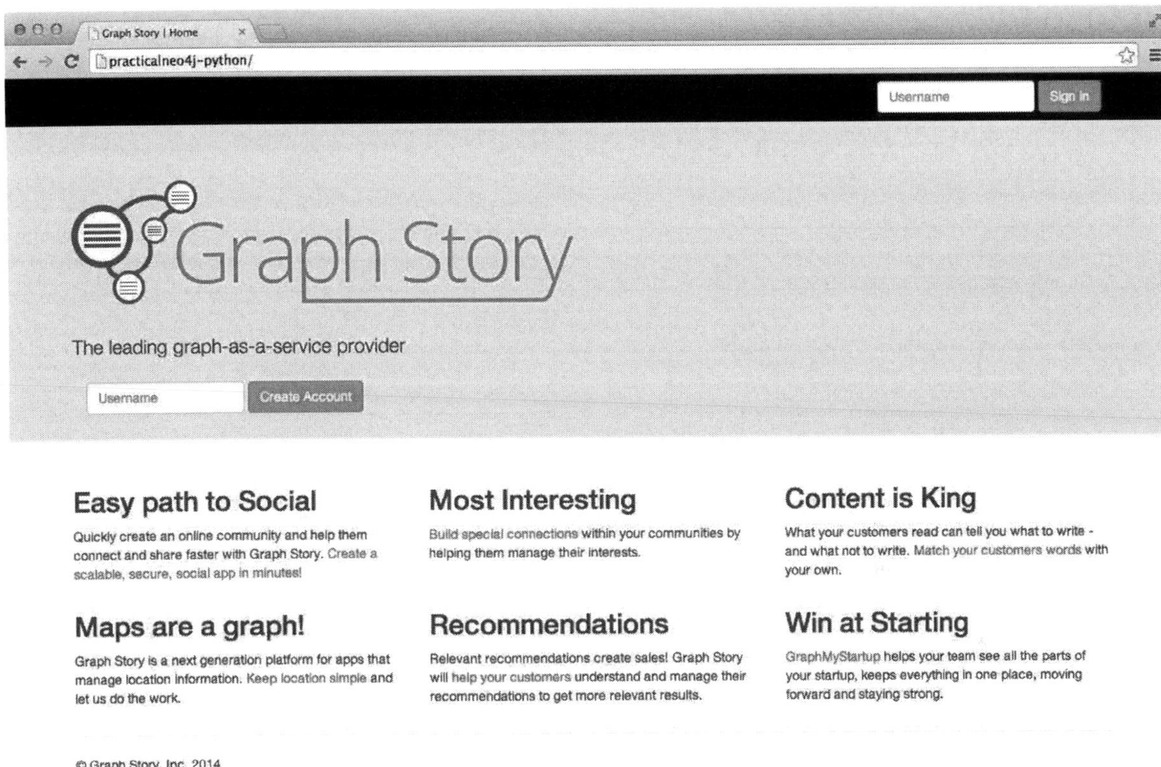

Figure 9-6. *The Python sample application home page*

Social Graph Model

This section explores the social graph model and a few of the operations that typically accompany it. In particular, this section looks at the following:

- Sign-up and login
- Updating a user
- Creating a relationship type through a user by following other users
- Managing user content, such as displaying, adding, updating, and removing status updates

---

■ **Note** The sample graph database used for these examples is loaded with data, so you can immediately begin working with representative data in each of the graph models. In the case of the social graph—and for other graph models, as well—you will login with the user **ajordan**. Going forward, please login with **ajordan** to see each of the working examples.

Sign-Up

The HTML required for the user sign-up form is shown in Listing 9-14 and can be found in the `{PROJECTROOT}/app/public/templates/home/index.html` file.

Listing 9-14. HTML Snippet of Sign-Up Form

```
<form class="navbar-form navbar-left" action="/signup/add" role="form"
        id="createaccountform" method="post">
                <div class="form-group">
                        <input type="text" placeholder="Username" name="username"
                        class="form-control">
                </div>
        <button type="submit" class="btn btn-success">Create Account</button>  
</form>
```

■ **Note** While the sample application creates a user without a password, I am certainly not suggesting or advocating this approach for a production application. Excluding the password property was done in order to create a simple sign-up and login that helps keep the focus on the more salient aspects of the Py2Neo library.

Sign-Up Route

In the sign-up route, start by doing a lookup on the `username` passed in the request and see if it already exists in the database using the `get_user_by_username` method found in the `User` class, as provided in Listing 9-15. If no match is found, the username is passed on to the `save_user` method within else statement.

If no errors are returned during the save attempt, the request is redirected via `redirect` and a message is passed to thank the user for signing up. Otherwise, the error message back to the home view informs the user of the problem.

Listing 9-15. The Sign-Up Route

```
@route('/signup/add', method='POST')
def signup():
    username = request.forms.get('username').strip().lower()

    # make sure username was passed
    if username:

        # check if username exists
        user = User().get_user_by_username(graph_db, username)
        if user:

            # user found, show message
            return template('public/templates/home/index.html', layout=homelayout, title="Home",
                            error='The username ' + username + ' already exists. Please use a
                            different username.')
        else:

            # save user
            User().save_user(graph_db, username)
            redirect("/msg?u=" + username)

    # otherwise send back
    else:
        return template('public/templates/home/index.html', layout=homelayout,
                        title="Home", error="Please enter a username.")
```

Adding a User

In each part of the five graph areas covered in this chapter, the domain object has a corresponding service class to manage the persistence operations within the database. In this case, the User class covers the management of the application's user nodes, using a mix of py2neo convenience methods and executing Cypher queries.

To save a node and label it as a User, the save_user method, shown in Listing 9-16, makes use of the create method by passing in the username param and value. Once the node is created, the add_labels method applies the User label.

Listing 9-16. The save_user Method in the User Class

```
def save_user(self, graph_db, username):
        # create user
        newuser, = graph_db.create({"username": username})
        # add the label
        newuser.add_labels("User")
        return newuser
```

Login

This section reviews the login process for the sample application. To execute the login process, you will also use the login route as well as User class. Before reviewing the controller and service layer, take a quick look at the front-end code for the login.

Login Form

The HTML required for the user login form is shown in Listing 9-17 and can be found in the {PROJECTROOT}/app/public/templates/global/base-home.html layout file.

Listing 9-17. The Login Form

```
<form class="navbar-form navbar-right" action="/login" role="form" method="post">
<div class="form-group">
<input type="text" placeholder="Username" name="username" class="form-control">
</div>
<button type="submit" class="btn btn-success">Sign in</button>
</form>
```

Login Route

In the graphstory application, use the login route to control the flow of the login process, as shown in Listing 9-18. Inside the login route, use the get_user_by_username method to check if the user exists in the database.

Listing 9-18. The login Route

```
@route('/login', method='POST')
def login():
    # make sure username was passed
    username = request.forms.get('username').strip().lower()

    if username:

        # look for username
        user = User().get_user_by_username(graph_db, username)
        if user:
            # user found, set cookie and redirect
            response.set_cookie(graphstoryUserAuthKey, user["username"], path="/")
            redirect("/social")

        else:
            # otherwise send back with not found message
            return template("public/templates/home/index.html", layout=homelayout, title="Home",
                            error="The username you entered was not found.")
    # otherwise send back
    else:
        return template('public/templates/home/index.html', layout=homelayout, title="Home",
                        error="Please enter a username.")
```

If the user is found during the login attempt, a cookie is added to the response and the request is redirected via redirect the social home page, shown in Figure 9-7. Otherwise, the route will specify the HTML page to return and will add the error messages that need to be displayed back to the view.

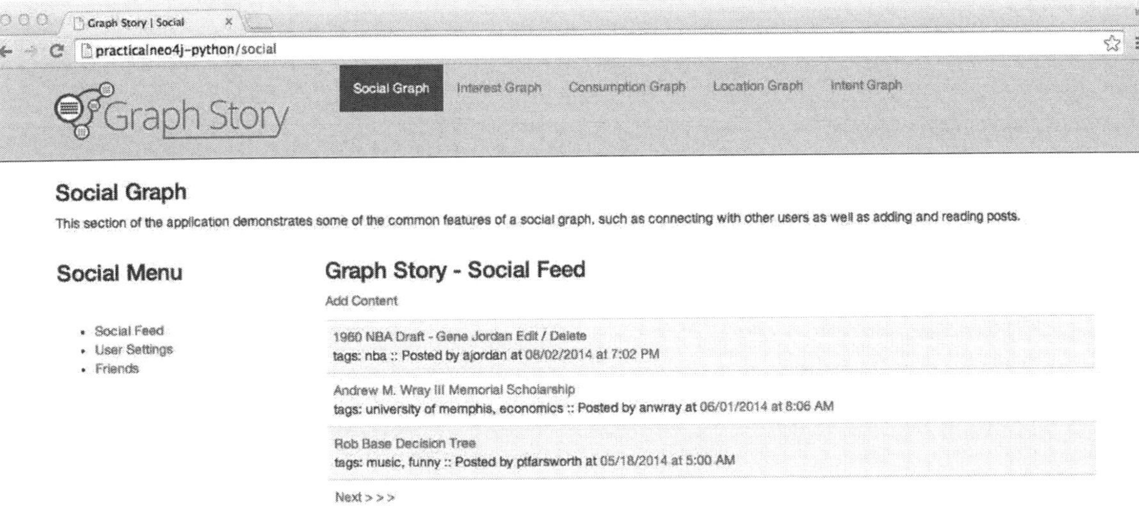

Figure 9-7. *The social graph home page*

Login Service

To check to see if the user values being passed through are connected to a valid user combination in the database, the application uses the `get_user_by_username` method in the `User` class. As shown in Listing 9-19, the result of the `get_user_by_username` method is assigned to the `user` variable.

If the result is not null or empty, the result is set on the `User` object and returned to the controller layer of the application.

Listing 9-19. The `get_user_by_username` Method in the `User` Class

```
def get_user_by_username(self, graph_db, username):
    query = neo4j.CypherQuery(graph_db,
                              " MATCH (user:User {username: {username}}) " +
                              " RETURN user ")
    params = {"username": username}
    result = query.execute_one(**params)
    return result
```

Now that the user is logged in, he can edit his settings, create relationships with other users in the graph, and create his own content.

Updating a User

To access the page for updating a user, click on the "User Settings" link in the social graph section, as shown in Figure 9-8. In this example, the front-end code uses an AJAX request via PUT and adds—or, in the case of the **ajordan** user, updates—the first and last name of the user.

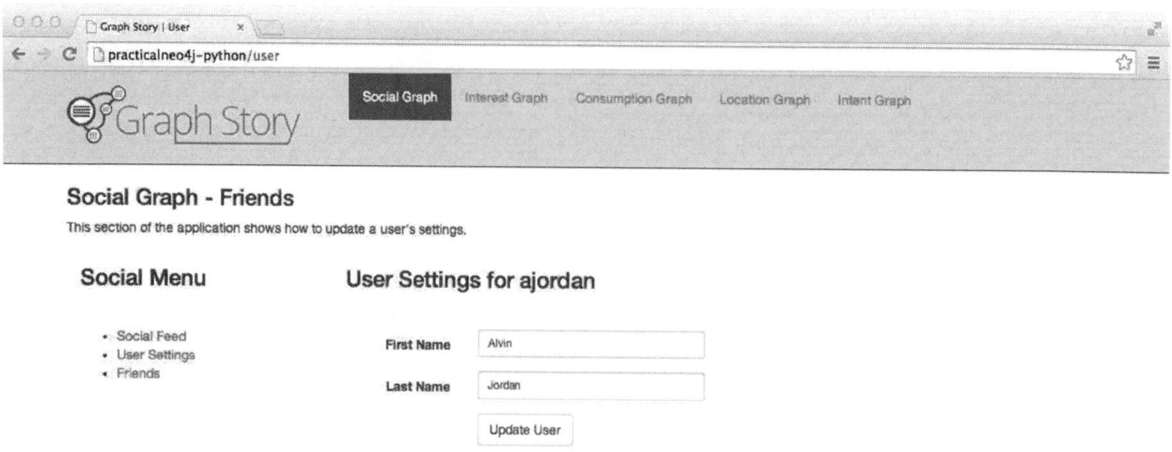

Figure 9-8. *The User Settings page*

User Update Form

The user settings form is located in `{PROJECTROOT}/app/public/templates/graphs/social/user.html` and is similar in structure to the other forms presented in the Sign Up and Login sections. One difference is that you have added the `value` property to the input element as well as the variables for displaying the respective stored values. If none exist, the form fields will be empty (Listing 9-20).

Listing 9-20. User Update Form

```
<form class="form-horizontal" id="userform" action="/user/edit" method="put">
  <div class="form-group">
    <label for="firstname" class="col-sm-2 control-label">First Name</label>
    <div class="col-sm-10">
      <input type="text" class="form-control input-sm" id="firstname" name="user.firstname"
      value="{{user.firstname}}" />
    </div>
  </div>
  <div class="form-group">
    <label for="lastname" class="col-sm-2 control-label">Last Name</label>
    <div class="col-sm-10">
      <input type="text" class="form-control input-sm" id="lastname" name="user.lastname"
      value="{{user.lastname}}" />
    </div>
  </div>
  <div class="form-group">
    <div class="col-sm-offset-2 col-sm-10">
      <button type="submit" id="updateUser" class="btn btn-default">Update User</button>
    </div>
  </div>
</form>
```

User Edit Route

The graphstory application contains a route with the path /user/edit, which takes the JSON object argument. The User object is converted from a JSON string and returns a User object as JSON. The response could be used to update the form elements, but because the values are already set within the form there is no need to update the values. In this case, the application uses the JSON response to let the user know if the update succeeded or not via a standard JavaScript alert message (Listing 9-21).

Listing 9-21. user_edit Route

```
@route('/user/edit', method='PUT')
def user_edit():
    User().update_user(graph_db, request.get_cookie(graphstoryUserAuthKey),
                       request.json["firstname"], request.json["lastname"])

    response.content_type = 'application/json'

    return {"msg": "ok"}
```

User Update Method

To complete the update, the controller layer calls the update_user method in User class. Because the object being passed into the update method did nothing more than modify the first and last name of an existing entity, you can use the SET clause via Cypher to update the properties in the graph, as shown in Listing 9-22.

This Cypher statement also makes use of the MATCH clause to retrieve the User node. You could also complete this feature by executing a find or using the get_user_by_username method, and then updating the first and last name via the update_properties method of the py2neo Node class.

Listing 9-22. The update_user Method in the User Class

```
def update_user(self, graph_db, username, firstname, lastname):
    query = neo4j.CypherQuery(graph_db,
                              "MATCH (user:User {username:{u}} )  " +
                              "SET user.firstname = {fn}, user.lastname = {ln}")
    params = {"u": username, "fn": firstname, "ln": lastname}
    result = query.execute(**params)
    return result
```

Connecting Users

A common feature in social media applications is to allow users to connect to each other through an explicit relationship. In the sample application, you will use the directed relationship type called FOLLOWS. By going to the "Friends" page within the social graph section, you can see the list of the users the current user is following, search for new friends to follow, add them and remove friends the current user is following.

The user management section of graphstory.py contains each of the routes to control the flow for these features, specifically the routes that cover friends, search_by_username, follow and unfollow.

To display the list of the users the current user is following, the friends route, showing in Listing 9-23, in the graphstory application calls the following method in User class. The following method in User class, also shown in Listing 9-23, creates a list of users by matching the current user's username with directed relationship FOLLOWS on the variable user.

Listing 9-23. The friends Route and the following Method

```
@route('/friends', method='GET')
def friends():
    following = User().following(graph_db, request.get_cookie(graphstoryUserAuthKey))

    return template('public/templates/graphs/social/friends.html',
                    following=following, layout=applayout, title="Friends")

# the following method in the User class
    def following(self, graph_db, username):
        query = neo4j.CypherQuery(graph_db,
                                  " MATCH (user { username:{u}})-[:FOLLOWS]->(users) " +
                                  " RETURN users.firstname as firstname, users.lastname as
                                  lastname,"+
                                  " users.username as username " +
                                  " ORDER BY users.username")
        params = {"u": username}
        result = query.execute(**params)
        return result
```

If the list contains users, it will be returned to the controller and displayed as on the right-hand part of Figure 9-9. The display code for showing the list of users can be found in `{PROJECTROOT}/app/public/templates/graphs/social/friends.html` and is shown in the code snippet in Listing 9-24.

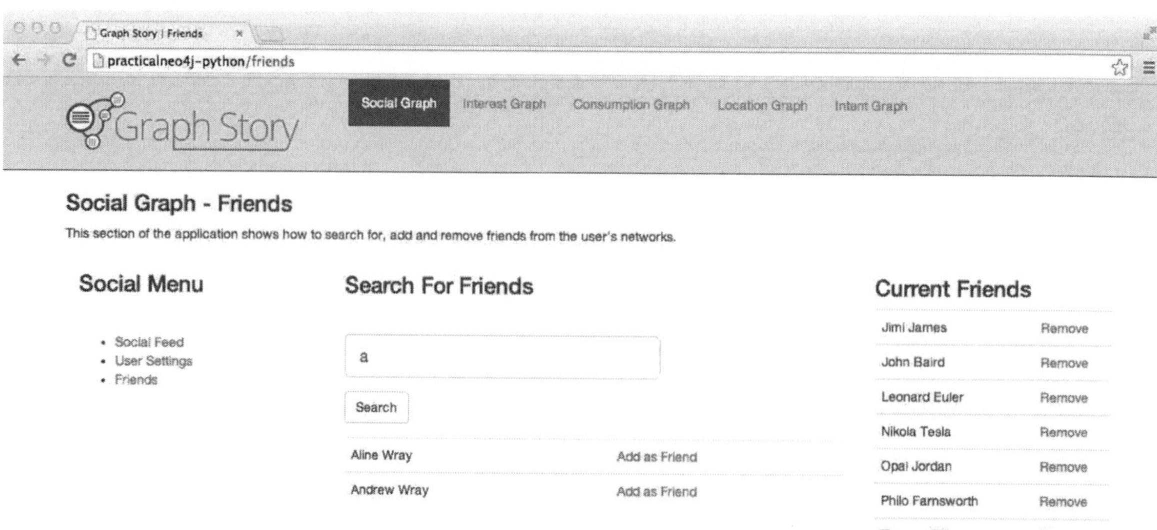

Figure 9-9. *The Friends page*

Listing 9-24. The HTML Code Snippet for Displaying the List of Friends

```
<div class="col-md-3">
        <h3>Current Friends</h3>
        <table class="table" id="following">
                {{#following}}
                                <tr><td>{{firstname}} {{lastname}}</td><td><a href="#"
                                id="{{username}}"
                        class="removefriend">Remove</a></td></tr>
                        {{/following}}
                        {{^following}}
                                No friends :(
                {{/following}}
        </table>
</div>
```

To search for users to follow, the user section of graphstory contains a GET route /searchbyusername and passes in a username value as part of the path. This route executes the search_by_username_not_following method found in User class, showing the second section of Listing 9-25. The first part of the WHERE clause in search_by_username_not_following returns users whose username matches on a wildcard String value. The second part of the WHERE clause in search_by_username_not_following checks to make sure the users in the MATCH clause are not already being followed by the current user.

Listing 9-25. The searchbyusername Route and service Method

```
@route('/searchbyusername/<username>', method='GET')
def search_by_username(username):
    # get the users' the current user is following
    users = User().search_by_username_not_following(graph_db,
                                                    request.get_cookie(graphstoryUserAuthKey),
                                                    username)


    response.content_type = 'application/json'

    # return as json
    return dumps({"users": User().users_results_as_array(users)})

# search by user returns users in the network that aren't already being followed
def search_by_username_not_following(self, graph_db, currentusername, username):
    username = username.lower() + ".*"
    query = neo4j.CypherQuery(graph_db,
                              " MATCH (n:User), (user { username:{cu}}) " +
                              " WHERE (n.username =~ {u} AND n <> user) " +
                              " AND (NOT (user)-[:FOLLOWS]->(n)) " +
                              " RETURN n.firstname as firstname, n.lastname as lastname,"+
                              " n.username as username")
    params = {"u": username, "cu": currentusername}
    result = query.execute(**params)
    return result
```

The searchByUsername in {PROJECTROOT}/app/public/js/graphstory.js uses an AJAX request and formats the response in renderSearchByUsername. If the list contains users, it is displayed in the center of the page under the search form, as shown in Figure 9-9. Otherwise, the response displays "No Users Found".

Once the search returns results, the next action is to click on the "Add as Friend" link, which calls the addfriend method in graphstory.js. This performs an AJAX request to the follow method in the UserController and calls follow in UserService. The follow method in UserService, shown in Listing 9-26, will create the relationship between the two users by first finding each entity via the MATCH clause and then using the CreateUnique clause to create the directed FOLLOWS relationship. Once the operation is completed, the next part of the query then runs a MATCH on the users being followed to return the full list of followers ordered by the username.

Listing 9-26. The follow Route and follow service Method

```
# follow a user
@route('/follow/<username>', method='GET')
def follow(username):
    following = User().follow(graph_db, request.get_cookie(graphstoryUserAuthKey), username)

    response.content_type = 'application/json'

    return dumps({"following": User().users_results_as_array(following)})

# the follow method in the User class
def follow(self, graph_db, currentusername, username):
        query = neo4j.CypherQuery(graph_db,
                                  " MATCH (user1:User {username:{cu}} ), (user2:User
                                  {username:{u}} ) " +
                                  " CREATE UNIQUE user1-[:FOLLOWS]->user2 " +
                                  " WITH user1" +
                                  " MATCH (user1)-[f:FOLLOWS]->(users)" +
                                  " RETURN users.firstname as firstname, users.lastname
                                  as lastname, " +
                                  " users.username as username " +
                                  " ORDER BY users.username")
        params = {"cu": currentusername,"u": username}
        result = query.execute(**params)
        return result
```

The unfollow feature for the FOLLOWS relationships uses a nearly identical application flow as follows feature. In the unfollow method, shown in Listing 9-27, the controller passes in two arguments—the current username and username to be unfollowed. As with the follows method, once the operation is completed, the next part of the query then runs a MATCH on the users being followed to return the full list of followers ordered by the username.

Listing 9-27. The unfollow Route and unfollow Method

```
@route('/unfollow/<username>', method='GET')
def unfollow(username):
    following = User().unfollow(graph_db, request.get_cookie(graphstoryUserAuthKey), username)

    response.content_type = 'application/json'

    return dumps({"following": User().users_results_as_array(following)})
```

```
# unfollow a user
def unfollow(self, graph_db, currentusername, username):
    query = neo4j.CypherQuery(graph_db,
                              " MATCH (user1:User {username:{cu}} )-[f:FOLLOWS]->(user2:User
                              {username:{u}} ) " +
                              " DELETE f " +
                              " WITH user1" +
                              " MATCH (user1)-[f:FOLLOWS]->(users)" +
                              " RETURN users.firstname as firstname, users.lastname as lastname, "+
                              " users.username as username " +
                              " ORDER BY users.username")
    params = {"cu": currentusername, "u": username}
    result = query.execute(**params)
    return result
```

User-Generated Content

Another important feature in social media applications is being able to have users view, add, edit, and remove content—sometimes referred to as *user-generated content*. In the case of this content, you will not be creating connections between the content and its owner, but creating a linked list of status updates. In other words, you are connecting a User to their most recent status update and then connecting each subsequent status to the next update through the CURRENTPOST and NEXTPOST directed relationship types, respectively.

This approach is used for two reasons. First, the sample application displays a given number of posts at a time, and using a limited linked list is more efficient than getting all status updates connected directly to a user and then sorting and limiting the number of items to return. Second, it also helps to limit the number of relationships that are placed on the User and Content entities. Therefore, the overall graph operations should be made more efficient by using the linked list approach.

Getting the Status Updates

To display the first set of status updates, start with the `social` route of the social section of `grapstory.py`. This method accesses the get_content method within Content service class, which takes an argument of the current user's username and the page being requested. The page refers to set number of objects within a collection. In this instance the paging is zero-based, and so you will request page 0 and limit the page size to 4 in order to return the first page.

The get_content method in Content class, shown in Listing 9-28, will first determine whom the user is following and then match that set of user with the status updates starting with the CURRENTPOST. The CURRENTPOST is then matched on the next three status updates via the `[:NEXTPOST*0..3]` section of the query. Finally, the method uses a loop to add a readable date and time string property—based on the timestamp—on the results returned to the controller and view.

Listing 9-28. The get_content Method in Content Class

```
def get_content(self, graph_db, username, skip):
    query = neo4j.CypherQuery(graph_db,
                " MATCH (u:User {username: {u} })-[:FOLLOWS*0..1]->f  " +
                " WITH DISTINCT f,u " +
                " MATCH f-[:CURRENTPOST]-lp-[:NEXTPOST*0..3]-p   " +
                " RETURN  p.contentId as contentId, p.title as title, " +
                " p.tagstr as tagstr, p.timestamp as timestamp, " +
                " p.url as url, f.username as username, f=u as owner  " +
                " ORDER BY p.timestamp desc SKIP {s} LIMIT 4 ")
```

```
    params = {"u": username, "s": skip}
    result = query.execute(**params)
    for r in result:
        setattr(r, "timestampAsStr",
                datetime.fromtimestamp(int(r.timestamp)).strftime('%m/%d/%Y') + " at " +
                datetime.fromtimestamp(int(r.timestamp)).strftime('%I:%M %p')
        )
    return result
```

Adding a Status Update

The page shown in Figure 9-10 shows the form to add a status update for the current user, which is displayed when clicking on the "Add Content" link just under the "Graph Story—Social Feed" header. The HTML for the form can be found in `{PROJECTROOT}/app/public/templates/graphs/social/posts.html`. The form uses the `addContent` function in `graphstory.js` to `POST` a new status update as well as return the response and add it to the top of the status update content stream.

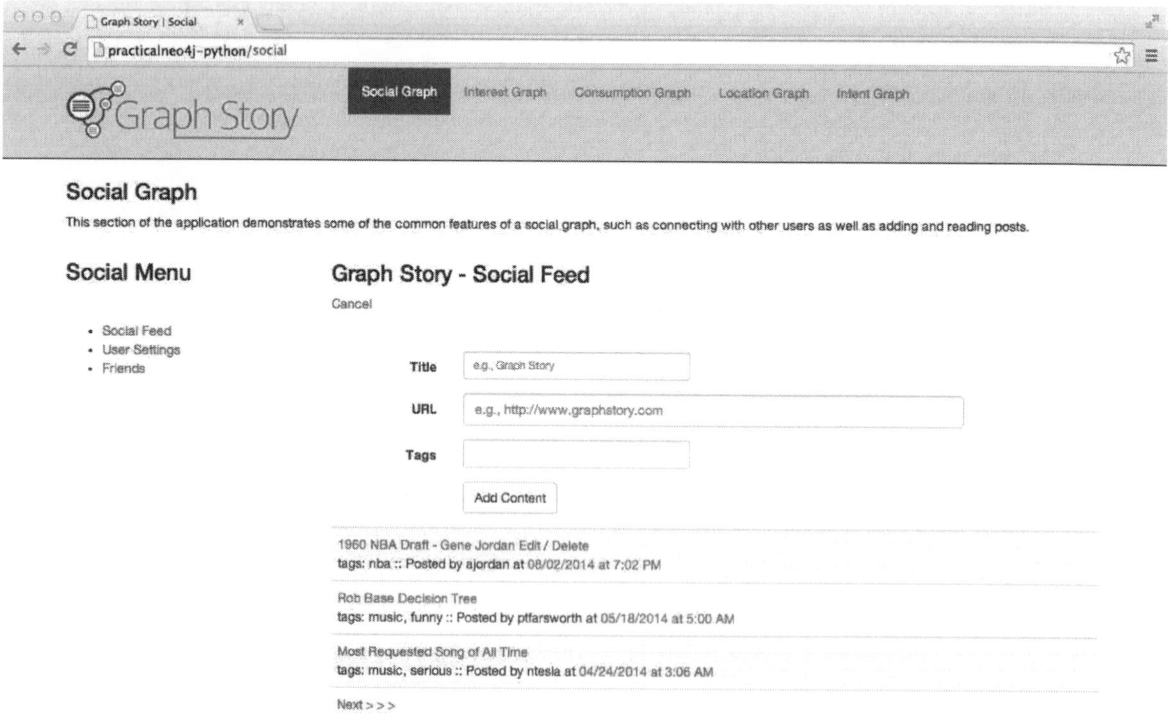

Figure 9-10. *Adding a status update*

The add_content route and add_content method are shown in Listing 9-29. When a new status update is created, in addition to its graph id, the add_content method also generates a contentId, which performs using the uuid1 method.

The add_content method also make the status the CURRENTPOST. Determine whether a previous CURRENTPOST exists and, if one does, change its relationship type to NEXTPOST. In addition, the tags connected to the status update are merged into the graph and connected to the status update via the HAS relationship type.

Listing 9-29. add_content Route and add_content Method for a Status Update

```
# add status update
@route('/posts/add', method='POST')
def add_content():

    # get json from the request
    content = request.json

    #save the status update
    content=Content().add_content(graph_db, request.get_cookie(graphstoryUserAuthKey), content)

    # set response type
    response.content_type = 'application/json'

    # return the saved content
    return dumps(content)

# add a status update
def add_content(self, graph_db, username, content):

    tagstr=self.trim_content_tags(content["tagstr"])
    tags = tagstr.split(",")
    ts = time.time()

    query = neo4j.CypherQuery(graph_db,
      " MATCH (user { username: {u}}) " +
      " CREATE UNIQUE (user)-[:CURRENTPOST]->(newLP:Content { title:{title}, " +
      " url:{url}, tagstr:{tagstr}, timestamp:{timestamp}, contentId:{contentId} }) " +
      " WITH user, newLP" +
      " FOREACH (tagName in {tags} |  " +
      " MERGE (t:Tag {wordPhrase:tagName}) " +
      " MERGE (newLP)-[:HAS]->(t) " +
      " )" +
      " WITH user, newLP " +
      " OPTIONAL MATCH  (newLP)<-[:CURRENTPOST]-(user)-[oldRel:CURRENTPOST]->(oldLP)" +
      " DELETE oldRel " +
      " CREATE (newLP)-[:NEXTPOST]->(oldLP) " +
      " RETURN newLP.contentId as contentId, newLP.title as title, newLP.tagstr as tagstr, " +
      " newLP.timestamp as timestamp, newLP.url as url, {u} as username, true as owner ")
    params = {"u": username, "title": contentItem["title"].strip(),
              "url": contentItem["url"].strip(),
              "tagstr":tagstr, "timestamp":ts,"contentId": uuid.uuid1(), "tags":tags}
```

```
    result = query.execute(**params)
    for r in result:
        setattr(r, "timestampAsStr",
                datetime.fromtimestamp(int(r.timestamp)).strftime('%m/%d/%Y') + " at " +
                datetime.fromtimestamp(int(r.timestamp)).strftime('%I:%M %p')
        )
    return result
```

Editing a Status Update

When status updates are displayed, the current user's status updates will contain a link to "Edit" the status. Once clicked, it will open the form, similar to the "Add Content" link, but will populate the form with the status update values and modify the form button to read "Edit Content", as shown in Figure 9-11. As with many similar UI features, clicking "Cancel" under the heading will remove the values and return the form to its ready state.

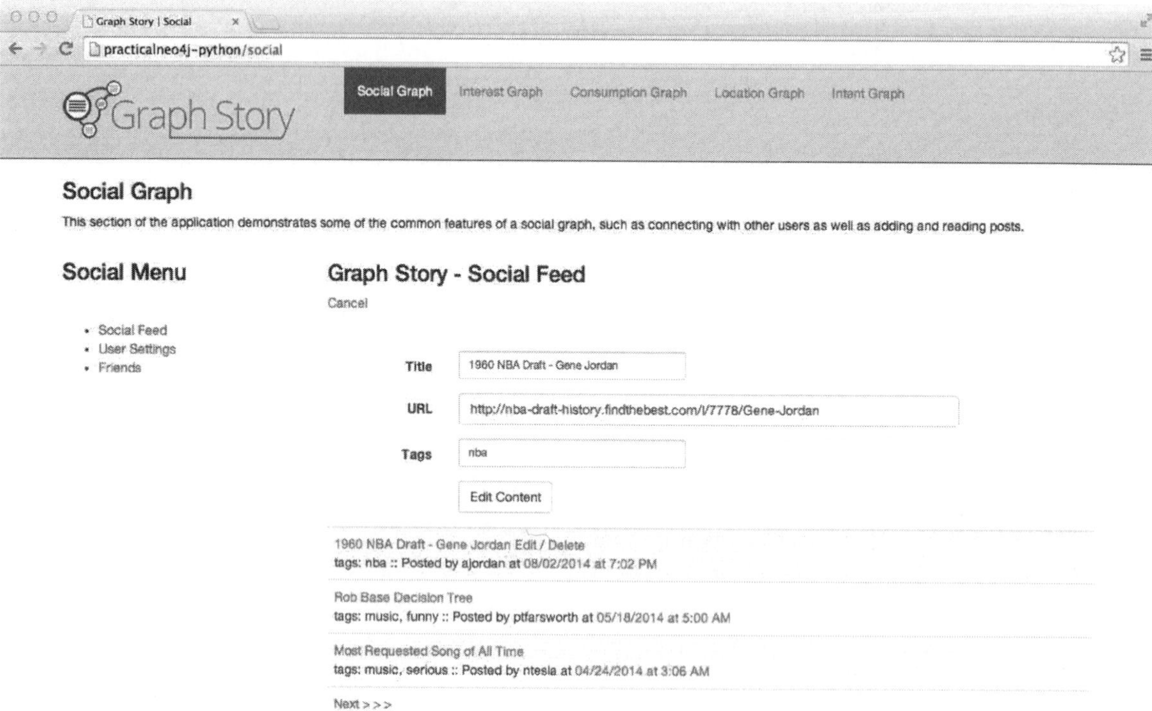

***Figure 9-11.** Editing a status update*

The edit feature, like the add feature, uses a route in the graphstory application and a function in graphstory.js, which are edit_ and updateContent, respectively. The edit_content route passes in the content object, with its content id, and then calls the edit_content method in Content class, as shown in Listing 9-30.

In the case of the edit feature, you do not need to update relationships. Instead, simply retrieve the existing node by its generated String Id (not its graph id), update its properties where necessary, and save it back to the graph.

Listing 9-30. edit_content Route and edit_content Method for a Status Update

```
# edit the status update
@route('/posts/edit', method='POST')
def edit_content():

    # get json from the request
    content = request.json

    #update the status update
    content=Content().edit_content(graph_db, request.get_cookie(graphstoryUserAuthKey), content)

    # set response type
    response.content_type = 'application/json'

    # return the saved content
    return dumps(content)

# edit a status update
def edit_content(self, graph_db, username, content):

    tagstr=self.trim_content_tags(content["tagstr"])
    tags = tagstr.split(",")

    query = neo4j.CypherQuery(graph_db,
      " MATCH (c:Content {contentId:{contentId}})-[:NEXTPOST*0..]-()-[:CURRENTPOST]-
      (user { username: {u}}) " +
      " SET c.title = {title}, c.url = {url}, c.tagstr = {tagstr}" +
      " FOREACH (tagName in {tags} |  " +
      " MERGE (t:Tag {wordPhrase:tagName}) " +
      " MERGE (c)-[:HAS]->(t) " +
      " )" +
      " RETURN c.contentId as contentId, c.title as title, c.tagstr as tagstr, " +
      " c.timestamp as timestamp, c.url as url, {u} as username, true as owner ")
    params = {"u": username, "contentId": content["contentId"],
              "title": content["title"].strip(), "url": content["url"].strip(),"tagstr":tagstr,
              "tags":tags}
    result = query.execute(**params)
    for r in result:
        setattr(r, "timestampAsStr",
                datetime.fromtimestamp(int(r.timestamp)).strftime('%m/%d/%Y') + " at " +
                datetime.fromtimestamp(int(r.timestamp)).strftime('%I:%M %p')
        )
    return result
```

Deleting a Status Update

As with the "edit" option, when status updates are displayed, the current user's status updates contain a link to "Delete" the status. Once clicked, it asks if you want it deleted (no regrets!) and, if accepted, generates an AJAX GET request to call the `delete_content` route and corresponding method in the `Content` class, shown in Listing 9-31.

The Cypher in the delete method begins by finding the user and content that will be used in the rest of the query. In the first `MATCH`, you can determine if this status update is the `CURRENTPOST` by checking to see if it is related to a `NEXTPOST`. If this relationship pattern matches, make the `NEXTPOST` into the CURRENTPOST with `CREATE UNIQUE`.

Next, the query will ask if the status update is somewhere the middle of the list, which is performed by determining if the status update has incoming and outgoing `NEXTPOST` relationships. If the pattern is matched, then connect the `before` and `after` status updates via `NEXTPOST`.

Regardless of the status update's location in the linked list, retrieve it and its relationships and then delete the node along with all of its relationships.

To recap, if one of the relationship patterns matches, replace that pattern with the nodes on either side of the status update in question. Once that has been performed, the node and its relationships can be removed from the graph.

Listing 9-31. `delete_content` Route and `delete_content` Method for a Status Update

```
# delete a status update
@route('/posts/delete/<contentId>', method='GET')
def delete_content(contentId):

    #delete the status update
    delete = Content().delete_content(graph_db, request.get_cookie(graphstoryUserAuthKey),
    contentId)

    # set response type
    response.content_type = 'application/json'

    # return the response
    return {"msg": "ok"}

# delete a status update
def delete_content(self, graph_db, username, contentId):
    query = neo4j.CypherQuery(graph_db,
      " MATCH (u:User { username: {u} }), (c:Content { contentId: {contentId} }) " +
      " WITH u,c " +
      " MATCH (u)-[:CURRENTPOST]->(c)-[:NEXTPOST]->(nextPost) " +
      " WHERE nextPost is not null " +
      " CREATE UNIQUE (u)-[:CURRENTPOST]->(nextPost) " +
      " WITH count(nextPost) as cnt " +
      " MATCH (before)-[:NEXTPOST]->(c:Content { contentId: {contentId}})-[:NEXTPOST]->(after) " +
      " WHERE before is not null AND after is not null " +
      " CREATE UNIQUE (before)-[:NEXTPOST]->(after) " +
      " WITH count(before) as cnt " +
      " MATCH (c:Content { contentId: {contentId} })-[r]-() " +
      " DELETE c, r")
    params = {"u": username, "contentId": contentId}
    result = query.execute(**params)
    return result
```

Interest Graph Model

This section looks at the interest graph and examines some basic ways it can be used to explicitly define a degree of interest. The following topics are covered:

- Adding filters for owned content
- Adding filters for connected content
- Analyzing connected content (count tags)

Interest in Aggregate

Inside the `interest` route of graphstory.py, we retrieve all of the user's tags and their friends' tags by calling, respectively, the `user_tags` and `tags__in_network` methods found in the Tag class. This is displayed in Figure 9-12 in the left-hand column.

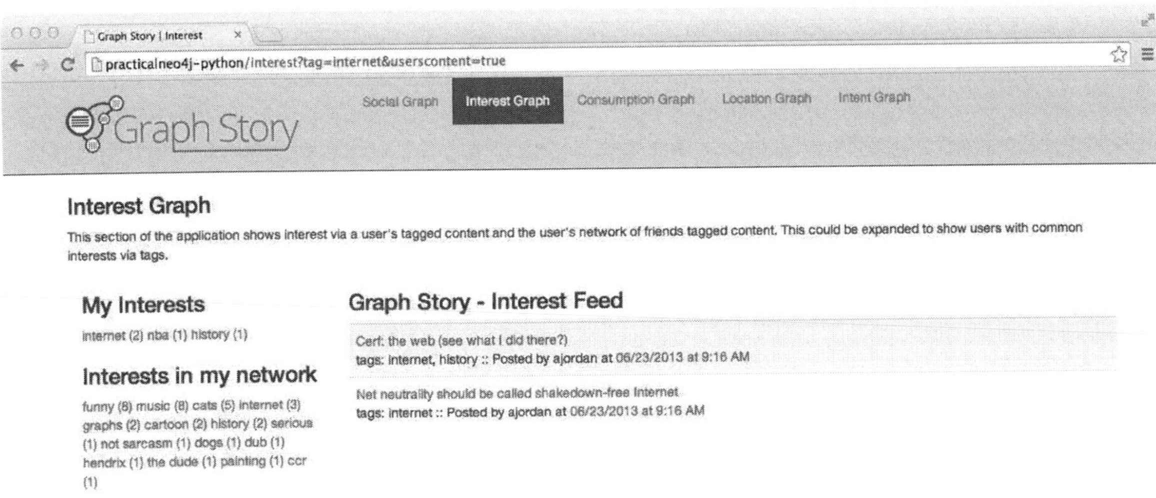

Figure 9-12. *Filtering the current user's content*

The display code is located in `{PROJECTROOT}/app/views/graphs/interest/index.html`. The `interest` route also uses two additional methods, which are shown in Listings 9-33 and 9-34. The `get_following_content_with_tag` finds users being followed, accesses all of their content, and finds connected tags through the `HAS` relationship type.

The `get_user_content_with_tag` method is similar but is concerned only with content and, subsequently, tags connected to the current user. As mentioned earlier, the methods return an array of content and tags, which supports an autosuggest plugin in the view and requires both a label and name to be provided in order to execute. This autosuggest feature is used in the status update form as well as some search forms found later in this chapter.

Listing 9-32. The `interest` Route

```
# show tags within the user's network (theirs and those being followed)
@route('/interest')
def interest():
    # get the user's tags
    userTags = Tag().user_tags(graph_db, request.get_cookie(graphstoryUserAuthKey))
```

```
    # get the tags of user's friends
    tagsInNetwork = Tag().tags_in_network(graph_db, request.get_cookie(graphstoryUserAuthKey))

    # if the user's content was requested
    if request.query.get('userscontent') == "true":
        contents = Content().get_user_content_with_tag(graph_db,
                                                    request.get_cookie(graphstoryUserAuthKey),
                                                    request.query.get('tag'))
    # if the user's friends' content was requested
    else:
        contents = Content().get_following_content_with_tag(graph_db,
                                                         request.get_cookie(graphstoryUserAuthKey),
                                                         request.query.get('tag'))

    return template('public/templates/graphs/interest/index.html', layout=applayout,
    userTags=userTags,
                    tagsInNetwork=tagsInNetwork, contents=contents, title="Interest")
```

Filtering Managed Content

Once the list of tags for the user and for the group she follows has been provided, the content can be filtered based on the generated tag links, which is shown in Figure 9-12. If a tag is clicked on the inside of the "My Interests" section, then the get_user_content_with_tag method, displayed in Listing 9-33, will be called.

Listing 9-33. Get the Content of the Current User Based on a Tag

```
def get_user_content_with_tag(self, graph_db, username, wordPhrase):
    query = neo4j.CypherQuery(graph_db,
                              " MATCH (u:User {username: {u} })-[:CURRENTPOST]-lp-[:NEXTPOST*0..]-p
                              " +
                              " WITH DISTINCT u,p" +
                              " MATCH p-[:HAS]-(t:Tag {wordPhrase : {wp} } )" +
                              " RETURN  p.contentId as contentId, p.title as title, p.tagstr as
                              tagstr, " +
                              " p.timestamp as timestamp, p.url as url, u.username as username, true
                              as owner" +
                              " ORDER BY p.timestamp DESC")
    params = {"u": username, "wp": wordPhrase}
    result = query.execute(**params)
    for r in result:
        setattr(r, "timestampAsStr",
                datetime.fromtimestamp(int(r.timestamp)).strftime('%m/%d/%Y') + " at " +
                datetime.fromtimestamp(int(r.timestamp)).strftime('%I:%M %p')
        )
    return result
```

Filtering Connected Content

If a tag is clicked on the inside of the "Interests in my Network" section, then get_following_content_with_tag method will be called, as shown in Listing 9-34. The second query is nearly identical the first query found in the interest route, except that it will factor in the users being followed and exclude the current user (Figure 9-13).

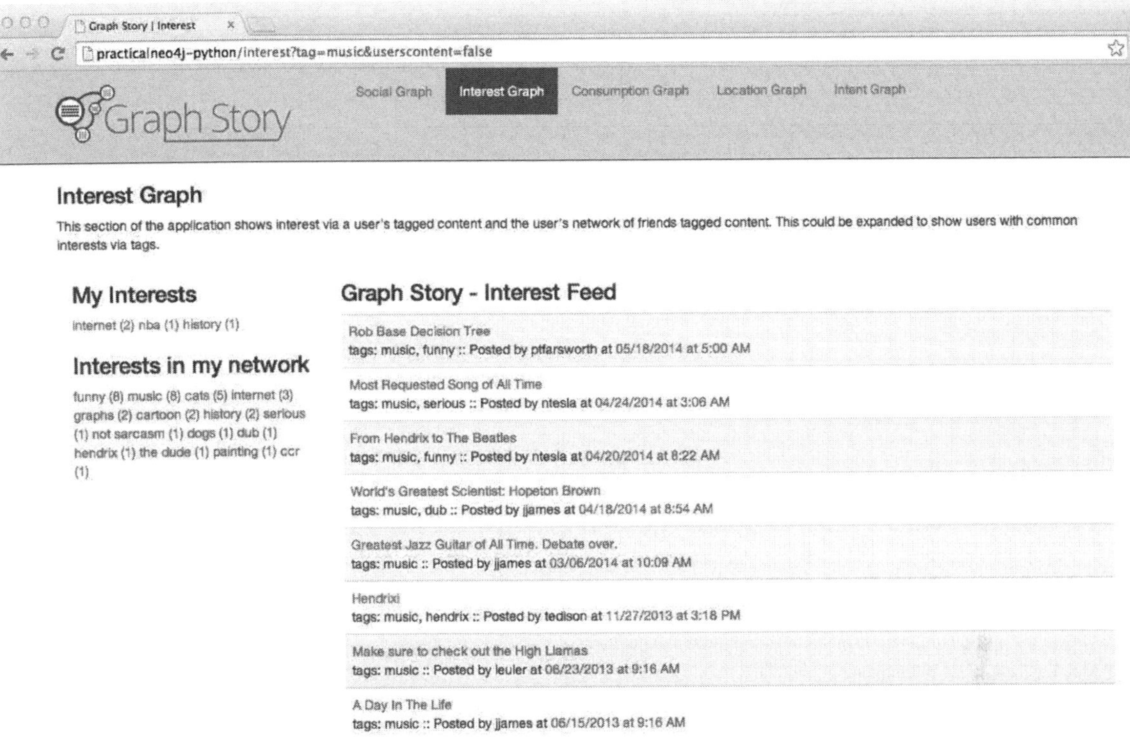

Figure 9-13. *Filtering content of the current user's friends*

The method also returns a collection of status updates based on the matching tag, placing no limit on the number of status updates to be returned. In addition, it marks the owner property as true, because you've determined ahead of time you are only returning the current user's content. The results of calling this method are shown in Figure 9-13.

Listing 9-34. Get the Content of the User's Being Followed Based on a Tag

```
def get_following_content_with_tag(self, graph_db, username, wordPhrase):
    query = neo4j.CypherQuery(graph_db,
                              " MATCH (u:User {username: {u} })-[:FOLLOWS]->f" +
                              " WITH DISTINCT f" +
                              " MATCH f-[:CURRENTPOST]-lp-[:NEXTPOST*0..]-p" +
                              " WITH DISTINCT f,p" +
                              " MATCH p-[:HAS]-(t:Tag {wordPhrase : {wp} } )" +
                              " RETURN  p.contentId as contentId, p.title as title, p.tagstr as
                              tagstr, " +
                              " p.timestamp as timestamp, p.url as url, f.username as username,
                              false as owner" +
                              " ORDER BY p.timestamp DESC")
    params = {"u": username, "wp": wordPhrase}
    result = query.execute(**params)
```

```
    for r in result:
        setattr(r, "timestampAsStr",
                datetime.fromtimestamp(int(r.timestamp)).strftime('%m/%d/%Y') + " at " +
                datetime.fromtimestamp(int(r.timestamp)).strftime('%I:%M %p')
        )
    return result
```

Consumption Graph Model

This section examines a few techniques to capture and use patterns of consumption generated implicitly by a user or users. For the purposes of your application, you will use the prepopulated set of products provided in the sample graph. The code required for the console will reinforce the standard persistence operations, this section focuses on the operations that take advantage of this model type, including:

- Capturing consumption
- Filtering consumption for users
- Filtering consumption for messaging

Capturing Consumption

The process above for creating code that directly captures consumption for a user could also be done by creating a graph-backed service to consume the webserver logs in real time or by creating another data store to create the relationships. The result would be the same in any event: a process that connects nodes to reveal a pattern of consumption (Listing 9-35).

Listing 9-35. Consumption Route to Show a List of Products and the Product Trail of the Current User

```
# show products and products VIEWED by user
@route('/consumption', method='GET')
def consumption():
    products = Product().get_products(graph_db, 0)
    next = True
    nextPageUrl = "/consumption/10"

    productTrail = Product().get_product_trail(graph_db, request.cookies[graphstoryUserAuthKey])

    return template('public/templates/graphs/consumption/index.html',
                    layout=applayout, products=products,
                    productTrail=productTrail, next=next, nextPageUrl=nextPageUrl,
                    title="Consumption")
```

The sample application used the `create_user_view_and_return_views` method in the `Product` class to first find the product being viewed and then create an explicit relationship type called `VIEWED`. As you may have noticed, this is the first relationship type in the application that also contains properties. In this case, you are creating a timestamp with a date and string value of the timestamp. The query, provided in Listing 9-36, checks to see if a `VIEWED` relationship already exists between the user and the product using `MERGE`.

In the `MERGE` section of the query, if the result of the `MERGE` is zero matches, then a relationship is created with key value pairs on the new relationship, specifically dateAsStr and timestamp. Finally, the query uses `MATCH` to return the existing product views.

Listing 9-36. Add consumption_add Route and create_user_view_and_return_views Method

```
# add a product via VIEWED relationship and return VIEWED products
@route('/consumption/add/<productNodeId:int>', method='GET')
def consumption_add(productNodeId):

    #save the view and return the full list of views
    productTrailAsJson=Product().create_user_view_and_return_views(graph_db, request.cookies
    [graphstoryUserAuthKey],  productNodeId)

    #set the response type
    response.content_type = 'application/json'

    #return the list of views
    return dumps(productTrailAsJson)

# the method to add a user view of a product
def create_user_view_and_return_views(self, graph_db, username, productNodeId):

    # create timestamp and string display
    ts = time.time()
    timestampAsStr = datetime.fromtimestamp(int(ts)).strftime(
        '%m/%d/%Y') + " at " + datetime.fromtimestamp(int(ts)).strftime('%I:%M %p')

    query = neo4j.CypherQuery(graph_db,
            " MATCH (p:Product), (u:User { username:{u} })" +
            " WHERE id(p) = {productNodeId}" +
            " WITH u,p" +
            " MERGE (u)-[r:VIEWED]->(p)" +
            " SET r.dateAsStr={timestampAsStr}, r.timestamp={ts}" +
            " WITH u " +
            " MATCH (u)-[r:VIEWED]->(p)" +
            " RETURN p.title as title,  r.dateAsStr as dateAsStr" +
            " ORDER BY r.timestamp desc")
    params = {"productNodeId": productNodeId,"u": username,
              "timestampAsStr": timestampAsStr,"ts": ts }
    result = query.execute(**params)

    result=self.get_product_trail_results_as_json(result)

    return result
```

Filtering Consumption for Users

One practical use of the consumption model is to create a content trail for users, as shown in Figure 9-14. As a user clicks on items in the scrolling product stream, the interaction is captured using `create_user_view_and_return_views`, which ultimately returns a `List` of relationship objects of the `VIEWED` type.

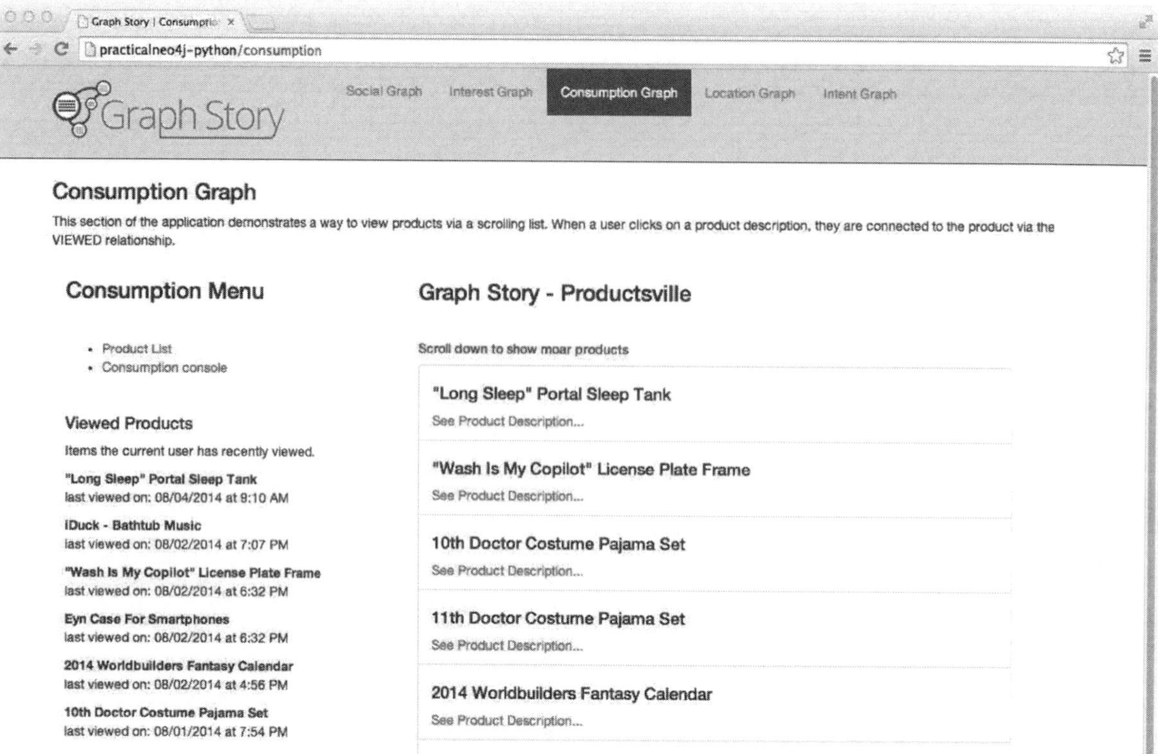

Figure 9-14. *The Scrolling Product and Product Trail page*

In the consumption graph section, you will take a look at the `consumption` route to see how the process begins inside the controller. The controller method first saves the view and then returns the complete history of views using the `get_product_trail`, which can be found in the `Product` class. The process is started when the `createUserProductViewRel` function is called, which is located in `graphstory.js`.

Filtering Consumption for Messaging

Another practical use of the consumption model is to create a personalized message for users, as displayed in Figure 9-15. In this case, you have a filter that allows the "Consumption Console" to narrow down to a very specific group of users who visited a product that was also tagged with a keyword or phrase each user had explicitly used (Listing 9-37).

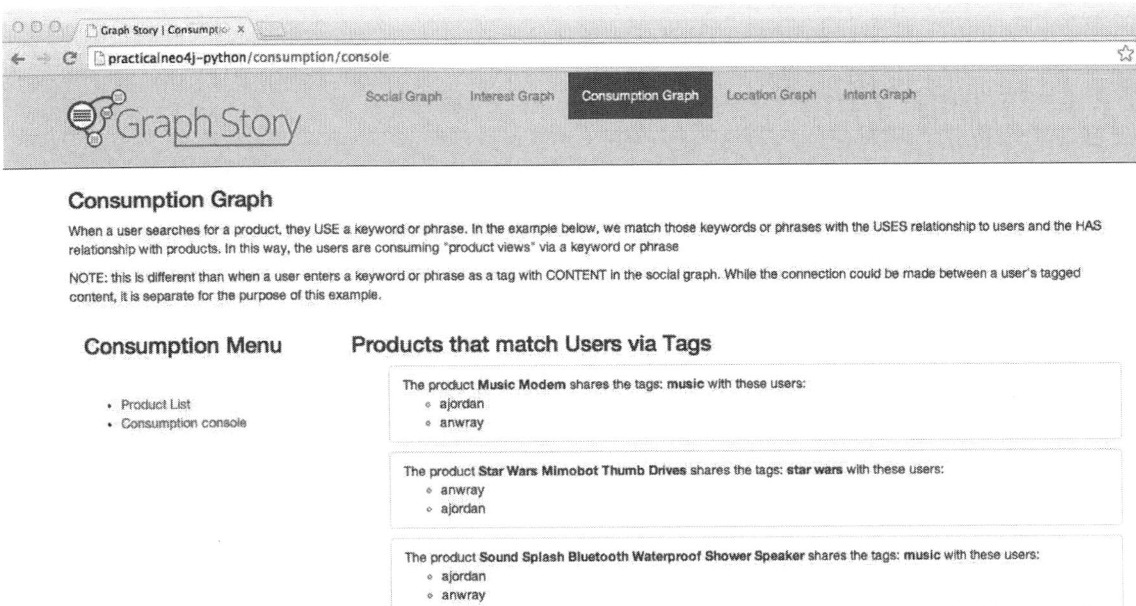

Figure 9-15. *The consumption console shows products connected to users via tags*

Listing 9-37. The `consumption console` Route and Methods to Get Connected Products and Users via Tags

```
# displays products that are connected to users via a tag relationship
@route('/consumption/console', method='GET')
def consumption_console():
    # was tag supplied, then get product matches based on specific tag
    if request.query.get('tag'):
      usersWithMatchingTags = Product().getProductsHasSpecificTagAndUserUsesSpecificTag(graph_db,
      request.query.get('tag'))
    # otherwise return all product matches as long as at least one tag matches against the users
    else:
      usersWithMatchingTags = Product().getProductsHasATagAndUserUsesAMatchingTag(graph_db)

    return template('public/templates/graphs/consumption/console.html', layout=applayout,
                usersWithMatchingTags=usersWithMatchingTags, title="Consumption Console")


# tags that match products and users
def getProductsHasATagAndUserUsesAMatchingTag(self, graph_db):
        query = neo4j.CypherQuery(graph_db,
        " MATCH (p:Product)-[:HAS]->(t)<-[:USES]-(u:User) "+
        " RETURN p.title as title , collect(u.username) as users, " +
        " collect(distinct t.wordPhrase) as tags ")
        result = query.execute()
        return result
```

```
# a specific tag that matches products and users
def getProductsHasSpecificTagAndUserUsesSpecificTag(self, graph_db, wp):
        query = neo4j.CypherQuery(graph_db,
        " MATCH (t:Tag { wordPhrase: {wp} }) " +
        " WITH t " +
        " MATCH (p:Product)-[:HAS]->(t)<-[:USES]-(u:User) " +
        " RETURN p.title as title,collect(u) as u, collect(distinct t) as t ")
        params= {"wp": wp}
        result = query.execute(**params)
        return result
```

Location Graph Model

This section explores the location graph model and a few of the operations that typically accompany it. In particular, it looks at the following:

- The spatial plugin
- Filtering on location
- Products based on location

The example demonstrates how to add a console to enable you to connect products to locations in an ad hoc manner (Listing 9-38).

Listing 9-38. Location Route for Showing Locations or Locations with Specific Products

```
# show locations nearby or locations that have a specific product
@route('/location')
def location():
    # get user location
    userlocations = UserLocation().get_user_location(graph_db,
    request.get_cookie(graphstoryUserAuthKey))

    distance = request.query.get('distance')

    # was distances provided
    if distance:

        # use first location
        ul = userlocations[0]

        productNodeId = request.query.get('productNodeId')

        # test for productNodeId
        if productNodeId:

            pnid = int(productNodeId)
            # get locations that have product
            locations = Location().locations_within_distance_with_product(graph_db,
            UserLocation().get_lq(ul, distance),  pnid, ul)
            productNode = graph_db.node(pnid)
            return template('public/templates/graphs/location/index.html',
```

```
                                layout=applayout, title="Location",
                                productTitle=productNode["title"], locations=locations,
                                mappedUserLocation=userlocations)
        # no product provided
        else:
            # get locations
            locations = Location().locations_within_distance(graph_db,
                                                             UserLocation().get_lq(ul, distance),
                                                             ul,"business")
            return template('public/templates/graphs/location/index.html',
                                layout=applayout, title="Location",
                                locations=locations, mappedUserLocation=userlocations)

    # return search template for locations
    else:
        return template('public/templates/graphs/location/index.html', layout=applayout,
        title="Location",
                        mappedUserLocation=userlocations)
```

Search for Nearby Locations

To search for nearby locations, as shown in Figure 9-16, use the current user's location, obtained by calling the `get_user_location` method in the `UserLocation` class, and then by calling the `locations_within_distance`. The `locations_within_distance` method in `Location` class uses a method called `distance` to return a string value of the distance between the starting point and the respective location (Listing 9-39).

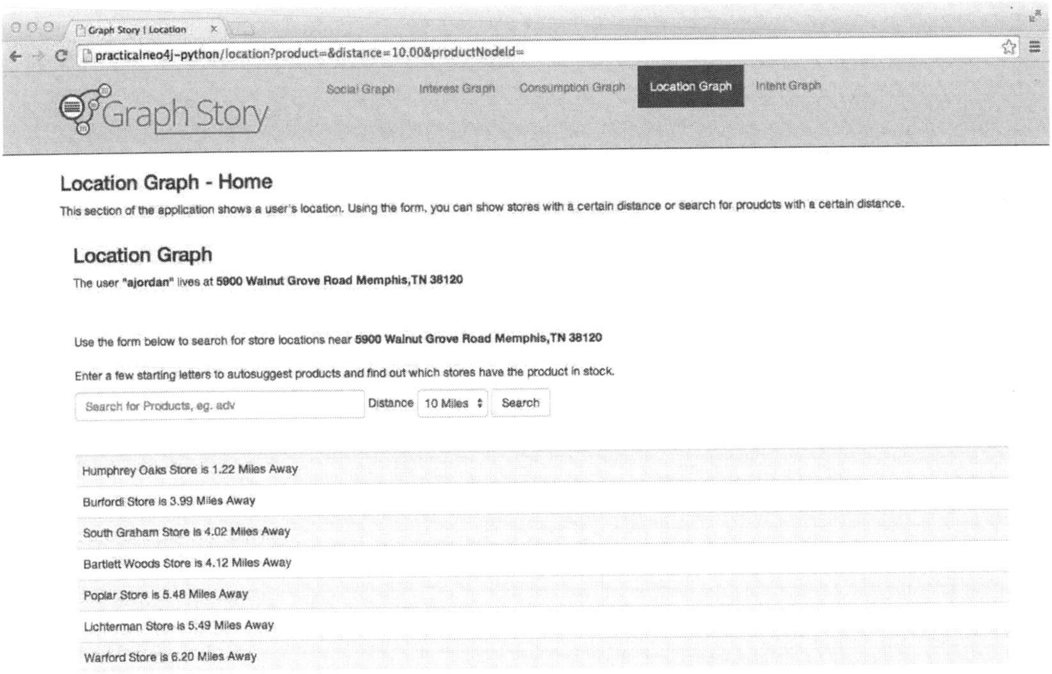

Figure 9-16. *Searching for Locations within a certain distance of User location*

Listing 9-39. The locations_within_distance Method in the Location Class

```
def locations_within_distance(self, graph_db, lq, mappedUserLocation,locationType):
    query = neo4j.CypherQuery(graph_db, " START n = node:geom({lq}) " +
                              " WHERE n.type = {locationType} " +
                              " RETURN n.locationId as locationId, n.address as address," +
                              " n.city as city,  n.state as state, n.zip as zip, n.name as name, " +
                              " n.lat as lat, n.lon as lon")
    params = {"lq": lq, "locationType":locationType}
    result = query.execute(**params)

    for r in result:
        # add the distance in miles
        setattr(r, "distanceToLocation", self.distance(float(r.lon), float(r.lat),
                                                        float(mappedUserLocation["lon"]),
                                                        float(mappedUserLocation["lat"])))
```

Locations with Product

To search for products nearby,as shown in Figure 9-17, the application makes use of an autosuggest AJAX request, which ultimately calls the search method in the Product service class. The method, shown in Listing 9-40, returns an array of objects to the product field in the search form and applies the selected product's productNodeId to the subsequent location search.

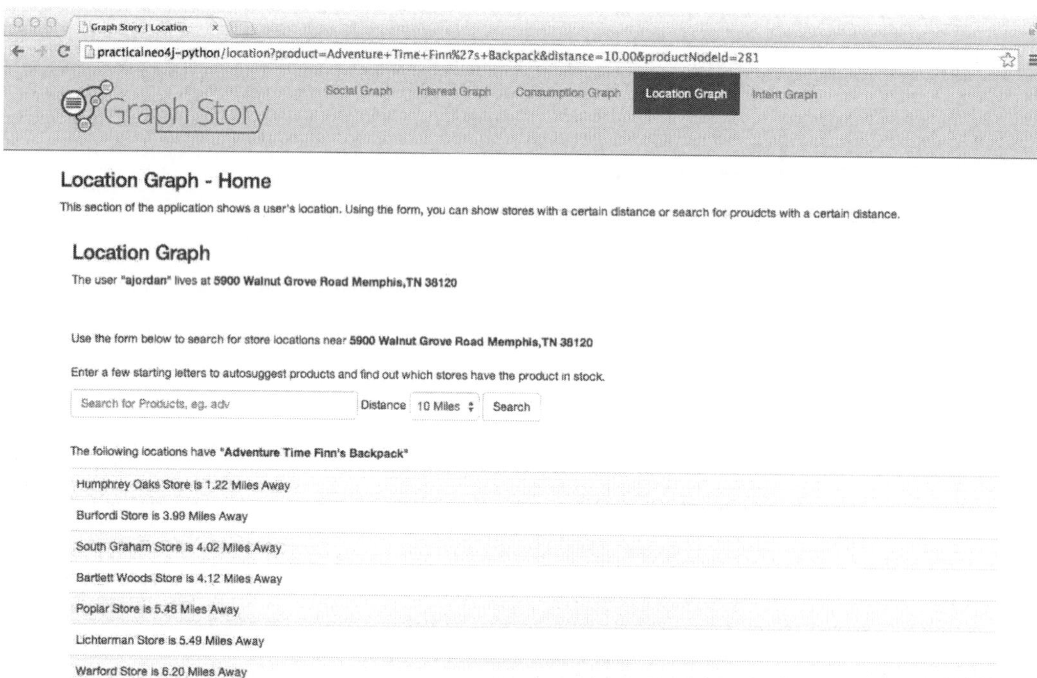

Figure 9-17. *Searching for Products in stock at Locations within a certain distance of the User location*

For almost all cases, it is recommended not to use the graphId because it can be recycled when its node is deleted. In this case, the productNodeId should be considered safe to use, because products would not be in danger of being deleted but only removed from a Location relationship.

Listing 9-40. The product_search Route and product_search Methods

```
# return product array as json
@route('/productsearch/<q>')
def product_search (q):
    # get matches
    productsFound = Product().product_search(graph_db, q + ".*")

    # create array
    products = Product().product_results_as_json(productsFound)

    # set response type
    response.content_type = 'application/json'

    # return as json
    return dumps(products)

# search for products
def product_search(self, graph_db, q):
    query = neo4j.CypherQuery(graph_db, "MATCH (p:Product) " +
                              " WHERE lower(p.title) =~ {q} " +
                              " RETURN TOSTRING(ID(p)) as id, count(*) as name, " +
                              " p.title as label  " +
                              " ORDER BY p.title LIMIT 5")
    params = {"q": q}
    result = query.execute(**params)
    return result

# return products as a list
def product_results_as_list (self, productsFound):
    products = []
    for r in productsFound:
        products.append({"id": r.id, "title": r.name, "label": r.label})
    return products
```

Once the product and distance have been set and the search is executed, the Location route tests to see if a productNodeId property has been set. If so, the locations_within_distance_with_product method is called from the Location class, as shown in Listing 9-41.

Listing 9-41. The locations_within_distance_with_product Method in the Location Class

```
def locations_within_distance_with_product(self, graph_db, lq, productNodeId, mappedUserLocation):
    query = neo4j.CypherQuery(graph_db,
                " START n = node:geom({lq}), " +
                " p=node({productNodeId}) " +
                " MATCH n-[:HAS]->p " +
```

```
                " RETURN n.locationId as locationId, n.address as address, " +
                " n.city as city,  n.state as state, n.zip as zip, n.name as name, " +
                " n.lat as lat, n.lon as lon")
    params = {"lq": lq, "productNodeId": productNodeId}
    result = query.execute(**params)
```

Intent Graph Model

The last part of the graph model exploration considers all the other graphs in order to suggest products based on the Purchase node type. The intent graph also considers the products, users, locations, and tags that are connected based on a Purchase.

Products Purchased by Friends

To get all of the products that have been purchased by friends, the `friends_purchase` method is called from Purchase class, which is shown in Listing 9-43. The corresponding route is first shown in Listing 9-42.

Listing 9-42. Intent Route to Show Purchases Made by Friends

```
# purchases by friends
@route('/intent', method='GET')
def intent():
    # get result set
    result = Purchase().friends_purchase(graph_db, request.get_cookie(graphstoryUserAuthKey))

    return template('public/templates/graphs/intent/index.html', layout=applayout,
                    title="Products Purchased by Friends",
                    mappedProductUserPurchaseList=result)
```

The query, show in Listing 9-43, finds the users being followed by the current user and then matches those users to a purchase that has been MADE which CONTAINS a product. The return value is a set of properties that identify the product title, the name of the friend or friends, as well the number of friends who have bought the product. The result is ordered by the number of friends who have purchased the product and then by product title, as shown in Figure 9-18.

Listing 9-43. The `friends_purchase` Method in the Purchase Class

```
# products purchased by friends
def friends_purchase(self, graph_db, username):
    query = neo4j.CypherQuery(graph_db,
              " MATCH (u:User {username: {u} } )-[:FOLLOWS]-(f)-[:MADE]->()-[:CONTAINS]->p" +
              " RETURN p.productId as productId,  " +
              " p.title as title, " +
              " collect(f.firstname + ' ' + f.lastname) as fullname, " +
              " null as wordPhrase, count(f) as cfriends " +
              " ORDER BY cfriends desc, p.title ")
    params = {"u": username}
    result = query.execute(**params)
    return result
```

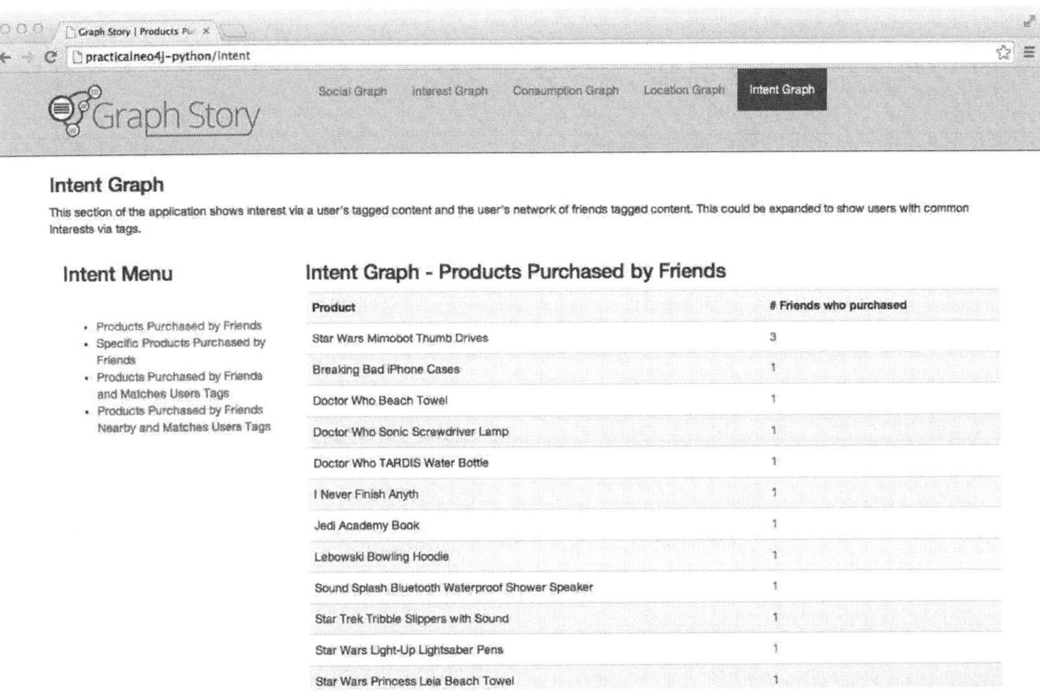

Figure 9-18. *Products Purchased By Friends*

Specific Products Purchased by Friends

If you click on the "Specific Products Purchased By Friends" link, you can specify a product, in this case "Star Wars Mimbot Thumb Drives", and then search for friends who have purchased this product, as shown in Figure 9-19. This is done via the `friends_purchase_by_product` method in `Purchase` service class, which is shown in Listing 9-44.

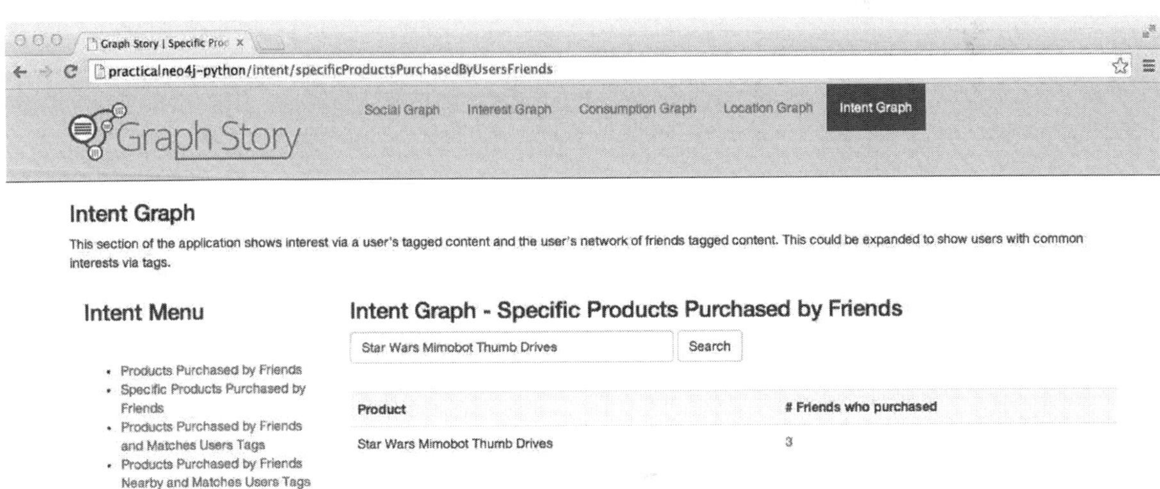

Figure 9-19. *Specific Products Purchased by Friends*

Listing 9-44. The `friends_purchase_by_product` Route and Method

```
# specific product purchases by friends
@route('/intent/friendsPurchaseByProduct', method='GET')
def friends_purchase_by_product():
    # get or use default product title
    producttitle = request.query.producttitle or 'Star Wars Mimobot Thumb Drives'
    # get result set
    result = Purchase().friends_purchase_by_product(graph_db, request.get_
    cookie(graphstoryUserAuthKey), producttitle)
    return template('public/templates/graphs/intent/index.html', layout=applayout,
                    title="Specific Products Purchased by Friends",
                    mappedProductUserPurchaseList=result, producttitle=producttitle)

# a specific product purchased by friends
def friends_purchase_by_product(self, graph_db, username, title):
    query = neo4j.CypherQuery(graph_db,
             " MATCH (p:Product) " +
             " WHERE lower(p.title) =lower({title}) " +
             " WITH p " +
             " MATCH (u:User {username: {u} } )-[:FOLLOWS]-(f)-[:MADE]->()-[:CONTAINS]->(p) " +
             " RETURN p.productId as productId,  " +
             " p.title as title, " +
             " collect(f.firstname + ' ' + f.lastname) as fullname, " +
             " null as wordPhrase, count(f) as cfriends " +
             " ORDER BY cfriends desc, p.title ")
    params = {"u": username, "title": title}
    result = query.execute(**params)
    return result
```

Products Purchased by Friends and Matches User's Tags

In this next instance, we want to determine products that have been purchased by friends but also have tags that are used by the current user (Listing 9-45). The result of the query is shown in Figure 9-20.

Listing 9-45. Product and Tag Similarity of the Current User's Friends

```
# friends bought specific products. match these products to tags of the current user
@route('/intent/friendsPurchaseTagSimilarity', method='GET')
def friends_purchase_tag_similarity():
    # get result set
    result = Purchase().friends_purchase_tag_similarity(graph_db, request.get_
cookie(graphstoryUserAuthKey))
    return template('public/templates/graphs/intent/index.html', layout=applayout,
                    title="Products Purchased by Friends and Matches User's Tags",
                    mappedProductUserPurchaseList=result)
```

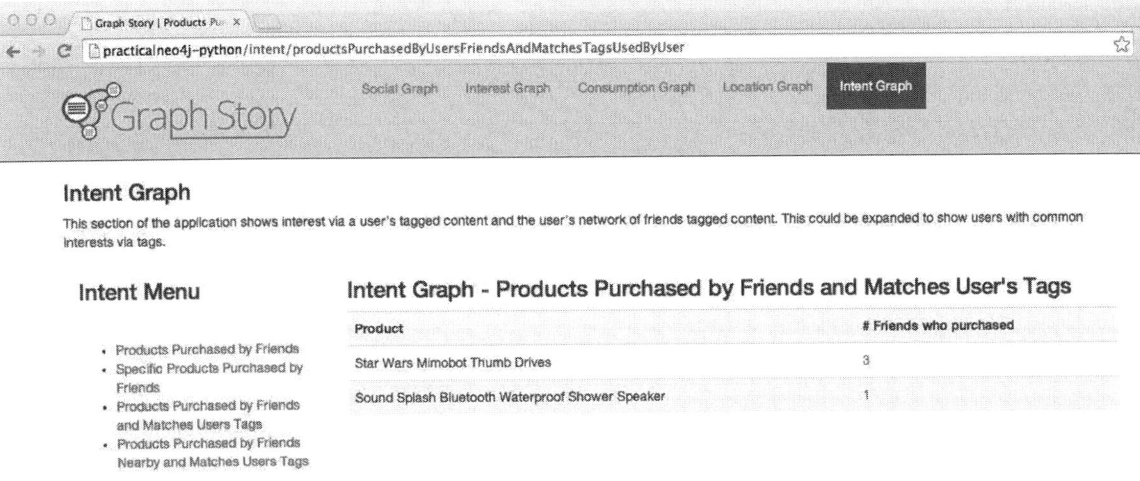

Figure 9-20. *Products Purchased by Friends and Matches User's Tags*

Using `friends_purchase_tag_similarity` in `Purchase` service class, shown in Listing 9-46, the application provides the `username` to the query and uses the `FOLLOWS`, `MADE`, and `CONTAINS` relationships to return products purchases by users being followed. The subsequent `MATCH` statement takes the `USES` and `HAS` directed relationship types to determine the tag relationships the resulting products and the current user have in common.

Listing 9-46. The Method to Find Products Purchased by Friends and Matches Current User's Tags

```
# products purchased by friends that match the user's tags
def friends_purchase_tag_similarity(self, graph_db, username):
    query = neo4j.CypherQuery(graph_db,
              " MATCH (u:User {username: {u} } )-[:FOLLOWS]-(f)-[:MADE]->()-[:CONTAINS]->p " +
              " WITH u,p,f " +
              " MATCH u-[:USES]->(t)<-[:HAS]-p " +
              " RETURN p.productId as productId,  " +
              " p.title as title, " +
              " collect(f.firstname + ' ' + f.lastname) as fullname, " +
              " t.wordPhrase as wordPhrase, " +
              " count(f) as cfriends " +
              " ORDER BY cfriends desc, p.title ")
    params = {"u": username}
    result = query.execute(**params)
    return result
```

Products Purchased by Friends Nearby and Matches User's Tags

Finding products that match with a specific user's tags and have been purchased by friends who live within a set distance of the user is performed by the `friends_purchase_tag_similarity_and_proximity_to_location` method, easily the world's longest method name, and is located in `Purchase` class(Listing 9-47).

Listing 9-47. Route to Find Products of Nearby Friends and Matches Tags of Current User

```
# friends that are nearby bought this product.
# the product should also matches tags of the current user
@route('/intent/friendsPurchaseTagSimilarityAndProximityToLocation', method='GET')
def friends_purchase_tag_similarity_and_proximity_to_location():
    # get user location
    userlocations = UserLocation().get_user_location(graph_db, request.get_
    cookie(graphstoryUserAuthKey))
    # use first location
    ul = userlocations[0]

    # get result set
    result = Purchase().friends_purchase_tag_similarity_and_proximity_to_location(graph_db,
    request.get_cookie(graphstoryUserAuthKey), UserLocation().get_lq_distance_set(ul))

    return template('public/templates/graphs/intent/index.html', layout=applayout,
                    title="Products Purchased by Friends Nearby and Matches User's Tags",
                    mappedProductUserPurchaseList=result, mappedUserLocation=userlocations)
```

The `friends_purchase_tag_similarity_and_proximity_to_location` route calls the `friends_purchase_tag_similarity_and_proximity_to_location` method shown in Listing 9-48.

Listing 9-48. `friendsPurchaseTagSimilarityAndProximityToLocation` Method in the Purchase Class

```
# user's friends' purchases who are nearby and the products match the user's tags
def friends_purchase_tag_similarity_and_proximity_to_location(self, graph_db, username, lq):
    query = neo4j.CypherQuery(graph_db,
              " START n = node:geom({lq}) " +
              " WITH n " +
              " MATCH (u:User {username: {u} } )-[:USES]->(t)<-[:HAS]-p " +
              " WITH n,u,p,t " +
              " MATCH u-[:FOLLOWS]->(f)-[:HAS]->(n) " +
              " WITH p,f,t " +
              " MATCH f-[:MADE]->()-[:CONTAINS]->(p) " +
              " RETURN p.productId as productId, " +
              " p.title as title, " +
              " collect(f.firstname + ' ' + f.lastname) as fullname, " +
              " t.wordPhrase as wordPhrase, " +
              " count(f) as cfriends " +
              " ORDER BY cfriends desc, p.title ")
    params = {"u": username, "lq": lq}
    result = query.execute(**params)
    return result
```

The query begins with a location search within a certain distance, then matches the current user's tags to products. Next, the query matches friends based on the location search. The resulting friends are matched against products that are in the set of user tag matches. The result of the query is shown in Figure 9-21.

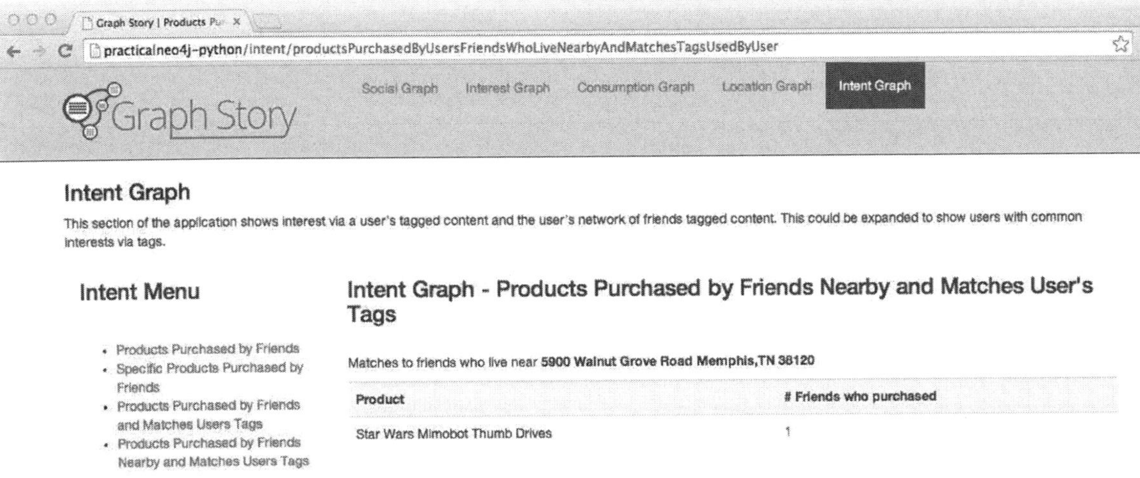

Figure 9-21. Products Purchased by Friends Nearby and Matches User's Tags

Summary

This chapter presented the setup for a development environment for Python and Neo4j and sample code using the py2neo driver. It proceeded to look at sample code for setting up a social network and examining interest within the network. It then looked at the sample code for capturing and viewing consumption—in this case, product views—and the queries for understanding the relationship between consumption and a user's interest. Finally, it looked at using geospatial matching for locations and examples of methods for understanding user intent within the context of user location, social network, and interests.

The next chapter will review using Ruby and Neo4j, covering the same concepts presented in this chapter but in the context of a Ruby driver for Neo4j.

CHAPTER 10

Neo4j + Ruby

This chapter focuses on using Ruby with Neo4j and reviewing the code for a working application that integrates the five graph model types covered in Chapter 3. As with other languages that offer a driver for Neo4j, the integration takes place using a Neo4j server instance with the Neo4j REST API. This chapter is divided into the following topics:

- Ruby and Neo4j Development Environment
- Neography
- Developing a Ruby and Neo4j application

In each chapter that explores a particular language paired with Neo4j, I recommend that you start a free trial on `www.graphstory.com` or have installed a local Neo4j server instance, as shown in Chapter 2.

Tip To quickly set up a server instance with the sample data and plugins for this chapter, go to `graphstory.com/practicalneo4j`. You will be provided with your own free trial instance, a knowledge base, and email support from Graph Story.

For this chapter, I expect that you have at least a beginning knowledge of Ruby and a basic understanding of how to configure Ruby for your preferred operating system. While the examples should work with later versions of Ruby, Ruby 1.9.2 is the version used in this chapter. In addition, the sample application uses the Apache HTTP server and Passenger (also known as mod_rails).

Do This If you do not have Apache HTTP installed, it is highly recommended that you follow the instructions at `http://httpd.apache.org/` based on your operating system. Configuring Ruby and Passenger with a local instance of Apache HTTP is beyond the scope of this book, but the basic steps can be found at `http://recipes.sinatrarb.com/p/deployment/apache_with_passenger`.

I also assume that you have a basic understanding of the model-view-controller (MVC) pattern and some knowledge of Ruby frameworks that provide an MVC pattern. There are, of course, a number of excellent Ruby frameworks from which to choose, but I had to pick one for the illustrative purposes of the application in this chapter. I chose the Sinatra framework because it is limited in its scope and allows the focus to remain on the application to the greatest extent possible. This chapter is focused on integrating Neo4j into your Ruby skill set and projects and does not dive deeply into the best practices of developing with Ruby or Ruby frameworks.

Ruby and Neo4j Development Environment

Preliminary to this chapter's discussion of the Ruby and Neo4j application, this section covers the basics of configuring a development environment.

■ **Readme** Although each language chapter walks through the process of configuring the development environment based on the particular language, certain steps are covered repeatedly in multiple chapters. While the initial development environment setup in each chapter is somewhat redundant, it allows each language chapter to stand on its own. Bearing this in mind, if you have already configured Eclipse with Aptana while working through another chapter, you can skip ahead to the section "Adding the Project to Eclipse."

IDE

The reasons behind the choice of an IDE vary from developer to developer and are often tied to the choice of programming language. I chose the Eclipse IDE for a number of reasons but mainly because it is freely available and versatile enough to work with most of the programming languages featured in this book.

Although you are welcome to choose a different IDE or other programming tool for building your application, I recommend that you install and use Eclipse to be able to follow the Ruby and Neo4j examples and the related examples found throughout the book and online.

■ **Tip** If you do not have Eclipse, please visit `http://www.eclipse.org/downloads/` and download the Indigo package, titled "Eclipse IDE for Java EE Developers" or "Version 3.7".

Once you have installed Eclipse, open it and select a workspace for your application. A *workspace* in Eclipse is simply an arbitrary directory on your computer. As shown in Figure 10-1, when you first open Eclipse, the program will ask you to specify which workspace you want to use. Choose the path that works best for you. If you are working through all of the language chapters, you can use the same workspace for each project.

Figure 10-1. *Opening Eclipse and choosing a workspace*

Aptana Plugin

The Eclipse IDE offers a convenient way to add new tools through their plugin platform. The process for adding new plugins to Eclipse is straightforward and usually involves only a few steps to install a new plugin, as you will see in this section.

A specific web-tool plugin called Aptana provides support for server-side languages such as Python as well as client languages such as CSS and JavaScript. This chapter and the other programming language chapters use the plugin to edit both server- and client-side languages. A benefit of using a plugin such as Aptana is that it can provide code-assist tools and code suggestions based on the type of file you are editing, such as CSS, JS, or HTML. The time saved with code-assist tools is usually significant enough to warrant their use. Again, if you feel comfortable exploring within your preferred IDE or other program, please do so.

To install the Aptana plugin, you need to have Eclipse installed and opened. Then proceed through the following steps:

1. From the Help menu, select "Install New Software" to open the dialog, which will look like the one in Figure 10-2.

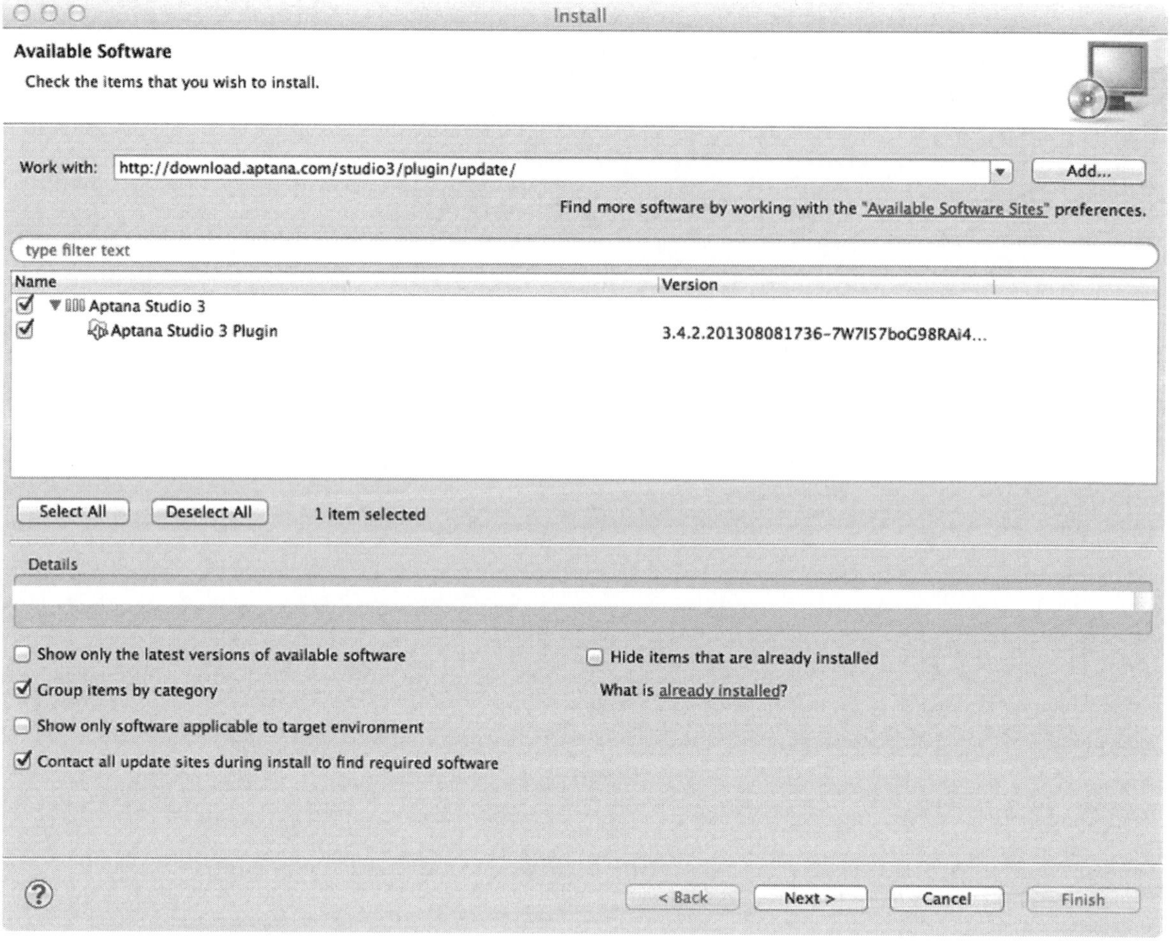

Figure 10-2. *Installing the Aptana plugin*

2. Paste the URL for the update site, `http://download.aptana.com/studio3/plugin/install`, into the "Work With" text box, and hit the Enter (or Return) key.
3. In the populated table below, check the box next to the name of the plugin, and then click the Next button.
4. Click the Next button to go to the license page.
5. Choose the option to accept the terms of the license agreement, and click the Finish button.
6. You may need to restart Eclipse to continue.

Adding the Project to Eclipse

After installing Eclipse and the Aptana plugin, you have the minimum requirements to work with your project in the workspace. To keep the workflow as fluid as possible for each of the language example application, use the project import tool with Eclipse. To import the project into your workspace, follow these steps:

1. Go to `www.graphstory.com/practicalneo4j` and download the archive file for "Practical Neo4j for Ruby." Unzip the archive file on to your computer.
2. In Eclipse, select File ➤ Import and type project in the "Select an import source."
3. Under the "General" heading, select "Existing Projects into Workspace." You should now see a window similar to Figure 10-3.

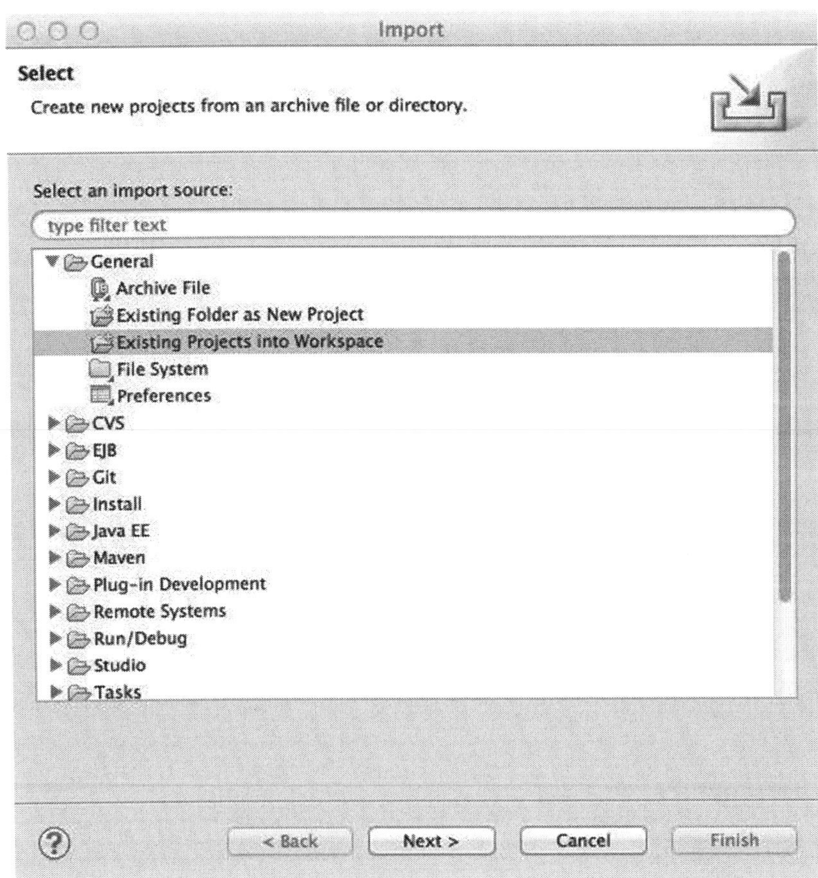

Figure 10-3. *Importing the project into Eclipse*

4. Now that you have selected "Existing Projects into Workspace", click the "Next >" button. The dialogue should now show an option to "Select root directory." Click the "Browse" button and find the root path of the "practicalneo4j-ruby" archive.

5. Next, check the option for "Copy project into workspace" and click the "Finish" button, as shown in Figure 10-4.

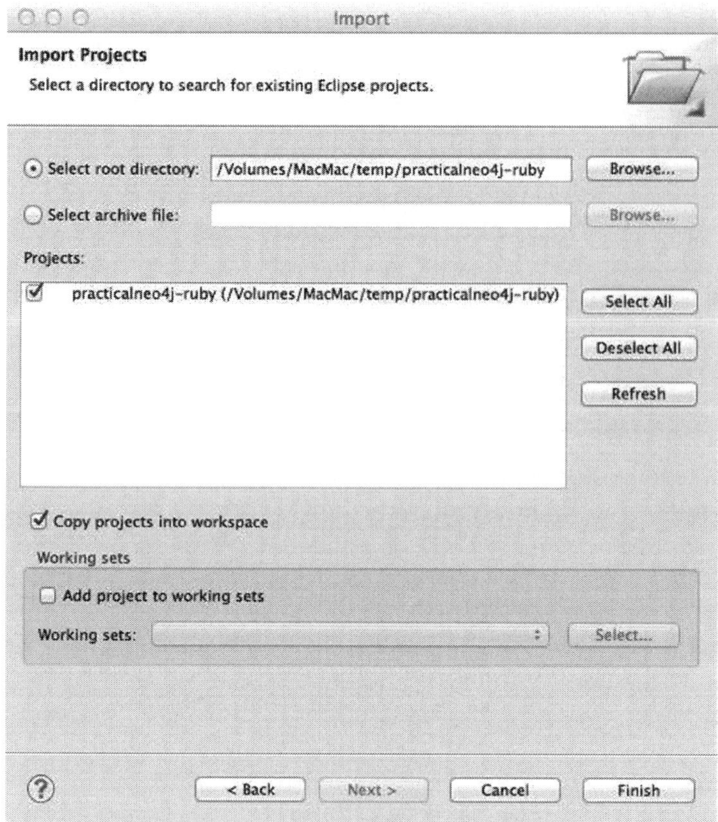

Figure 10-4. *Selecting the project location*

6. Once the project is finished importing into your workspace, you should have a directory structure that looks similar to the one shown in Figure 10-5.

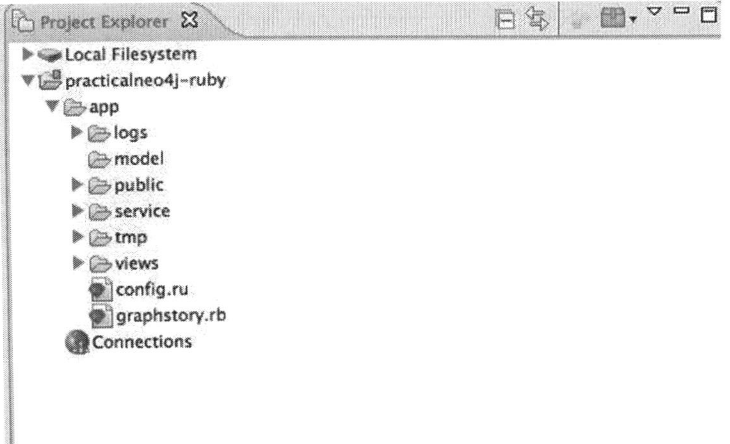

Figure 10-5. *Snapshot of the imported project*

Sinatra Web Framework for Ruby

Sinatra is a Ruby implementation of what is often called a *micro framework*. The aim of a micro framework is to help you quickly build out powerful web applications and APIs only using what is absolutely necessary to get the job done (Listing 10-1).

Listing 10-1. Sinatra Example of GET Route

```
# home page
get '/' do
  @title = "Home"
  mustache :"home/index"
end
```

Note Sinatra is maintained by Blake Mizerany and supported by a number of equally outstanding committers. If you would like to get involved with Sinatra, please visit `https://github.com/sinatra/sinatra`.

The starting point for the Sinatra application is the `{PROJECTROOT}/app/config.ru` file, which is shown in Listing 10-2.

Listing 10-2. The `config.ru` File

```
root = ::File.dirname(__FILE__)
require ::File.join( root, 'graphstory' )
run App.new
```

The `{PROJECTROOT}/app/graphstory.rb` file contains the global application settings, such as the database connection and the requests routes. An abbreviated version of the file is shown in Listing 10-3.

Listing 10-3. The graphstory.rb File

```
require 'rubygems'
require 'ostruct'
require 'sinatra/base'
require 'sinatra/mustache'
require "sinatra/cookies"
require "sinatra/json"
require 'neography'
require 'logger'

require './service/content'
require './service/location'
require './service/product'
require './service/purchase'
require './service/tags'
require './service/user'
require './service/userlocation'

class App < Sinatra::Base

  helpers Sinatra::Cookies
  helpers Sinatra::Content
  helpers Sinatra::Location
  helpers Sinatra::Product
  helpers Sinatra::Purchase
  helpers Sinatra::Tags
  helpers Sinatra::User
  helpers Sinatra::Userlocation

  set :views, 'views'

  Excon.defaults[:ssl_verify_peer] = false

  graphstoryUserAuthKey = "graphstoryUserAuthKey"

  log = Logger.new('logs/practicalneo4j-ruby-debug.log')

  neo = Neography::Rest.new("http://localhost:7474/db/data")

  #routes start here...
  # home page
  get '/' do
    @title = "Home"
    mustache :"home/index"
  end

  #...more routes...

end
```

Local Apache Configuration

To follow the sample application found later in this chapter, you will need to properly configure your local Apache webserver to use the workspace project in Eclipse as the document root. One way to accomplish this is by adding a virtual host to Apache. Listing 10-4 covers the basic configuration for adding a virtual host to the `httpd-vhosts.conf` file.

Listing 10-4. Minimum Configuration for `httpd-vhosts.conf`

```
NameVirtualHost *:80
<VirtualHost *:80>
        ServerName practicalneo4j-ruby
          DocumentRoot /Users/username/somepath/practicalneo4j-ruby/app/public

          <Directory /Users/username/somepath/practicalneo4j-ruby/app/public>
                        Options None
                        AllowOverride None
                        Order allow,deny
                        allow from all
        </Directory>
        ErrorLog /Users/username/somepath/practicalneo4j-ruby/app/logs/error.log
        LogLevel warn
</VirtualHost>
```

■ **Important** If you do not have Apache HTTP installed, go to `http://httpd.apache.org/` and follow the instructions based on your operating system. Configuring Ruby + Sinatra with a local instance of Apache HTTP is out of the scope of this book, but you can find the basic configuration steps at `http://recipes.sinatrarb.com/p/deployment/apache_with_passenger`.

Neography

As with most of the language drivers and libraries available for Neo4j, the purpose of Neography is to provide a degree of abstraction over the Neo4j REST API. In addition, the Neography API provides some additional enhancements that might otherwise be required at some other stage in the development of your Ruby application, such as caching.

This section reviews the operations and usage of the Neography library with the goal of understanding the library before implementing it within an application. Then the "Developing a Ruby and Neo4j Application" section will walk you through a sample application with specific graph goals and models.

■ **Note** Neography is maintained by the super-awesome Max De Marzi and supported by a number of great Ruby graphistas. If you would like to get involved with Neography, go to `https://github.com/maxdemarzi/neography`.

Each of the following brief sections covers concepts that tie either directly or indirectly to features and functionality found within the Neo4j Server and REST API. If you choose to go through each language chapter, then you should notice how each library covers those features and functionality in similar ways but takes advantage of the language-specific capabilities to ensure the API is flexible and performant.

Managing Nodes and Relationships

Chapters 1 and 2 covered the elements of a graph database, which includes the most basic of graph concepts: the node. Managing nodes and their properties and relationships will probably account for the bulk of your application's graph-related code.

Creating a Node

The maintenance of nodes is set in motion with the creation process, as shown in Listing 10-5. Creating a node begins with setting up a connection to the database and making the node instance. The node properties are set next, and then the node can be saved to the database.

Listing 10-5. Creating a Node

```
require 'neography'

neo = Neography::Rest.new({ :protocol => 'http://', :server => 'localhost', :port => 7474,
:directory => '/db/data'})

node = neo.create_node("username" => "Greg")
neo.add_label(node, "User")
```

Retrieving and Updating a Node

Once nodes have been added to the database, you will need a way to retrieve and modify them. Listing 10-6 shows the process for finding a node by its node id value and updating it.

Listing 10-6. Retrieving and Updating a Node

```
require 'neography'

neo = Neography::Rest.new({ :protocol => 'http://', :server => 'localhost', :port => 7474,
:directory => '/db/data'})

greg = neo.get_node(1)
neo.set_node_properties greg, {"business" => "Graph Story"}
```

Removing a Node

Once a node's graph id has been set and saved into the database, it becomes eligible to be removed when necessary. To remove a node, set a variable as a node object instance and then call the delete method for the node (Listing 10-7).

Listing 10-7. Deleting a Node

```
require 'neography'

neo = Neography::Rest.new({ :protocol => 'http://', :server => 'localhost', :port => 7474,
:directory => '/db/data'})

greg=neo.get_node(1)
```

```
# Delete node that has no relationships
neo.delete_node(greg)

# Delete an unrelated node
neo.delete_node!(greg)
```

Note You cannot delete any node that is currently set as the start point or end point of any relationship. You must remove the relationship before you can delete the node.

Creating a Relationship

Neography offers two different methods to create relationships, one using the *relateTo* method and another using the *makeRelationship* method. In the example in Listing 10-8, it sets up the relationship using the *relateTo* method, which is the less verbose of the two options.

Listing 10-8. Relating Two Nodes

```
require 'neography'

neo = Neography::Rest.new({ :protocol => 'http://', :server => 'localhost', :port => 7474,
:directory => '/db/data'})

greg = neo.get_node(1)
daniel = neo.get_node(10)

neo.create_relationship("FOLLOWS", greg, daniel)
```

Note Both the start and end nodes of a relationship must already be established within the database before the relationship can be saved.

Retrieving Relationships

Once a relationship has been created between one or more nodes, the relationship can be retrieved based on a node (Listing 10-9).

Listing 10-9. Retreiving relationships.

```
require 'neography'

neo = Neography::Rest.new({ :protocol => 'http://', :server => 'localhost', :port => 7474,
:directory => '/db/data'})

# get the related nodes
greg = neo.get_node(1)
daniel = neo.get_node(10)

# find their directed relationship
rels = neo.get_node_relationships_to(greg, daniel, "in", "FOLLOWS")
```

Deleting a Relationship

Once a relationship's graph id has been set and saved into the database, it becomes eligible to be removed when necessary. To remove a relationship, set it as a relationship object instance and then call the delete method for the relationship (Listing 10-10).

Listing 10-10. Deleting a Relationship

```
require 'neography'

neo = Neography::Rest.new({ :protocol => 'http://', :server => 'localhost', :port => 7474,
:directory => '/db/data'})

# get the related nodes
greg = neo.get_node(1)
daniel = neo.get_node(10)

# find their directed relationship
rels = neo.get_node_relationships_to(greg, daniel, "in", "FOLLOWS")

# delete the relationship
rels.each { |rel_id| neo.delete_relationship(rel_id) }
```

Using Labels

Labels function as specific meta-descriptions that can be applied to nodes. Labels were introduced in Neo4j 2.0 in order to help in querying and can also function as a way to quickly create a subgraph.

Adding a Label to Nodes

In Neography, you can add one more labels to a node. As Listing 10-11 shows, the *addLabels* function takes one or more labels as argument. You can return each of the labels on a node by calling its *getLabels* function. The value used for the label should be any nonempty string or numeric value.

Listing 10-11. Creating a Label and Adding It to a Node

```
require 'neography'

neo = Neography::Rest.new({ :protocol => 'http://', :server => 'localhost', :port => 7474,
:directory => '/db/data'})

greg = neo.get_node(1)

# add single label
neo.add_label(greg, "User")

# add multiple labels
neo.add_label(greg, ["User ", "Developer"])
```

■ **Caution** A label will not exist on the database server until it has been added to at least one node.

Removing a Label

Removing a label uses similar syntax as adding a label to a node. After the given label has been removed from the node (Listing 10-12), the return value is a list of labels still on the node.

Listing 10-12. Removing a Label from a Node

```
require 'neography'

neo = Neography::Rest.new({ :protocol => 'http://', :server => 'localhost', :port => 7474,
:directory => '/db/data'})

greg = neo.get_node(1)

# delete single label
neo.delete_label greg, "Developer"
```

Querying with a Label

To get nodes that use a specific label, use the function called *getNodes*. This function returns value is a result Row object, which can be iterated over like an array (Listing 10-13).

Listing 10-13. Querying with a Label

```
require 'neography'

neo = Neography::Rest.new({ :protocol => 'http://', :server => 'localhost', :port => 7474,
:directory => '/db/data'})

# find all developers
developers = neo.get_nodes_labeled("Developer")

# find all developers named Daniel
developers = neo. find_nodes_labeled("Developer", username: "Daniel")
```

Developing a Ruby and Neo4j Application

Preliminary to building out your first Ruby and Neo4j application, this section covers the basics of configuring a development environment.

Again, if you have not worked through the installation steps in Chapter 2, please take a few minutes to do so.

Preparing the Graph

In order to spend more time highlighting code examples for each of the more common graph models, we will use a preloaded instance of Neo4j including necessary plugins, such as the spatial plugin.

■ **Tip** To quickly set up a server instance with the sample data and plugins for this chapter, go to `graphstory.com/practicalneo4j`. You will be provided with your own free trial instance, a knowledge base, and email support from Graph Story. Alternatively, you may run a local Neo4j database instance with the sample data by going to `graphstory.com/practicalneo4j`, downloading the zip file containing the sample database and plugins, and adding them to your local instance.

Using the Sample Application

If you have already downloaded the sample application from `graphstory.com/practicalneo4j` for Ruby and configured it with your local application environment, you can skip ahead to the "Sinatra Application Configuration" section. Otherwise, you will need to go back to the section in this chapter titled "`Ruby and Neo4j Development Environment`" and set up your local environment in order to follow the examples in the sample application.

■ **Note** The sample application also contains a readme file with instructions on configuration as well as contact information at `graphstory.com` for support.

Sinatra Application Configuration

Before diving into the code examples, you need to update the configuration for the Sinatra application. In Eclipse (or the IDE you are using), open the file `{PROJECTROOT}/app/graphstory.rb` and edit the GraphStory connection string information. If you are using a free account from graphstory.com, you will change the username, password, and URL in Listing 10-14 with the one provided in your graph console on `graphstory.com`.

Listing 10-14. Database Connection Settings for a Remote Service such as Graph Story

```
neo = Neography::Rest.new("https://username:password@theURL:7473/db/data/")
```

If you have installed a local Neo4j server instance, you can modify the configuration to use the local address and port that you specified during the installation, as shown in Listing 10-15.

Listing 10-15. Database Connection Settings for Local Environment

```
neo = Neography::Rest.new("http://localhost:7474/db/data")
```

Once the environment is properly configured and started, you can open a browser to `graphstory.com/practicalneo4j`, and you should see a page like the one shown in Figure 10-6.

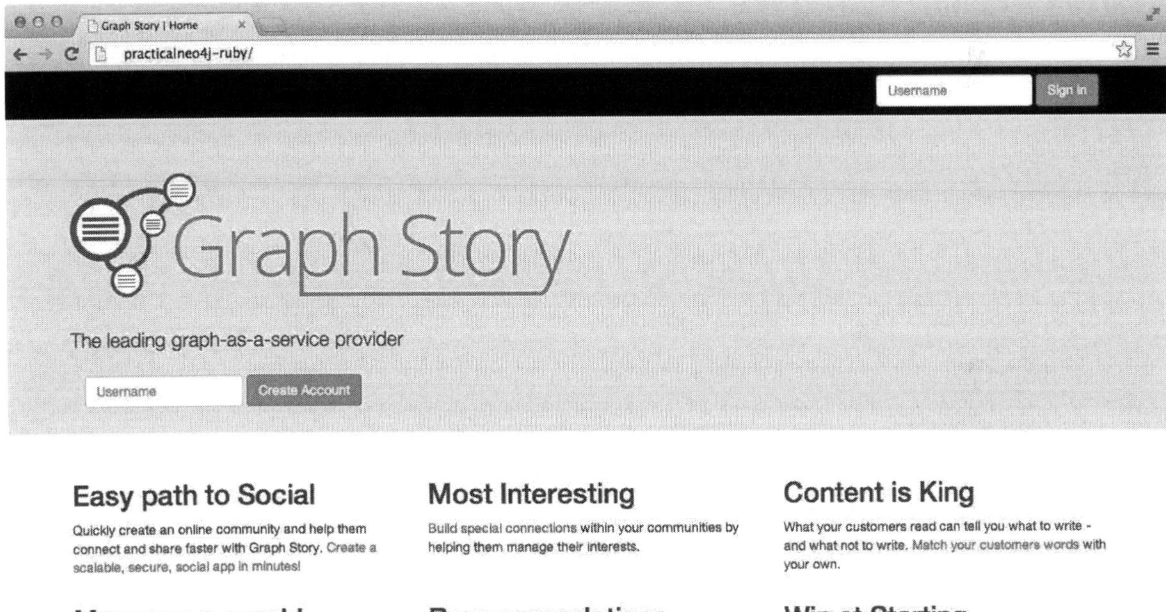

Figure 10-6. *The Ruby sample application home page*

Social Graph Model

This section explores the social graph model and a few of the operations that typically accompany it. In particular, this section looks at the following:

- The User Entity
- Sign-up and login
- Updating a user
- Creating a relationship type through a user by following other users
- Managing user content, such as displaying, adding, updating, and removing status updates

---

■ **Note** The sample graph database used for these examples is loaded with data, so you can immediately begin working with representative data in each of the graph models. In the case of the social graph—and for other graph models, as well—you will log in with the user **ajordan**. Going forward, please log in with **ajordan** to see each of the working examples.

Sign Up

The HTML required for the user sign-up form is shown in Listing 10-16 and can be found in the `{PROJECTROOT}/app/views/home/index.mustache` file.

Listing 10-16. HTML Snippet of Sign-Up Form

```
<form class="navbar-form navbar-left" action="/signup/add" role="form"
        id="createaccountform" method="post">
                <div class="form-group">
                        <input type="text" placeholder=
                        "Username" name="username" class="form-control">
                </div>
        <button type="submit" class="btn btn-success">Create Account</button>   
</form>
```

■ **Note** Although the sample application creates a user without a password, I am certainly not suggesting or advocating this approach for a production application. Excluding the password property was done in order to create a simple sign-up and login that helps keep the focus on the more salient aspects of the Neography library.

Sign-Up Route

In the sign-up route, start by doing a lookup on the `username` passed in the request and see if it already exists in the database using the `get_user_by_user_name` method found in the `User` service layer, as provided in Listing 10-17. If no match is found, the username is passed on to the `save_user` method.

If no errors are returned during the save attempt, the request is redirected via redirect and a message is passed to thank the user for signing up. Otherwise, the error message back to the home view informs the user of the problem.

Listing 10-17. The Sign-Up Controller Route

```
# sign up
post '/signup/add' do
  # search db for user
    user = get_user_by_user_name(neo,params[:username])

    # found a match. need to use another username
    if !!user.nil  && !user.empty?
      @title = "Home"
      @error ="The username " +params[:username]+ " already exists. Please use a different username"
      mustache :"home/index"
    #save the user
    else
      save_user(neo,params[:username])
      redirect to("/msg?u="+params[:username])
    end
end
```

Adding a User

In each part of the five graph areas covered in the chapter, the domain object will have a corresponding service to manage the persistence operations within the database. In this case, the `User` class covers the management of the application's user nodes using a mix of Neography convenience methods and executing Cypher queries.

To save a node and label it as a User, the `save_user` method, shown in Listing 10-18, makes use of the `create_node` method by passing in the username param and value. Once the node is created, then the `add_label` method applies the User label.

Listing 10-18. The save_user Method in the User Class

```
def save_user(neo, username)
        node = neo.create_node("username" => username)
        neo.add_label(node, "User")
end
```

Login

This section reviews the login process for the sample application. To execute the login process, we also use the login route as well as User class. Before reviewing the controller and service layer, take a quick look at the front-end code for the login.

Login Form

The HTML required for the user login form is shown in Listing 10-19 and can be found in the {PROJECTROOT}/ app/ views/global/homeheader.mustache layout file.

Listing 10-19. The Login Form

```
<form class="navbar-form navbar-right" action="/login" role="form" method="post">
<div class="form-group">
<input type="text" placeholder="Username" name="username" class="form-control">
                    </div>
<button type="submit" class="btn btn-success">Sign in</button>
</form>
```

Login Route

In the App class, use the login route to control the flow of the login process, as shown in Listing 10-20. Inside the login route, use the get_user_by_user_name method to check if the user exists in the database.

Listing 10-20. The login Route

```
# login
post '/login' do
    # search db for user
    user = get_user_by_user_name(neo,params[:username])

    # found it!  set cookie and redirect
    if !user.nil?  && !user.empty?
      @user = user
      response.set_cookie(graphstoryUserAuthKey, :value => @user["username"], :path => "/", :expires
      => Time.now + 86400000)
      redirect to('/social')

    # not found. show message
    else
      @title = "Home"
      @error ="The username you entered was not found."
      mustache :"home/index"
    end
end
```

If the user is found during the login attempt, a cookie is added to the response and the request is redirected via `redirect to` the social home page, shown in Figure 10-7. Otherwise, the route will specify the HTML page to return and will add the error messages that need to be displayed back to the view.

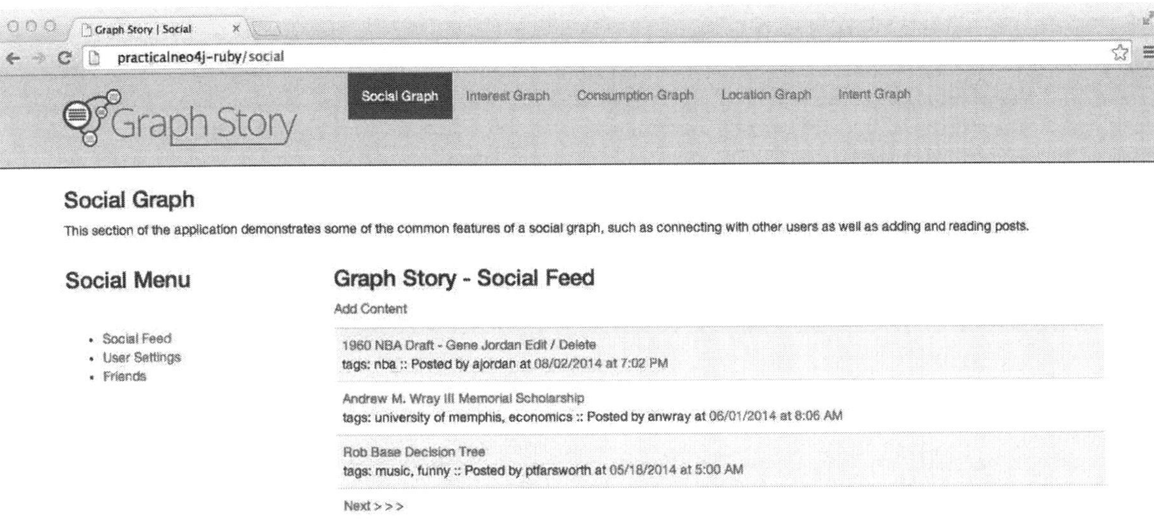

Figure 10-7. *The social graph home page*

Login Service

To check to see if the user values being passed through are connected to a valid user combination in the database, the application uses the `get_user_by_user_name` method in the `User` class. As shown in Listing 10-21, the result of the `get_user_by_user_name` method is assigned to the `user` variable.

Listing 10-21. The get_user_by_user_name Method in the User class

```
def get_user_by_user_name(neo, username)
  user=""
  users = neo.find_nodes_labeled("User", username: username)
    if !!users  && users.any?
      user = users.first["data"]
    end
  user
end
```

If the result is not null or empty, the result is set on the User object and returned to the controller layer of the application.

Now that the user is logged in, he can edit his settings, create relationships with other users in the graph, and create his own content.

Updating a User

To access the page for updating a user, click on the "User Settings" link in the social graph section, as shown in Figure 10-8. In this example, the front-end code uses an AJAX request via PUT and inserts—or, in the case of the **ajordan** user, updates—the first and last name.

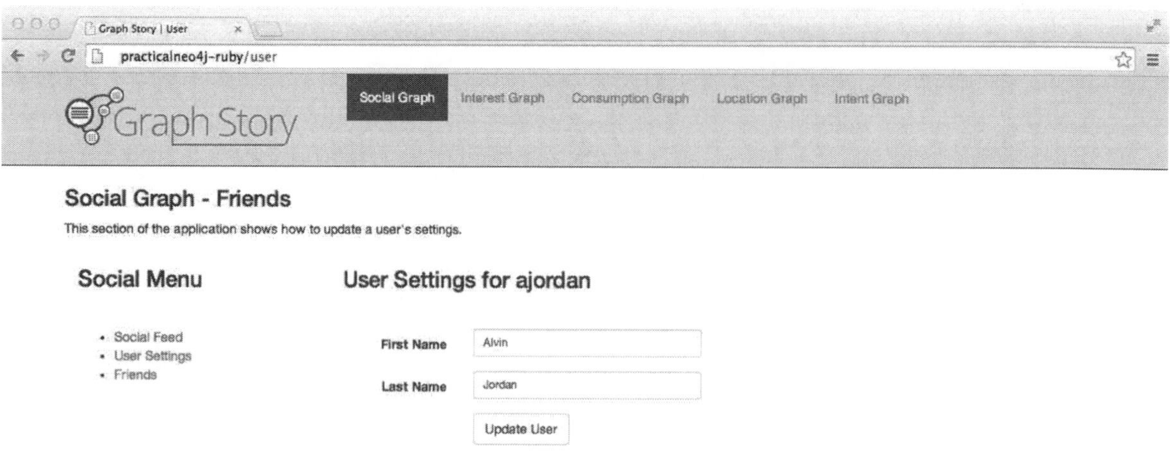

Figure 10-8. *The User Settings page*

User Update Form

The user settings form is located in `{PROJECTROOT}/ app/views/graphs/social/user.mustache` and is similar in structure to the other forms presented in the Sign Up and Login sections. One difference is that we have added the `value` property to the input element as well as the variables for displaying the respective stored values. If none exist, the form fields will be empty (Listing 10-22).

Listing 10-22. User Update Form

```
<form class="form-horizontal" id="userform">
  <div class="form-group">
    <label for="firstname" class="col-sm-2 control-label">First Name</label>
    <div class="col-sm-10">
      <input type="text" class="form-control input-sm" id="firstname" name="user.firstname"
      value="{{user.firstname}}" />
    </div>
  </div>
  <div class="form-group">
    <label for="lastname" class="col-sm-2 control-label">Last Name</label>
    <div class="col-sm-10">
      <input type="text" class="form-control input-sm" id="lastname" name="user.lastname"
      value="{{user.lastname}}" />
    </div>
  </div>
```

```
  <div class="form-group">
    <div class="col-sm-offset-2 col-sm-10">
      <button type="submit" id="updateUser" class="btn btn-default">Update User</button>
    </div>
  </div>
</form>
```

User Edit Route

The App class contains a route with the path /user/edit, which takes the JSON object argument. The User object is converted from a JSON string and returns a User object as JSON. The response could be used to update the form elements, but because the values are already set within the form, there is no need to update the values. In this case, the application uses the JSON response to let the user know if the update succeeded or not via a standard JavaScript alert message (Listing 10-23).

Listing 10-23. /user/edit Route

```
# edit user's first/last name
put '/user/edit' do
  user = JSON.parse(request.body.read)
  update_user(neo,user,request.cookies[graphstoryUserAuthKey])
  json user
end
```

User Update Method

To complete the update, the controller layer calls the update_user method in User class. Because the object being passed into the update method did nothing more than modify the first and last name of an existing entity, you can use the SET clause via Cypher to update the properties in the graph, as shown in Listing 10-24. This Cypher statement also makes use of the MATCH clause to retrieve the User node.

Listing 10-24. The update_user Method in the User Class

```
def update_user(neo,user,username)
  cypher =  "MATCH (user:User {username:{u}} )  " +
            "SET user.firstname = {fn}, user.lastname = {ln}"
  neo.execute_query(cypher, {:fn => user["firstname"],:ln => user["lastname"], :u => username} )
end
```

Connecting Users

A common feature in social media applications is to allow users to connect to each other through an explicit relationship. In the sample application, we use the directed relationship type called FOLLOWS. By going to the "Friends" page within the social graph section, you can see the list of the users the current user is following, search for new friends to follow, add them and remove friends the current user is following. The user management section of the App class contains each of the routes to control the flow for these features, specifically the routes that cover friends, search_by_user_name, follow, and unfollow.

To display the list of the users the current user is following, the `/friends` route, showing in Listing 10-25, in the App class calls the `following` method in the `User` class.

Listing 10-25. The `/friends` Route

```
# friends route that shows connected users via FOLLOW relationship
get '/friends' do
    @title = "Friends"
    @following = following(neo, request.cookies[graphstoryUserAuthKey])
    mustache :"graphs/social/friends"
end
```

The method shown in Listing 10-26 creates a list of users by matching the current user's username with directed relationship FOLLOWS on the variable user.

Listing 10-26. The `following` Method in the `User` Class

```
def following(neo,username)
      cypher =  " MATCH (user { username:{u}})-[:FOLLOWS]->(users) "+
      " RETURN users.firstname as firstname, users.lastname as lastname, " +
      " users.username as username " +
      " ORDER BY users.username"
      results = neo.execute_query(cypher, u: username})
      results["data"].map {|row| Hash[*results["columns"].zip(row).flatten] }
end
```

If the list contains users, it will be returned to the controller and displayed in the right-hand part of the page, as shown in Figure 10-9. The display code for showing the list of users can be found in `{PROJECTROOT}/ app/views/graphs/social/friends.mustache` and is shown in the code snippet in Listing 10-27.

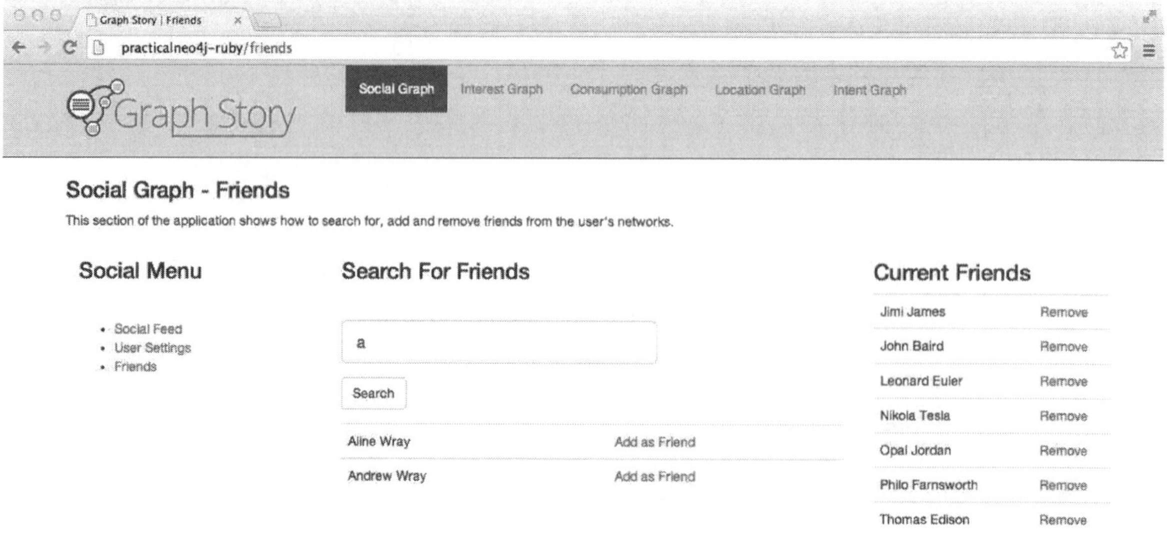

Figure 10-9. *The Friends page*

Listing 10-27. The HTML Code Snippet for Displaying the List of Friends

```
<div class="col-md-3">
<h3>Current Friends</h3>
<table class="table" id="following">
        {{#following}}
              <tr><td>{{firstname}} {{lastname}}</td><td><a href="#" id="{{username}}"
              class="removefriend">Remove</a></td></tr>
        {{/following}}
        {{^following}}
               No friends :(
        {{/following}}
        </table>
</div>
```

To search for users to follow, the user section of App contains a GET route /searchbyusername and passes in a username value as part of the path. This route executes the `search_by_user_name` method found in `User` class, showing the second part of Listing 10-28. The first part of the `WHERE` clause in the method returns users whose username matches on a wildcard String value. The second part of the `WHERE` clause in the method checks to make sure the users in the MATCH clause are not already being followed by the current user.

Listing 10-28. The searchbyusername Route and service Method

```
# search for users / returns collection of users as json
get '/searchbyusername/:username' do
  content_type :json
  username=params[:username]
  json :users => search_by_user_name(neo, request.cookies[graphstoryUserAuthKey],username)
end

# search by user returns users in the network that aren't already being followed
def search_by_user_name(neo,currentusername,username)
  username=username.downcase+".*"

  cypher =  " MATCH (n:User), (user { username:{c}}) " +
            " WHERE (n.username =~ {u} AND n <> user) " +
            " AND (NOT (user)-[:FOLLOWS]->(n)) " +
            " RETURN n.firstname as firstname, n.lastname as lastname, n.username as username"
  results=neo.execute_query(cypher, {:c => currentusername, :u => username} )
  results["data"].map {|row| Hash[*results["columns"].zip(row).flatten] }
end
```

The `searchByUsername` in `{PROJECTROOT}/app/public/js/graphstory.js` uses an AJAX request and formats the response in `render SearchByUsername`. If the list contains users, it will be displayed in the center of the page under the search form, as shown in Figure 10-9. Otherwise, the response will display "No Users Found."

Once the search returns results, the next action would be to click on the "Add as Friend" link, which will call the `addfriend` method in `graphstory.js`. This performs an AJAX request to the `follow` route, which then calls the `follow` method in the `User` class. The `follow` method in `User` shown in Listing 10-29 will create the relationship between the two users by first finding each entity via the `MATCH` clause and then using the `CreateUnique` clause to create the directed `FOLLOWS` relationship. Once the operation is completed, the next part of the query then runs a `MATCH` on the users being followed to return the full list of followers ordered by the username.

Listing 10-29. The `follow` Route and `follow service` Method

```
# follow a user & return the updated list of users being followed
get '/follow/:username' do
  content_type :json
  json :following => follow(neo,request.cookies[graphstoryUserAuthKey],params[:username])
end

# the follow method in the User class
def follow(neo,currentusername,username)
  cypher =  " MATCH (user1:User {username:{cu}} ), (user2:User {username:{u}} ) " +
            " CREATE UNIQUE user1-[:FOLLOWS]->user2 " +
            " WITH user1" +
            " MATCH (user1)-[f:FOLLOWS]->(users)" +
            " RETURN users.firstname as firstname, users.lastname as lastname, "+
            " users.username as username " +
            " ORDER BY users.username"
  results=neo.execute_query(cypher, {:cu => currentusername, :u => username} )
  results["data"].map {|row| Hash[*results["columns"].zip(row).flatten] }
end
```

The unfollow feature for the `FOLLOWS` relationships uses a nearly identical application flow as follows feature. In the `unfollow` method, shown in Listing 10-30, the controller passes in two arguments—the current username and username to be unfollowed. As with the `follow` method, once the operation is completed, the next part of the query then runs a `MATCH` on the users being followed to return the full list of followers ordered by the username.

Listing 10-30. The `unfollow` Route and `unfollow service` Method

```
# unfollow a user & return the updated list of users being followed
get '/unfollow/:username' do
  content_type :json
  json :following => unfollow(neo,request.cookies[graphstoryUserAuthKey],params[:username])
end

# the unfollow method in the User class
def unfollow(neo,currentusername,username)
  cypher =  "MATCH (user1:User {username:{cu}} )-[f:FOLLOWS]->(user2:User {username:{u}} ) " +
            " DELETE f " +
            " WITH user1" +
            " MATCH (user1)-[f:FOLLOWS]->(users)" +
            " RETURN users.firstname as firstname, users.lastname as lastname, "+
            " users.username as username " +
            " ORDER BY users.username"
  results=neo.execute_query(cypher, {:cu => currentusername, :u => username} )
  results["data"].map {|row| Hash[*results["columns"].zip(row).flatten] }
end
```

User-Generated Content

Another important feature in social media applications is being able to have users view, add, edit, and remove content—sometimes referred to as *user-generated content*. In the case of this content, you will not be creating connections between the content and its owner but creating a linked list of status updates. In other words, you are connecting a User to their most recent status update and then connecting each subsequent status to the next update through the CURRENTPOST and NEXTPOST directed relationship types, respectively.

This approach is used for two reasons. First, the sample application displays a given number of posts at a time, and using a limited linked list is more efficient than getting all status updates connected directly to a user and then sorting and limiting the number of items to return. In addition, it also helps to limit the number of relationships that are placed on the User and Content entities. Therefore, the overall graph operations should be made more efficient by using the linked list approach.

Getting the Status Updates

To display the first set of status updates start with the social route of the social section of grapstory.py. This method accesses the get_content method within Content service class, which takes an argument of the current user's username and the page being requested. The page refers to set number of objects within a collection. In this instance, the paging is zero-based, and so we will request page 0 and limit the page size to 4 in order to return the first page.

The get_content method in Content class shown in Listing 9-28 will first determine whom the user is following and then match that set of user with the status updates starting with the CURRENTPOST. The CURRENTPOST is then matched on the next three status updates via the [:NEXTPOST*0..3] section of the query. Finally, the method uses a loop to add a readable date and time string property—based on the timestamp—on the results returned to the controller and view.

Listing 10-31. The get_content Method in the Content Service Class

```
def get_content(neo,username,skip)
  cypher =  " MATCH (u:User {username: {u} })-[:FOLLOWS*0..1]->f  "+
            " WITH DISTINCT f,u "+
            " MATCH f-[:CURRENTPOST]-lp-[:NEXTPOST*0..3]-p   "+
            " RETURN  p.contentId as contentId, p.title as title, "+
            " p.tagstr as tagstr, p.timestamp as timestamp, "+
            " p.url as url, f.username as username, f=u as owner  "+
            " ORDER BY p.timestamp desc SKIP {s} LIMIT 4 "
  results=neo.execute_query(cypher, {:u => username, :s => skip} )
  r=results["data"].map {|row| Hash[*results["columns"].zip(row).flatten] }
  r.each do |e|
    #convert the timestamp to readable date and time
    e.merge!("timestampAsStr" => Time.at(e["timestamp"]).strftime("%m/%d/%Y") +
    " at " +
    Time.at(e["timestamp"]).strftime("%l:%M %p"))
  end
  r
end
```

Adding a Status Update

The page shown in Figure 10-10 shows the form to add a status update for the current user, which is displayed when clicking on the "Add Content" link just under the "Graph Story - Social Feed" header. The HTML for the form can be found in {PROJECTROOT}/app/views/graphs/social/posts.mustache. The form uses the add_content function in graphstory.js to POST a new status update as well as return the response and add it to the top of the status update stream.

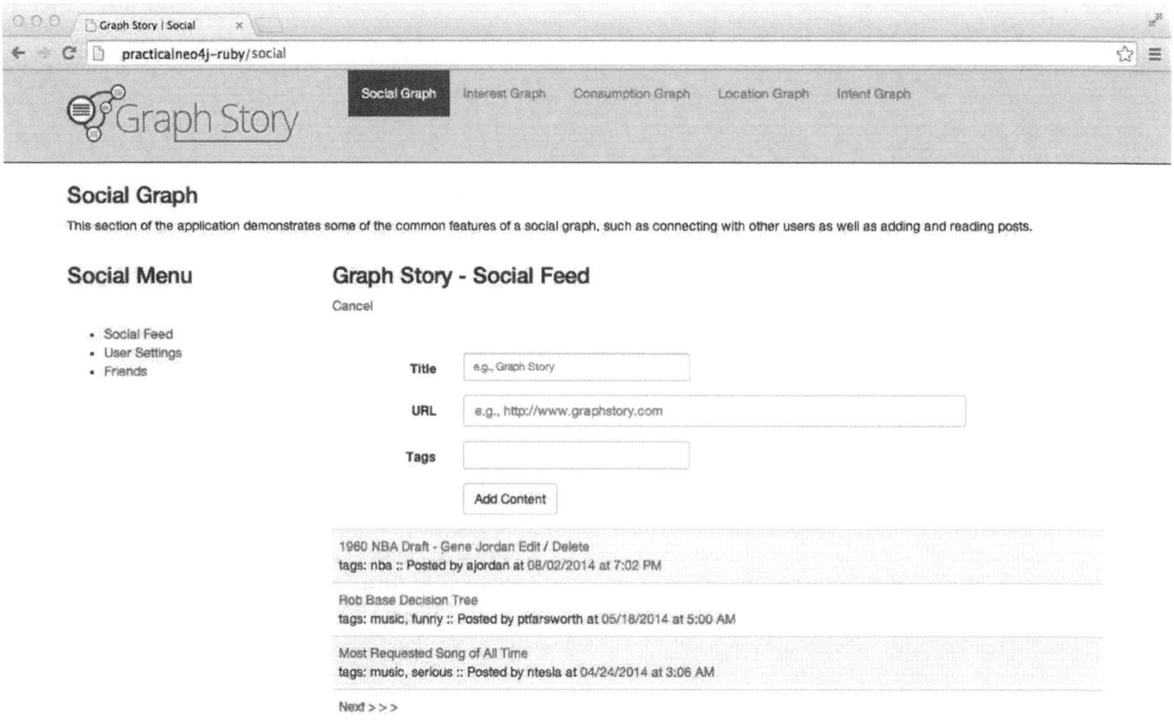

Figure 10-10. Adding a status update

The add_content route and add_content method are shown in Listing 10-32. When a new status update is created, in addition to its graph id, the add_content method also generates a contentId, which performs using the SecureRandom.uuid method.

Listing 10-32. add Route and save Method for a Status Update

```
# add a status update - route
post '/posts/add' do
  contentItem = JSON.parse(request.body.read)

  # save and return content
  contentItem=add_content(neo,contentItem,request.cookies[graphstoryUserAuthKey])

  json contentItem

end
```

The add_content method also makes the status the CURRENTPOST. determine whether a previous CURRENTPOST exists and, if one does, change its relationship type to NEXTPOST. In addition, the tags connected to the status update are merged into the graph and connected to the status update via the HAS relationship type.

```
# add a status update
def add_content(neo,contentItem,username)

  tagstr=trim_content_tags(contentItem["tagstr"])
  tags=tagstr.split(",")
  time = Time.now.to_i

  cypher =  " MATCH (user { username: {u}}) " +
            " CREATE UNIQUE (user)-[:CURRENTPOST]->(newLP:Content { title:{title}, url:{url}, " +
            " tagstr:{tagstr}, timestamp:{timestamp}, contentId:{contentId} }) " +
            " WITH user, newLP" +
            " FOREACH (tagName in {tags} |  " +
            " MERGE (t:Tag {wordPhrase:tagName}) " +
            " MERGE (newLP)-[:HAS]->(t) " +
            " )" +
            " WITH user, newLP " +
            " OPTIONAL MATCH  (newLP)<-[:CURRENTPOST]-(user)-[oldRel:CURRENTPOST]->(oldLP)" +
            " DELETE oldRel " +
            " CREATE (newLP)-[:NEXTPOST]->(oldLP) " +
            " RETURN newLP.contentId as contentId, newLP.title as title, newLP.tagstr as tagstr, " +
            " newLP.timestamp as timestamp, newLP.url as url, {u} as username, true as owner "

  results=neo.execute_query(cypher, { :u => username,
                                      :title => contentItem["title"].strip,
                                      :url => contentItem["url"].strip,
                                      :tagstr => tagstr,
                                      :timestamp => time,
                                      :contentId => SecureRandom.uuid,
                                      :tags => tags } )
  r=results["data"].map {|row| Hash[*results["columns"].zip(row).flatten] }
  r.each do |e|
    #convert the timestamp to readable date and time
    e.merge!("timestampAsStr" => Time.at(e["timestamp"]).strftime("%m/%d/%Y") +
    " at " +
    Time.at(e["timestamp"]).strftime("%l:%M %p"))
  end
  r
end
```

Editing a Status Update

When status updates are displayed, the current user's status updates will contain a link to "Edit" the status. Once clicked, it will open the form, similar to the "Add Content" link, but will populate the form with the status update values as well as modify the form button to read "Edit Content", as shown in Figure 10-11. Clicking "Cancel" under the heading will remove the values and return the form to its ready state.

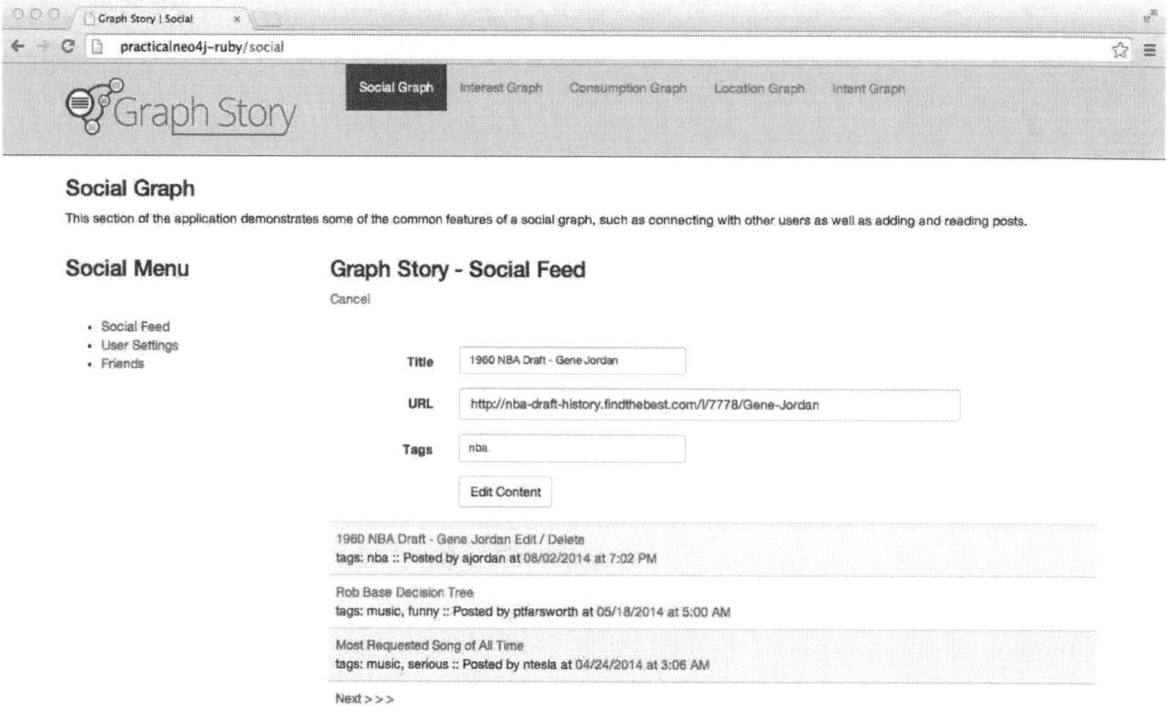

Figure 10-11. *Editing a status update*

Similar to the add feature, the edit feature will use a route in the App as well as a function in `graphstory.js`, which are `edit` and `edit_content`, respectively. The edit content route passes in the content object, with its content id, and then calls the `edit_content` method in Content class, which is shown in Listing 10-33.

Listing 10-33. edit Route and Method for a Status Update

```
# edit a status update - route
post '/posts/edit' do
  contentItem = JSON.parse(request.body.read)
  # edit content
  contentItem = edit_content(neo,contentItem,request.cookies[graphstoryUserAuthKey])

  json contentItem
end

# edit a status update
def edit_content(neo,contentItem,username)

  tagstr=trim_content_tags(contentItem["tagstr"])
  tags=tagstr.split(",")

  cypher =  " MATCH (c:Content {contentId:{contentId}})-[:NEXTPOST*0..]-()-[:CURRENTPOST]-(user
  { username: {u}}) " +
            " SET c.title = {title}, c.url = {url}, c.tagstr = {tagstr}" +
            " FOREACH (tagName in {tags} |  " +
            " MERGE (t:Tag {wordPhrase:tagName}) " +
```

```
            " MERGE (c)-[:HAS]->(t) " +
            " )" +
            " RETURN c.contentId as contentId, c.title as title, c.tagstr as tagstr, " +
            " c.timestamp as timestamp, c.url as url, {u} as username, true as owner "
  results=neo.execute_query(cypher, { :u => username,
                                      :title => contentItem["title"].strip,
                                      :url => contentItem["url"].strip,
                                      :tagstr => tagstr,
                                      :contentId => contentItem["contentId"],
                                      :tags => tags } )
  r=results["data"].map {|row| Hash[*results["columns"].zip(row).flatten] }
  r.each do |e|
    #convert the timestamp to readable date and time
    e.merge!("timestampAsStr" => Time.at(e["timestamp"]).strftime("%m/%d/%Y") +
    " at " +
    Time.at(e["timestamp"]).strftime("%l:%M %p"))
  end
  r
end
```

In the case of the edit feature, you do not need to update relationships. Instead, simply retrieve the existing node by its generated String Id (not its graph id), update its properties where necessary, and save it back to the graph.

Deleting a Status Update

As with the “edit” option, when status updates are displayed, the current user’s status updates will contain a link to “Delete” the status. Once clicked, it will ask if you want it deleted (no regrets!) and, if accepted, generate an AJAX GET request to call the delete route and corresponding method in the Content class, shown in Listing 10-34.

Listing 10-34. Deleting a Status Update

```
# delete post
get '/posts/delete/:contentId' do
  delete_content(neo,request.cookies[graphstoryUserAuthKey],params[:contentId])
end

# delete a status update
def delete_content(neo,username,contentId)

   cypher =  " MATCH (u:User { username: {u} }), (c:Content { contentId: {contentId} }) " +
            " WITH u,c " +
            " MATCH (u)-[:CURRENTPOST]->(c)-[:NEXTPOST]->(nextPost) " +
            " WHERE nextPost is not null " +
            " CREATE UNIQUE (u)-[:CURRENTPOST]->(nextPost) " +
            " WITH count(nextPost) as cnt " +
            " MATCH (before)-[:NEXTPOST]->(c:Content { contentId: {contentId}})-[:NEXTPOST]->(after) " +
            " WHERE before is not null AND after is not null " +
            " CREATE UNIQUE (before)-[:NEXTPOST]->(after) " +
            " WITH count(before) as cnt " +
            " MATCH (c:Content { contentId: {contentId} })-[r]-() " +
            " DELETE c, r"
  results=neo.execute_query(cypher, {:u => username, :contentId => contentId})
end
```

The Cypher in the delete method begins by finding the user and content that will be used in the rest of the query. In the first MATCH, you can determine if this status update is the CURRENTPOST by checking to see if it is related to a NEXTPOST. If this relationship pattern matches, make the NEXTPOST into the CURRENTPOST with CREATE UNIQUE.

Next, the query will ask if the status update is somewhere the middle of the list, which is performed by determining if the status update has incoming and outgoing NEXTPOST relationships. If the pattern is matched, then connect the before and after status updates via NEXTPOST.

Regardless of the status update's location in the linked list, retrieve it and its relationships and then delete the node along with all of its relationships.

To recap, if one of the relationship patterns matches, replace that pattern with the nodes on either side of the status update in question. Once that has been performed, the node and its relationships can be removed from the graph.

Interest Graph Model

This section looks at the interest graph and examines some basic ways it can be used to explicitly define a degree of interest. The following topics are covered:

- Adding filters for owned content
- Adding filters for connected content
- Analyzing connected content (count tags)

Interest in Aggregate

Using the /interest route, we retrieve all of the user's tags and their friends' tags by calling, respectively, the user_tags and tags_in_network methods, which can be found in the Tag service class. This is displayed in Figure 10-12 in the left-hand column.

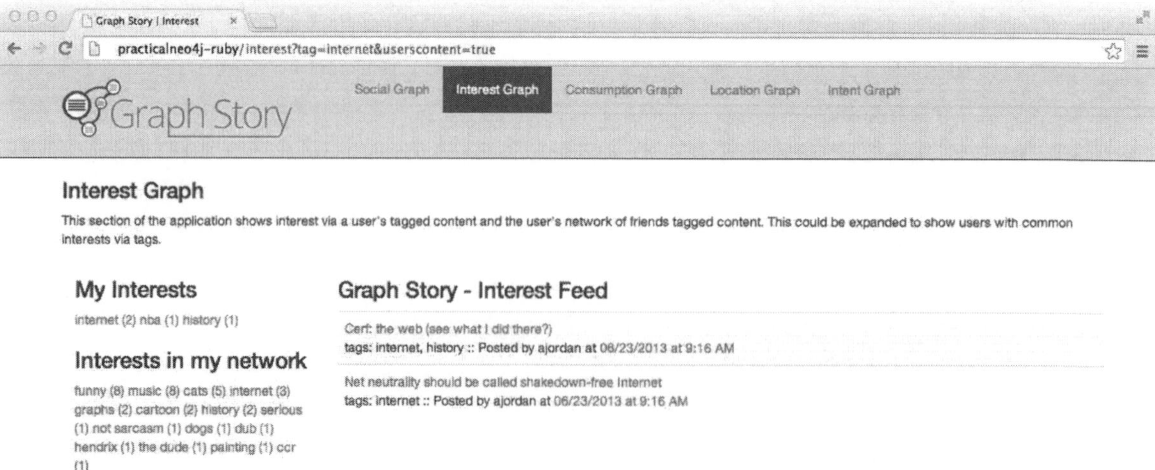

Figure 10-12. *Filtering the current user's content*

The display code is located in {PROJECTROOT}/ app/views/graphs/interest/index.mustache. The interest route uses two queries, which are shown in Listing 10-36 and 10-37. The get_following_content_with_tag finds users being followed, accesses all of their content, and finds connected tags through the HAS relationship type.

The get_user_content_with_tag method is similar but is concerned only with content and, subsequently, tags connected to the current user. Both methods limit the results to 30 items. As mentioned earlier, the methods return an array of content and tags, which supports autosuggest plugin in the view and requires both a label and name to be provided in order to execute. This autosuggest feature is used in the status update form as well as some search forms found later in this chapter.

Listing 10-35. The interest Route

```
# show tags within the user's network (theirs and those being followed)
get '/interest' do
  @title = "Interest"

  @tagsInNetwork = tags_in_network(neo,request.cookies[graphstoryUserAuthKey])
  @userTags = user_tags(neo,request.cookies[graphstoryUserAuthKey])

  if params[:userscontent] == "true"
    @contents = get_user_content_with_tag(neo,request.cookies[graphstoryUserAuthKey],params[:tag] )
  else
    @contents = get_following_content_with_tag(neo,request.cookies[graphstoryUserAuthKey],
    params[:tag] )
  end

  mustache :"graphs/interest/index"
end
```

Filtering Managed Content

Once the list of tags for the user and for the group she follows has been provided, then the content can be filtered based of the generated tag links, which is shown in Figure 10-12. If a tag is clicked on inside of "My Interests" section, then the get_user_content_with_tag method, displayed in Listing 10-34, will be called.

Listing 10-36. Get the Content of the Current User Based on a Tag

```
def get_user_content_with_tag(neo,username,wordPhrase)
  cypher =  " MATCH (u:User {username: {u} })-[:CURRENTPOST]-lp-[:NEXTPOST*0..]-p " +
            " WITH DISTINCT u,p" +
            " MATCH p-[:HAS]-(t:Tag {wordPhrase : {wp} } )" +
            " RETURN  p.contentId as contentId, p.title as title, p.tagstr as tagstr, " +
            " p.timestamp as timestamp, p.url as url, u.username as username, true as owner" +
            " ORDER BY p.timestamp DESC"
   results=neo.execute_query(cypher, {:u => username, :wp => wordPhrase} )
   r=results["data"].map {|row| Hash[*results["columns"].zip(row).flatten] }
  r.each do |e|
    #convert the timestamp to readable date and time
    e.merge!("timestampAsStr" => Time.at(e["timestamp"]).strftime("%m/%d/%Y") +
    " at " +
    Time.at(e["timestamp"]).strftime("%l:%M %p"))
  end
  r
end
```

Filtering Connected Content

If a tag is clicked on the inside of the "Interests in my Network" section, then `get_following_content_with_tag` method will be called, as shown in Listing 10-37. The second query is nearly identical the first query found in the `interest` route, except that it will factor in the users being followed and exclude the current user. The method also returns a collection of status updates based on the matching tag, placing no limit on the number of status updates to be returned. In addition, it marks the owner property as true, because you've determined ahead of time you are only returning the current user's content. The results of calling this method are shown in Figure 10-13.

Listing 10-37. Get the Content of the User's Being Followed Based on a Tag

```
def get_following_content_with_tag(neo,username,wordPhrase)
  cypher =  " MATCH (u:User {username: {u} })-[:FOLLOWS]->f" +
            " WITH DISTINCT f" +
            " MATCH f-[:CURRENTPOST]-lp-[:NEXTPOST*0..]-p" +
            " WITH DISTINCT f,p" +
            " MATCH p-[:HAS]-(t:Tag {wordPhrase : {wp} } )" +
            " RETURN  p.contentId as contentId, p.title as title, p.tagstr as tagstr, " +
            " p.timestamp as timestamp, p.url as url, f.username as username, false as owner" +
            " ORDER BY p.timestamp DESC"
   results=neo.execute_query(cypher, {:u => username, :wp => wordPhrase} )
   r=results["data"].map {|row| Hash[*results["columns"].zip(row).flatten] }
  r.each do |e|
```

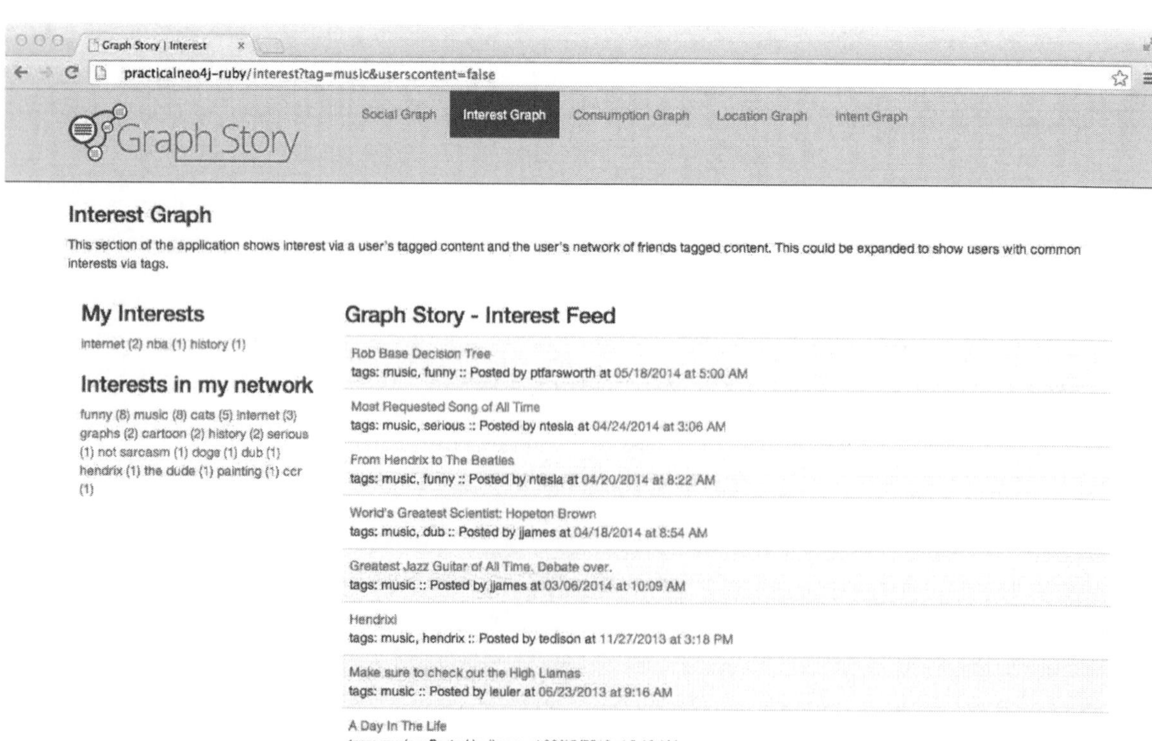

Figure 10-13. *Filtering content of the current user's friends*

```
    #convert the timestamp to readable date and time
    e.merge!("timestampAsStr" => Time.at(e["timestamp"]).strftime("%m/%d/%Y") +
    " at " +
    Time.at(e["timestamp"]).strftime("%l:%M %p"))
  end
  r
end
```

Consumption Graph Model

This section examines a few techniques to capture and use patterns of consumption generated implicitly by a user or users. For the purposes of your application, you will use the pre-populated set of products provided in the sample graph. The code required for the console will reinforce the standard persistence operations, this section focuses on the operations that take advantage of this model type, including:

- Capturing consumption
- Filtering consumption for users
- Filtering consumption for messaging

Capturing Consumption

The process above for creating code that directly captures consumption for a user could also be done by creating a graph-backed service to consume the webserver logs in real time, or by creating another data store to create the relationships. The result would be the same in any event: a process that connects nodes to reveal a pattern of consumption (Listing 10-38).

Listing 10-38. Consumption route to show a list of products and the product trail of the current user

```
# add a product via VIEWED relationship and return VIEWED products
get '/consumption' do
  @title="Consumption"

  @products=get_products(neo,0)
  @next = true
  @nextPageUrl="/consumption/1"

  @productTrail = get_product_trail(neo,request.cookies[graphstoryUserAuthKey])

  mustache :"graphs/consumption/index"
end
```

The sample application used the `create_user_view_and_return_views` method in the `Product` class to first find the product being viewed and then create an explicit relationship type called `VIEWED`. As you may have noticed, this is the first relationship type in the application that also contains properties. In this case, we are creating a timestamp with a date and string value of the timestamp. The query, shown in Listing 10-39, will check to see if a `VIEWED` relationship already exists between the user and the product using `MERGE`.

Listing 10-39. Add consumption_add Route and create_user_view_and_return_views Method

```
#add a product via VIEWED relationship and return VIEWED products
get '/consumption/add/:productNodeId' do
  # productNodeId to integer
  productNodeId=params[:productNodeId].to_i

  #create or update the user view and
  #return the product trail as JSON
  json :productTrail => create_user_view_and_return_views(neo,
                                                          request.cookies[graphstoryUserAuthKey],
                                                          productNodeId)
end

# the method to add a user view of a product and return all views
def create_user_view_and_return_views(neo,username,productNodeId)

  # create timestamp and string display
  time = Time.now
  tsAsInt = time.to_i
  timestampAsStr= time.strftime("%m/%d/%Y") +
        " at " + time.strftime("%l:%M %p")

  cypher =  " MATCH (p:Product), (u:User { username:{u} })" +
            " WHERE id(p) = {productNodeId}" +
            " WITH u,p" +
            " MERGE (u)-[r:VIEWED]->(p)" +
            " SET r.dateAsStr={timestampAsStr}, r.timestamp={ts}" +
            " WITH u " +
            " MATCH (u)-[r:VIEWED]->(p)" +
            " RETURN p.title as title,  r.dateAsStr as dateAsStr" +
            " ORDER BY r.timestamp desc"

  results=neo.execute_query(cypher, {:u => username,
                                     :productNodeId => productNodeId,
                                     :timestampAsStr => timestampAsStr,
                                     :ts => ts} )
  results["data"].map {|row| Hash[*results["columns"].zip(row).flatten] }

end
```

In the MERGE section of the query, if the result of the MERGE is zero matches, then a relationship is created with key value pairs on the new relationship, specifically dateAsStr and timestamp. Finally, the query uses MATCH to return the existing product views.

Filtering Consumption for Users

One practical use of the consumption model is to create a content trail for users, as shown in Figure 10-14. As a user clicks on items in the scrolling product stream, the interaction is captured using create_user_view_and_return_views, which ultimately returns a List of relationship objects of the VIEWED type.

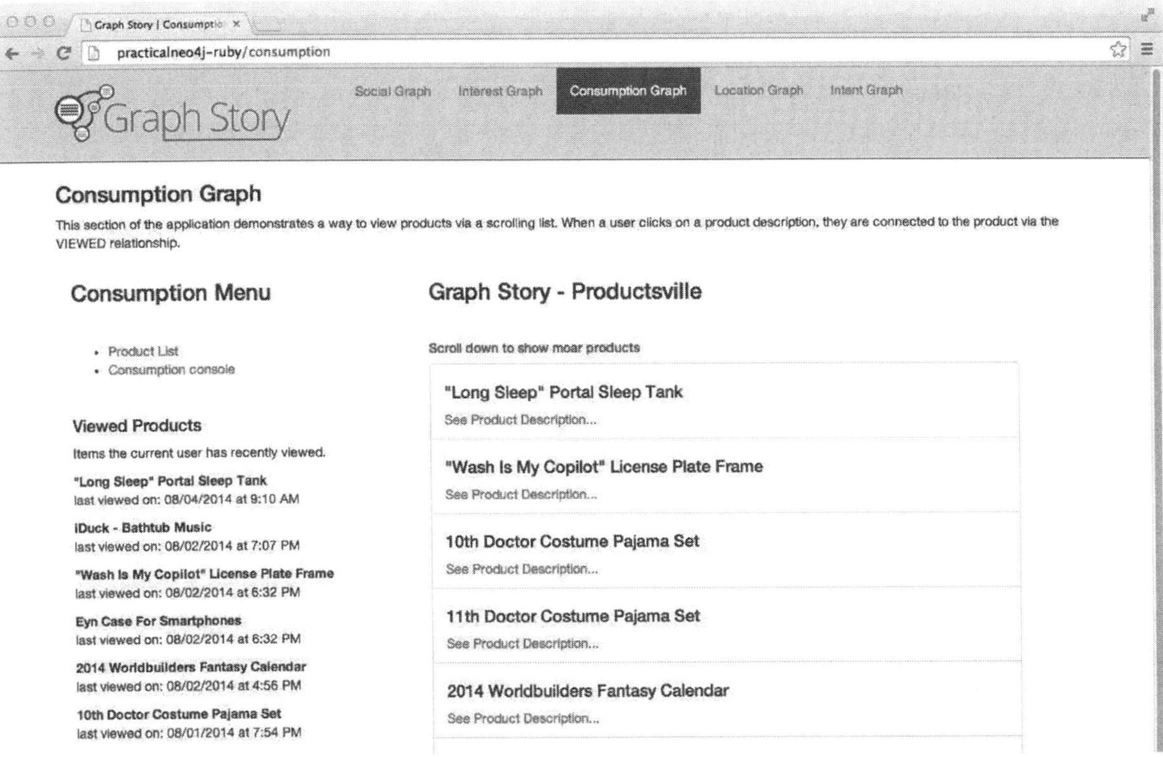

Figure 10-14. *The Scrolling Product and Product Trail page*

In the consumption graph section, we take a look at the `consumption` route to see how the process begins inside the controller. The controller method first saves the view and then returns the complete history of views using the `get_product_trail`, which can be found in the `Product` class. The process is started when the `createUserProductViewRel` function is called, which is located in `graphstory.js`.

Filtering Consumption for Messaging

Another practical use of the consumption model is to create a personalized message for users, as displayed in Figure 10-15. In this case, you have a filter that allows the "Consumption Console" to narrow down to a very specific group of users who visited a product that was also tagged with a keyword or phrase each user had explicitly used (Listing 10-40).

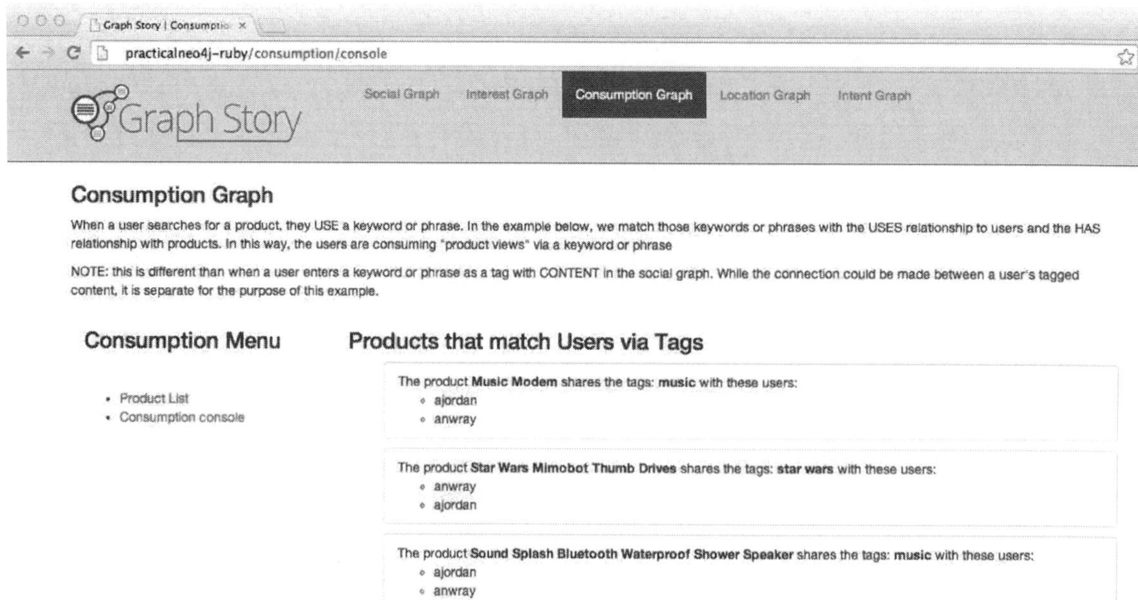

Figure 10-15. *The consumption console*

Listing 10-40. The `consumption console` Route and Methods to Get Connected Products and Users via Tags

```
# displays products that are connected to users via a tag relationship
get '/consumption/console' do
  @title="Consumption Console"

  if params[:tag] && !params[:tag].empty?
    @usersWithMatchingTags  = get_products_has_specific_tag_and_user_users_specific_
    tag(neo,params[:tag])
  else
    @usersWithMatchingTags = get_products_has_a_tag_and_user_users_a_matching_tag(neo)
  end

  mustache :"graphs/consumption/console"
end

# products that share any tag with a user
def get_products_has_a_tag_and_user_users_a_matching_tag(neo)
  cypher =  " MATCH (p:Product)-[:HAS]->(t)<-[:USES]-(u:User) "+
            " RETURN p.title as title , collect(u.username) as users, " +
            " collect(distinct t.wordPhrase) as tags "
  results=neo.execute_query(cypher)
  results["data"].map {|row| Hash[results["columns"].zip(row)] }
end
```

```
# products that share a specific tag with a user
def get_products_has_specific_tag_and_user_users_specific_tag(neo, wp)
  cypher =  " MATCH (t:Tag { wordPhrase: {wp} }) " +
            " WITH t " +
            " MATCH (p:Product)-[:HAS]->(t)<-[:USES]-(u:User) " +
            " RETURN p.title as title,collect(u) as u, collect(distinct t) as t "
  results=neo.execute_query(cypher, {:wp => wp} )
  results["data"].map {|row| Hash[results["columns"].zip(row)] }
end
```

Location Graph Model

This section explores the location graph model and a few of the operations that typically accompany it. In particular, it looks at the following:

- The spatial plugin
- Filtering on location
- Products based on location

The example demonstrates how to add a console to enable you to connect products to locations in an ad hoc manner (Listing 10-41).

Listing 10-41. Location Route for Showing Locations or Locations with Specific Product

```
# show locations nearby or locations that have a specific product
get '/location' do
  @title="Location"
  #get their primary location
  @mappedUserLocation=get_user_location(neo,request.cookies[graphstoryUserAuthKey])

  # was a distance param provided?
  if(params[:distance])
    #make the location query
    lq = get_lq(@mappedUserLocation[0],params[:distance].to_s)
    # was a product node id provided?
    if(params[:productNodeId].empty?)
      # if no, just get locations of type 'business'
      @locations=locations_within_distance(neo, lq, @mappedUserLocation[0],"business")
    else
      #otherwise find locations that have this product
      pnid=params[:productNodeId].to_i
      @productnode=neo.get_node(pnid)["data"]
      @locations=locations_within_distance_with_product(neo,lq,pnid, @mappedUserLocation[0])
    end
  end

  mustache :"graphs/location/index"
end
```

Search for Nearby Locations

To search for nearby locations (Figure 10-16), use the current user's location, obtained with `get_user_location`, and then use the `locations_within_distance`. The `Locations_within_distance` method in `Location` service class uses a method called `distance` to return a string value of the distance between the starting point and the respective location (Listing 10-42).

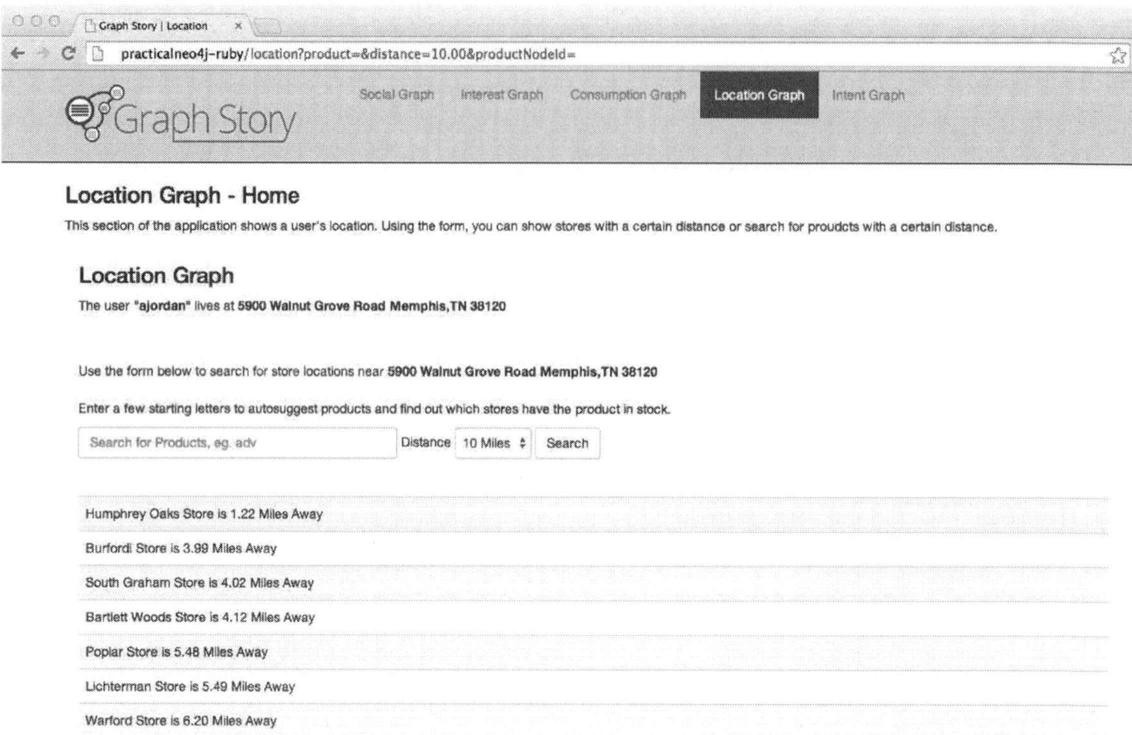

Figure 10-16. *Searching for Locations within a certain distance of User location*

Listing 10-42. The locations_within_distance Method in the Location class

```
def locations_within_distance(neo, lq, mappedUserLocation,locationType)
    cypher = " START n = node:geom({lq}) WHERE n.type = {locationType}  " +
    " RETURN n.locationId as locationId, n.address as address, n.city as city, " +
    " n.state as state, n.zip as zip, n.name as name, n.lat as lat, n.lon as lon"
    results = neo.execute_query(cypher, {:lq => lq,:locationType => locationType} )
    r=results["data"].map {|row| Hash[*results["columns"].zip(row).flatten] }
    r.each do |e|
        d = distance [e["lat"].to_f,e["lon"].to_f],[mappedUserLocation["lat"].
to_f,mappedUserLocation["lon"].to_f]
        e.merge!("distanceToLocation" => d.to_s + " Miles Away")
    end
    r
end
```

Locations with Product

To search for products nearby (Figure 10-17), the application makes use of an autosuggest AJAX request, which ultimately calls the search method in the Product service class. The method, shown in Listing 10-43, returns an array of objects to the product field in the search form and applies the selected product's productNodeId to the subsequent location search.

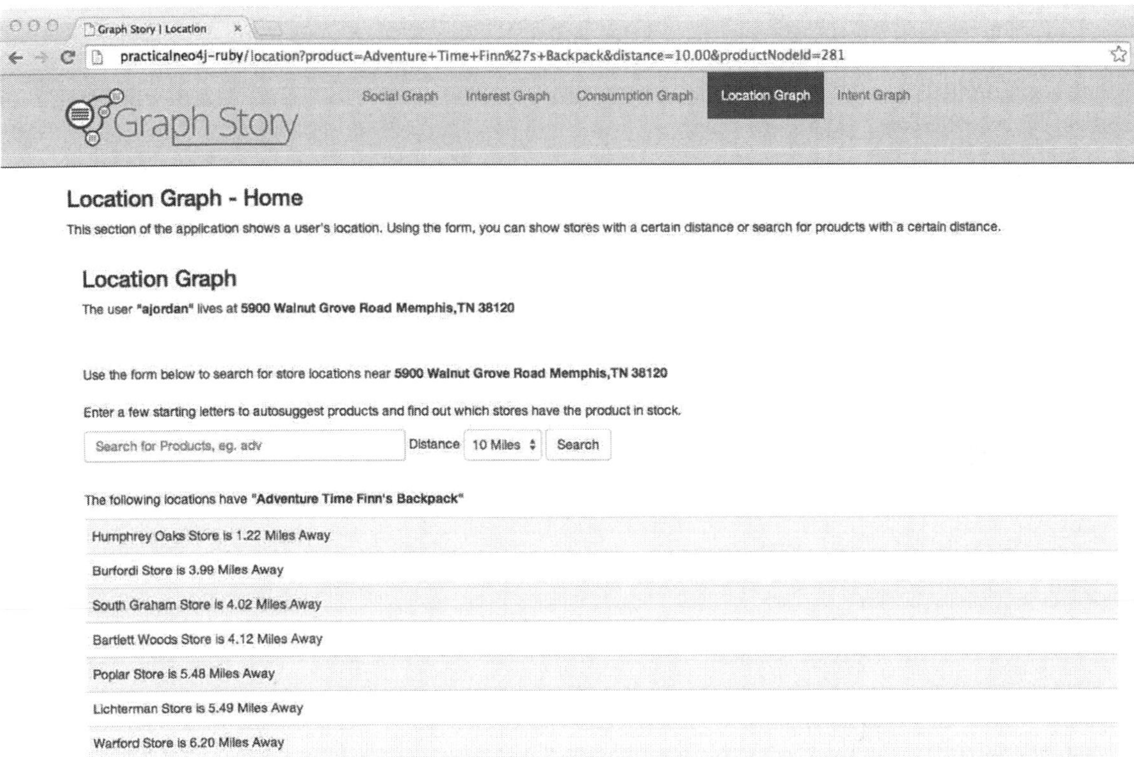

Figure 10-17. *Searching for Products in stock at Locations within a certain distance of the User location.*

Listing 10-43. The product_search Route and product_search Methods

```
# return product array as json
get '/productsearch/:q' do
  json product_search(neo,params[:q].to_s)
end

# product_search method - located in the Product service class.
def product_search(neo,q)
  q= q + ".*"
  cypher =  " MATCH (p:Product) WHERE lower(p.title) =~ {q}"+
            " RETURN count(*) as name, TOSTRING(ID(p)) as id, p.title as label " +
            " ORDER BY p.title " +
            " LIMIT 5 "
```

```
  results=neo.execute_query(cypher, {:q => q} )
  results["data"].map {|row| Hash[results["columns"].zip(row)] }
end
```

For almost all cases, it is recommended that you do not to use the graphId because it can be recycled when its node is deleted. In this case, the productNodeId should be considered safe to use, because products would not be in danger of being deleted but only removed from a Location relationship.

Once the product and distance have been set and the search is executed, the Location route tests to see if a productNodeId property has been set. If so, the locations_within_distance_with_product method is called from the Location class, which is shown in Listing 10-44.

Listing 10-44. The `locations_within_distance_with_product` Method in the Location Class

```
def locations_within_distance_with_product(neo,lq,productNodeId, mappedUserLocation)
    cypher = " START n = node:geom({lq}), p=node({productNodeId}) " +
    " MATCH n-[:HAS]->p " +
    " RETURN n.locationId as locationId, n.address as address, n.city as city, " +
    " n.state as state, n.zip as zip, n.name as name, n.lat as lat, n.lon as lon"
    results = neo.execute_query(cypher, {:lq => lq, :productNodeId => productNodeId} )
    r=results["data"].map {|row| Hash[*results["columns"].zip(row).flatten] }
    r.each do |e|
        d = distance [e["lat"].to_f,e["lon"].to_f],[mappedUserLocation["lat"].
        to_f,mappedUserLocation["lon"].to_f]
        e.merge!("distanceToLocation" => d.to_s + " Miles Away")
    end
    r
end
```

Intent Graph Model

The last part of the graph model exploration considers all the other graphs in order to suggest products based on the `Purchase` node type. The intent graph also considers the products, users, locations, and tags that are connected based on a purchase.

Products Purchased by Friends

To get all of the products that have been purchased by friends, the `friends_purchase` method is called from the `Purchase` class, shown in Listing 10-46. The corresponding route is first shown in Listing 10-45.

Listing 10-45. Intent Route to Show Purchases Made by Friends

```
#purchases by friends
get '/intent' do
  @title = "Products Purchased by Friends"
  #get products purchased by Friends
  @mappedProductUserPurchaseList =friends_purchase(neo,request.cookies[graphstoryUserAuthKey])
  mustache :"graphs/intent/index"
end
```

Listing 10-46. The `friends_purchase` Method in the Purchase Class

```
# products purchased by friends
def friends_purchase(neo,username)
  cypher = " MATCH (u:User { username: {u} } )-[:FOLLOWS]-(f)-[:MADE]->()-[:CONTAINS]->p" +
           " RETURN p.productId as productId,  p.title as title, " +
           " collect(f.firstname + ' ' + f.lastname) as fullname, " +
           " null as wordPhrase, count(f) as cfriends " +
           " ORDER BY cfriends desc, p.title "
   results=neo.execute_query(cypher, {:u => username} )
   results["data"].map {|row| Hash[results["columns"].zip(row)] }
end
```

The query shown in Listing 10-46 finds the users being followed by the current user and then matches those users to a purchase that has been `MADE` which `CONTAINS` a product. The return value is a set of properties that identify the product title, the name of the friend or friends, as well the number of friends who have bought the product. The result is ordered by the number of friends who have purchased the product and then by product title, as shown in Figure 10-18.

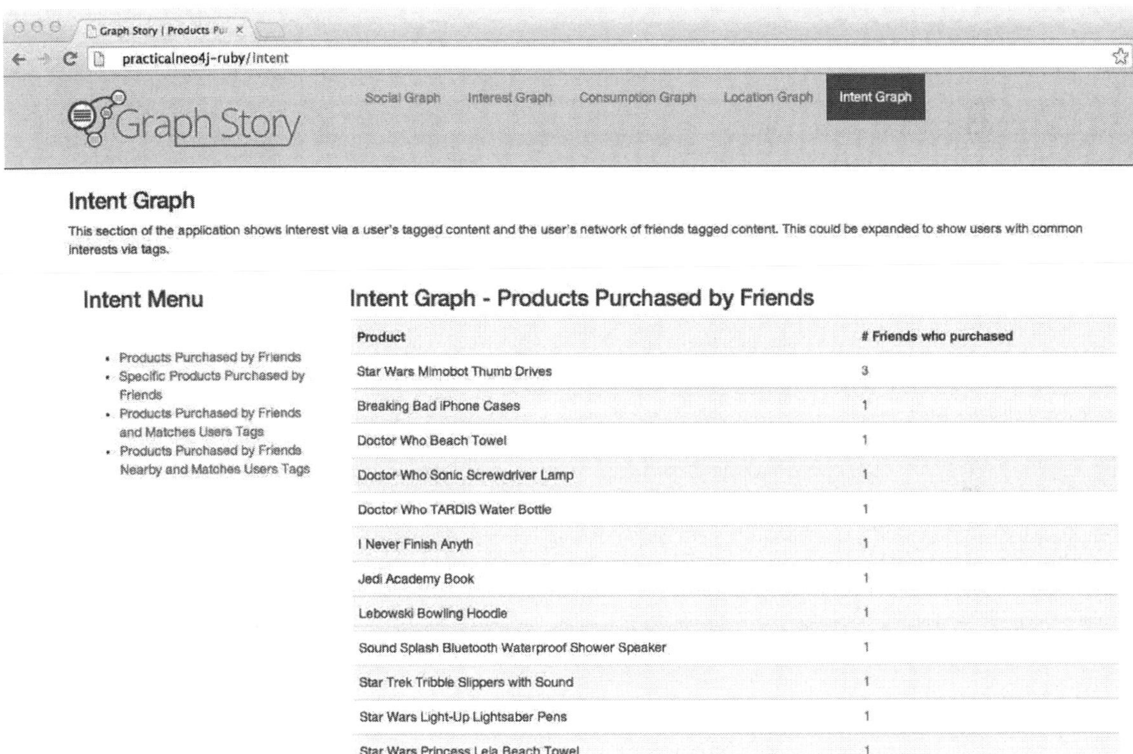

Figure 10-18. *Products Purchased By Friends*

Specific Products Purchased by Friends

If you click on the "Specific Products Purchased By Friends" link, you can specify a product, in this case "Star Wars Mimobot Thumb Drives", and then search for friends who have purchased this product (Figure 10-19). This is done via the `friends_purchase_by_product` route and method of the same name in `Purchase` service class, both of which are shown in Listing 10-47.

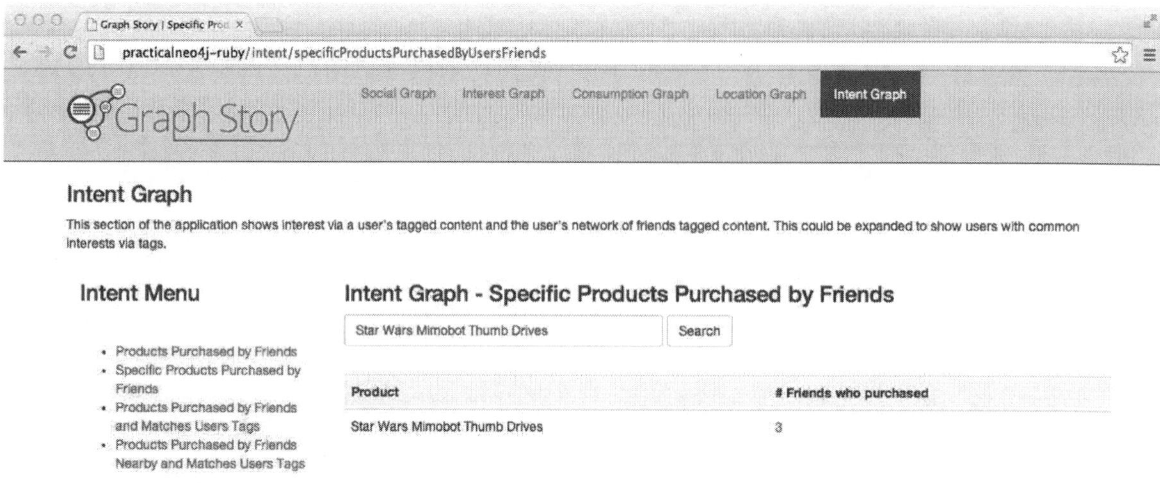

Figure 10-19. *Specific Products Purchased by Friends*

Listing 10-47. The `friends_purchase_by_product` Route and Method

```
# specific product purchases by friends
  get '/intent/friends_purchase_by_product' do
  @title = "Specific Products Purchased by Friends"
  @producttitle = 'Star Wars Mimobot Thumb Drives'
  @mappedProductUserPurchaseList = friends_purchase_by_product(neo,request.
  cookies[graphstoryUserAuthKey], @producttitle)
  mustache :"graphs/intent/index"
end

# a specific product purchased by friends
def friends_purchase_by_product(neo,username,title)
    cypher =  " MATCH (p:Product) " +
              " WHERE lower(p.title) =lower({title}) " +
              " WITH p " +
              " MATCH (u:User { username: {u} } )-[:FOLLOWS]-(f)-[:MADE]->()-[:CONTAINS]->(p) " +
              " RETURN p.productId as productId,  p.title as title, " +
              " collect(f.firstname + ' ' + f.lastname) as fullname, " +
              " null as wordPhrase, count(f) as cfriends " +
              " ORDER BY cfriends desc, p.title "
    results=neo.execute_query(cypher, {:u => username, :title => title } )
    results["data"].map {|row| Hash[results["columns"].zip(row)] }
end
```

Products Purchased by Friends and Matches User's Tags

In this next instance, we want to determine products that have been purchased by friends but that also have tags used by the current user (Listing 10-48). The result of the query is shown in Figure 10-20.

Listing 10-48. Product and Tag Similarity of the Current Users's Friends.

```
# friends bought specific products. match these products to tags of the current user
get '/intent/friends_purchase_tag_similarity' do
  @title = "Products Purchased by Friends and Matches User's Tags"
  @mappedProductUserPurchaseList = friends_purchase_tag_similarity(neo,request.
cookies[graphstoryUserAuthKey])
  mustache :"graphs/intent/index"
end
```

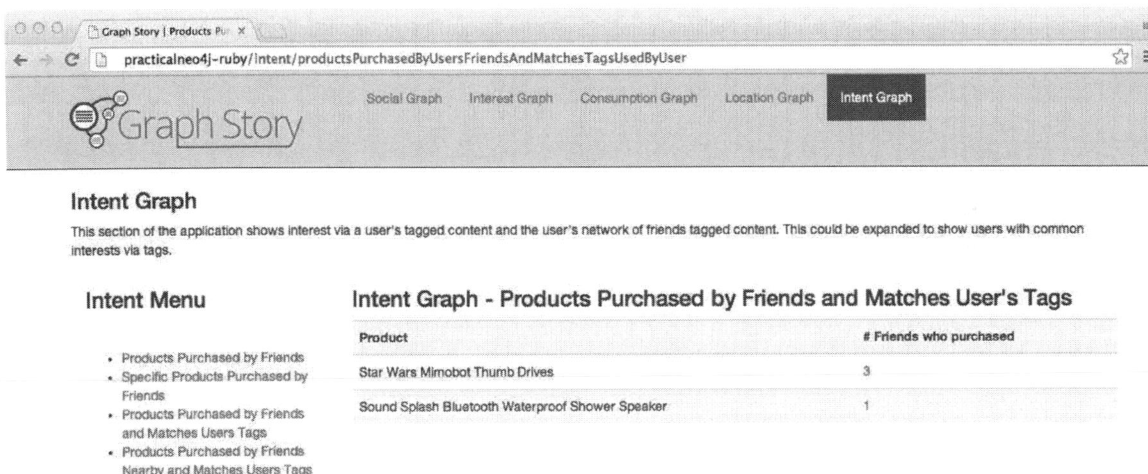

Figure 10-20. *Products Purchased by Friends and Matches User's Tags*

Using `friends_purchase_tag_similarity` in the `Purchase` service class, shown in Listing 10-49, the application provides the userId to the query and uses the `FOLLOWS`, `MADE` and the `CONTAINS` relationships to return products purchases by users being followed. The subsequent `MATCH` statement takes the `USES` and `HAS` directed relationship types to determine the tag relationships the resulting products and the current user have in common.

Listing 10-49. The Method to Find Products Purchased by Friends and Matches Current User's Tags.

```
# products purchased by friends that match the user's tags
def friends_purchase_tag_similarity(neo,username)
    cypher =  " MATCH (u:User { username: {u} } )-[:FOLLOWS]-(f)-[:MADE]->()-[:CONTAINS]->p " +
              " WITH u,p,f " +
              " MATCH u-[:USES]->(t)<-[:HAS]-p " +
              " RETURN p.productId as productId,  p.title as title, " +
              " collect(f.firstname + ' ' + f.lastname) as fullname, " +
              " t.wordPhrase as wordPhrase, " +
```

```
                " count(f) as cfriends " +
                " ORDER BY cfriends desc, p.title "
    results=neo.execute_query(cypher, {:u => username} )
    results["data"].map {|row| Hash[results["columns"].zip(row)] }
end
```

Products Purchased by Friends Nearby and Matches User's Tags

Finding products that match with a specific user's tags and have been purchased by friends who live within a set distance of the user is performed by the friends_purchase_tag_similarity_and_proximity_to_location method, easily the world's longest method name, and is located in the Purchase class (Listing 10-50).

Listing 10-50. The friendsPurchaseTagSimilarityAndProximityToLocation Route

```
# friends that are nearby bought this product. the product should also matches tags of the current
user
get '/intent/friends_purchase_tag_similarity_and_proximity_to_location' do
  @title = "Products Purchased by Friends Nearby and Matches User's Tags"
  @mappedUserLocation=get_user_location(neo,request.cookies[graphstoryUserAuthKey])
  lq = get_lq(@mappedUserLocation[0],"10.00")
  @mappedProductUserPurchaseList=friends_purchase_tag_similarity_and_proximity_to_
  location(neo,request.cookies[graphstoryUserAuthKey],lq)
  mustache :"graphs/intent/index"
end
```

The `friendsPurchaseTagSimilarityAndProximityToLocation` route calls the `friends_purchase_tag_similarity_and_proximity_to_location` method shown in Listing 10-51.

Listing 10-51. The friends_purchase_tag_similarity_and_proximity_to_location Method in Purchase

```
# user's friends' purchases who are nearby and the products match the user's tags
def friends_purchase_tag_similarity_and_proximity_to_location(neo,username,lq)
    cypher =  " START n = node:geom({lq}) " +
              " WITH n " +
              " MATCH (u:User { username: {u} } )-[:USES]->(t)<-[:HAS]-p " +
              " WITH n,u,p,t " +
              " MATCH u-[:FOLLOWS]->(f)-[:HAS]->(n) " +
              " WITH p,f,t " +
              " MATCH f-[:MADE]->()-[:CONTAINS]->(p) " +
              " RETURN p.productId as productId,  p.title as title, " +
              " collect(f.firstname + ' ' + f.lastname) as fullname, " +
              " t.wordPhrase as wordPhrase, " +
              " count(f) as cfriends " +
              " ORDER BY cfriends desc, p.title "
    results=neo.execute_query(cypher, {:u => username, :lq => lq} )
    results["data"].map {|row| Hash[results["columns"].zip(row)] }
end
```

The query begins with a location search within a certain distance, then matches the current user's tags to products. Next, the query matches friends based on the location search. The resulting friends are matched against products that are in the set of user tag matches. The result of the query is shown in Figure 10-21.

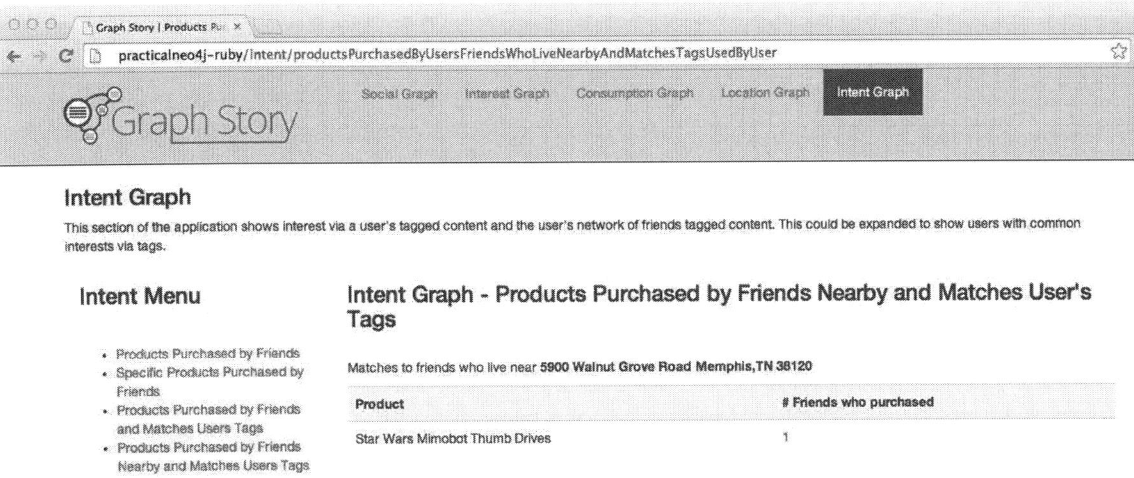

Figure 10-21. *Products Purchased by Friends Nearby and Matches User's Tags*

Summary

This chapter presented the setup for a development environment for Ruby and Neo4j and sample code using the Neography driver. It proceeded to look at sample code for setting up a social network and examining interest within the network. It then looked at the sample code for capturing and viewing consumption—in this case, product views—and the queries for understanding the relationship between consumption and a user's interest. Finally, it looked at using geospatial matching for locations and examples of methods for understanding user intent within the context of user location, social network, and interests.

The next chapter will review using Spring Data and Neo4j, covering the same concepts presented in this chapter but in the context of the Spring Data driver for Neo4j.

CHAPTER 11

Spring Data Neo4j

This chapter will focus on using Spring Data Neo4j as well as creating a working application that integrates the five graph model types covered in Chapter 3. As with other languages that offer drivers for Neo4j, the integration takes place using a Neo4j server instance with Spring Data Neo4j (SDN) API and related libraries (henceforth referred to collectively as *SDN*. The chapter will be divided into the following topics:

- Spring Data Neoj4 Development Environment
- Spring Data Neo4j API
- Developing a Spring Data Neo4j web application

In each chapter that explores a particular language paired with Neo4j, I recommend that you start a free trial on `www.graphstory.com` or have installed a local Neo4j server instance as shown in Chapter 2.

Tip To quickly setup a server instance with the sample data and plugins for this chapter, go to `graphstory.com/practicalneo4j`. You will be provided with your own free trial instance, a knowledge base, and email support from Graph Story.

For this chapter, I assume that you have at minimum a good understanding of HTML, JavaScript, and CSS and of Java web application development with Spring Web MVC. You will also need to understand the basics of configuring the Apache Tomcat servlet container for your preferred operating system. To proceed with the examples in this chapter, you will need to have Tomcat 7 installed and configured.

Do This If you do not have Apache Tomcat installed, please visit `http://tomcat.apache.org/` and download Tomcat version 7. The configuration steps of Tomcat are beyond the scope of this book, but the wiki section on the Apache Tomcat site provides a detailed guide to guide you through more detailed configuration and optimization techniques.

I also assume that you have a basic understanding of the *model-view-controller* (MVC) pattern and some knowledge of Java web frameworks that provide an MVC pattern. Because you are using Spring Data Neo4j, it makes sense to take advantage of Spring Web MVC and other libraries in the Spring family. This chapter is focused on integrating Neo4j into your Spring skill set and does not dive deeply into the best practices of developing with Spring Web MVC or Spring libraries.

Spring Data Neo4j Development Environment

This section covers the basics of configuring a development environment preliminary to building out your first Spring Data Neo4j web application.

■ **Readme** Although each language chapter walks through the process of configuring the development environment based on the particular language, certain steps are covered repeatedly in multiple chapters. While the initial development environment setup in each chapter is somewhat redundant, it allows each language chapter to stand on its own. Bearing this in mind, if you have already configured Eclipse with the necessary plugins while working through another chapter, you can skip ahead to the section "Adding the Project to Eclipse."

IDE

The reasons behind the choice of an IDE vary from developer to developer and are often tied to the choice of programming language. I chose the Eclipse IDE for a number of reasons but mainly because it is freely available and versatile enough to work with most of the programming languages featured in this book.

Although you are welcome to choose a different IDE or other programming tool for building your application, I recommend that you install and use Eclipse to be able to follow the SDN examples and the related examples found throughout the book and online.

■ **Tip** If you do not have Eclipse, please visit `http://www.eclipse.org/downloads/` and download the Indigo package that is titled "Eclipse IDE for Java EE Developers." The Indigo package is also labeled "Version 3.7."

Once you have installed Eclipse, open it and select a workspace for your application. A *workspace* in Eclipse is simply an arbitrary directory on your computer. As shown in Figure 11-1, when you first open Eclipse, the program will ask you to specify which workspace you want to use. Choose the path that works best for you. If you are working through all of the language chapters, you can use the same workspace for each project.

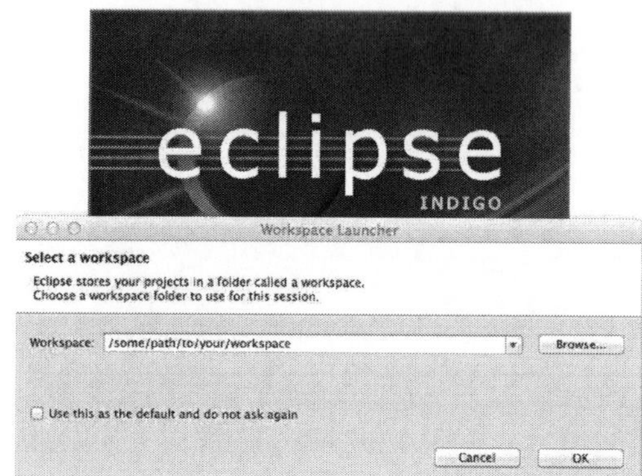

Figure 11-1. *Opening Eclipse and choosing a workspace*

Aptana Plugin

The Eclipse IDE offers a convenient way to add new tools through their plugin platform. The process for adding new plugins to Eclipse is straightforward and usually involves only a few steps to install a new plugin—as you will see in this section.

An Eclipse plugin named Aptana provides support for server-side languages like PHP as well as client-side languages such as CSS and JavaScript. This chapter and the other programming language chapters use the plugin to edit both server- and client-side languages. A benefit of using a plugin such as Aptana is that it can provide code-assist tools and code suggestions based on the type of file you are editing, such as CSS, JS, or HTML. The time saved with code-assist tools is usually significant enough to warrant their use. Again, if you feel comfortable exploring within your preferred IDE or other program, please do so.

To install the Aptana plugin, you need to have Eclipse installed and opened. Then proceed through the following steps:

1. From the Help menu, select "Install New Software" to open the dialog, which will look like the one in Figure 11-2.
2. Paste the URL for the update site, `http://download.aptana.com/studio3/plugin/install`, into the "Work With" text box, and hit the Enter (or Return) key.
3. In the populated table below, check the box next to the name of the plugin, and then click the Next button.
4. Click the Next button to go to the license page.
5. Choose the option to accept the terms of the license agreement, and click the Finish button.
6. You may need to restart Eclipse to continue.

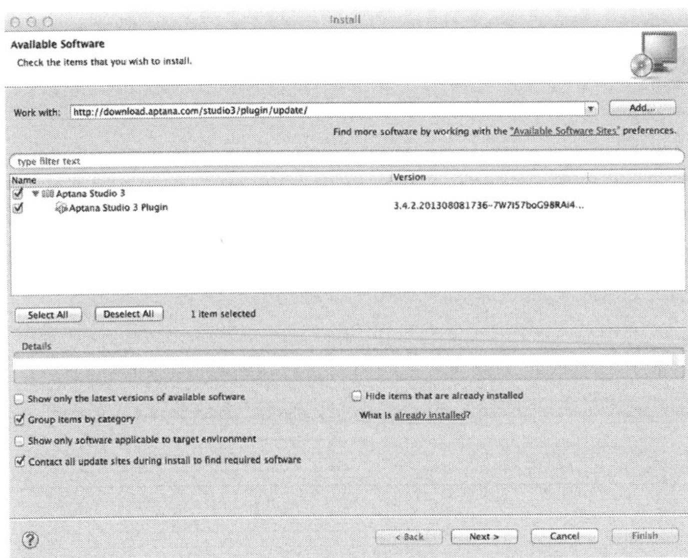

Figure 11-2. *Installing the Aptana plugin*

LogWatcher

When working with applications, it is often helpful to have a way to view application output through server logs. There are a few plugins available for Eclipse for this purpose, such as LogWatcher. With LogWatcher, you can watch output for multiple files inside or outside of Eclipse as well as filters to highlight or skip over specific patterns. At time of writing, the LogWatcher does not have an update URL for quick installation. To manually install LogWatcher, visit `http://graysky.sourceforge.net/` and follow the quick installation steps and setup the view to suit your development environment.

Adding the Project to Eclipse

After installing Eclipse plugin, you will have met the minimum requirements to work with your project in the workspace. To keep the workflow as fluid as possible for each of the language example application, use the project import tool with Eclipse. To import the project into your workspace, follow these steps:

1. Go to `www.graphstory.com/practicalneo4j` and download the archive file for "Practical Neo4j for Spring." Unzip the archive file on to your computer.
2. In Eclipse, select File ➤ Import and type "project" in the "Select an import source" field.
3. Under the "General" heading, select "Existing Projects into Workspace". You should now see a window similar to the one in Figure 11-3.

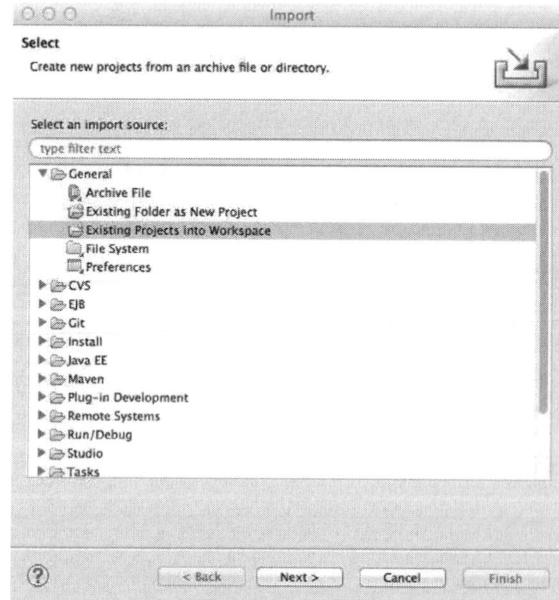

Figure 11-3. *Importing the project into Eclipse*

4. Now that you have selected "Existing Projects into Workspace", click the "Next ➤ " button. The dialogue should now show an option to "Select root directory". Click the "Browse" button and find the root path of the "practicalneo4j-springdata" archive.
5. Next, check the option for "Copy project into workspace" and click the "Finish" button, as shown in Figure 11-4.

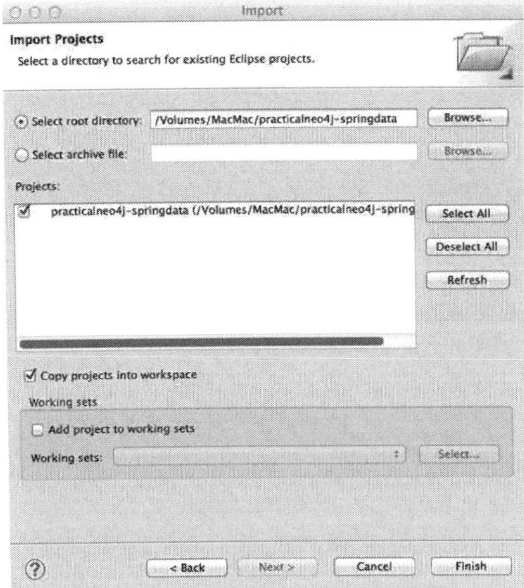

Figure 11-4. *Selecting the project location*

6. Once the project is finished importing into your workspace, you should have a directory structure that looks like the one shown in Figure 11-5.

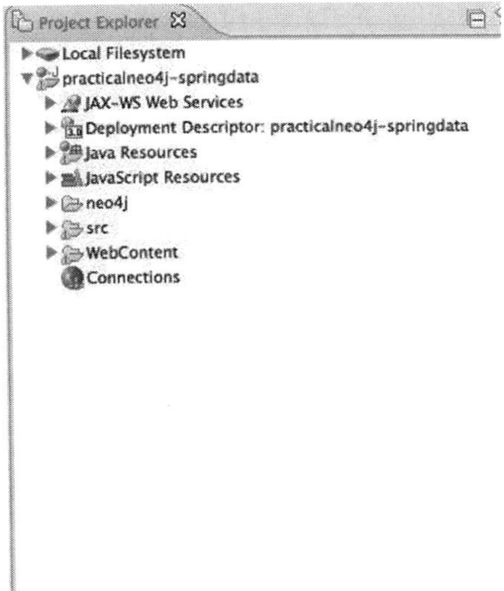

Figure 11-5. *Snapshot of imported project*

Spring Web MVC

The *Spring Web model-view-controller* (SWMVC) is the Spring implementation of a *model-view-controller* (MVC) framework. The aim of the framework is to help you quickly build out powerful web applications and APIs using only what is absolutely necessary to get the job done. The SWMVC library and its dependencies are included with the sample application and should not require any additional configuration beyond what is provided in this chapter to run the application.

As with other MVC frameworks, one of the most important aspects of SWMVC is the handling of routing. The use of annotations allows routing to be placed directly within the controller class. Listing 11-1 shows that the `HomeController` uses the `@RequestMapping` annotation and sets its path as root. The home method is the default method executed in this example. In addition to enabling you to see the mapping settings at a glance, it allows you to configure and view the specific methods and results within the class file.

Listing 11-1. Example of a Controller and Its Annotations

```
@Controller
@RequestMapping("/")
public class HomeController extends GraphStoryController {

        @RequestMapping(method = RequestMethod.GET)
        public String home(Locale locale, Model model) {
                // add page title
                model.addAttribute("title", "Home");
                // return page to display
                return "/mustache/html/home/index.html";
        }
}
```

The sample application will use a file named `applicationContext.xml`, which resides in the /WEB-INF directory. I will cover its configuration in the sample application section of this chapter.

Hosts File

To keep each chapter separated in terms of the webserver or container configuration, add a host name to your local hosts file. The process for modifying the hosts file depends on your preferred operating system. For this chapter, please add an entry to point 127.0.0.1 to practicalneo4j-spring.

Local Apache Tomcat Configuration

To follow the sample application later in this chapter, you need to configure your local Apache Tomcat to use the workspace project in Eclipse as the document root. To do this, you need to modify the server.xml file, which can be found at /TOMCAT-INSTALLATION-DIR/conf/server.xml, as shown in Listing 11-2. The most important changes are adding a HOST and CONTEXT, as shown in the listing.

■ **Note** Using the method of pointing your HOST's appbase to your project within the workspace is one way to "hot reload" code changes. This method is very helpful for most developers because server startup and restart times can be a significant drain on productivity. The process of "deploy and run" has its positive aspects, but the minutes add up quickly.

Listing 11-2. Example of Annotation Configuration

```
<?xml version='1.0' encoding='utf-8'?>
<Server port="8005" shutdown="SHUTDOWN">
<!--
        Listener and GlobalNamingResources excluded for brevity
-->
<Service name="Catalina">
        <Connector port="8090" protocol="HTTP/1.1" connectionTimeout="20000" redirectPort="8443"
                URIEncoding="UTF-8" useBodyEncodingForURI="true" />
        <Connector port="8009" protocol="AJP/1.3" redirectPort="8443" URIEncoding="UTF-8"
                useBodyEncodingForURI="true"/>
        <Engine name="Catalina" defaultHost="localhost">
                <Realm className="org.apache.catalina.realm.LockOutRealm">
                <Realm className="org.apache.catalina.realm.UserDatabaseRealm"
                        resourceName="UserDatabase"/>
        </Realm>
        <Host name="practicalneo4j-java"
                appBase="/path-to-workspace/practicalneo4j-springdata/WebContent"
                unpackWARs="true" autoDeploy="true" >
        <Context path="" docBase=""
        aliases="/resources=/path-to-workspace/practicalneo4j- springdata/WebContent/resources"
        reloadable="true" swallowOutput="true" />
        </Host>
        </Engine>
</Service>
</Server>
```

Apache Tomcat and Apache HTTP

If you already have Apache HTTP installed (or some other webserver) and configured on port 80, you need to make sure that you do one of the following:

- Ensure that Apache HTTP (or other service on port 80) has been stopped. You can then configure and run Tomcat on port 80.
- Enable and configure ProxyPass in your virtual hosts file, as shown in Listing 11-3.
- Use the default Apache Tomcat port of 8080.

If you use Apache HTTP with many other projects and do not want spend time starting and stopping Apache HTTP, I recommend the second option, which is shown in Listing 11-3.

Listing 11-3. Minimum Configuration for `httpd-vhosts.conf`

```
<VirtualHost *:80>
        ServerName practicalneo4j-java
        ProxyPreserveHost On
        ProxyPass        / http://practicalneo4j-spring:8080/
        ProxyPassReverse / http://practicalneo4j-spring:8080/
</VirtualHost>
```

Spring Data Neo4j

This section covers basic operations and usage of *Spring Data Neo4j* (SDN) with the goal of reviewing the specific code examples before implementing it within an application. The next section will walk you through a sample application with specific graph goals and models.

As for the other language drivers and libraries available for Neo4j, one goal of SDN is to provide a degree of abstraction over the Neo4j REST API. In addition, the SDN provides many additional utility classes and methods that might otherwise be required to be coded at some other stage in the development of your application.

■ **Note** Spring Data Neo4j is maintained by the undeniably awesome and helpful Michael Hunger and supported by a number of great Spring Data Neo4j developers. If you would like to get involved with SDN, go to `https://github.com/spring-projects/spring-data-neo4j`.

Each of the following brief sections covers concepts that tie either directly or indirectly to features and functionality found within the Neo4j Server and REST API. If you choose to go through each language chapter, notice how each library covers those features and functionality in similar ways but takes advantage of the language-specific capabilities to ensure that the API is flexible and performant.

■ **Important** The code examples shown in this section are deliberately brief, being provided to familiarize you with basic operations. For example, many of the examples make use of the Neo4jOperations class to perform operations. Notwithstanding, Spring Data Neo4j is an extremely rich library and provides additional classes and methods to handle basic operations. To give you a sense of their scope, I expand on a selection of capabilities in the sample application.

Managing Nodes and Relationships

Chapters 1 and 2 covered the elements of a graph database, which includes the most basic of graph concepts: the node. Managing nodes and their properties and relationships will probably account for the bulk of your application's graph-related code.

In SDN, there are a few ways to manage creation and retrieval of nodes and relationships. This section covers some basic methods, and the sample application provides some additional ways.

Creating a Node

The maintenance of nodes is set in motion with the creation process, as shown in Listing 11-4. Creating a node begins with setting up a connection to the database. As is the case with most Spring projects that use a database, the configuration of the database properties can be set in a configuration file via XML. The sample application uses a file named `applicationContext.xml`, which resides in the /WEB-INF directory. The next section of this chapter will cover the configuration.

In addition, we will add the @Autowired annotation on the Neo4jOperations class. This instantiates the Neo4jOperations bean for use inside each method in the class. The sample SDN project extends a parent Service class in order to reuse the Neo4jOperations bean. Next, the properties are put into a Map, and then the Node can be saved to the database using the createNode method and adding its Map parameter.

Listing 11-4. Creating a Node

```
import java.util.HashMap;
import java.util.Map;

import org.neo4j.graphdb.Node;
import org.springframework.beans.factory.annotation.Autowired;
import org.springframework.data.neo4j.template.Neo4jOperations;

// class
public class SDNServiceClass {

        @Autowired
        public Neo4jOperations neo4jTemplate;

        public Node createNode(){
                // create map
                Map props=new HashMap<>();
                props.put("id", 100);
                props.put("name","firstNode");

                Node node = neo4jTemplate.createNode(props);

                return node;
        }
}
```

Retrieving and Updating a Node

Once nodes have been added to the database, you need a way to retrieve and modify them. Listing 11-5 shows one way to find a node by its node id and update it. As mentioned earlier, there are a few ways to manage the retrieval of a node and modify its properties.

Listing 11-5. Retrieving and Updating a Node

```
public class SDNServiceClass {

        @Autowired
        public Neo4jOperations neo4jTemplate;

        public void updateNode(){
                // get the node
                Node node = neo4jTemplate.getNode(10);

                // update node properties
                node.setProperty("firstname","Greg");
                node.setProperty("lastname","Jordan");

                neo4jTemplate.save(node);
        }
}
```

Removing a Node

Once a node's graph id has been set and saved into the database, it becomes eligible to be removed when necessary. To remove a node, set a variable as a node object instance and then call the delete method for the node (Listing 11-6).

Listing 11-6. Deleting a Node

```
public class SDNServiceClass {

        @Autowired
        public Neo4jOperations neo4jTemplate;

        public void deleteNode(){
                // get the node
                Node node = neo4jTemplate.getNode(10);

                // delete node
                neo4jTemplate.delete(node);
        }
}
```

■ **Note** You cannot delete any node that is currently set as the start point or end point of any relationship. You must remove the relationship before you can delete the node.

Creating a Relationship

SDN offers a few methods to create relationships, one using the `createRelationshipBetween` method and another using the `getOrCreateRelationship` method. The example in Listing 11-7 sets up the relationship using the `createRelationshipBetween` method.

Listing 11-7. Relating Two Nodes

```
public class SDNServiceClass {

        @Autowired
        public Neo4jOperations neo4jTemplate;

        public void relateNodes(){
                // retrieve the node by its node id value, in this case 10
                Node greg = neo4jTemplate.getNode(10);

                // retrieve the node by its node id value, in this case 1
                Node jeremy = neo4jTemplate.getNode(1);

                // populate & save the relationship (greg follows jeremy)
                neo4jTemplate.createRelationshipBetween(greg, jeremy, "FOLLOWS", null);
        }
}
```

■ **Note** Both the start and end nodes of a relationship must already be established within the database before the relationship can be saved.

Retrieving Relationships

Once a relationship has been created between one or more nodes, the relationship can be retrieved based on the nodes relating to it. If no relationship exists, the relationship will be set to null (Listing 11-8).

Listing 11-8. Retrieving Relationships

```
public class SDNServiceClass {

        @Autowired
        public Neo4jOperations neo4jTemplate;

        public void retrieveRelationship(){
                // retrieve the node by its node id value, in this case 10
                Node greg = neo4jTemplate.getNode(10);

                // retrieve the node by its node id value, in this case 1
                Node jeremy = neo4jTemplate.getNode(1);

                // retrieve the relationship (greg follows jeremy)
                Relationship rel = neo4jTemplate.getRelationshipBetween(greg,jeremy,"FOLLOWS");

        }
}
```

Deleting a Relationship

Once a relationship's graph id has been set and saved into the database, it becomes eligible to be removed when necessary. To remove a relationship, set it as a relationship object instance and then call the delete method for the relationship (Listing 11-9).

Listing 11-9. Deleting a Relationship

```
public class SDNServiceClass {

        @Autowired
        public Neo4jOperations neo4jTemplate;

        public void deleteRelationship(){

                // retrieve the Relationship by its Relationship id value, in this case 20
                Relationship relationship = neo4jTemplate.getRelationship(20);
```

```
                neo4jTemplate.delete(relationship);

                //alternatively you could delete the relationship between two nodes

                // retrieve the node by its node id value, in this case 10
                Node greg = neo4jTemplate.getNode(10);

                // retrieve the node by its node id value, in this case 1
                Node jeremy = neo4jTemplate.getNode(1);

                neo4jTemplate.deleteRelationshipBetween(greg, jeremy, "FOLLOWS");

        }
}
```

Using Labels

Labels function as specific meta-descriptions that can be applied to nodes. Labels were introduced in Neo4j 2.0 in order to help in querying and can also function as a way to quickly create a subgraph.

Adding a Label to Nodes

In SDN, you can add one more labels to a node using `LabelBasedStrategyCypherHelper`. As shown in Listing 11-10, the `setLabelsOnNode` function takes one or more labels as argument. You can return each of the labels on a node by calling its `getLabels` function. The value used for the label should be any nonempty string or numeric value.

Listing 11-10. Adding Labels to a Node

```
public class SDNServiceClass {

        @Autowired
        public Neo4jOperations neo4jTemplate;

        public void addLabels(){

                // retrieve the node by its node id value, in this case 10
                Node greg = neo4jTemplate.getNode(10);

                // array of labels
                String[] labelArray = {"Admin","Developer"};

                //setup CypherQueryEngine
                CypherQueryEngine cqe = neo4jTemplate.getGraphDatabase().queryEngine();

                // instantiate LabelBasedStrategyCypherHelper
                LabelBasedStrategyCypherHelper lbsch = new LabelBasedStrategyCypherHelper(cqe);

                // set the labels
                lbsch.setLabelsOnNode(greg.getId(),new ArrayList<String>(Arrays.
                asList(labelArray)));

        }
}
```

■ **Caution** A label will not exist on the database server until it has been added to at least one node.

Removing a Label

Removing a label uses similar syntax as adding a label to a node. After the given label has been removed from the node (Listing 11-11), the return value is a list of labels still on the node.

Listing 11-11. Removing a Label from a Node

```
public class SDNServiceClass {

        @Autowired
        public Neo4jOperations neo4jTemplate;

        public void removeLabel(){

                // retrieve the node by its node id value, in this case 10
                Node greg = neo4jTemplate.getNode(10);

                greg.removeLabel(DynamicLabel.label("Admin"));

        }
}
```

Querying with a Label

To get nodes that use a specific label, use the method called `getNodesWithLabel`. This method's returns value is an iterable (Listing 11-12).

Listing 11-12. Querying with a Label

```
public class SDNServiceClass {

        @Autowired
        public Neo4jOperations neo4jTemplate;

        public Iterable<Node> getNodesWithLabel(){

                CypherQueryEngine cqe = neo4jTemplate.getGraphDatabase().queryEngine();

                LabelBasedStrategyCypherHelper lbsch = new LabelBasedStrategyCypherHelper(cqe);

                Iterable<Node> nodes = lbsch.getNodesWithLabel("Developer");

                return nodes;
        }
}
```

Developing a Spring Data Neo4j Application

This section covers a few more items for configuring a development environment, preliminary to walking through the Spring Data Neo4j application.

Preparing the Graph

To spend more time highlighting code examples for each of the more common graph models, we will use a preloaded instance of Neo4j including necessary plugins, such as the spatial plugin.

■ **Tip** To quickly set up a server instance with the sample data and plugins for this chapter, go to `graphstory.com/practicalneo4j`. You will be provided with your own free trial instance, a knowledge base, and email support from Graph Story. Alternatively, you may run a local Neo4j database instance with the sample data by going to `graphstory.com/practicalneo4j`, downloading the zip file containing the sample database and plugins, and adding them to your local instance.

Using the Sample Application

If you have already downloaded the sample application from `www.graphstory.com/practicalneo4j` for Spring Data Neo4j and configured it with your local application environment, you can skip ahead to the "Spring Application Configuration" section.

Otherwise, you will need to go back to the "Spring Data Neo4j Development Environment" section and set up your local environment in order to follow the examples in the sample application.

In Eclipse (or the IDE you are using), open the file `package.properties`, which is located in the `com.practicalneo4j.graphstory.service`, and edit the GraphStory connection string information. If you are using a free account from `graphstory.com`, change the username, password, and URL in Listing 11-13 with the one provided in your graph console on `graphstory.com`.

Listing 11-13. Database Connection Settings

```
rootNeo4jServiceUrl=https://username:password@theURL:7473
```

If you have installed a local Neo4j server instance, you can modify the configuration to use the local address and port that you specified during the installation, as in the example shown in Listing 11-14.

Listing 11-14. Database Connection Settings for Local Environment

```
rootNeo4jServiceUrl=http://localhost:7474
```

Once the environment is properly configured and started, you can go the local address `http://practicalneo4j-spring` and you should see a page like the one shown in Figure 11-6.

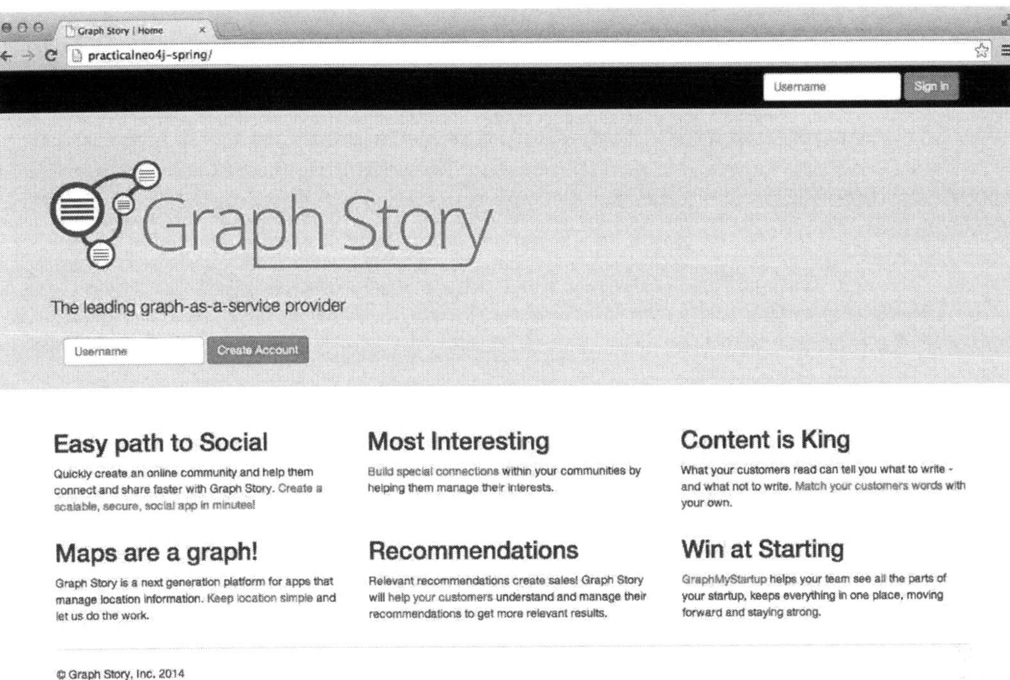

Figure 11-6. *The Spring Data Neo4j sample application home page*

Spring Application Configuration

The Spring application configuration can be completed in one of two ways: (1) using a XML configuration or (2) by using a Java-based configuration. In this section, I will review the XML configuration used for the sample application and briefly cover the important settings.

First, each XML configuration will contain schema references required for the application and will depend upon your application. The references have been removed in Listing 11-15, but they can be reviewed by opening the application-context.xml file located in WebContent/WEB-INF directory of your project.

Listing 11-15. The `applicationContext.xml` Configuration File

```
<?xml version="1.0" encoding="UTF-8"?>

...bean references omitted for brevity...

        <context:annotation-config/>
        <context:spring-configured/>
        <context:component-scan base-package="com.practicalneo4j.graphstory.controller"/>
        <context:component-scan base-package="com.practicalneo4j.graphstory.service"/>

        <mvc:annotation-driven/>

        <!-- static web resources -->
        <mvc:resources mapping="/resources/**" location="/resources/" />
```

```
        <!-- used to check login before accessing certain pages -->
        <mvc:interceptors>
                <mvc:interceptor>
                        <mvc:mapping path="/social/**" />
                        <mvc:mapping path="/user/**" />
                        <mvc:mapping path="/interest/**" />
                        <mvc:mapping path="/consumption/**" />
                        <mvc:mapping path="/location/**" />
                        <mvc:mapping path="/intent/**" />
                        <bean class="com.practicalneo4j.graphstory.interceptor.SecurityInterceptor" />
                </mvc:interceptor>
        </mvc:interceptors>

        <!-- get properties for use in the configuration -->
        <bean id="projectPropertyConfigurer" class="org.springframework.beans.factory.config.
        PropertyPlaceholderConfigurer">
                <property name="location">
                <value>classpath:/com/practicalneo4j/graphstory/service/package.properties</value>
                </property>
        </bean>

        <!-- mustache.java -->
        <bean id="viewResolver" class="com.practicalneo4j.graphstory.util.NMustacheViewResolver">
            <property name="cache" value="false" />
            <property name="templateFactory">
                        <bean class="com.practicalneo4j.graphstory.util.NMustacheJTemplateFactory" />
            </property>
        </bean>

        <!-- DB Connection to Neo4j server -->
        <bean id="graphDatabaseService" class="org.springframework.data.neo4j.rest.
        SpringRestGraphDatabase" scope="singleton">
                <constructor-arg value="${rootNeo4jServiceUrl}/db/data"  index="0"/>
                <constructor-arg value="${username}"  index="1"/>
                <constructor-arg value="${password}"  index="2"/>

        <!-- domain entity classes -->
        <neo4j:config graphDatabaseService="graphDatabaseService" base-package="com.practicalneo4j.
        graphstory.domain"/>

        <!-- Package repositories -->
        <neo4j:repositories base-package="com.practicalneo4j.graphstory.repository" />

        <tx:annotation-driven mode="proxy"/>
</beans>
```

Next, the configuration applies context and mvc specific settings, such as the package location of the application's controllers. The MCV bean also sets the location for static assets, such as CSS, JavaScript, and images that are used within the application. The mvc:interceptors reference can be used before each request to run specific code prior to completing the request, such as check if a user is logged in before accessing certain pages in certain paths. Following the interceptor, the projectPropertyConfigurer supplies the location for application properties, and the viewResolver bean handles the integration with the Mustache templating language.

Finally, the `graphDatabaseService` bean provides the location and authentication information for the graph database, and the `neo4j:config` and `neo4j:repositories` settings set the entity package location and the package location of repository interfaces, respectively.

Controller and Service Layers

All of the controllers in the sample application extend a parent controller called `GraphStoryController`. The `GraphStoryController` provides access to the `GraphStory` bean, the `GraphStoryInterface` service, and a method called `currentuser`, which allows for quick access to the currently logged-in user.

The `GraphStory` bean encapsulates the domain objects for the sample application and is primarily used for convenience. This object will allow domain objects to be sent to the service layer and returned—in some cases—with additional objects and properties.

The `GraphStoryInterface` service provides access to each of the individual service interfaces that support persistence and other service-level operations on each of the domain objects. For example, if an exception is raised in the service layer, such as a when attempting to create a User that matches an existing User's username, then the `GraphStory` object can be returned with message information, such as an error message, which can then be used to determine the next part of the application flow as well as return messages to the view.

■ **Head's-Up** Spring MVC and the front-end code, such as Mustache, help run the sample application, but extended coverage of those concepts will be limited to the Social Graph section. In the Social Graph section, I will focus on the non-obvious but important aspects of those concepts. As you go through the rest of the application, controllers as well as the front-end code will use similar syntax—so they will be referenced but not listed in the chapter, because repetitive coverage of that syntax would distract from the discrete, specific Spring Data Neo4j examples.

Social Graph Model

This section explores the social graph model and a few of the operations that typically accompany it. In particular, this section looks at the following:

- The User Entity
- Sign-up and Login
- Updating a user
- Creating a relationship type through a user by following other users
- Managing user content, such as displaying, adding, updating, and removing status updates

---

■ **Note** The sample graph database used for these examples is loaded with data so that you can immediately begin working with representative data in each of the graph models. In the case of the social graph—and for other graph models, as well—you will login with the user **ajordan**. Going forward, please login with **ajordan** to see each of the working examples.

User Node Entity

We will begin the social graph model by reviewing the code for creating a `User` node in the graph via the sign-up process. Later in this section, I will briefly review the code to validate a user upon attempting to login. In each case, the code contains brief validation routines to demonstrate the basics of running checks against data. In the case of sign-up, the code will check to see if a `User` already exists with the same username.

Node Entities

To begin, open the `User` class located in the `com.practicalneo4j.graphstory.domain` package. First, you should notice that the `User` class—as with each Node Entity—is annotated with `@NodeEntity`, as shown in Listing 11-29. You can also use the `@TypeAlias` to specify the alias name, which could be helpful if or when refactoring occurs. Each of the entities should have a `@GraphId` annotation to set the property that will contain the node's ID.

Listing 11-16. The User Entity

```
@NodeEntity
@TypeAlias("User")
public class User {

        @GraphId
        private Long nodeId;

        @Indexed
        private String userId;

        @Indexed
        private String username;

        private String firstname;

        private String lastname;

        @RelatedTo(type = GraphStoryConstants.MADE, direction = Direction.OUTGOING,
        elementClass = Purchase.class)
        private Purchase purchase;

        @RelatedTo(type = GraphStoryConstants.USES, direction = Direction.OUTGOING,
        elementClass = Tag.class)
        private Set<Tag> tags;

        @RelatedTo(type = GraphStoryConstants.HAS, direction = Direction.OUTGOING,
        elementClass = Location.class)
        private Set<Location> locations;

        // getters and setters
}
```

Next, properties that require index lookups should use the `@Indexed` annotation. In most cases, simply setting the annotation will suffice in order to do future lookups. However—as noted earlier in this chapter—it is also possible to use the annotation property "unique=true" with `@Indexed` to help ensure no duplicates can be added to the index. Node Entities in SDN are only allowed one unique index regardless of the type of index being used. In the case of a unique index, the value is checked at creation time and re-uses the existing entity if the key-value pair already exists.

After the Node properties are created, the User class has a number of encapsulated domain objects that have the @RelatedTo annotation. The @RelatedTo has a type, such as MADE, and a direction, such as OUTGOING or INCOMING, as well as specifying the class on the other side of the relationship.

As suggested in the chapter on modeling, one way to think about directed relationships is by first constructing a Cypher snippet or a short phrase to consider direction, such as "user-[:made]->purchase" or "a user made a purchase". In some cases, the relationship will be bidirectional, such as FOLLOWS. Although it is possible to analyze the relationship without direction in this case, the direction serves as an expression of the relationship.

Spring Data Repositories

For each object type in the domain, the sample application has at least one corresponding Spring Data repository interface. One of the intentions of the Spring Data repositories is to save you from coding methods for the most commonly used data operations.

For the sample application, all of the repository interfaces are located in the com.practicalneo4j.graphstory.repository package and extend the GraphRepository interface. By extending the GraphRepository interface, the repositories will have access to a number of commonly used methods, such as a save method. In addition, repositories can include (1) your own methods via a @Query annotation, which takes a Cypher query as a property, and (2) the very handy and flexible derived finder methods.

Each of the derived methods begins with prefix, like findBy in the case of the finder methods, and then is followed by the necessary properties, conjunctions, and operators to create a Cypher query. For example, the findByUsername method, shown in Listing 11-17, will use the @Indexed field username to form a Cypher query as start user=node:User(username = {0}) return user.

In the case of the additional methods in UserRepository, you will use Cypher queries with parameters supplied by the method. For example, the searchByUsername method in Listing 11-30 looks for users to follow based on a search of the User entities. It performs a MATCH on the currentusername parameter, which is set via @Param("c").

The query also performs a wild card search using WHERE on the username, which is set via @Param("u"). This part of the WHERE also ignores the user found in the MATCH currentusername part of the query. Finally, the query also ignores all of the users the currentusername is *already* following by using the Boolean operator NOT and the directional relationship of FOLLOWS.

Listing 11-17. The UserRepository Interface

```
public interface UserRepository extends GraphRepository<User> {

User findByUsername(String username);

@Query(

        // match users and user by username via param 'c'
        // where n.username WILDCARD on param 'u'
        // but is not the current user
        // and don't return users already being followed
        // return list of users
        " MATCH (n:User), (user { username:{c}}) " +
        " WHERE (n.username =~ {u} AND n <> user) " +
        " AND (NOT (user)-[:FOLLOWS]->(n)) " +
        " RETURN n")
        List<User> searchByUsername(@Param("c") String currentusername,
                @Param("u") String username);
```

```
    @Query("MATCH (user { username:{u}})-[:FOLLOWS]->(users) " +
            " RETURN users " +
            " ORDER BY users.username")
    LinkedList<User> following(@Param("u") String username);

}
```

Sign-Up

The HTML required for the user sign-up form is shown in Listing 11-18 and can be found in the `{PROJECTROOT}/WebContent/mustache/html/home/index.html` file. The important item to note in the HTML form is that the **bean name** then **property** are used to specify what is passed to controller and, subsequently, to the service layer for saving to the database.

Listing 11-18. Sign-Up HTML Form

```
<form class="navbar-form navbar-left" action="/signup/add" role="form"  id="createaccountform"
method="post">
<div class="form-group">
  <input type="text" placeholder="Username" name="user.username" class="form-control">
</div>
<button type="submit" class="btn btn-success">Create Account</button>   
</form>
```

■ **Note** The sample application creates a user without a password, but I am certainly not suggesting or advocating this approach for a production application. Excluding the password property was done in order to create a simple sign-up and login that helps keep the focus on the more salient aspects of SDN.

Sign-Up Controller

In the `SignupController` class, located in the `com.practicalneo4j.graphstory.controller`, you will use a method called *adduser* to control the flow of the sign-up process, shown in Listing 11-19. The controller instantiates a `ModelAndView` object, which returns properties to the view layer. Next, the `GraphStoryInterface` accesses the save method of the `UserInterface` and returns a `GraphStory` object.

If no errors are returned during the save attempt, the request is redirected to a message view to thank the user for signing up. Otherwise, the `ModelAndView` specifies the HTML page to return and the error messages that need to be displayed.

Listing 11-19. Sign-Up Controller

```
@RequestMapping(value = "/signup/add", method = RequestMethod.POST)
public ModelAndView addUser(@ModelAttribute("graphStory") GraphStory graphStory) {

        ModelAndView modelAndView;

        try {
                graphStory = graphStoryInterface.getUserInterface().save(graphStory);
```

```
            // no errors occurred, so send to the thank you page
            if (CollectionUtils.isEmpty(graphStory.getErrorMsgs())) {

                    modelAndView = new ModelAndView("redirect:/msg");
                    modelAndView.addObject("msg", "Thank you, " + graphStory.getUser().
                    getUsername());

            // send the errors that occurred to the view
            } else {
                    modelAndView = new ModelAndView("/mustache/html/home/index.html");
                    modelAndView.addObject("title", "Home");
                    modelAndView.addObject(graphStory.getErrorMsgs());
            }

            return modelAndView;

        }
        catch (Exception e) {
                log.error(e);
                return null;
        }
}
```

Adding the User

Each domain object has a corresponding interface and implementation to manage the object. As a part of the architecture, each interface is part of the main service layer created with the `GraphStoryImpl` class, which implements the `GraphStoryInterface`. In addition, each of the implementation classes extends a class called `GraphStoryService` in order to have access to commonly used beans and methods, such as the Spring Data repositories and the `Neo4jOperations` class.

In this case, the `UserImpl` class implements the methods found in `UserInterface`, both of which are located in the `com.practicalneo4j.graphstory.service.main` package. An abbreviated version of `UserInterface` is shown in Listing 11-20.

Listing 11-20. UserInterface

```
public interface UserInterface {
        ...
        public GraphStory save(GraphStory graphStory) throws Exception;
        ...
}
```

■ **Note** This chapter does not dive into the details of the `GraphStoryService` and `GraphStoryImpl classes`, but both of these service classes will be reused throughout the application. The `GraphStoryImpl` class is used for convenience in order to have access to each specific interface by using a single service interface.

In the UserImpl class, you will notice several implemented methods to manage the User object. To add the User object to the database, use the save method, which will first check to see if a username has already been added to the database. If no user exists, then the user is saved to the database.

The UserImpl class, shown in Listing 11-21, will also use the @Service annotation to set the interface name as well as provide its scope through the @Scope annotation. To save the user to the database, the application calls the save method from UserRepository.

Listing 11-21. UserImpl

```
@Service("userInterface")
@Scope("prototype")
public class UserImpl extends GraphStoryService implements UserInterface {

        static Logger log = Logger.getLogger(UserImpl.class);

        private User tempUser;

        public GraphStory save(GraphStory graphStory) throws Exception {

                // trim and lower case the username
                graphStory.getUser().setUsername(graphStory.getUser().getUsername()
                .toLowerCase().trim());

                // check to see if the username has already been taken
                if (!userExists(graphStory.getUser())) {
                        graphStory.setUser(userRepository.save(graphStory.getUser()));
                } else {
                        addErrorMsg(graphStory, "The username you entered already exists.");
                }

                return graphStory;

        }

        private boolean userExists(User user) throws Exception {

                boolean userFound = false;

                if (getByUserName(user.getUsername()) != null) {
                        userFound = true;
                }

                return userFound;
        }

        public User getByUserName(String username) throws Exception {

                User u = userRepository.findByUsername(username);
                return u;
        }
}
```

Login

This section reviews the login process for the sample application. To execute the login process, use the LoginController and User, UserInterface, and UserImpl classes.

Login Form

The HTML required for the user login form is shown in Listing 11-22 and can be found in the {PROJECTROOT}/WebContent/mustache/html/global/base-home.html file. Again, the important item to note in the form is that the **bean name** and **property** are used to specify what is passed to controller and, subsequently, to the service layer for querying the database.

Listing 11-22. The login Form

```
<form class="navbar-form navbar-right" action="/login" role="form" method="post">
        <div class="form-group">
        <input type="text" placeholder="Username" name="user.username" class="form-control">
        </div>
        <button type="submit" class="btn btn-success">Sign in</button>
</form>
```

Login Controller

In the LoginController class, you will use a method called *login* to control the flow of the login process, as shown in Listing 11-23. The controller instantiates a ModelAndView object and returns properties to the view layer. Next, the GraphStoryInterface accesses the login method of the UserInterface and returns a GraphStory object.

If no errors are returned during the login attempt, a cookie is added to the response and the request is redirected to the social home page, as shown in Figure 11-7. Otherwise, the ModelAndView specifies the HTML page to return and the error messages that need to be displayed.

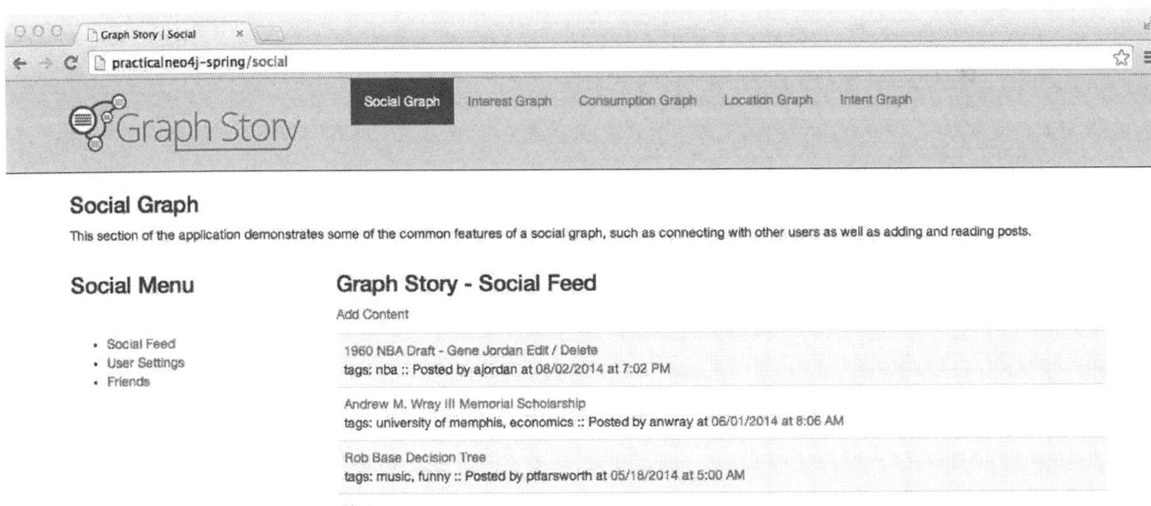

Figure 11-7. *The Social Graph home page*

Listing 11-23. login Controller

```
@RequestMapping(value = "/login", method = RequestMethod.POST)
public ModelAndView addUser(@ModelAttribute("graphStory") GraphStory graphStory, HttpServletResponse
response) {

        ModelAndView modelAndView;

        try {
                graphStory = graphStoryInterface.getUserInterface().login(graphStory);

                // no errors, user was found
                if (CollectionUtils.isEmpty(graphStory.getErrorMsgs())) {

                        response.addCookie(graphStoryInterface.getHelperInterface().
                        addCookie(GraphStoryConstants.graphstoryUserAuthKey, graphStory.getUser().
                        getUsername()));

                        modelAndView = new ModelAndView("redirect:/social");

                // user was not found
                } else {

                        modelAndView = new ModelAndView("/mustache/html/home/message.html");
                        modelAndView.addObject("title", "Tell Yours");
                        modelAndView.addObject(graphStory.getErrorMsgs());
                }

                return modelAndView;
        }
        catch (Exception e) {
                log.error(e);
                return null;
        }

}
```

Login Service

To check to see if the user attempting to log in is a valid user, the application uses the login method in UserImpl, which implements in UserInterface. An abbreviated version of UserInterface is shown in Listing 11-24.

Listing 11-24. UserInterface with the login Method

```
public interface UserInterface {
        ...

        public GraphStory login(GraphStory graphStory) throws Exception;

        ...
}
```

As shown in the UserImpl code in Listing 11-25, the result of the findByUsername method from the UserRepository is assigned to the tempUser variable. If the result is not null, the result is set on the User object of the GraphStory service bean. Otherwise, a message is added to the GraphStory bean through the inherited addErrorMsg method and returned to the controller along with the original User object.

Listing 11-25. UserImpl

```
public class UserImpl extends GraphStoryService implements UserInterface {

        ...
        private User tempUser;

        @Override
        public GraphStory login(GraphStory graphStory) throws Exception {
                tempUser = userRepository.findByUsername(graphStory.getUser().getUsername());

                // user was found
                if (tempUser != null) {
                        graphStory.setUser(tempUser);
                }

                // user was not found
                else {
                        addErrorMsg(graphStory, "The username you entered does not exist.");
                }

                return graphStory;
        }
         ...
}
```

Updating a User

To access the page for updating a user, click on the "User Settings" link in the social graph section, as show in Figure 11-8. In this example, you will simply add or update the first and last name of the user using an AJAX request via PUT. If no errors were return during the login attempt, a cookie is added to the response and the request is redirected to the social home page, as shown in Figure 11-8. Otherwise, the ModelAndView specifies the HTML page to return and the error messages that need to be displayed.

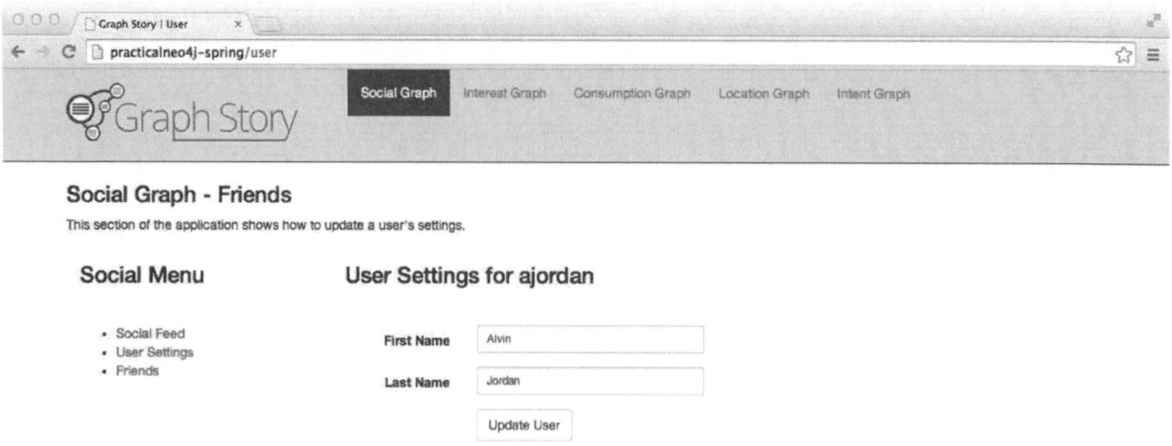

Figure 11-8. *The User Settings page*

User Update Form

The user update form in {PROJECTROOT}/WebContent/mustache/html/graphs/social/user.html is similar in structure to the other forms presented in the "Sign Up" and "Login" sections. One difference is that you have added the value property to the input element as well as the variables for displaying the respective stored values. If none exist, the form fields will be empty.

Listing 11-26. User Update Form

```
<form class="form-horizontal" id="userform">
        <div class="form-group">
            <label for="firstname" class="col-sm-2 control-label">First Name</label>
            <div class="col-sm-10">
                <input type="text" class="form-control input-sm" id="firstname"
                name="user.firstname"
                value="{{user.firstname}}" />
            </div>
        </div>
        <div class="form-group">
                <label for="lastname" class="col-sm-2 control-label">Last Name</label>
                <div class="col-sm-10">
                       <input type="text" class="form-control input-sm" id="lastname"
                       name="user.lastname" value="{{user.lastname}}" />
                </div>
        </div>
        <div class="form-group">
                <div class="col-sm-offset-2 col-sm-10">
                <button type="submit" id="updateUser" class="btn btn-default">Update User</button>
                </div>
         </div>
</form>
```

User Controller

The UserController class contains a method called *edit*, which takes several arguments including a User object. The User object is converted from a JSON string and returns a User object. The response could be used to update the form elements, but the values are already set within the form. In this case, the application uses the JSON response to let the user know whether the update succeeded or not.

Listing 11-27. UserController Edit Method

```
@RequestMapping(value = "/user/edit", method = RequestMethod.PUT)
public @ResponseBody User edit(Model model, @ModelAttribute("currentuser") User currentuser,
@RequestBody User jsonString) {

        try {

                if (jsonString != null) {
                        currentuser.setFirstname(jsonString.getFirstname());
                        currentuser.setLastname(jsonString.getLastname());
                        currentuser = graphStoryInterface.getUserInterface().update(currentuser);
                }
        }
        catch (Exception e) {
                log.error(e);
        }

        return currentuser;
}
```

User Update Method

To complete the update, the UserController edit method calls the update method in UserImpl. Because the object being passed into the update method simply modified the first and last name of the existing entity, the save method can be used to update the properties in the graph.

Listing 11-28. The update Method in UserImpl

```
// UserImpl...

@Override
public User update(User user) throws Exception {
        user = userRepository.save(user);
        return user;
}
```

■ **Note** Recall that each of the controllers and the front-end code make use of similar syntax. For this reason, subsequent sections will not feature the controller and front-end code so as to focus on the Spring Data Neo4j aspects of the application. The controllers and front-end code will be referenced but not listed directly in the sections.

Connecting Users

A common feature in social media applications is to allow users to connect to each other through an explicit relationship. The sample application uses the relationship type called `FOLLOWS`. By going to the "Friends" page within the social graph section, you can see the list of the users the current user is following, search for new friends to follow, add them, and remove friends the current user is following. The `UserController` contains each of the methods to control the flow for these features, including `friends`, `searchbyusername`, `follow` and `unfollow`.

To display the list of the users the current user is following, the `friends` method in the `UserController` calls the `following` method in `UserImpl`. The `following` method in `UserImpl`, shown in the first part of Listing 11-29, calls the `following` method in the `UserRepository`, shown the second part of Listing 11-29. Each takes an argument of username, which results in a `LinkedList` of users. If the list contains users, it will be displayed in the right-hand part of the page, as shown in Figure 11-9. The display code for showing the list of users can be found in `{PROJECTROOT}/WebContent/mustache/html/graphs/social/friends.html.`

Listing 11-29. The Respective Following Methods for `UserImpl` and `UserRepository`

```
// UserImpl

public List<User> following(String username) throws Exception {

        LinkedList<User> following = userRepository.following(username);

        return following;
}

// UserRepository

@Query("MATCH (user { username:{u}})-[:FOLLOWS]->(users) RETURN users " +
        " ORDER BY users.username")
LinkedList<User> following(@Param("u") String username);
```

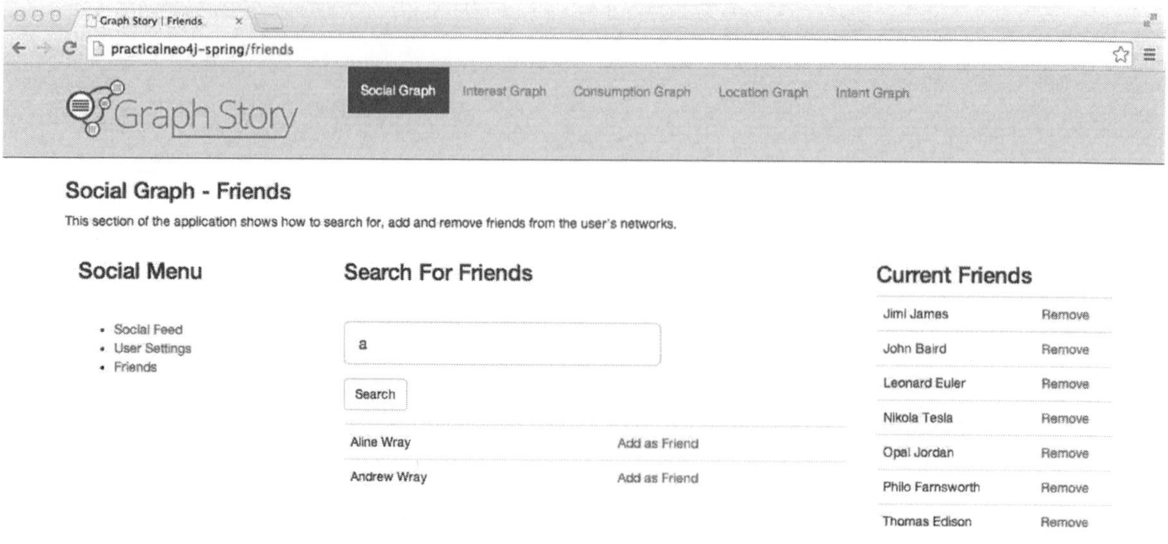

Graph Story | Friends

practicalneo4j-spring/friends

Graph Story

Social Graph | Interest Graph | Consumption Graph | Location Graph | Intent Graph

Social Graph - Friends

This section of the application shows how to search for, add and remove friends from the user's networks.

Social Menu

- Social Feed
- User Settings
- Friends

Search For Friends

a

Search

Aline Wray	Add as Friend
Andrew Wray	Add as Friend

Current Friends

Jimi James	Remove
John Baird	Remove
Leonard Euler	Remove
Nikola Tesla	Remove
Opal Jordan	Remove
Philo Farnsworth	Remove
Thomas Edison	Remove

Figure 11-9. *The Friends page*

To search for users to follow, the UserController uses the searchbyusername method, which calls the searchByUserName method in UserImpl. The searchByUserName method requests the searchByUserName method in the UserRepository, which is shown in the second part of Listing 11-30 and was also covered in more detail in Listing 11-17 of the "Spring Repositories" section. The searchByUserName method in UserRepository matches the current user and then returns a List of users not already being followed by the current user and whose username matches on a wildcard String value, which is created in the searchByUserName method in UserImpl.

Listing 11-30. The searchByUsername Method in UserImpl

```
// UserImpl

public List<User> searchByUsername(String currentusername, String username) throws Exception {
        username = username.toLowerCase() + ".*";

        LinkedList<User> users =
        new LinkedList<User>(userRepository.searchByUsername(currentusername, username));

        return users;
}

// UserRepository

@Query(" MATCH (n:User), (user { username:{c}}) " +
        " WHERE (n.username =~ {u} AND n <> user) " +
        " AND (NOT (user)-[:FOLLOWS]->(n)) " +
        " RETURN n")
List<User> searchByUsername(@Param("c") String currentusername, @Param("u") String username);
```

The searchByUsername in {PROJECTROOT}/WebContent/resources/js/graphstory.js uses an AJAX request and formats the response in renderSearchByUsername. If the list contains users, it will be displayed in the center of the page under the search form, as shown in Figure 11-9. Otherwise, the response will display "No Users Found". The display code for showing the list of users found can be reviewed by opening the friends.html file in {PROJECTROOT}/WebContent/mustache/html/graphs/social/.

Once the search returns results, the next action would be to click on the "Add as Friend" link, which will call the addfriend method in graphstory.js. This will perform an AJAX request to the follow method in the UserController and call follow in UserImpl. The follow method in UserImpl, shown in Listing 11-31, will create the relationship between the two users by first finding each entity via getByUserName and then use createRelationshipBetween provided by the neo4jTemplate.

Listing 11-31. The follow Method in UserImpl

```
// UserImpl

public void follow(String currentusername, String username) throws Exception {

        User cu = getByUserName(currentusername);
        User toFollow = getByUserName(username);

        neo4jTemplate.createRelationshipBetween(neo4jTemplate.getNode(cu.getNodeId()),
        neo4jTemplate.getNode(toFollow.getNodeId()), GraphStoryConstants.FOLLOWS, null);
}
```

The createRelationshipBetween method takes four arguments: the node of the current user, the node of the user being followed, the String value of the relationship type, and, optionally, any properties that need to be added the Relationship being created. In this specific example, you also will use the getNode method in neo4jTemplate, which takes an argument of the node ID and returns a Node object.

Once the operation is completed, the controller requests the `following` method in `UserImpl` to return the full list of followers ordered by the username.

The "unfollow" operation for the `FOLLOWS` relationships uses a nearly identical application flow as "follows". In the `unfollow` method, shown in Listing 11-32, the first step is to use the `getByUsername` to find each node in the expected relationship. To remove the relationship, call deleteRelationshipBetween with three arguments—both nodes in the relationship and the String value of the relationship. Once completed, the `UserController` executes the `following` method and returns the current list of users being followed.

Listing 11-32. The `unfollow` method in `UserImpl`

```
// UserImpl

public void unfollow(String currentusername, String username) throws Exception {

        User cu = getByUserName(currentusername);
        User toUnfollow = getByUserName(username);

        neo4jTemplate.deleteRelationshipBetween(cu, toUnfollow, GraphStoryConstants.FOLLOWS);

}
```

User-Generated Content

Another important feature in social media applications is being able to have users view, add, edit, and remove content—sometimes referred to as *user-generated content*. In the case of this content, you will not be creating connections between the content and its owner but creating a linked list of status updates. In other words, you are connecting a User to their most recent status update and then connecting each subsequent status to the next update through the `CURRENTPOST` and `NEXTPOST` directed relationship types, respectively.

This approach is used for two reasons. First, the sample application displays a given number of posts at a time. A modeled list is more efficient than getting all status updates connected to a user and then sorting and limiting the return. With this relationship approach, you also help to limit the number of relationships that are placed on the User and Content entities. Overall, the graph operations should be more efficient using this approach.

As shown in Listing 11-33, the `User` is tied the `Content` object through the `CURRENTPOST` relationship type as well as a `Content` object connected to another `Content` object through the `NEXTPOST`.

Listing 11-33. The `Content` entity

```
@NodeEntity
@TypeAlias("Content")
public class Content {

        @GraphId
        private Long nodeId;

        @Indexed
        private String contentId;

        private String title;
```

```
    private String url;

    private String tagstr;

    private Long timestamp;

    @Transient
    private String userNameForPost;

    @Transient
    private String timestampAsStr;

    @RelatedTo(type = GraphStoryConstants.HAS, direction =
    Direction.OUTGOING, elementClass = Tag.class)
    @JsonInclude(Include.NON_NULL)
    private Set<Tag> tags;

    @RelatedTo(type = GraphStoryConstants.CURRENTPOST, direction =
    Direction.INCOMING, elementClass = User.class)
    @JsonIgnore
    private User user;

    @RelatedTo(type = GraphStoryConstants.NEXTPOST, direction =
    Direction.OUTGOING, elementClass = Content.class)
    @JsonIgnore
    private Content next;

    // getters and setters
}
```

Getting the Status Updates

To display the first set of status updates, start with the home method inside of the SocialController. This method accesses the getContent method within ContentImpl, which takes an argument of the GraphStory bean, the current user's username, the page being requested, and the page size. The page refers to set number of objects within a collection. In this instance the paging is zero-based, so we will request page 0 and limit the page size to 3 in order to return the first page.

The MappedContentRepository contains a method that is also called getContent. This method, shown in the first part of Listing 11-35, first determines whom the user is following and then matches that set of users with the status updates starting with the CURRENTPOST. The CURRENTPOST is then matched on the next three status updates via the [:NEXTPOST*0..3] section of the query.

Listing 11-34. The getContent Method in ContentImpl

```
public GraphStory getContent(GraphStory graphStory, String username, Integer page, Integer pagesize)
{

    Page<MappedContent> mappedContent = mappedContentRepository.getContent(username,
    new PageRequest(page, pagesize, new Sort(Direction.DESC, "p.timestamp")));
```

```
        // return the mapped content
        graphStory.setContent(Lists.newLinkedList(mappedContent.getContent()));

        // is there more content?
        graphStory.setNext(mappedContent.hasNext());

        return graphStory;

}
```

Mapped Query Results

Query Results are a convenient way to convert results from a Cypher query into POJO interfaces or objects. The MappedContentRepository's getContent method first determines the user via a MATCH, then whom the user is following, and finally the list of status updates to be returned. Using a PageRequest, the query will be provided with a page, page size, and the sort preference of the sub-graph that is created by the Cypher query.

Using the MappedContent object, the query will map discrete properties that are to be used. In addition to being able to specify only what needs to be returned, the QueryResult is a more efficient way of reading from the graph. If the query simply returned each status update as a node, it would require multiple calls to the database and result in a much slower operation.

To create a QueryResult, you need to apply the @QueryResult annotation as well as @NodeEnity. Next, you need provide @GraphId for the object and annotate each property with a @ResultColumn that specifies the alias or property name used within the query. In cases in which you are using aliases for properties, be aware that the @ResultColumn value must match, including case, exactly to the alias name.

Listing 11-35. The MappedContentRepository Interface and MappedContent Class

```
// MappedContentRepository

public interface MappedContentRepository extends GraphRepository<MappedContent> {

        @Query(" MATCH (u:User {username: {u} }) " +
                " WITH u " +
                " MATCH (u)-[:FOLLOWS*0..1]->f " +
                " WITH DISTINCT f,u " +
                " MATCH f-[:CURRENTPOST]-lp-[:NEXTPOST*0..3]-p " +
                " RETURN p.contentId as contentId, p.title as title, p.tagstr as tagstr, " +
                " p.timestamp as timestamp, p.url as url, f.username as username, f=u as owner ")
        Page<MappedContent> getContent(@Param("u") String username, Pageable pageable);
}

// MappedContent

@QueryResult
@NodeEntity
public class MappedContent {

        @GraphId
        private Long nodeId;
```

```
    @ResultColumn("contentId")
    private String contentId;

    @ResultColumn("title")
    private String title;

    @ResultColumn("url")
    private String url;

    @ResultColumn("tagstr")
    private String tagstr;

    @ResultColumn("timestamp")
    private Long timestamp;

    @ResultColumn("username")
    private String userNameForPost;

    private String timestampAsStr;

    @ResultColumn("owner")
    private Boolean owner;

    // getters and setters
}
```

Adding a Status Update

The page shown in Figure 11-10 shows the form to add a status update for the current user, which is displayed when clicking on the "Add Content" link just under the "Graph Story - Social Feed" header. The HTML for the form can be found in `{PROJECTROOT}/WebContent/mustache/html/graphs/social/posts.html`. The form uses the `addContent` function in `graphstory.js` to `POST` a new status update and to return the response and add it to the top of the status update stream.

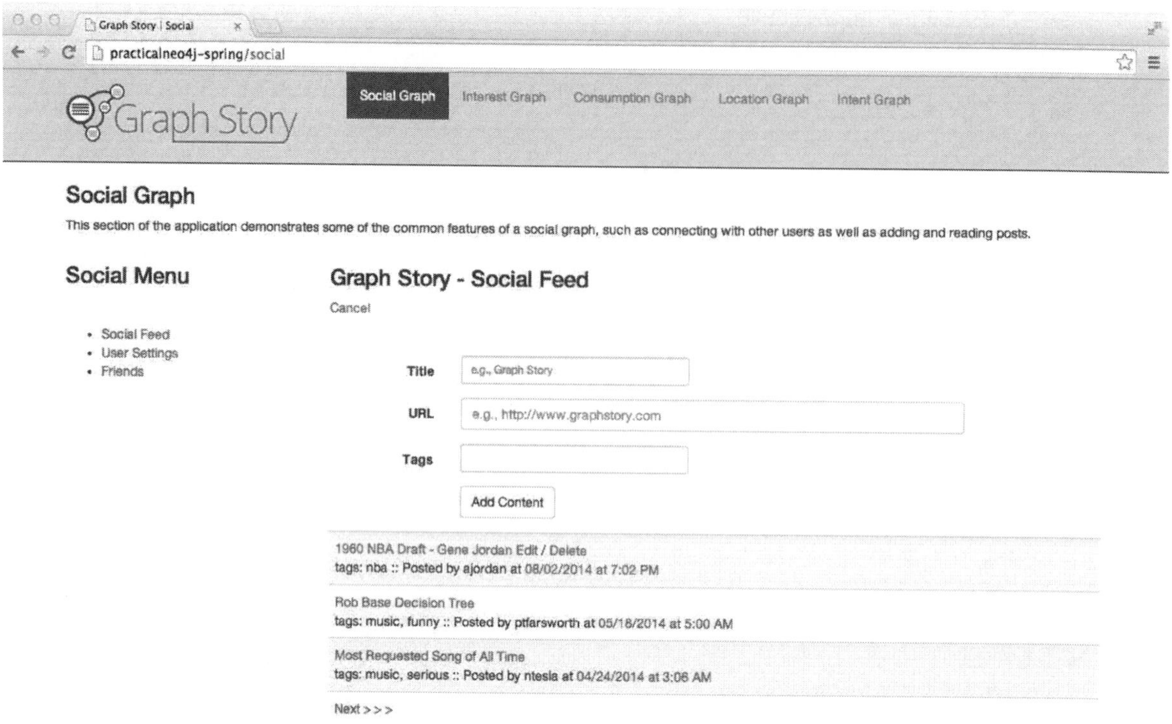

Figure 11-10. *Adding a status update*

In the SocialController, you will use the add method to first check and see if any tags are being added. If so, the tags are first saved individually through the saveTags method in TagsImpl (more on Tags in later sections), which returns a SET of tags, which will be added to the Content object via setTags. Next, you will send the Content object to the add method of ContentImpl along with a User object via currentuser.

The add method for ContentImpl is shown in Listing 11-36. When a new status update is created, in addition to its graph id, the save method also generates a contentId, which is performed using the uuidGenWithTimeStamp method. The save method will also make the status the CURRENTPOST, determines whether a previous CURRENTPOST exists, and, if one does, changes its relationship type to NEXTPOST.

Listing 11-36. The add Method in ContentImpl

```
public Content add(Content content, User user) {

        content.setContentId(uuidGenWithTimeStamp());
        content.setTimestamp(new Date().getTime() / 1000);
        content.setTagstr(removeTrailingComma(content.getTagstr()));

        // has the user posted content before?
        // if so, then get the "currentPost", remove that REL,
        // set this post as CURRENTPOST by creating REL with user,
        // then make currentPost the "next" post and save it all

        Content currentPost = contentRepository.currentpost(user.getNodeId());
```

```
        if (currentPost != null) {
                neo4jTemplate.deleteRelationshipBetween(user, currentPost,
                GraphStoryConstants.CURRENTPOST);
                content.setUser(user);
                content.setNext(currentPost);
                content = contentRepository.save(content);
        }

        // or is the first content post for this user?
        else {
                content.setUser(user);
                content = contentRepository.save(content);
        }

        return content;
}
```

Editing a Status Update

When status updates are displayed, the current user's status updates contain a link to "Edit" the status. Once clicked, it opens the form, similar to the "Add Content" link, but it populates the form with the status update values and modifies the form button to read "Edit Content", as shown in Figure 11-11. As an aside, clicking "Cancel" under the heading removes the values and returns the form to its ready state.

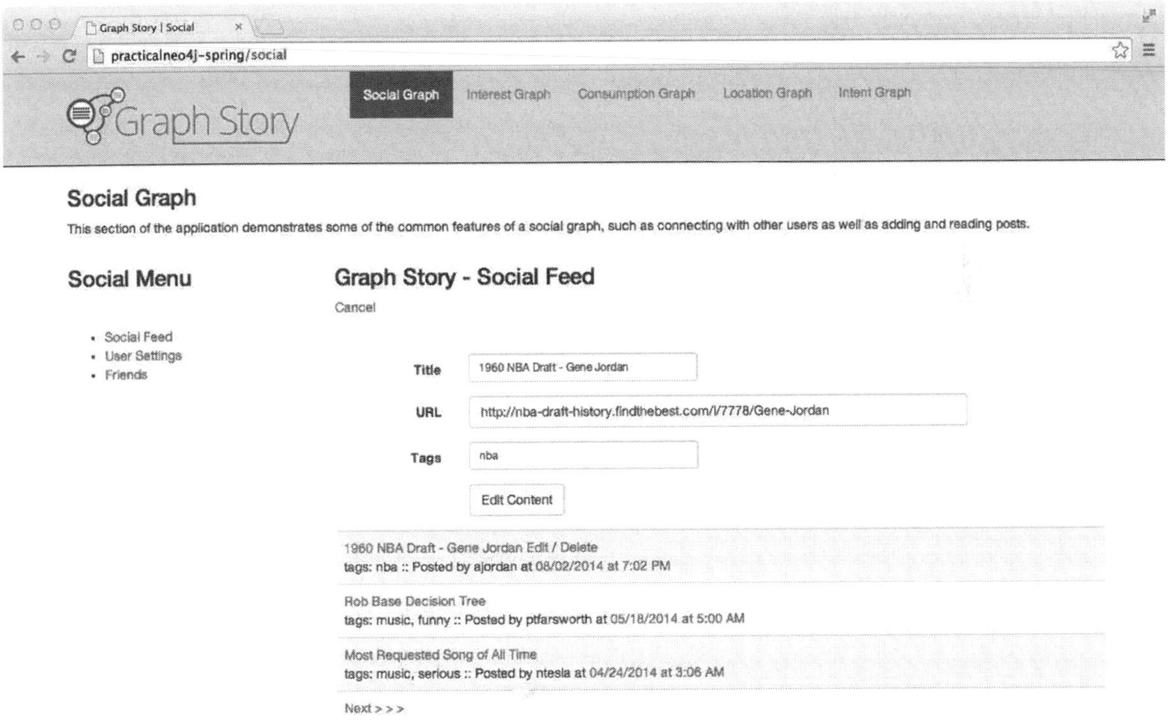

Figure 11-11. Editing a status update

The edit feature, like the add feature, uses a method in the SocialController and a function in graphstory.js, which are edit and updateContent, respectively. The edit method will first determine whether the tag set should be updated, and then call the edit method in ContentImpl, which is shown in Listing 11-34. In the case of the edit feature, you will not need to update relationships. Instead, you will simply retrieve the existing node by its generated String Id (not graph id), update its properties where necessary, and save it back to the graph.

Listing 11-37. The edit Method for ContentImpl

```
public Content edit(Content content, User user) {

        Content c = contentRepository.findByContentId(content.getContentId());

        // just update the essentials. it will NOT be re-ordered.
        c.setTitle(content.getTitle());
        c.setUrl(content.getUrl());

        if (content.getTags() != null) {
                c.setTags(content.getTags());
                c.setTagstr(removeTrailingComma(content.getTagstr()));
        }

        content = contentRepository.save(c);
        return content;
}
```

Deleting a Status Update

As with the "edit" option, when status updates are displayed, the current user's status updates will contain a link to "Delete" the status. Once clicked, it immediately (you wanted it gone, so no regrets!) generates an AJAX GET request to call the delete method in the SocialController. This method then calls the delete method in ContentImpl, shown in Listing 11-38.

The delete method in ContentImpl first determines where in the status update chain the provided status exists. If the status was the CURRENTPOST, which the currentpost method in the ContentRepository interface returns, then you need to "promote" the NEXTPOST in the chain to the CURRENTPOST relationship.

If the status is connected to CURRENTPOST, you need to remove the relationship, find the subsequent NEXTPOST, and make it connected to the CURRENTPOST. If neither of these conditions exists, then the status is further down the chain. So, you will remove its relationship to the NEXTPOST and then connect the status updates that were previously on either side of the soon-to-be-deleted status update. Once the relationships have been rearranged, the entity can be removed through the neo4jTemplate's delete method.

Listing 11-38. Deleting a status update

```
public void delete(String contentId, User user) {

        // find the content
        Content content = getContentItem(contentId);

        // get the CURRENTPOST
        Content currentPost = contentRepository.currentpost(user.getNodeId());
```

```
// was this content also the last post?
if (content.getContentId().equals(currentPost.getContentId())) {

        // get the next post
        // remove the rel between currentpost and profile
        neo4jTemplate.deleteRelationshipBetween(user, content,
        GraphStoryConstants.CURRENTPOST);

        // remove the rel between currentpost and next post
        if (content.getNext() != null) {
                Content nextPost = contentRepository.findOne(content.getNext().getNodeId());

                neo4jTemplate.deleteRelationshipBetween(content, nextPost,
                GraphStoryConstants.NEXTPOST);

                // make nextpost the currentpost
                neo4jTemplate.createRelationshipBetween(
                neo4jTemplate.getNode(user.getNodeId()), neo4jTemplate.getNode(nextPost.
                getNodeId()), GraphStoryConstants.CURRENTPOST, null);

                // set the profile
                nextPost.setUser(user);

                // save it
                contentRepository.save(nextPost);
        }

}

// OK, then this is NEXT content
else
{
        // is next to currentpost?
        if (currentPost.getNext().getNodeId().equals(content.getNodeId())) {

                // remove the rel between currentpost and the next to last content
                neo4jTemplate.deleteRelationshipBetween(currentPost, content,
                GraphStoryConstants.NEXTPOST);

                if (content.getNext().getNodeId() != null) {

                        // get the next content
                        Content newNextToLastPost = contentRepository.findOne(content.
                        getNext().getNodeId());

                        // remove the rel between the now former next to last content and
                        // new next to last content
                        neo4jTemplate.deleteRelationshipBetween(content,
                        newNextToLastPost, GraphStoryConstants.NEXTPOST);
```

```
                    // create rel bewteen the last content and
                    // now new next to last content
                    neo4jTemplate.createRelationshipBetween(
                    neo4jTemplate.getNode(currentPost.getNodeId()),
                    neo4jTemplate.getNode(newNextToLastPost.getNodeId()),
                    GraphStoryConstants.NEXTPOST, null);

                    // set the next
                    currentPost.setNext(newNextToLastPost);

                      // save it
                    contentRepository.save(currentPost);
                }

            } else {

                Content previousPost = contentRepository.prevpost(content.getNodeId());


                // remove the rel between prevpost and content
                neo4jTemplate.deleteRelationshipBetween(previousPost, content,
                GraphStoryConstants.NEXTPOST);

                if (content.getNext().getNodeId() != null) {
                    Content newNextPost =
                    contentRepository.findOne(content.getNext().getNodeId());

                    neo4jTemplate.deleteRelationshipBetween(content, newNextPost,
                    GraphStoryConstants.NEXTPOST);

                    neo4jTemplate.createRelationshipBetween(
                    neo4jTemplate.getNode(previousPost.getNodeId()),
                    neo4jTemplate.getNode(newNextPost.getNodeId()),
                    GraphStoryConstants.NEXTPOST, null);

                    // set the next
                    previousPost.setNext(newNextPost);

                    // save it
                    contentRepository.save(previousPost);
                }

            }
        }

        // delete the content
        neo4jTemplate.delete(content);
}
```

Interest Graph Model

This section looks at the interest graph and examines some basic ways it can be used to explicitly define a degree of interest. The following topics are covered:

- Interest in Aggregate
- Filtering managed content
- Filtering connected content

Tag Entity

Listing 11-39 displays the Tag entity, which will be used to determine a user's interest and network of interest based on users she follows. The tag entity also has incoming relationships with Users and Products, but the relationship is defined using the other entities. It is not necessary to explicitly annotate the relationships on both entities, because one implies the other.

Listing 11-39. The Tag Entity

```
@NodeEntity
@TypeAlias("Tag")
public class Tag {

        public Tag() {

        }

        public Tag(String wordPhrase) {
                this.setWordPhrase(wordPhrase);
        }

        @GraphId
        private Long nodeId;

        @Indexed(unique = true)
        private String wordPhrase;

        @Transient
        private Integer tagCount;

        // getters and setters
}
```

Interest in Aggregate

Inside the view method of the `InterestController`, you will retrieve all of the use tags connected to a user and their friends using the `tagsInMyNetwork` method found in the `TagImpl` class. This is displayed in Figure 11-12 in the left-hand column. The display code is located in `{PROJECTROOT}/WebContent/mustache/html/graphs/interest/index.html`.

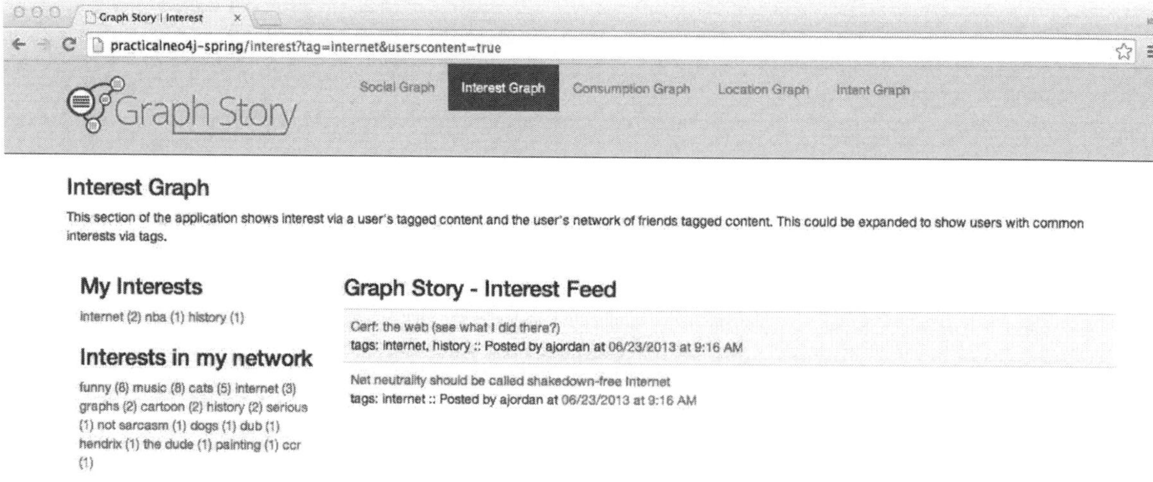

Figure 11-12. *Filtering the current user's content*

Listing 11-40. TagImpl

```
public GraphStory tagsInMyNetwork(GraphStory graphStory) {
        try {
                graphStory.setTagsInNetwork(Lists.newLinkedList(
                mappedContentTagRepository.tagsInNetwork(graphStory.getUser().getNodeId())));

                graphStory.setUserTags(Lists.newLinkedList(
                mappedContentTagRepository.userTags(graphStory.getUser().getNodeId())));

        }
        catch (Exception e) {
                log.error(e);
        }

        return graphStory;
}
```

The tagsInMyNetwork method uses two methods inside MappedContentTagRepository, which is shown in Listing 11-41. The tagsInNetwork finds users being followed, accesses all of their content, finds connected tags through the HAS relationship type. Finally, the method returns an Iterable of MappedContentTag.

The userTags method is similar but is concerned only with content and, subsequently, tags connected to the current user. Both methods limit the results to 30 items.

Listing 11-41. MappedContentTagRepository

```
public interface MappedContentTagRepository extends GraphRepository<MappedContentTag> {

@Query("START u=node({nodeId})" +
        " MATCH u-[:FOLLOWS]->f " +
        " WITH distinct f " +
        " MATCH f-[:CURRENTPOST]-lp-[:NEXTPOST*0..]-c " +
```

```
        " WITH distinct c " +
        " MATCH c-[ct:HAS]->(t) " +
        " WITH distinct ct,t " +
        " RETURN t.wordPhrase as name, count(ct) as count " +
        " ORDER BY count desc " +
        " SKIP 0 LIMIT 30")
Iterable<MappedContentTag> tagsInNetwork(@Param("nodeId") Long nodeId);

@Query("START u=node({nodeId})" +
        " MATCH u-[:CURRENTPOST]-lp-[:NEXTPOST*0..]-c " +
        " WITH distinct c " +
        " MATCH c-[ct:HAS]->(t) " +
        " WITH distinct ct,t " +
        " RETURN t.wordPhrase as name, count(ct) as count " +
        " ORDER BY count desc " +
        " SKIP 0 LIMIT 30")
Iterable<MappedContentTag> userTags(@Param("nodeId") Long nodeId);

}
```

The methods return `MappedContentTag`, which is located inside the `MappedContentTagRepository` interface. Notice that the `MappedContentTag` uses two getter methods with the same result column: name. This is done to support a specific autosuggest plugin in the view, which requires both a label and name to be provided in order to execute. This autosuggest feature is used in the status update form and in some search forms presented later in this chapter.

Listing 11-42. The `MappedContent` Interface

```
@QueryResult
@JsonPropertyOrder(alphabetic = true)
@NodeEntity
public interface MappedContentTag {

        @ResultColumn("count")
        String getId();

        @ResultColumn("name")
        String getLabel();

        @ResultColumn("name")
        String getName();
}
```

Filtering Managed Content

Once the list of tags for the user and for the group she follows has been provided, the content can be filtered based on the generated tag links, as shown in Figure 11-12. If one of the user's tags is clicked, then the `getContentByTag` method, displayed in Listing 11-43, will be called with the `userscontent` value set to true.

Listing 11-43. getContentByTag in ContentImpl

```
public List<MappedContent> getContentByTag(String username, String tag, Boolean getuserscontent) {

        if (getuserscontent) {
                return mappedContentRepository.getUserContentWithTag(username, tag);
        } else {
                return mappedContentRepository.getFollowingContentWithTag(username, tag);
        }
}
```

In turn, this will call the `getUserContentWithTag`, shown in listing 11-44. Similarly to the query for the `getContent` method in `MappedContentRepository`, the query for `getUserContentWithTag` returns a collection of `MappedContent` items, but matches resulting content to a provide tag, via `@Param("wp")`, and places no limit on the number of status updates to be returned. In addition, it marks the `owner` property as true, because we've determined ahead of time we are only returning the current user's content.

Listing 11-44. getUserContentWithTag in the MappedContentRepository

```
@Query("MATCH (u:User {username: {u} })" +
        " MATCH u-[:CURRENTPOST]-lp-[:NEXTPOST*0..]-p " +
        " WITH DISTINCT u,p " +
        " MATCH p-[:HAS]-(t:Tag {wordPhrase : {wp} } ) " +
        " RETURN  p.contentId as contentId, p.title as title, p.tagstr as tagstr, " +
        " p.timestamp as timestamp, p.url as url, u.username as username, true as owner" +
        " ORDER BY p.timestamp DESC")
List<MappedContent> getUserContentWithTag(@Param("u") String username, @Param("wp") String
wordPhrase);
```

Filtering Connected Content

If a tag is clicked on inside of the “Interests in my Network” section, then the `getContentByTag` method will be called be with the `userscontent` value set to false. In turn, this will call the `getFollowingContentWithTag` method, shown in Listing 11-45.

The query for the `getFollowingContentWithTag` method is nearly identical to the query found in `getUserContentWithTag`, except it factors in the users being followed and exclude the current user. The method also returns a collection of `MappedContent` items and matches resulting content to a provide tag, via `@Param("wp")`, placing no limit on the number of status updates to be returned. In addition, it marks the owner property as false. The results of calling this method are shown in Figure 11-13.

Listing 11-45. getFollowingContentWithTag in the MappedContentRepository

```
@Query("MATCH (u:User {username: {u} }) " +
        " WITH u " +
        " MATCH (u)-[:FOLLOWS]->f " +
        " WITH DISTINCT f " +
        " MATCH f-[:CURRENTPOST]-lp-[:NEXTPOST*0..]-p " +
        " WITH DISTINCT f,p " +
        " MATCH p-[:HAS]-(t:Tag {wordPhrase : {wp} } ) " +
        " RETURN  p.contentId as contentId, p.title as title, p.tagstr as tagstr, " +
        " p.timestamp as timestamp, p.url as url, f.username as username, false as owner" +
        " ORDER BY p.timestamp DESC")
List<MappedContent> getFollowingContentWithTag(@Param("u") String username, @Param("wp") String
wordPhrase);
```

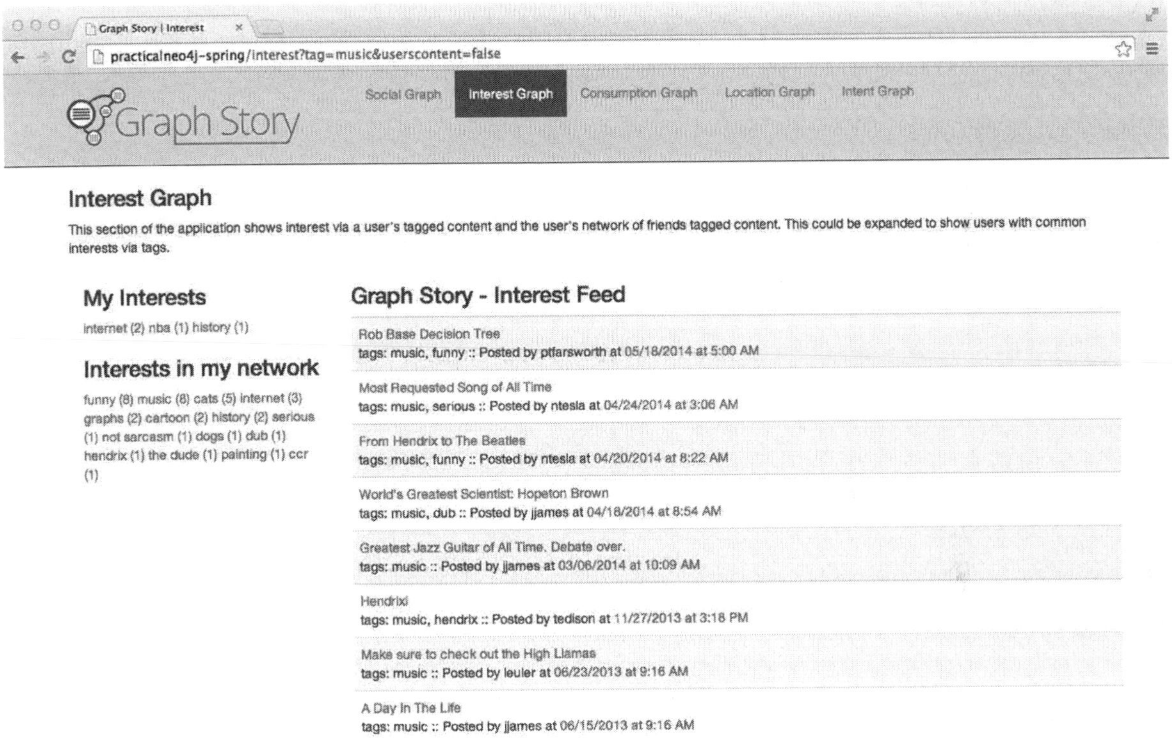

Figure 11-13. *Filtering content of the current user's friends*

Consumption Graph Model

This section examines a few techniques to capture and use patterns of consumption generated implicitly by a user or users. For the purposes of your application, you will use the prepopulated set of products provided in the sample graph. The code required for the console reinforces the standard persistence operations, but I will focus on the operations that take advantage of this model type, including:

- Capturing consumption
- Filtering consumption for users
- Filtering consumption for messaging

Product Entity

The Product entity is similar to the other entities that I have reviewed for this chapter, except that I have added an indexType of FULLTEXT and specified the name for the index (Listing 11-46).

Listing 11-46. Product Entity

```
@NodeEntity
@TypeAlias("Product")
public class Product {

        @GraphId
        private Long nodeId;

        @Indexed
        private String productId;

        private String title;

        private String description;

        private String tagstr;

        @Indexed(indexType = IndexType.FULLTEXT, indexName = "productcontent")
        private String content;

        private String price;

        @RelatedTo(type = GraphStoryConstants.HAS, direction =
        Direction.OUTGOING, elementClass = Tag.class)
        private Set<Tag> tags;

        // getters and setters
}
```

Capturing Consumption

You are creating code that directly captures consumption for a user, but the process could also be done by creating a graph-backed service to consume the webserver logs in real time or another data store to create the relationships. The result would be the same in either event: a process that connects nodes to reveal a pattern of consumption.

For the sample application, you used the `createUserView` method, shown in Listing 11-47, in `ProductImpl` to first find the Product entity being viewed and then create an explicit relationship type called `VIEWED`. Notice that this is the first relationship type in the application that also contains properties. In this case, you are creating a timestamp with a `Date` object and String value of the timestamp. Use the `getRelationshipBetween` method of the `neo4jTemplate` to determine if the relationship already exists.

Listing 11-47. The `createUserView` in `ProductImpl`

```
public void createUserView(User user, Long productNodeId) {

        Product product = productRepository.findOne(productNodeId);

        try {
                Relationship r = neo4jTemplate.getRelationshipBetween(user, product,
                GraphStoryConstants.VIEWED);

                Long d = new Date().getTime() / 1000;

                Date timestamp = new Date(d * 1000);
                SimpleDateFormat dformatter = new SimpleDateFormat("MM/dd/yyyy");
                SimpleDateFormat tformatter = new SimpleDateFormat("h:mm a");
                String timestampAsStr = dformatter.format(timestamp) + " at " +
                tformatter.format(timestamp);

                if (r == null) {
                        Map<String, Object> map = new HashMap<String, Object>();
                        map.put("timestamp", d);
                        map.put("dateAsStr", timestampAsStr);

                        neo4jTemplate.createRelationshipBetween(neo4jTemplate.getNode
                        (user.getNodeId()), neo4jTemplate.getNode(productNodeId),
                        GraphStoryConstants.VIEWED, map);
                } else {

                        r.setProperty("timestamp", d);
                        r.setProperty("dateAsStr", timestampAsStr);
                        neo4jTemplate.save(r);
                }

        }
        catch (Exception e) {
                log.error(e);
        }

}
```

If the result of `getRelationshipBetween` is null, a map is created with key value pairs to create properties on the new relationship, specifically `timestamp` and `dateAsStr`. Otherwise, you can use setProperty and specify the property names and their respective values as arguments.

Filtering Consumption for Users

One practical use of the consumption model is to create a content trail for users, as shown in Figure 11-14. As a user clicks on items in the scrolling product stream, the interaction is captured using `createUserView`, which ultimately returns a `List` of relationship objects of the `VIEWED` type called `MappedProductUserViews`, which are located in the `MappedProductUserViewsRepository`.

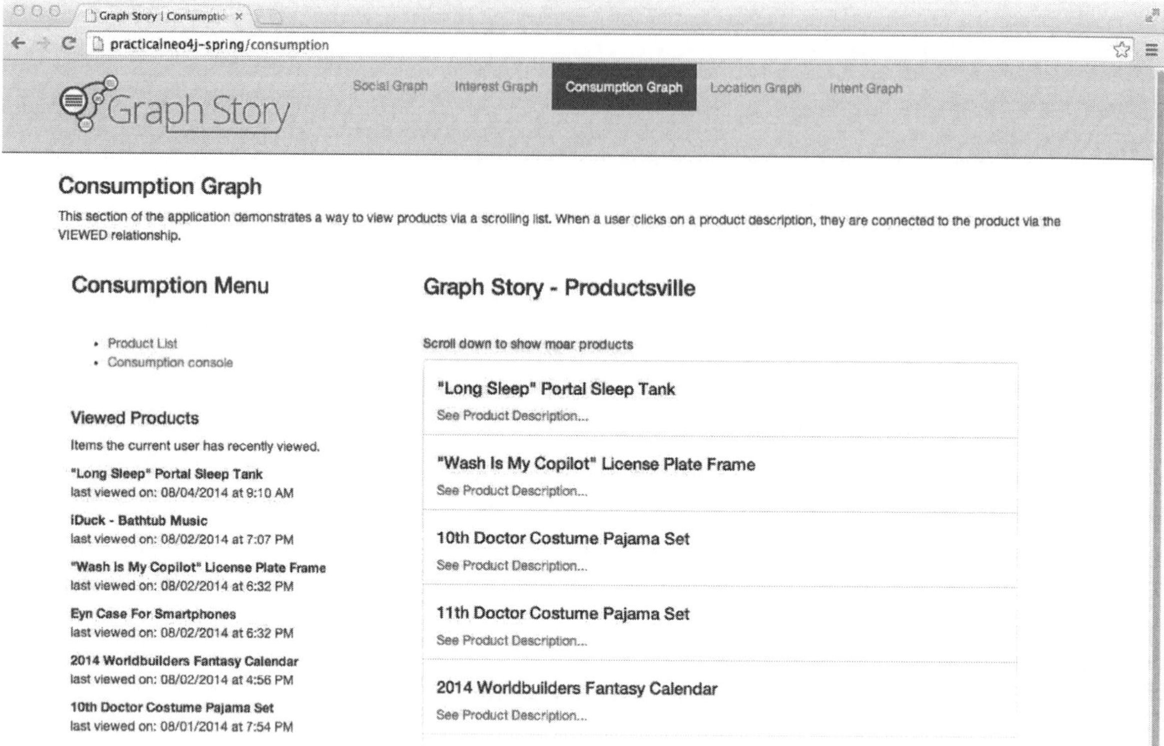

Figure 11-14. *The Scrolling Product and Product Trail page*

In the `ConsumptionController`, take a look at the `createUserProductViewRel` method to see how the process begins inside the controller. The controller method first saves the view and then returns the complete history of views using the `getProductTrail`, which can be found in the `MappedProductUserViewsRepository` interface and is shown in Listing 11-48. The process is started when the `createUserProductViewRel` function is called, which is located in `graphstory.js`.

Listing 11-48. `getProductTrail` in the `MappedProductUserViewsRepository`

```
@Query("MATCH (u:User { username: {username} })-[r:VIEWED]->(p) " +
        " RETURN p.title as title, r.dateAsStr as dateAsStr " +
        " ORDER BY r.timestamp DESC ")
List<MappedProductUserViews> getProductTrail(@Param("username") String username);
```

```
@QueryResult
@NodeEntity
public interface MappedProductUserViews {

        @ResultColumn("title")
        String getTitle();

        @ResultColumn("dateAsStr")
        String getDateAsStr();
}
```

Filtering Consumption for Messaging

Another practical use of the consumption model is to create a personalized message for users, as displayed in Figure 11-15. In this case, a filter allows the "Consumption Console" to drill down to a very specific group of users who visited a product that was also tagged with a keyword or phrase each user had explicitly used.

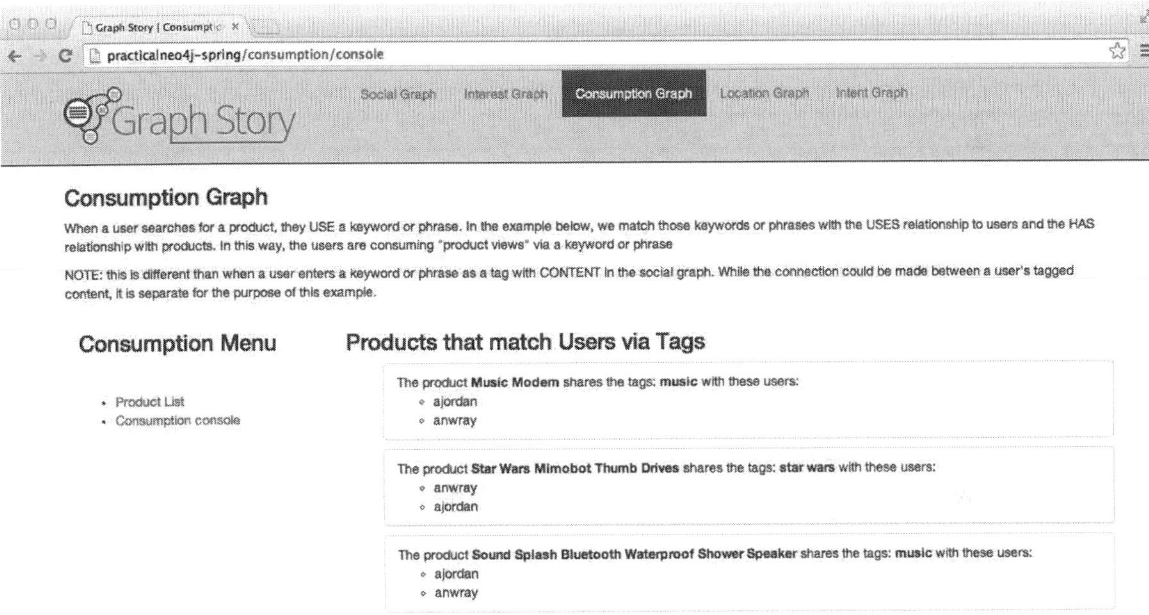

Figure 11-15. The consumption console

Both getProductsHasATagAndUserUsesAMatchingTag and getProductsHasTagAndUserUsesTag methods in the MappedProductUserTagRepository interface return a List of MappedProductUserTag objects. The getProductsHasATagAndUserUsesAMatchingTag does not require any arguments and will simply return the product title as well as the user and tags that are a match. However, the getProductsHasTagAndUserUsesTag, which is shown in Listing 11-49, requires a word/phrase as well as a username. In addition, this will result in a list of MappedProducts as opposed to MappedProductUserTag.

Listing 11-49. The Products Matching User Tags Methods and the MappedProductUserTag Interface in the MappedProductUserTagRepository Interface

```
// getProductsHasATagAndUserUsesAMatchingTag

@Query("MATCH (p:Product)-[:HAS]->(t)<-[:USES]-(u:User)        " +
       " RETURN p.title as title, collect(u.username) as u, collect(distinct t.wordPhrase) as t ")
List<MappedProductUserTag> getProductsHasATagAndUserUsesAMatchingTag();

// getProductsHasTagAndUserUsesTag

@Query("MATCH (t:Tag { wordPhrase: {wp} }),(u:User { username: {username} })  " +
       " WITH t,u " +
       " MATCH (p:Product)-[:HAS]->(t)<-[:USES]-(u)   " +
       " RETURN ID(p) as nodeId, p.title, p.description, p.tagstr ")
List<MappedProduct> getProductsHasTagAndUserUsesTag(@Param("wp") String wp, @Param("username")
String username);

// MappedProductUserTag

@QueryResult
@NodeEntity
public interface MappedProductUserTag {

        @ResultColumn("title")
        String getTitle();

        @ResultColumn("u")
        List<String> getUsers();

        @ResultColumn("t")
        List<String> getTags();
}
```

Location Graph Model

This section explores the location graph model and a few of the operations that typically accompany it. In particular, it looks at the following:

- The spatial plugin
- Filtering on location
- Products based on location

The example demonstrates how to add a console to enable you to connect products to locations in an ad hoc manner.

Location Entity

The Location entity, shown in Listing 11-50, has an outgoing relationship to Product that allows a location to have multiple products. In addition, the entity includes a @Transient value. Transient values are not persisted or managed in the database but contain values that an entity could use for display or other purposes. In this case, you will use the distanceToLocation property to display a String value of the location's distance relative to the starting point in the search.

Listing 11-50. The Location Entity

```
@NodeEntity
@TypeAlias("Location")
public class Location {

        @GraphId
        private Long nodeId;

        @Indexed
        private String locationId;

        private String name;

        private String address;

        private String city;

        private String state;

        private String zip;

        private Double lat;

        private Double lon;

        @RelatedTo(type = GraphStoryConstants.HAS, direction =
        Direction.OUTGOING, elementClass = Product.class)
        private Set<Product> products;

        @Transient
        private String distanceToLocation;

        // getters and setters
}
```

The User object also contains a relationship to Location via the HAS relationship type. User locations are retrieved through the getUserLocation method, shown in Listing 11-51, which is located in the UserImpl class.

Listing 11-51. getUserLocation in UserImpl

```
public MappedUserLocation getUserLocation(String currentusername) {
        MappedUserLocation mappedUserLocation = null;

        List<MappedUserLocation> mappedUserLocations = mappedUserLocationRepository.getUserLocation
        (currentusername);

        if (mappedUserLocations.size() > 0) {
                mappedUserLocation = mappedUserLocations.get(0);
        }

        return mappedUserLocation;
}
```

Search for Nearby Locations

To search for nearby locations (Figure 11-16), use the current user's location, obtained with `getUserLocation`, and then use the `returnLocationsWithinDistance` method. The `returnLocationsWithinDistance` method in `LocationImpl` (Listing 11-52) also uses a method called `addDistanceTo` to place a string value of the distance between the starting point and the respective location.

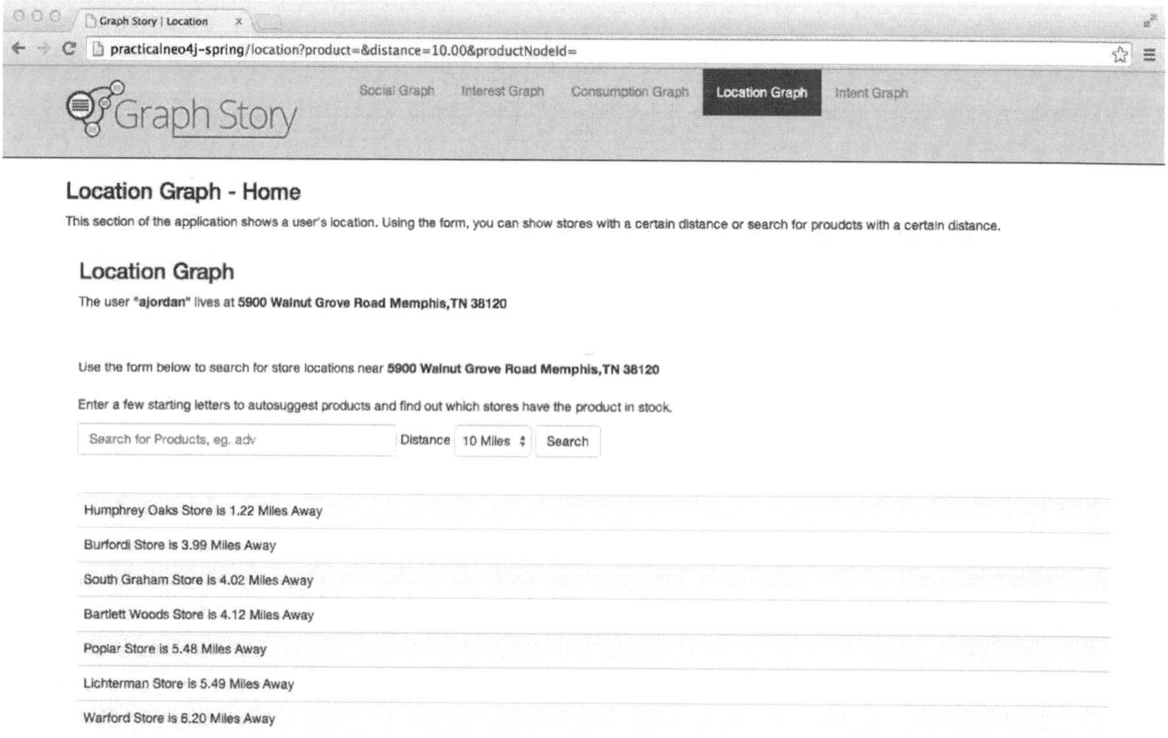

Figure 11-16. *Searching for Locations within a certain distance of User location*

Listing 11-52. returnLocationsWithinDistance in the LocationImpl interface

```
public List<MappedLocation> returnLocationsWithinDistance(Double lat, Double lon, Double distance) {
          List<MappedLocation> locations =
          mappedLocationRepository.locationsWithinDistance(distanceQueryAsString(lat, lon,
          distance));

        // add the distance in miles to locations
        addDistanceTo(locations, lat, lon);

        return locations;
}
```

Locations with Product

To search for products nearby (Figure 11-17), the application makes use of an autosuggest AJAX request, which ultimately calls the search method (Listing 11-53) in the MappedProductSearchRespository interface. The method, shown in Listing 11-54, returns an array of MappedProductSearch objects to the product field in the search form. It applies the selected product's productNodeId.

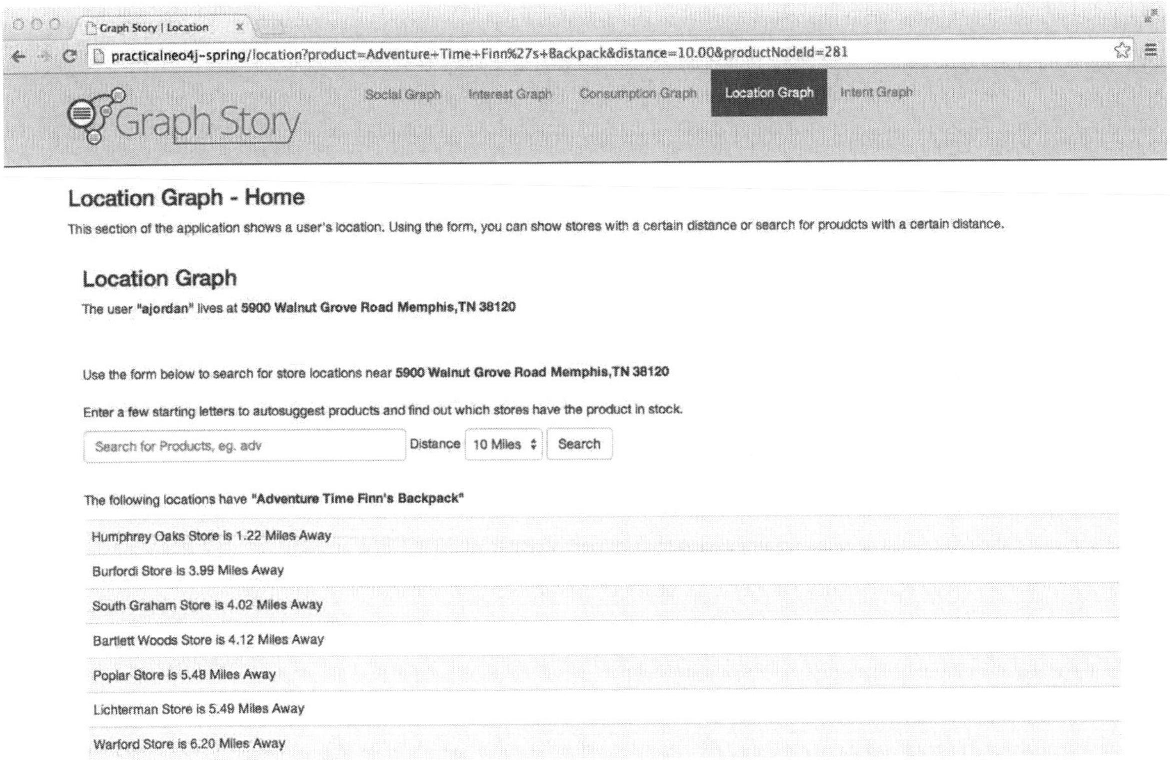

Figure 11-17. *Searching for Products in stock at Locations within a certain distance of the User location*

Listing 11-53. The Search Method to Find Products

```
public MappedProductSearch[] search(String q) {

        q = q.trim().toLowerCase() + ".*";

        return Iterables.toArray(MappedProductSearch.class, mappedProductSearchRespository.search(q));
}
```

Listing 11-54. The Search Method in the `MappedProductSearchRespository`

```
@Query(value = "MATCH (p:Product) " +
                " WHERE lower(p.title) =~ {q} " +
                " RETURN count(*) as count, TOSTRING(ID(p)) as productNodeId, " +
                " p.title as name  " +
                " ORDER BY p.title LIMIT 5")
Iterable<MappedProductSearch> search(@Param("q") String q);

@QueryResult
@JsonPropertyOrder(alphabetic = true)
@NodeEntity
public interface MappedProductSearch {

        @ResultColumn("productNodeId")
        String getId();

        @ResultColumn("name")
        String getLabel();

        @ResultColumn("count")
        String getName();
}
```

In many cases, it is recommended not to use the graphId because it can be recycled when its node is deleted. In this case, the `productNodeId` is safe to use, because products would not be in danger of being deleted but only removed from a Location relationship.

Once the product and distance have been set and the search is executed, the `LocationController` tests to see if a `prouctNodeId` property has been set. If so, the `returnLocationsWithinDistanceAndHasProduct` method is called from LocationImpl, which in turn calls the `returnLocationsWithinDistanceAndHasProduct` method, shown in Listing 11-55, from the `MappedLocationRepository` interface is called.

Listing 11-55. The returnLocationsWithinDistanceAndHasProduct Method

```
public GraphStory returnLocationsWithinDistanceAndHasProduct(GraphStory graphStory, Double lat,
Double lon, Double distance, Long productNodeId) {

        List<MappedLocation> locations = mappedLocationRepository.locationsWithinDistanceWithProduct
        (distanceQueryAsString(lat, lon, distance), productNodeId);

        // add the distance in miles to locations
        addDistanceTo(locations, lat, lon);

        graphStory.setMappedLocations(locations);
        graphStory.setProduct(productRepository.findOne(productNodeId));

        return graphStory;
}
```

Intent Graph Model

The last part of the graph model exploration considers all the other graphs in order to suggest products based on the Purchase entity, shown in Listing 11-56. The intent graph also considers the products, users, locations, and tags that are connected based on the Purchase entity.

In addition, each one of the following examples makes use of the MappedProductUserPurchase interface found in the MappedProductUserPurchaseRepository, as shown in Listing 11-57.

Listing 11-56. The Purchase entity

```
@NodeEntity
@TypeAlias("Purchase")
public class Purchase {

        @GraphId
        private Long nodeId;

        @Indexed
        private String purchaseId;

        @RelatedTo(type = GraphStoryConstants.CONTAINS, direction =
        Direction.OUTGOING, elementClass = Product.class)
        private Set<Product> products;

        private Date timestamp;
        // getters and setters
}
```

Listing 11-57. The MappedProductUserPurchase Interface

```
@QueryResult
@NodeEntity
public interface MappedProductUserPurchase {

        @ResultColumn("productId")
        String getProductId();

        @ResultColumn("title")
        String getTitle();

        @ResultColumn("fullname")
        List<String> getFullname();

        @ResultColumn("wordPhrase")
        String getWordPhrase();

        @ResultColumn("cfriends")
        Integer getCfriends();
}
```

Products Purchased by Friends

To get all of the products that have been purchased by friends, the `friendsPurchase` method is called from `PurchaseImpl`, which then makes use of the `friendsPurchase` in the `MappedProductUserPurchaseRepository`. The `getProductsPurchasedByUsersFriends` is shown in Listing 11-58.

The query in `getProductsPurchasedByUsersFriends` finds the users being followed by the current user and then matches those users to a purchase that has been `MADE` which `CONTAINS` a product. The return value is a set of properties that identify the product title and the name of the friend or friends, as well the number of friends who have bought the product. The result is ordered by the number of friends who have purchased the product and then by product title, as shown in Figure 11-18.

Listing 11-58. The `friendsPurchase` Method

```
@Query("MATCH (u:User { userId : {userId} } )-[:FOLLOWS]-(f)-[:MADE]->()-[:CONTAINS]->p " +
        " RETURN p.productId as productId, " +
        " p.title as title, " +
        " collect(f.firstname + ' ' + f.lastname) as fullname, " +
        " null as wordPhrase, " +
        " count(f) as cfriends " +
        " ORDER BY cfriends desc, p.title ")
List<MappedProductUserPurchase> friendsPurchase (@Param("userId") String userId);
```

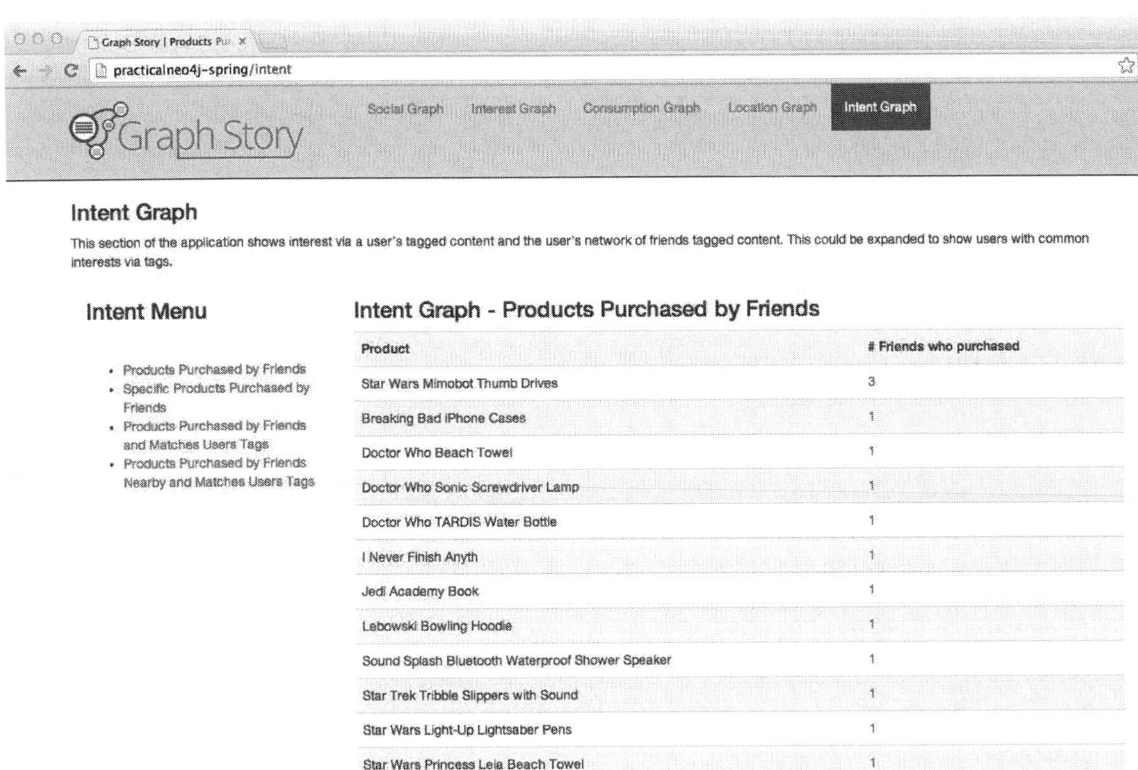

Figure 11-18. *Products Purchased by Friends*

Specific Products Purchased by Friends

If you click on the "Specific Products Purchased By Friends" link, you can specify a product, in this case "Star Wars Mimbot Thumb Drives", and then search for friends who have purchased this product, as shown in Figure 11-19. This is done via the `friendsPurchaseByProduct` method in `PurchaseImpl`, which then makes use of the `friendsPurchaseByProduct` in the `MappedProductUserPurchaseRepository` interface, as shown in Listing 11-59.

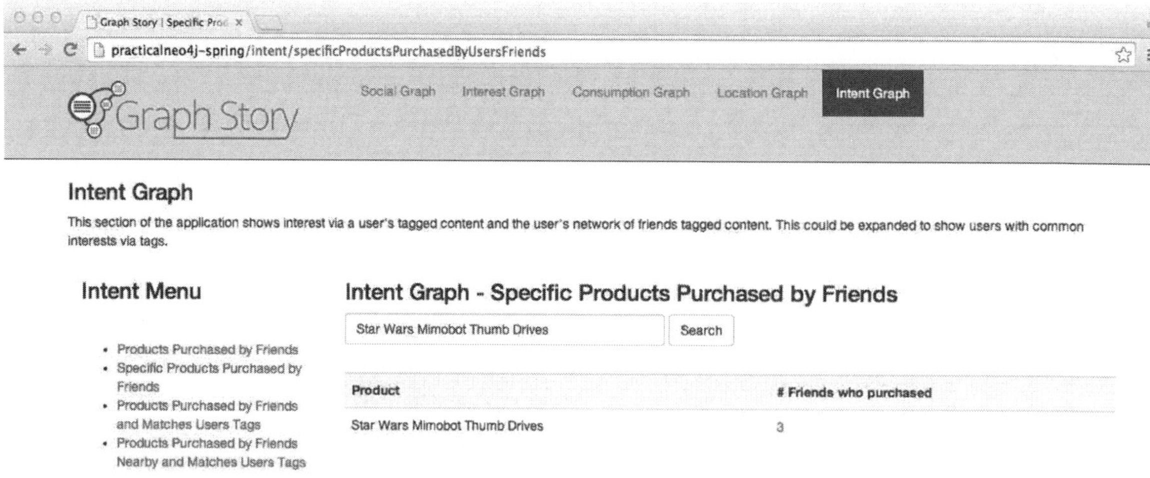

Figure 11-19. *Specific Products Purchased by Friends*

Listing 11-59. The friendsPurchaseByProduct Method

```
@Query("MATCH (p:Product) " +
        " WHERE lower(p.title) =lower({title}) " +
        " WITH p " +
        " MATCH (u:User { userId : {userId} } )-[:FOLLOWS]-(f)-[:MADE]->()-[:CONTAINS]->(p) " +
        " RETURN p.productId as productId,  " +
        " p.title as title, " +
        " collect(f.firstname + ' ' + f.lastname) as fullname, " +
        " null as wordPhrase, count(f) as cfriends " +
        "ORDER BY cfriends desc, p.title ")
List<MappedProductUserPurchase> friendsPurchaseByProduct (@Param("userId") String userId,
@Param("title") String title);
```

Products Purchased by Friends and Matches User's Tags

In this next instance, we want to determine products that have been purchased by friends but also have tags that are used by the current user. The result of the query is shown in Figure 11-20.

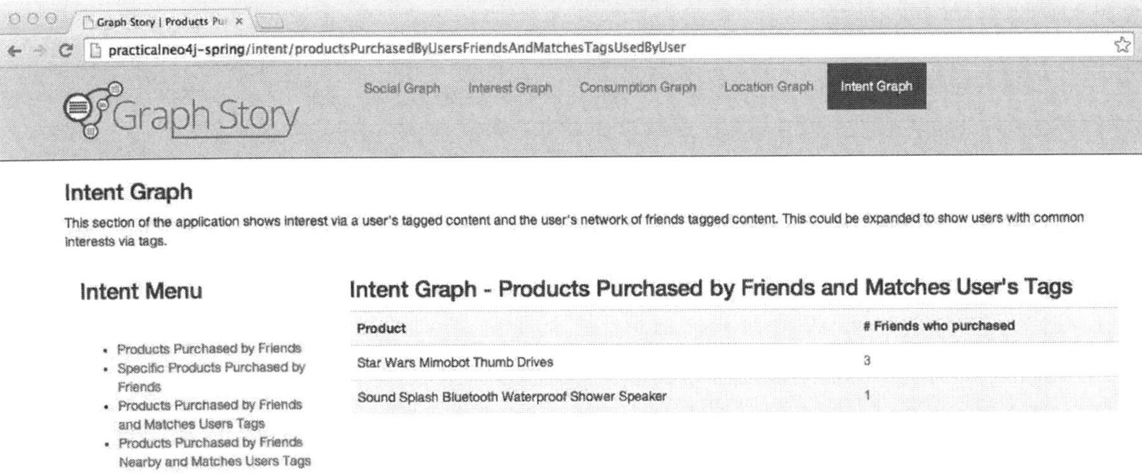

Figure 11-20. *Products Purchased by Friends and Matches User's Tags*

Using `friendsPurchaseTagSimilarity` in `PurchaseImpl`, the method `friendsPurchaseTagSimilarity` is called, which is located in the `MappedProductUserPurchaseRepository` and shown in Listing 11-60.

Listing 11-60. The friendsPurchaseTagSimilarity Method

```
@Query("MATCH (u:User { userId : {userId} } )-[:FOLLOWS]-(f)-[:MADE]->()-[:CONTAINS]->p " +
       " WITH u,p,f " +
       " MATCH u-[:USES]->(t)<-[:HAS]-p " +
       " RETURN p.productId as productId,  " +
       " p.title as title, " +
       " collect(f.firstname + ' ' + f.lastname) as fullname, " +
       " t.wordPhrase as wordPhrase, " +
       " count(f) as cfriends " +
       " ORDER BY cfriends desc, p.title ")
List<MappedProductUserPurchase> friendsPurchaseTagSimilarity (@Param("userId") String userId);
```

Products Purchased by Friends Nearby and Matches User's Tags

Finding products that match with a specific user's tags and have been purchased by friends who live within a set distance of the user is performed by `friendsPurchaseTagSimilarityAndProximityToLocation` method, easily the world's longest method name and is located in `PurchaseImpl`.

The query starts with a location search within a certain distance, then matches the current user's tags to products. Next, the query matches friends based the location search. The resulting friends are matched against products that are in the set of user tag matches. The result of the query is shown in Figure 11-21.

Listing 11-61. The `friendsPurchaseTagSimilarityAndProximityToLocation` Method

```
@Query("START n = node:geom({lq}) " +
        " WITH n " +
        " MATCH (u:User { userId : {userId} } )-[:USES]->(t)<-[:HAS]-p " +
        " WITH n,u,p,t " +
        " MATCH u-[:FOLLOWS]->(f)-[:HAS]->(n) " +
        " WITH p,f,t " +
        " MATCH f-[:MADE]->()-[:CONTAINS]->(p) " +
        " RETURN p.productId as productId, " +
        " p.title as title, " +
        " collect(f.firstname + ' ' + f.lastname) as fullname, " +
        " t.wordPhrase as wordPhrase, " +
        " count(f) as cfriends " +
        " ORDER BY cfriends desc, p.title ")
List<MappedProductUserPurchase> friendsPurchaseTagSimilarityAndProximityToLocation (@Param("userId")
String userId, @Param("lq") String lq);
```

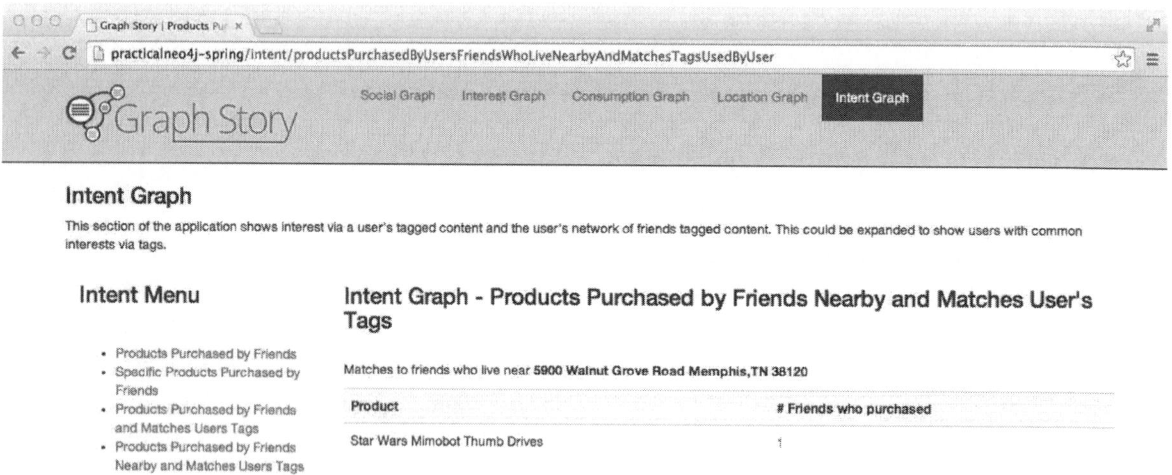

Figure 11-21. *Products Purchased by Friends Nearby and Matches User's Tags*

Summary

This chapter presented the setup for a development environment for Spring Data and Neo4j and sample code using the Spring Data Neo4j driver. It proceeded to look at sample code for setting up a social network and examining interest within the network. It then looked at the sample code for capturing and viewing consumption—in this case, product views—and the queries for understanding the relationship between consumption and a user's interest. Finally, it looked at using geospatial matching for locations and examples of methods for understanding user intent within the context of user location, social network, and interests.

The next chapter will review using Java and Neo4j, covering the same concepts presented in this chapter but in the context of a Java driver for Neo4j.

CHAPTER 12

Neo4j + Java

This chapter focuses on using Java with Neo4j and reviewing the code for a working application that integrates the five graph model types covered in Chapter 4. The Java integration takes place using a Neo4j server instance with the Neo4j JDBC driver, henceforth referred to as *Neo4j JDBC* or simply *NJDBC*. This chapter is divided into the following topics:

- Java & Neo4j Development Environment
- Common operations using Java and Neo4j JDBC
- Developing a Java and Neo4j web application

In each chapter that explores a particular language paired with Neo4j, I recommend that you start a free trial at `www.graphstory.com` or have installed a local Neo4j server instance as shown in Chapter 2.

Tip To quickly setup a server instance with the sample data and plugins for this chapter, go to `graphstory.com/practicalneo4j`. You will be provided with your own free trial instance, a knowledge base, and email support from Graph Story.

For this chapter, I expect that you have at least a beginning knowledge of Java web application development and a basic understanding of how to configure the Apache Tomcat servlet container for your preferred operating system. You should be able to run the web application in other servlet containers, as well. To follow the examples in this chapter, you will need to have Tomcat 7 or higher installed and configured.

Do This If you do not have Apache Tomcat installed, please visit `http://tomcat.apache.org/` and download Tomcat version 7. The configuration steps of Tomcat are beyond the scope of this book, but the wiki section on the Apache Tomcat site provides a detailed guide to guide you through more detailed configuration and optimization techniques.

I also expect that you have a basic understanding of the *model-view-controller* (MVC) pattern as well as some knowledge of Java web frameworks that provide an MVC pattern. There are, of course, a number of excellent Java frameworks from which to choose, but I had to pick one. For the purposes of the application in this chapter, I chose the Struts2 framework because of its stability, which helps keep the focus on the important aspects of this application as it relates to NJDBC and Neo4j. This chapter is focused on integrating Neo4j into your Java skill set and projects and does not dive deeply into the best practices of developing with Java or Java web frameworks.

Java and Neo4j Development Environment

This section covers the basics of configuring a development environment preliminary to reviewing the Java and Neo4j application presented in this chapter.

■ **Readme** Although each language chapter walks through the process of configuring the development environment based on the particular language, certain steps are covered repeatedly in multiple chapters. While the initial development environment setup in each chapter is somewhat redundant, it allows each language chapter to stand on its own. Bearing this in mind, if you have already configured Eclipse with the necessary plugins while working through another chapter, you can skip ahead to the section "Adding the Project to Eclipse."

IDE

The reasons behind the choice of an IDE vary from developer to developer and are often tied to the choice of programming language. I chose the Eclipse IDE for a number of reasons but mainly because it is freely available and versatile enough to work with most of the programming languages featured in this book.

Although you are welcome to choose a different IDE or other programming tool for building your application, I recommend that you install and use Eclipse to be able to follow the Java and Neo4j examples and the related examples found throughout the book and online.

■ **Tip** If you do not have Eclipse, please visit `http://www.eclipse.org/downloads/` and download the Indigo package that is titled "Eclipse IDE for Java EE Developers." The Indigo package is also labeled "Version 3.7."

Once you have installed Eclipse, open it and select a workspace for your application. A *workspace* in Eclipse is simply an arbitrary directory on your computer. As shown in Figure 12-1, when you first open Eclipse, the program will ask you to specify which workspace you want to use. Choose the path that works best for you. If you are working through all of the language chapters, you can use the same workspace for each project.

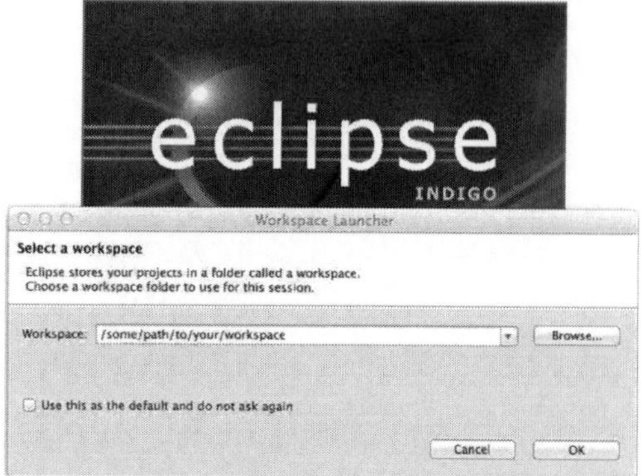

Figure 12-1. *Opening Eclipse and choosing a workspace*

Aptana Plugin

The Eclipse IDE offers a convenient way to add new tools via their plugin platform. The process for adding new plugins to Eclipse is straightforward and usually involves only a few steps to install a new plugin, as you will see in this section.

A specific web-tool plugin called Aptana provides support for server-side languages like Java as well as client languages such as CSS and JavaScript. This chapter and the other programming language chapters use the plugin to edit both server- and client-side languages. A benefit of using a plugin such as Aptana is that it can provide code-assist tools and code suggestions based on the type of file you are editing, such as CSS, JS, or HTML. The time saved with code-assist tools is usually significant enough to warrant their use. Again, if you feel comfortable exploring within your preferred IDE or other program, please do so.

To install the Aptana plugin, you need to have Eclipse installed and opened. Then proceed through the following steps:

1. From the Help menu, select "Install New Software" to open the dialog, which will look like the one in Figure 12-2.
2. Paste the URL for the update site, `http://download.aptana.com/studio3/plugin/install`, into the "Work With" text box, and hit the Enter (or Return) key.
3. In the populated table below, check the box next to the name of the plugin, and then click the Next button.
4. Click the Next button to go to the license page.
5. Choose the option to accept the terms of the license agreement, and click the Finish button.
6. You may need to restart Eclipse to continue.

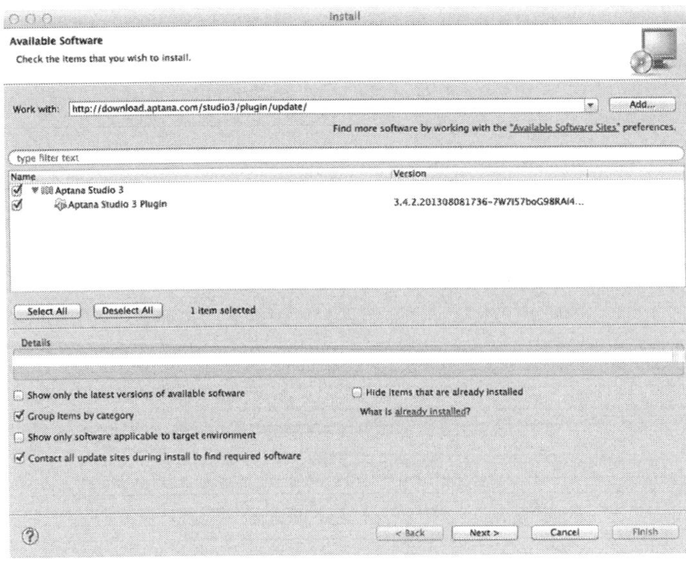

Figure 12-2. *Installing the Aptana plugin*

LogWatcher

When working with applications, it is often helpful to have a way to view application output through server logs. There are a few plugins available for Eclipse for this purpose, such as LogWatcher. With LogWatcher, you can watch output for multiple files inside or outside of Eclipse as well as filters to highlight or skip over specific patterns. At time of writing, the LogWatcher does not have an update URL for quick installation. To manually install LogWatcher, visit `http://graysky.sourceforge.net/` and follow the quick installation steps and set up the view to suit your development environment.

Adding the Project to Eclipse

After installing Eclipse plugin, you have met the minimum requirements to work with your project in the workspace. To keep the workflow as fluid as possible for each of the language sample applications, use the project import tool with Eclipse. To import the project into your workspace, follow these steps:

1. Go to `www.graphstory.com/practicalneo4j` and download the archive file for "Practical Neo4j for Java." Unzip the archive file on to your computer.
2. In Eclipse, select File>Import and type "project" in the "Select an import source" field.
3. Under the "General" heading, select "Existing Projects into Workspace". You should now see a window similar to Figure 12-3.

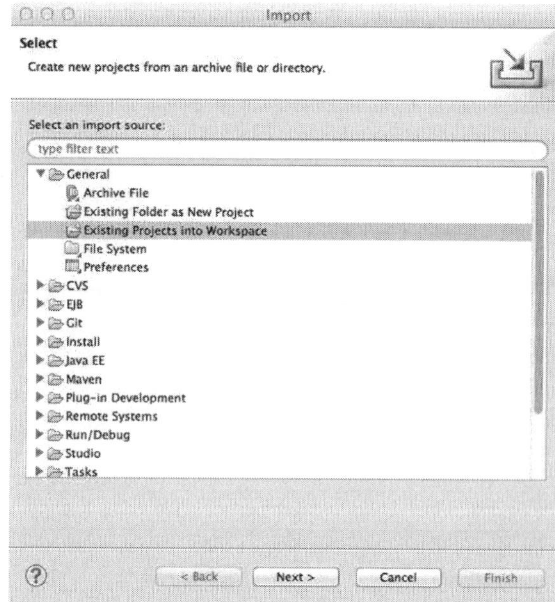

Figure 12-3. *Importing the project into Eclipse*

4. Now that you have selected "Existing Projects into Workspace", click the "Next >" button. The dialogue should now show an option to "Select root directory". Click the "Browse" button and find the root path of the "practicalneo4j-java" archive.
5. Next, check the option for "Copy project into workspace" and click the "Finish" button, as shown in Figure 12-4.

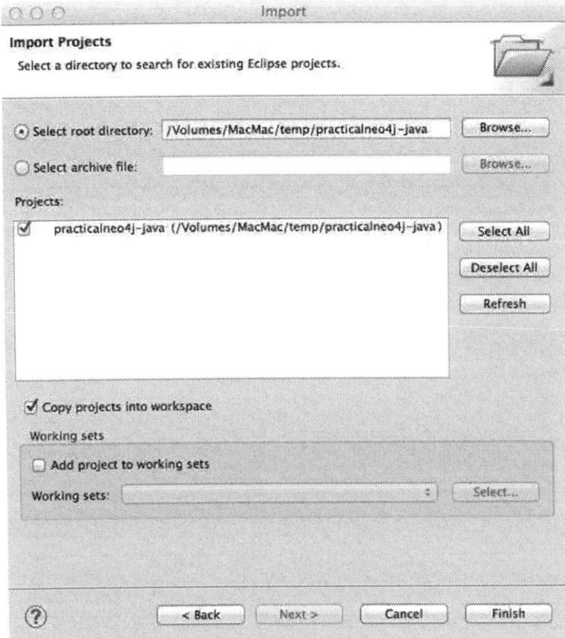

Figure 12-4. *Selecting the project location*

6. Once the project is finished importing into your workspace, you should have a directory structure that looks similar to the one shown in Figure 12-5.

Figure 12-5. *Snapshot of imported project*

Apache Struts 2

Apache Struts 2 is a Java implementation of an MVC framework. The aim of the framework is to help you quickly build out powerful web applications and APIs using only what is absolutely necessary to get the job done. The Struts 2 library and its dependencies are included with the sample application and should not require any additional configuration to run the application.

As with other MVC frameworks, one of the most important aspects of Struts 2 is the handling of request routing. Listing 12-1 demonstrates the basics of Struts 2 with the XML configuration option.

Listing 12-1. Example of `struts.xml` Configuration for a Package and Its Actions

```
<struts>
    <package name="default" extends="struts-default">
        <action name="Logon" class="mailreader2.Logon">
            <result name="input">/pages/Logon.jsp</result>
            <result name="cancel" type="redirectAction">Welcome</result>
            <result type="redirectAction">MainMenu</result>
            <result name="expired" type="chain">ChangePassword</result>
        </action>
        <action name="Logoff" class="mailreader2.Logoff">
            <result type="redirectAction">Welcome</result>
        </action>
    </package>
</struts>
```

However, the addition of annotations to Struts 2 has allowed request routing to be placed directly within the controller class. Most of the sample code uses the annotation method to keep the configuration variables closer to the action to which it is connected. As with the XML configuration, you can set up parent packages that set up top-level configuration that can then be reused within child packages. In Listing 12-2, you will see that the “HomeAction” uses the root namespace and extends the parent package that is named “practicalneo4j-struts-default”. In addition to being able to see the package and namespace settings at a glance, it allows you to configure and view the specific actions and results within the class file.

Listing 12-2. Example of Annotation Configuration

```
@ParentPackage("practicalneo4j-struts-default")
public class HomeAction extends GraphStoryAction {

        private static final long serialVersionUID = 1L;

        @Actions({
                @Action(value = "home", results = {
                        @Result(name = "success", type = "mustache", location = "/filepath")})
        })
        public String home() {
                 setTitle("Home");
                return SUCCESS;
        }
}
```

Hosts File

To keep each chapter separated in terms of the webserver and container configuration, I recommend that you add a host name to your local hosts file. The process for modifying the hosts file depends on your preferred operating system. For this chapter, add an entry that points 127.0.0.1 to practicalneo4j-java.

Local Apache Tomcat Configuration

To follow the sample application found later in this chapter, you will need to configure your local Apache Tomcat to use the workspace project in Eclipse as the document root. To do this, you will need to modify the server.xml file, which can be found at /TOMCAT-INSTALLATION/conf/server.xml, as shown in Listing 12-3. The most important changes are adding a HOST and CONTEXT as shown in the listing.

Listing 12-3. Example of Tomcat Configuration

```
<?xml version='1.0' encoding='utf-8'?>
<Server port="8005" shutdown="SHUTDOWN">
<!--
Listener and GlobalNamingResources excluded for brevity
-->
<Service name="Catalina">
<Connector port="8090" protocol="HTTP/1.1" connectionTimeout="20000" redirectPort="8443"
URIEncoding="UTF-8" useBodyEncodingForURI="true" />
        <Connector port="8009" protocol="AJP/1.3" redirectPort="8443" URIEncoding="UTF-8"
        useBodyEncodingForURI="true"/>
        <Engine name="Catalina" defaultHost="localhost">
                <Realm className="org.apache.catalina.realm.LockOutRealm">
        <               Realm className="org.apache.catalina.realm.UserDatabaseRealm"
        resourceName="UserDatabase"/>
        </Realm>
        <Host name="practicalneo4j-java"
        appBase="/path-to-workspace/practicalneo4j-java/WebContent"
        unpackWARs="true" autoDeploy="true" >
        <Context path="" docBase=""
        aliases="/resources=/path-to-workspace/practicalneo4j-java/WebContent/resources"
        reloadable="true" swallowOutput="true" />
        </Host>
        </Engine>
</Service>
</Server>
```

■ **Note** Using the method of pointing your HOST's appbase to your project within the workspace is one way to "hot reload" code changes. This method is very helpful for most developers because server startup and restart times can be a significant drain on productivity. The process of "deploy and run" has its positive aspects, but the minutes add up quickly.

Apache Tomcat and Apache HTTP

If you already have Apache HTTP installed (or some other webserver) and configured on port 80, you need to make sure that you do one of the following:

1. Ensure that Apache HTTP (or other service on port 80) has been stopped. You can then configure and run Tomcat on port 80.
2. Enable and configure ProxyPass in your virtual hosts file, as shown in Listing 12-4.
3. Use the default Apache Tomcat port of 8080.

If you use Apache HTTP with many other projects and do not want spend time starting and stopping Apache HTTP, I recommend the second option. A sample virtual host configuration is shown in Listing 12-4.

Listing 12-4. Minimum Configuration for `httpd-vhosts.conf`

```
<VirtualHost *:80>
        ServerName practicalneo4j-java
        ProxyPreserveHost On
        ProxyPass / http://practicalneo4j-java:8080/
        ProxyPassReverse / http://practicalneo4j-java:8080/
</VirtualHost>
```

Neo4j JDBC Driver

This section covers basic operations and usage of the Neo4j JDBC driver (NJDBC) with the goal of reviewing the small code examples before implementing it within an application. The next section of this chapter walks through a sample application with specific graph goals and models.

As for the other language drivers and libraries available for Neo4j, one goal of NJDBC is to provide a degree of abstraction over the Neo4j REST API. In addition, NJDBC provides some additional enhancements that you might otherwise be required write yourself at some other stage in the development of your Java application.

The Neo4j JDBC driver is maintained by the undeniably awesome and helpful Michael Hunger and supported by a number of great Java graphistas. If you would like to contribute to the Neo4j JDBC driver, go to `https://github.com/neo4j-contrib/neo4j-jdbc`.

Each of the following brief sections covers concepts that tie either directly or indirectly to features and functionality found within NJDBC and Neo4j Server. If you choose to go through each language chapter, notice how each library covers those features and functionality in similar ways but takes advantage of the language-specific capabilities to ensure the language-specific API is flexible and performant.

Managing Nodes and Relationships

Chapters 1 and 2 covered the elements of a graph database, which includes the most basic of graph concepts: the node. Managing nodes and their properties and relationships will probably account for the bulk of your application's graph-related code.

Creating a Node

The maintenance of nodes is set in motion with the creation process, as shown in Listing 12-5. Creating a node begins with setting up a connection to the database. Next, the properties are put into a Map, and then the Node can be saved to the database.

Listing 12-5. Creating a Node

```
import static org.neo4j.helpers.collection.MapUtil.map;
// other imports

// class
public void createUserNode(){

        // Make sure Neo4j Driver is registered
        Class.forName("org.neo4j.jdbc.Driver");

        // Connect
        Connection conn = DriverManager.getConnection("jdbc:neo4j://localhost:7474/");

        // create map
        HashMap<String, Object> userMap=new HashMap<String, Object>();
        userMap.put("name", "Greg");
        userMap.put("business","Graph Story");

        Map<String, Object> params = map("1", userMap);

        String query= " CREATE (user:User {1}) ";

        final PreparedStatement statement = conn.prepareStatement(query);

        for (Map.Entry<String, Object> entry : params.entrySet()) {
                int index = Integer.parseInt(entry.getKey());
                statement.setObject(index, entry.getValue());
        }

        final ResultSet result = statement.executeQuery();
}
```

■ **Note** The map keys (parameter index) that are passed into a prepared statement should use numbers and begin with "{1}" and so on.

Retrieving and Updating a Node

Once nodes have been added to the database, you need a way to retrieve and modify them. Listing 12-6 shows the process for finding a node by its node id value and updating it.

Listing 12-6. Retrieving and Updating a Node

```
//class
public void updateNode() {
        // Make sure Neo4j Driver is registered
        Class.forName("org.neo4j.jdbc.Driver");

        // Connect
        Connection conn = DriverManager.getConnection("jdbc:neo4j://localhost:7474/");

        Map<String, Object> params = map("1", "Greg", "2", "Greg", "3", "Jordan");

        String query= " MATCH (user:User {name:{1}}) " +
                      " SET user.firstname={2},  user.lastname={3}  " +
                      " RETURN user ";

        final PreparedStatement statement = conn.prepareStatement(query);

        for (Map.Entry<String, Object> entry : params.entrySet()) {
                int index = Integer.parseInt(entry.getKey());
                statement.setObject(index, entry.getValue());
        }

        final ResultSet result = statement.executeQuery();

        // result contains user data, which can be mapped to bean
}
```

Removing a Node

Once a node's graph id has been set and saved into the database, it becomes eligible to be removed when necessary. To remove a node, set a variable as a node object instance and then call the delete method for the node (Listing 12-7).

■ **Note** You cannot delete any node that is currently set as the start point or end point of any relationship. You must remove the relationship before you can delete the node.

Listing 12-7. Deleting a Node

```
public void DeleteNode() {
        // Make sure Neo4j Driver is registered
        Class.forName("org.neo4j.jdbc.Driver");

        // Connect
        Connection conn = DriverManager.getConnection("jdbc:neo4j://localhost:7474/");


        Map<String, Object> params = map("1", "Greg");

        String query= " MATCH (user:User {name:{1}}) " +
                      " DELETE user  ";

        final PreparedStatement statement = conn.prepareStatement(query);

        for (Map.Entry<String, Object> entry : params.entrySet()) {
                int index = Integer.parseInt(entry.getKey());
                statement.setObject(index, entry.getValue());
        }

        final ResultSet result = statement.executeQuery();

}
```

Creating a Relationship

To create a basic relationship, you need at a minimum one distinct node and to know ahead of time the name of the relationship you would like to use. Listing 12-8 creates a relationship called FOLLOWS between two user nodes by matching on their names and using CREATE UNIQUE to establish the relationship.

■ **Note** Both the start and end nodes of a relationship must already be established within the database before the relationship can be saved.

Listing 12-8. Relating Two Nodes

```
public void CreateRelationship() {

        // Make sure Neo4j Driver is registered
        Class.forName("org.neo4j.jdbc.Driver");

        // Connect
        Connection conn = DriverManager.getConnection("jdbc:neo4j://localhost:7474/");

        Map<String, Object> params = map("1", "Greg", "2", "Jeremy");
```

```
        String query= " CREATE UNIQUE (u1:User { name:{1}})-[r:FOLLOWS]->(u2:User { name:{2}}) " +
                      " RETURN r ";

        final PreparedStatement statement = conn.prepareStatement(query);

        for (Map.Entry<String, Object> entry : params.entrySet()) {
                int index = Integer.parseInt(entry.getKey());
                statement.setObject(index, entry.getValue());
        }

        final ResultSet result = statement.executeQuery();
}
```

Retrieving Relationships

Once a relationship has been created between one or more nodes, the relationship can be retrieved using the nodes and the relationship type (Listing 12-9).

Listing 12-9. Retrieving Relationships

```
public void GetRelationshipsByName() {

        // Make sure Neo4j Driver is registered
        Class.forName("org.neo4j.jdbc.Driver");

        // Connect
        Connection conn = DriverManager.getConnection("jdbc:neo4j://localhost:7474/");

        Map<String, Object> params = map("1", "Greg", "2", "Jeremy");

        String query= " MATCH (u1:User { name:{1}})-[rel:FOLLOWS]->(u2:User { name:{2}}) " +
                      " RETURN rel ";

        final PreparedStatement statement = conn.prepareStatement(query);

        for (Map.Entry<String, Object> entry : params.entrySet()) {
                int index = Integer.parseInt(entry.getKey());
                statement.setObject(index, entry.getValue());
        }

        final ResultSet result = statement.executeQuery();
}
```

Deleting a Relationship

Once a relationship's graph id has been set and saved into the database, it becomes eligible to be removed when necessary (Listing 12-10).

Listing 12-10. Deleting a Relationship

```
public void DeleteRelationship() {

        // Make sure Neo4j Driver is registered
        Class.forName("org.neo4j.jdbc.Driver");

        // Connect
        Connection conn = DriverManager.getConnection("jdbc:neo4j://localhost:7474/");

        Map<String, Object> params = map("1", "Greg", "2", "Jeremy");

        String query= " MATCH (u1:User { name:{1}})-[rel:FOLLOWS]->(u2:User { name:{2}}) " +
                      " DELETE rel ";

        final PreparedStatement statement = conn.prepareStatement(query);

        for (Map.Entry<String, Object> entry : params.entrySet()) {
                int index = Integer.parseInt(entry.getKey());
                statement.setObject(index, entry.getValue());
        }

        final ResultSet result = statement.executeQuery();

}
```

Using Labels

Labels function as specific meta-descriptions that can be applied to nodes. Labels were introduced in Neo4j 2.0 in order to support index querying and can also function as a way to quickly create a subgraph.

Adding a Label to Nodes

For existing nodes, you can add one more labels by using the SET clause. As Listing 12-11 shows, you first find the node using the MATCH clause and then SET one (or more) labels.

■ **Caution** A label will not exist on the database server until it has been added to at least one node.

Listing 12-11. Adding Labels to a Node

```
public void AddLabels() {

        // Make sure Neo4j Driver is registered
        Class.forName("org.neo4j.jdbc.Driver");

        // Connect
        Connection conn = DriverManager.getConnection("jdbc:neo4j://localhost:7474/");

        // uses a Node Id for the param in the WHERE clause
        Map<String, Object> params = map("1", 1);

        String query= " MATCH (n) "+
                      " WHERE id(n) = {1} "+
                      " SET n :Developer :Admin "+
                      " RETURN n ";

        final PreparedStatement statement = conn.prepareStatement(query);

        for (Map.Entry<String, Object> entry : params.entrySet()) {
                int index = Integer.parseInt(entry.getKey());
                statement.setObject(index, entry.getValue());
        }

        final ResultSet result = statement.executeQuery();

}
```

Removing a Label

Removing a label uses nearly identical syntax as adding labels to a node, except that you change the SET clause to a REMOVE clause. After the given label has been removed from the node, the return value is the node (Listing 12-12).

Listing 12-12. Removing a Label from a Node

```
public void RemoveLabels() {

        // Make sure Neo4j Driver is registered
        Class.forName("org.neo4j.jdbc.Driver");

        // Connect
        Connection conn = DriverManager.getConnection("jdbc:neo4j://localhost:7474/");

        // uses a Node Id for the param in the WHERE clause
        Map<String, Object> params = map("1", 1);

        String query= " MATCH (n) "+
                      " WHERE id(n) = {1} "+
                      " REMOVE n :Developer :Admin "+
                      " RETURN n ";
```

```
        final PreparedStatement statement = conn.prepareStatement(query);

        for (Map.Entry<String, Object> entry : params.entrySet()) {
                int index = Integer.parseInt(entry.getKey());
                statement.setObject(index, entry.getValue());
        }

        final ResultSet result = statement.executeQuery();

}
```

Querying with a Label

To get nodes that use a specific label, use a MATCH clause, similar to previous examples, and, in this instance, set a LIMIT of 50 nodes to be returned (Listing 12-13).

Listing 12-13. Querying with a Label

```
public Iterable GetNodesByLabel() {

        // Make sure Neo4j Driver is registered
        Class.forName("org.neo4j.jdbc.Driver");

        // Connect
        Connection conn = DriverManager.getConnection("jdbc:neo4j://localhost:7474/");

        String query= " MATCH (users:User) " +
                      " RETURN users " +
                      " LIMIT 50 ";

        final PreparedStatement statement = conn.prepareStatement(query);

         final ResultSet result = statement.executeQuery();
}
```

Developing a Java and Neo4j Application

This section covers the basics of configuring a development environment, preliminary to building out your first Java and Neo4j application. Again, if you have not worked through the installation steps in Chapter 2, take a few minutes to review the steps and configure your development environment before continuing.

Preparing the Graph

In order to spend more time highlighting code examples for each of the more common graph models, you will use a preloaded instance of Neo4j including necessary plugins, such as the spatial plugin.

■ **Tip** To quickly setup a server instance with the sample data and plugins for this chapter, go to `graphstory.com/practicalneo4j`. You will be provided with your own free trial instance, a knowledge base, and email support from Graph Story. Alternatively, you may run a local Neo4j database instance with the sample data by going to `graphstory.com/practicalneo4j`, downloading the zip file containing the sample database and plugins, and adding them to your local instance.

Using the Sample Application

If you have already downloaded the sample application from `graphstory.com/practicalneo4j` for Java and configured it within your local application environment, you can skip ahead to the next section.

Otherwise, you will need to go back to the "`Java and Neo4j Development Environment`" section and set up your local environment in order to follow the examples in the sample application.

Struts2 Application Configuration

Before diving into the code examples, you need to update the configuration for the Struts2 application. In Eclipse (or the IDE you are using), open the file `GraphStoryConstants.java`, which is located in the `com.practicalneo4j.graphstory.util` package, and edit the GraphStory connection string information. If you are using a free account from graphstory.com, you will change the username, password, and URL in Listing 12-14 with the one provided in your graph console on `graphstory.com`.

Listing 12-14. Database Connection Settings for a Remote Service, such as Graph Story

```
public static final String DEFAULT_URL = " https:// username:password@theURL:7473";
```

If you have installed a local Neo4j server instance, you can modify the configuration to use the local address and port that you specified during the installation, as in the example shown in Listing 12-15.

Listing 12-15. Database Connection Settings for Local Enviroment

```
public static final String DEFAULT_URL = "http://localhost:7474";
```

Once the environment is properly configured and started, you can open a browser to the URL, such as `http://practicalneo4j-java`, and you should see a page like the one shown in Figure 12-6.

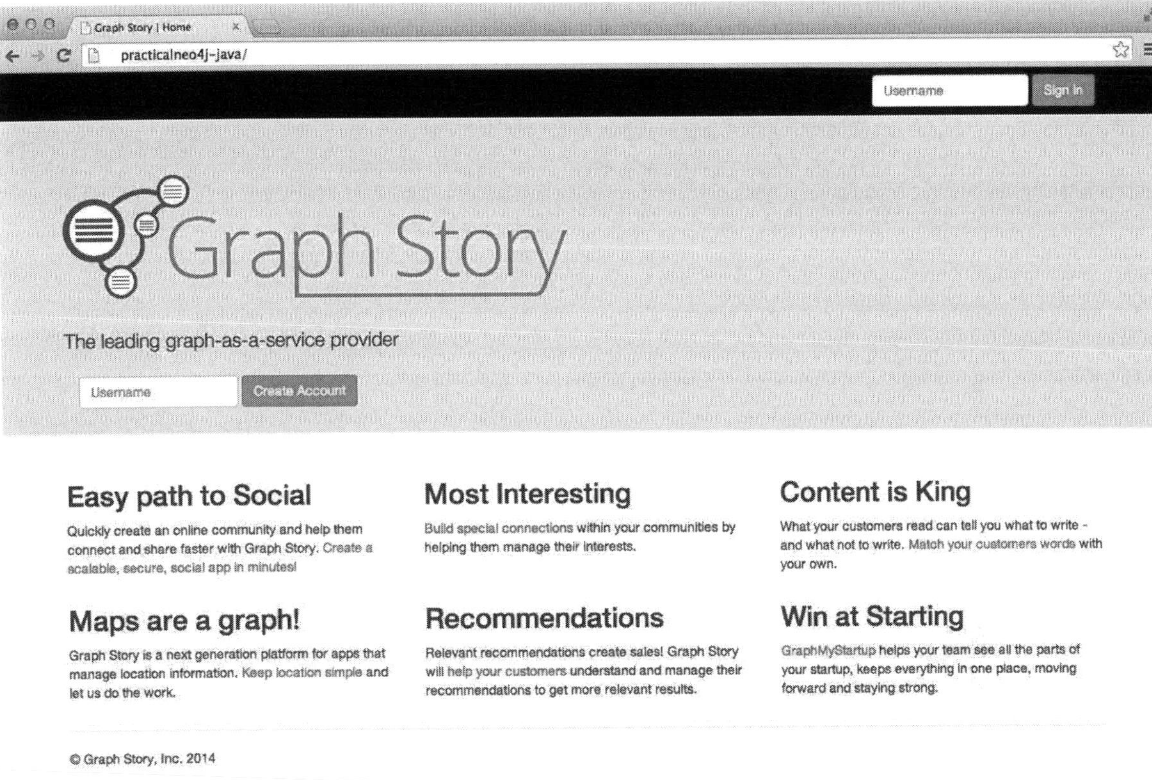

Figure 12-6. *The Java sample application home page*

Controller and Service Layers

In order to provide some common objects and methods at the controller layer, all of the action controllers in the sample application extend a parent controller called `GraphStoryAction`. The `GraphStoryAction controller` provides access to the `GraphStory` bean and the `GraphStoryDAO` service.

The `GraphStory` bean encapsulates the domain objects for the sample application and is primarily used for convenience. This object will allow domain objects to be sent to the service layer and returned—in some cases—with helper objects and properties, such as form and data validation messages to help users.

The `GraphStoryDAO` service provides access to each of the individual service classes that support persistence and other service-level operations on each of the domain objects. For example, if an exception is raised in the service layer, such as a when attempting to create a User that matches an existing User's username, then the `GraphStory` object can be returned with message information, such as an error message, which can then be used to determine the next part of the application flow as well as return messages to the view.

ResultSetMapper

A common need in many data-driven applications is to take results from a query and map them back to domain objects. To map database results back to the domain objects, you will use a specifically designed class called `ResultSetMapper`. ResultSetMapper contains four public methods and one private method:

- `mapLabelNodeToClass`—This method takes a `Map` from a query result, a `Class` type and an `ObjectMapper` to convert a single `Label` node into a domain object.
- `mapResultSetToObject`—This method takes a `ResultSet` and `Class` type and returns a List of domain objects based on the Class type.
- `mapResultSetToListMappedClass`—This method takes a `ResultSet` and `Class` type and returns a List of mapped objects based on the `Class` type. Mapped objects typically consist of a mix of properties that will be used for the view, such as a list of status updates.
- `mapResultSetToMappedClass`—This method takes a `Map` and `Class` type and returns a single mapped object based on the `Class` type. Again, a mapped object typically consists of a mix of properties that will be used for the view, such as a list of status updates.
- `query`—this private method is used to convert a `ResultSet` into an `Iterator` of `Map` objects.

■ **Head's-Up** Struts 2 and the front-end code, such as Mustache, help run the sample application, but I will limit extended coverage of those concepts to the Social Graph section. In the Social Graph section, I will focus on the non-obvious but important aspects of those concepts. As you go through the rest of the application, controllers as well as the front-end code will use similar syntax, so they will be referenced but not listed in the chapter as repetitive coverage of that syntax would distract from the discrete, specific Java and Neo4j examples.

Social Graph Model

This section explores the social graph model and a few of the operations that typically accompany it. In particular, this section looks at the following:

- Sign-up and Login
- Updating a user
- Creating a relationship type through a user by following other users
- Managing user content, such as displaying, adding, updating, and removing status updates

---

■ **Note** The sample graph database used for these examples comes loaded with social data, so you can immediately begin working with representative data in each of the graph models. In the case of the social graph—and for other graph models, as well—you will login with the user **ajordan**. Going forward, please login with **ajordan** to see each of the working examples.

Sign Up

The HTML required for the user sign-up form is shown in Listing 12-16 and can be found in the `{PROJECTROOT}/WebContent/mustache/html/home/index.html` file. The important item to note in the HTML form is that the **bean name** and **property** are used to specify what is passed to controller and, subsequently, to the service layer for saving to the database.

Listing 12-16. HTML Snippet of Sign-Up Form

```
<form class="navbar-form navbar-left" action="/signup/add" role="form"
        id="createaccountform" method="post">
        <div class="form-group">
        <input type="text" placeholder="Username" name="user.username" class="form-control">
        </div>
        <button type="submit" class="btn btn-success">Create Account</button>   
</form>
```

■ **Note** While the sample application creates a user without a password, I am certainly not suggesting or advocating this approach for a production application. I excluded the password property in order to create a simple sign-up and login that helps keep the focus on the more salient aspects of the Neo4j JDBC library.

Sign-Up Action

In the sign-up action, simply pass the GraphStory bean to the SignUpAction's add method, which in turn connects to the service layer via the save method in the UserDAO class. The save method will also perform a look up on the `username` passed in via the request to see if it already exists in the database using the `userExists` method found in the `UserDAO` class. If no match is found, the username is passed on to the save query within the if statement (Listing 12-17).

If no errors are returned during the save attempt, the request is redirected via `redirectAction` and a message is passed to thank the user for signing up. Otherwise, the user is redirected back to the home view along with an error message to inform the user of the problem.

Listing 12-17. The add Method in the `SignUpAction`

```
@Action(value = "add",
        results = {
                @Result(name = "success", type = "redirectAction", params = { "actionName",
                "thankyou",
                "namespace", "/" }),
                @Result(name = "userExists", type = "mustache", location = "/mustache/html/home/
                index.html")})
public String add() {
        try {
              graphStory = getGraphStoryDAO().getUserDAO().save(graphStory);

                if (graphStory.getErrorMsgs().isEmpty()) {
```

```
                setTitle("Thank you!");
                return SUCCESS;
            }
            else {
                setTitle("Home");
                        return "userExists";
            }
        }
        catch (Exception e) {
            log.error(e);
            return ERROR;
        }

}
```

Adding a User

In each part of the five graph areas covered in the chapter, the domain object, such as a User, will have a corresponding DAO class to manage the persistence operations within the database. In this case, the UserDAO class covers the management of the application's user nodes by executing cypher queries.

To save a node and label it as a User, the save method, shown in Listing 12-18, makes use of the CREATE clause by passing the user object through a convenience method called objectAsMap.

Listing 12-18. The save Method in the UserDAO Class

```
public GraphStory save(GraphStory graphStory) throws Exception {

        // no user match, so proceed with the saving
        if (userExists(graphStory.getUser()) == false) {

                // give user an id
                graphStory.getUser().setUserId(uuidGenWithTimeStamp());

                cypher.iteratorQuery(" CREATE (user:User {1}) ", map("1",
                      objectAsMap(graphStory.getUser())));

        } else {
                graphStory.getErrorMsgs().add("The username you entered already exists.");
        }

        return graphStory;
}
```

Login

Next, I will review the login process for the sample application. To execute the login process, you will use the login route and the UserDAO class. Before I review the controller and service layer, I will take a quick look at the front-end code for the login view.

Login Form

The HTML required for the user login form is shown in Listing 12-19 and can be found in the {PROJECTROOT}/ WebContent/mustache/html/global/base-home.html layout file. Again, an important item to note in the form is that the **bean name** and **property** are used to specify what is passed to controller and, subsequently, to the service layer for querying the database.

Listing 12-19. The login Form

```
<form class="navbar-form navbar-right" action="/login" role="form" method="post">
        <div class="form-group">
        <input type="text" placeholder="Username" name="user.username" class="form-control">
        </div>
<button type="submit" class="btn btn-success">Sign in</button>
</form>
```

Login Action

The LoginAction controller is used to handle the flow of the login process, as shown in Listing 12-20. Inside LoginAction, use the checkLogin method to check if the user exists in the database.

If the user was found during the login attempt, a cookie is added to the response and the request is redirected via redirectAction to the social home page, shown in Figure 12-7. Otherwise, the route specifies the HTML page to return and adds the error messages that need to be displayed back to the view.

Listing 12-20. The checkLogin Method in the LoginAction Controller

```
@Action(value = "login",
                results = {
                @Result(name = "success", type = "redirectAction", params = { "actionName",
                "social", "namespace", "" }),
               @Result(name = "loginfail", type = "mustache", location =
               "/mustache/html/home/message.html")
                })
public String checkLogin() {

        try {

                graphStory = graphStoryDAO.getUserDAO().login(graphStory);

                if (noGraphStoryErrors()) {
                        response.addCookie(addCookie(GraphStoryConstants.graphstoryUserAuthKey,
                                graphStory.getUser().getUsername()));

                        return SUCCESS;

                } else {

                            setTitle("Login Failed");
                        return "loginfail";
                }

        }
```

```
        catch (Exception e) {

                log.error(e);
                return ERROR;
        }
}
```

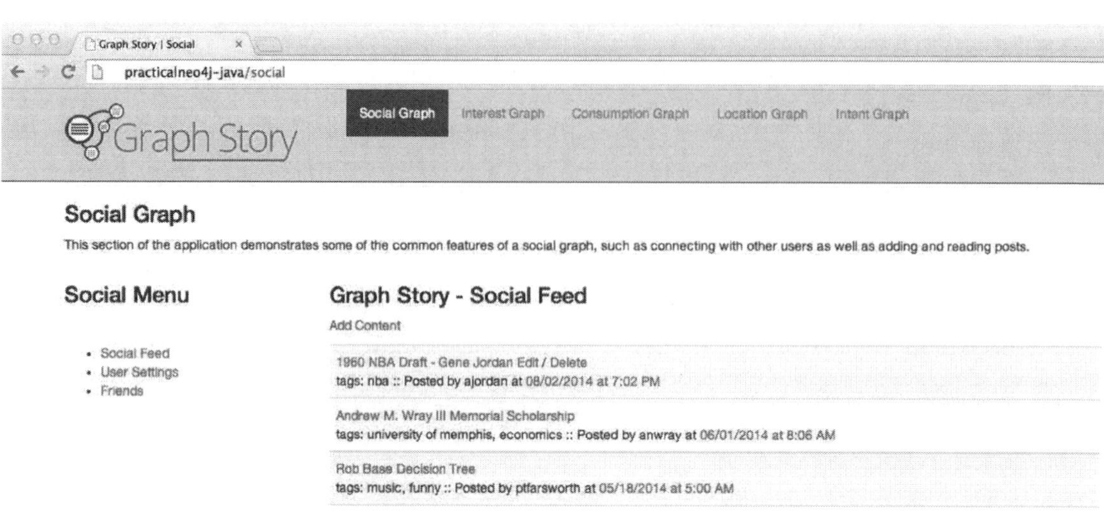

Figure 12-7. *The Social Graph home page*

Login Service

To check to see if the user values being passed through are connected to a valid user in the database, the application uses the `login` method in the `UserDAO` class. As shown in the Listing 12-21, the result of the `login` method is assigned to the `tempUser` variable.

If the result is not null, the result is set on the `graphStory User` object and returned to the controller layer of the application.

Listing 12-21. The `login` Method in the `UserDAO` Class

```
private User tempUser;

public GraphStory login(GraphStory graphStory) throws Exception {

        tempUser = getByUserName(graphStory.getUser());

        if (tempUser != null) {
                graphStory.setUser(tempUser);
        } else {
                addErrorMsg(graphStory, "The username you entered does not exist.");
        }

        return graphStory;
}
```

Now that the user is logged in, they can edit their settings, create relationships with other users in the graph and create their own content.

Updating a User

To access the page for updating a user, click on the "User Settings" link in the social graph section, as shown in Figure 12-8. In this example, the front-end code uses an AJAX request via POST and will add or—in the case of the **ajordan** user—update the first and last name of the user.

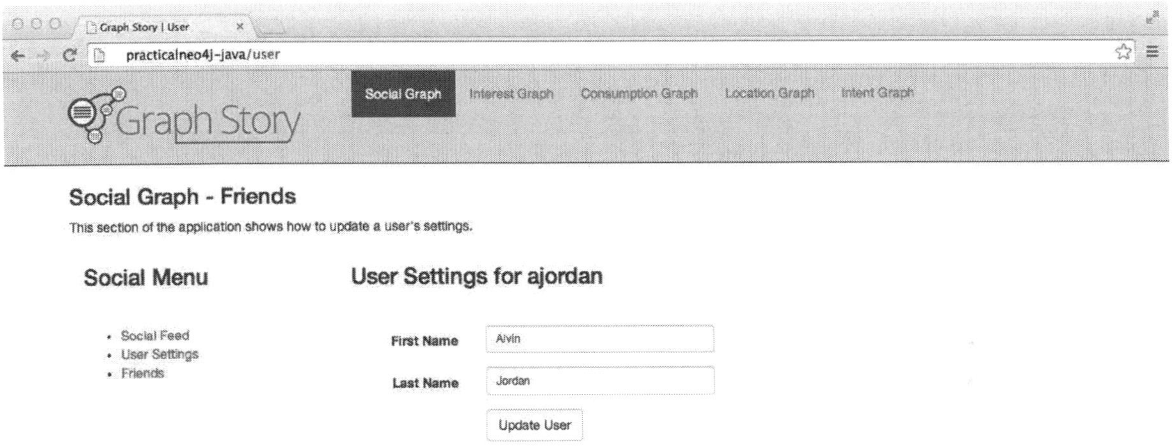

Figure 12-8. *The User Settings Page*

User Update Form

The user settings form is located in `{PROJECTROOT}/WebContent/mustache/html/graphs/social/user.html` and is similar in structure to the other forms presented in the Sign Up and Login sections. One difference is that I have added the `value` property to the input element and used Mustache variables for displaying the respective stored values. If none exist, the form fields will be empty (Listing 12-22).

Listing 12-22. User Update Form

```
<form class="form-horizontal" id="userform">
  <div class="form-group">
    <label for="firstname" class="col-sm-2 control-label">First Name</label>
    <div class="col-sm-10">
      <input type="text" class="form-control input-sm" id="firstname" name="user.firstname"
       value="{{ graphStory.user.firstname }}" />
    </div>
  </div>
  <div class="form-group">
    <label for="lastname" class="col-sm-2 control-label">Last Name</label>
    <div class="col-sm-10">
      <input type="text" class="form-control input-sm" id="lastname" name="user.lastname"
       value="{{ graphStory.user.lastname }}" />
    </div>
```

```
  </div>
  <div class="form-group">
    <div class="col-sm-offset-2 col-sm-10">
      <button type="submit" id="updateUser" class="btn btn-default">Update User</button>
    </div>
  </div>
</form>
```

User Action

The UserAction controller contains an edit method with the path /user/edit, which takes a JSON object as an argument. You should note that the User object is converted from a JSON string and returns a User object as JSON. The response could be used to update the form elements, but because the values are already set within the form there is no need to update the values. In this case, the application uses the JSON response to let the user know if the update succeeded or not via a standard JavaScript alert message (Listing 12-23).

Listing 12-23. The edit Method in the UserAction Class

```
@Action(value = "user/edit", interceptorRefs = {
        @InterceptorRef(value = "cookie", params = { "cookiesName", "graphstoryUserAuthKey" }),
        @InterceptorRef(value = "json", params = { "noCache", "true", "excludeNullProperties",
        "true" }) },
        results = {
        @Result(name = "success", type = "json", params = { "noCache", "true" })
        })
public String edit() {

        try {
                if (graphStory.getUser() != null) {

                graphStory.setUser(graphStoryDAO.getUserDAO()
                        .update(
                                cookiesMap.get(GraphStoryConstants.graphstoryUserAuthKey),
                                graphStory.getUser())
                        );
                }
        }
        catch (Exception e) {
                log.error(e);
        }

        return SUCCESS;
}
```

User Update Method

To complete the update, the controller layer calls the update method in UserDAO class. Because the object being passed into the update method did nothing more than modify the first and last name of an existing entity, you can use the SET clause via Cypher to update the properties in the graph, as shown in Listing 12-24. This Cypher statement also makes use of the MATCH clause to retrieve the User node.

Listing 12-24. The update Method in the UserDAO Class

```
public User update(String currentusername, User user) throws Exception {

        Map<String, Object> userMap = null;

        userMap = IteratorUtil.singleOrNull(cypher.iteratorQuery(
                " MATCH (user:User {username:{1}}) " +
                " SET user.firstname={2}, user.lastname={3} " +
                " RETURN user",
                map("1", currentusername, "2", user.getFirstname(), "3", user.getLastname())));

        ResultSetMapper<User> resultSetMapper = new ResultSetMapper<User>();

        return resultSetMapper.mapLabelNodeToClass(userMap, User.class, new ObjectMapper());
}
```

Connecting Users

A common feature in social media applications is to allow users to connect to each other through an explicit relationship. In the sample application, use the directed relationship type called FOLLOWS. By going to the "Friends" page within the social graph section, you can see the list of users the current user is following, search for new friends to follow and add and remove friends. The UserAction controller contains each of the methods and routes to control the flow for these features, specifically the routes named friends, searchbyusername, follow, and unfollow.

To display the list of the users the current user is following, the showFriends method, shown in Listing 12-23, in the UserAction class calls the following method in UserDAO class. The following method, also shown in Listing 12-25, creates a list of users by matching the current user's username with the directed relationship FOLLOWS on the variable user.

Listing 12-25. The showFriends Method in UserAction and the following Method in UserDAO

```
// showFriends in UserAction
@Action(value = "friends",
        results = {
                @Result(name = "success", type = "mustache", location =
                        "/mustache/html/graphs/social/friends.html"),
        })

public String showFriends() {

        try {
                setTitle("Friends");
```

```
            graphStory.setFollowing(graphStoryDAO.getUserDAO()
                    .following(cookiesMap.get(GraphStoryConstants.graphstoryUserAuthKey)));

        }
        catch (Exception e) {
            log.error(e);
        }

        return SUCCESS;
}

// following method in UserDAO
public List<User> following(String username) {

        try
        {
            ResultSet resultSet = cypher.resultSetQuery(
                    " MATCH (user { username:{1}})-[:FOLLOWS]->(users) " +
                    " RETURN users " +
                    " ORDER BY users.username",
                    map("1", username));

            ResultSetMapper<User> resultSetMapper = new ResultSetMapper<User>();
            return resultSetMapper.mapRersultSetToObject(resultSet, User.class);
        }
        catch (Exception e) {
            log.error(e);
            return null;
        }
}
```

If the List contains users, it will be returned to the controller and displayed in the right-hand side of the page, as shown in Figure 12-9. The display code for showing the list of users can be found in `{PROJECTROOT}/WebContent/mustache/html/graphs/social/friends.html` and is shown in the code snippet in Listing 12-26.

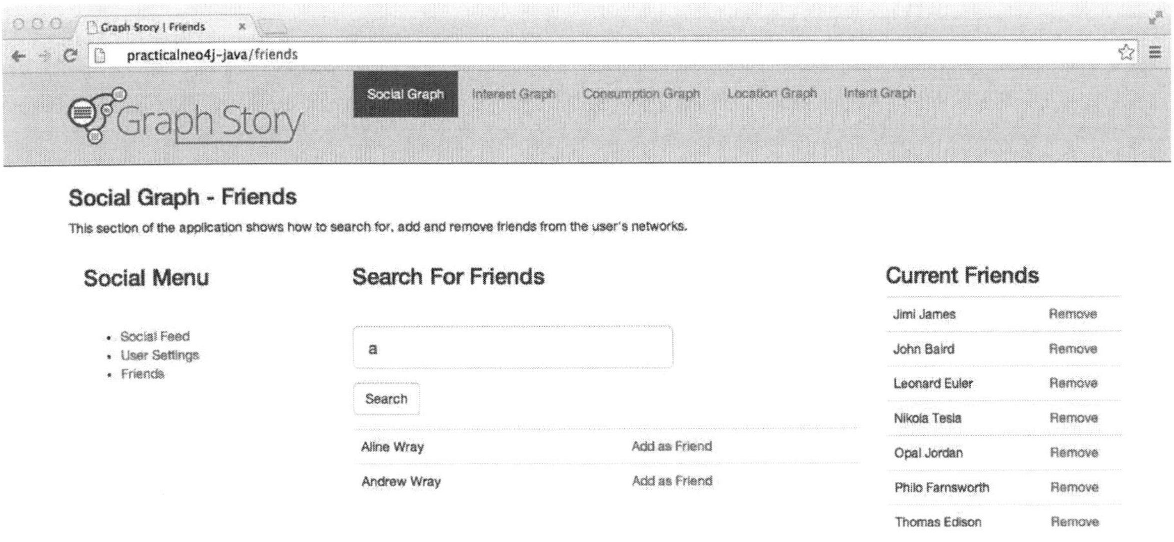

Figure 12-9. *The Friends page*

Listing 12-26. The HTML Code Snippet for Displaying the List of Friends

```
<div class="col-md-3">
        <h3>Current Friends</h3>
        <table class="table" id="following">
        {{#graphStory.following}}
                 <tr>
                 <td>{{firstname}} {{lastname}}</td>
                 <td><a href="#" id="{{username}}" class="removefriend">Remove</a></td>
                 </tr>
         {{/graphStory.following}}
         {{^graphStory.following}}
                        No friends :(
        {{/graphStory.following}}
        </table>
</div>
```

To search for users to follow, the searchByUsername method contains a GET route /searchbyusername and passes in a username value as part of the path. This route executes the searchNotFollowing method found in UserDAO class, showing the second section of Listing 12-27.

The first part of the WHERE clause in searchNotFollowing returns users whose username matches on a wildcard String value. The second part of the WHERE clause in searchNotFollowing checks to make sure that the users in the MATCH clause are not already being followed by the current user.

Listing 12-27. The searchByUsername Route and Service Method

```
@Action(value = "searchbyusername/{username}",
        results = {@Result(name = "success", type = "json")})
public String searchByUsername() {
        try {
```

```
                graphStory.setUsers(graphStoryDAO.getUserDAO()
               .searchNotFollowing(
                        cookiesMap.get(GraphStoryConstants.graphstoryUserAuthKey),
                         graphStory.getUsername()
                        ));
        }
        catch (Exception e) {
                        log.error(e);
        }

        return SUCCESS;
}

// the searchNotFollowing method returns users NOT being followed already
public List<User> searchNotFollowing(String currentusername, String username) {
         try
        {
                username = username.toLowerCase() + ".*";

                ResultSet resultSet = cypher.resultSetQuery(
                        " MATCH (users:User), (user { username:{1}}) " +

                        // where n.username WILDCARD on param 'u'
                        // but is not the current user
                        " WHERE (users.username =~ {2} AND users <> user) " +

                        // and don't return users already being followed
                        " AND (NOT (user)-[:FOLLOWS]->(users)) " +
                        " RETURN users" +
                        " ORDER BY users.username",
                        map("1", currentusername, "2", username));

                ResultSetMapper<User> resultSetMapper = new ResultSetMapper<User>();
                return resultSetMapper.mapRersultSetToObject(resultSet, User.class);
        }
        catch (Exception e) {
                log.error(e);
                return null;
        }
}
```

The searchByUsername in {PROJECTROOT}/WebContent/resources/js/graphstory.js uses an AJAX request and formats the response in renderSearchByUsername. If the list contains users, it will be displayed in the center of the page under the search form, as shown in Figure 12-9. Otherwise, the response will display "No Users Found".

Once the search returns results, the next action would be to click on the "Add as Friend" link, which calls the addfriend method in graphstory.js. This will perform an AJAX request to the follow method in the UserAction and calls the follow method in UserDAO. The follow method in UserDAO, shown in Listing 12-28, will create the relationship between the two users by first finding each entity via the MATCH clause and then by using the CREATE UNIQUE clause to create the directed FOLLOWS relationship. Once the operation is complete, the controller then requests the following method in UserService to return the full list of followers ordered by the username.

Listing 12-28. The `follow` Method in `UserAction` and `follow` Service Method in `UserDAO`

```
@Action(value = "follow/{username}",results = {@Result(name = "success", type = "json")})
public String follow() {
        try {

                graphStory.setFollowing(graphStoryDAO.getUserDAO()
                        .follow(
                                cookiesMap.get(GraphStoryConstants.graphstoryUserAuthKey),
                                graphStory.getUsername()
                        ));
        }
        catch (Exception e) {
                log.error(e);
        }

        return SUCCESS;
}

// follow and return new list of following
public List<User> follow(String currentusername, String username) {
        try
        {
                ResultSet resultSet = cypher.resultSetQuery(
                        " MATCH (user1:User {username:{1}} ),(user2:User {username:{2}} )" +
                        " CREATE UNIQUE user1-[:FOLLOWS]->user2" +
                        " WITH user1" +
                        " MATCH (user1)-[f:FOLLOWS]->(users)" +
                        " RETURN users " +
                        " ORDER BY users.username",
                        map("1", currentusername, "2", username));

                ResultSetMapper<User> resultSetMapper = new ResultSetMapper<User>();
                return resultSetMapper.mapRersultSetToObject(resultSet, User.class);
        }
        catch (Exception e) {
                log.error(e);
                return null;
        }
}
```

The unfollow feature uses an application flow nearly identical to the follows feature. In the `unfollow` method, shown in Listing 12-29, the controller passes in two arguments: the current username and username to be unfollowed. Once completed, the `unfollow` route returns the updated collection of users being followed.

Listing 12-29. The `unfollow` Route and `unfollow` Method

```
// unfollow a user
@Action(value = "unfollow/{username}",results = {@Result(name = "success", type = "json")})
public String unfollow() {
        try {

                graphStory.setFollowing(graphStoryDAO.getUserDAO()
                        .unfollow(
                                cookiesMap.get(GraphStoryConstants.graphstoryUserAuthKey),
                                graphStory.getUsername()
                        ));
        }
        catch (Exception e) {
                log.error(e);
        }

        return SUCCESS;
}

// unfollow (e.g. delete relationship) and return new list of following
public List<User> unfollow(String currentusername, String username) {
        try
        {
                ResultSet resultSet = cypher.resultSetQuery(
                " MATCH (user1:User {username:{1}} )-[f:FOLLOWS]->(user2:User {username:{2}} )" +
                " DELETE f" +
                " WITH user1" +
                " MATCH (user1)-[f:FOLLOWS]->(users)" +
                " RETURN users " +
                " ORDER BY users.username",
                map("1", currentusername, "2", username));

                ResultSetMapper<User> resultSetMapper = new ResultSetMapper<User>();
                return resultSetMapper.mapRersultSetToObject(resultSet, User.class);
        }
        catch (Exception e) {
                log.error(e);
                return null;
        }

}
```

User-Generated Content

Another important feature in social media applications is being able to have users view, add, edit, and remove content, sometimes referred to as User Generated Content. In the case of this content, you will not be creating connections between the content and its owner but creating a linked list of status updates. In other words, you will be connecting a User to their most recent status update and then connecting each subsequent status to the next update through the `CURRENTPOST` and `NEXTPOST` directed relationship types, respectively.

This approach is used for two reasons. First, the sample application displays a given number of posts at a time and using a limited linked list is more efficient than getting all status updates connected directly to a user and then sorting and limiting the number of items to return. Second, you will also help limit the number of relationships that are placed on the User and Content entities. Overall, the graph operations should be more efficient using the linked list approach.

Getting the Status Updates

To display the first set of status updates, start with the `social` route of the social section of the Java sample application `graphstory`. This method accesses the getContent method within `Content` service class, which takes an argument of the current user's username and the page being requested. The page refers to set number of objects within a collection. In this instance the paging is zero-based, so you will request page 0 and limit the page size to 4 in order to return the first page.

The `getContent` method in `Content` class, shown in Listing 12-30, first determines whom the user is following and then matches that set of users with the status updates starting with the `CURRENTPOST`. The `CURRENTPOST` is then matched on the next three status updates via the `[:NEXTPOST*0..3]` section of the query. Finally, the method uses a loop to add a readable date and time string property—based on the timestamp—on the results returned to the controller and view.

Listing 12-30. The `getContent` Method in `ContentDAO` Class

```
public GraphStory getContent(String username, int skip, GraphStory graphStory) {
        try {

                ResultSet rs = cypher.resultSetQuery(
                " MATCH (u:User {username: {1} }) " +
                " WITH u " +
                " MATCH (u)-[:FOLLOWS*0..1]->f " +
                " WITH DISTINCT f,u " +
                " MATCH f-[:CURRENTPOST]-lp-[:NEXTPOST*0..3]-p " +
                " RETURN  p.contentId as contentId, p.title as title, p.tagstr as tagstr, " +
                " p.timestamp as timestamp, p.url as url, f.username as username, f=u as owner " +
                " ORDER BY p.timestamp DESC " +
                " SKIP {2} LIMIT 4 ",
                map("1", username, "2", skip));

                 ResultSetMapper<MappedContent> resultSetMapper =
                 new ResultSetMapper<MappedContent>();

                graphStory.setContent(
                        resultSetMapper.mapResultSetToListMappedClass(rs,MappedContent.class));

                if (graphStory.getContent().size() >= 4) {
                        graphStory.setMorecontent(true);
                        if (skip == 0) {
                                graphStory.setContent(graphStory.getContent().subList(0, 3));
                        }

                } else {
                        graphStory.setMorecontent(false);
                }
        }
        catch (Exception e) {
                log.error(e);
        }

        return graphStory;
 }
```

Adding a Status Update

The page shown in Figure 12-10 shows the form to add a status update for the current user, which is displayed when clicking on the "Add Content" link just under the "Graph Story—Social Feed" header. The HTML for the form can be found in `{PROJECTROOT}/WebContent/mustache/html/graphs/social/posts.html`. The form uses the `addContent` function in `graphstory.js` to `POST` a new status update as well as return the response and add it to the top of the status update stream.

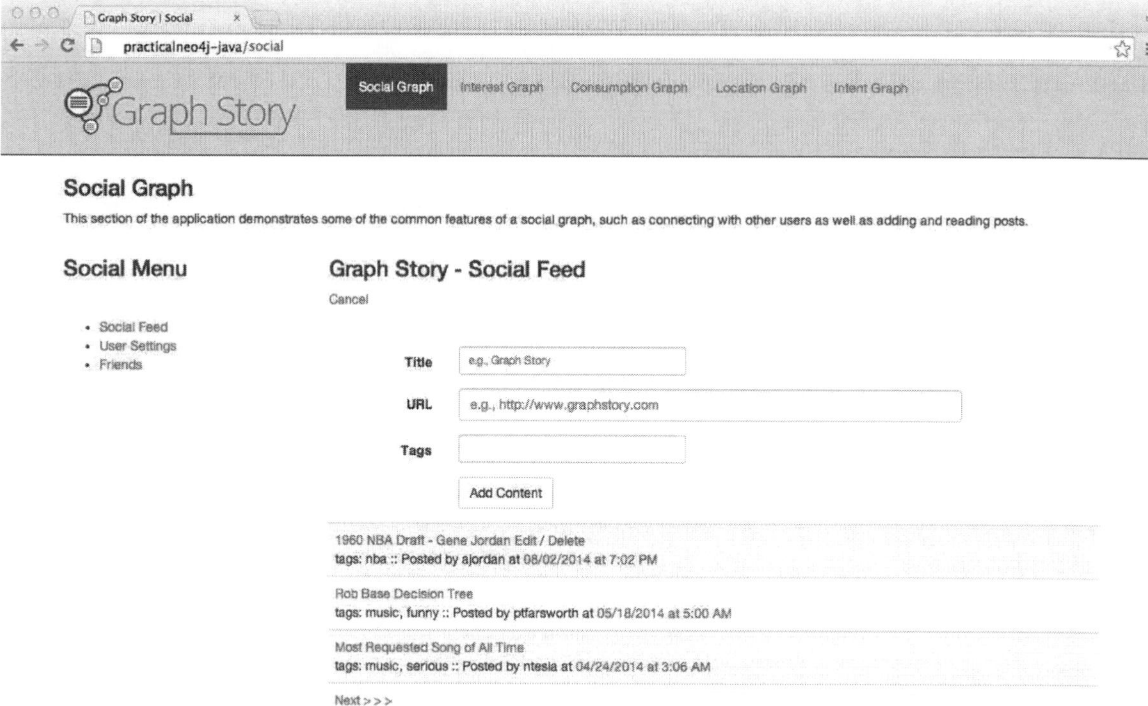

Figure 12-10. *Adding a status update*

The `addContent` method in `SocialAction` and the corresponding `addContent` method in `ContentDAO` are shown in Listing 12-31. When a new status update is created, in addition to its graph id, the `addContent` method also generates a contentId, which performed using the SecureRandom.uuid method.

The `addContent` method makes the status the `CURRENTPOST` and also determines whether a previous `CURRENTPOST` exists, and, if one does, changes its relationship type to `NEXTPOST`. In addition, the tags connected to the status update will be merged into the graph and connected to the status update via the `HAS` relationship type.

Listing 12-31. addContent Methods in SocialAction and ContentDAO

```
@Action(value = "posts/add", interceptorRefs = {
        @InterceptorRef(value = "cookie", params = { "cookiesName", "graphstoryUserAuthKey" }),
        @InterceptorRef(value = "json", params = { "noCache", "true", "excludeNullProperties",
        "true" }) },
        results = {
                @Result(name = "success", type = "json", params = { "noCache", "true" })
        })
public String addContent() {
        try {

                if (graphStory.getStatusUpdate() != null) {
                        graphStory.setMappedContent(graphStoryDAO.getContentDAO()
                        .addContent(
                                        graphStory.getStatusUpdate(),
                                        cookiesMap.get(GraphStoryConstants.graphstoryUserAuthKey)
                                        ));
                }
        }
        catch (Exception e) {
                log.error(e);
        }

        return SUCCESS;
}

//addContent method in ContentDAO
public MappedContent addContent(Content content, String username) {
        Date timestamp = new Date();

        String tagStr = trimContentTags(content.getTagstr());

        Map<String, Object> contentMap = IteratorUtil.singleOrNull(cypher.iteratorQuery(
        " MATCH (user { username: {1}}) " +
        " CREATE UNIQUE (user)-[:CURRENTPOST]->(newLP:Content { title:{2}, url:{3}, " +
        " tagstr:{4}, timestamp:{5}, contentId:{6} }) " +
        " WITH user, newLP, collect(distinct newLP.tagstr) as tstr" +
        " FOREACH (tagName in {7} |  " +
        " MERGE (t:Tag {wordPhrase: tagName })" +
        " MERGE (newLP)-[:HAS]->(t) )" +
        " WITH user, newLP " +
        " OPTIONAL MATCH  (newLP)<-[:CURRENTPOST]-(user)-[oldRel:CURRENTPOST]->(oldLP)" +
        " DELETE oldRel " +
        " CREATE (newLP)-[:NEXTPOST]->(oldLP) " +
        " RETURN newLP.contentId as contentId, newLP.title as title, " +
        " newLP.tagstr as tagstr, " +
        " newLP.timestamp as timestamp, newLP.url as url, " +
        "user.username as username, true as owner ",
        map("1", username, "2", content.getTitle(), "3", content.getUrl(), "4", tagStr, "5",
```

```
            timestamp.getTime() / 1000, "6", UUID.randomUUID().toString(), "7",
            tagList(tagStr))));
        ResultSetMapper<MappedContent> resultSetMapper = new ResultSetMapper<MappedContent>();
        return resultSetMapper.mapResultSetToMappedClass(contentMap, MappedContent.class);
}
```

Editing a Status Update

When status updates are displayed, the current user's status updates will contain a link to "Edit" the status. Once clicked, it will open the form, similar to the "Add Content" link, but will populate the form with the status update values as well as modify the form button to read "Edit Content", as shown in Figure 12-11. As with many similar UI features, clicking "Cancel" under the heading removes the values and returns the form to its ready state.

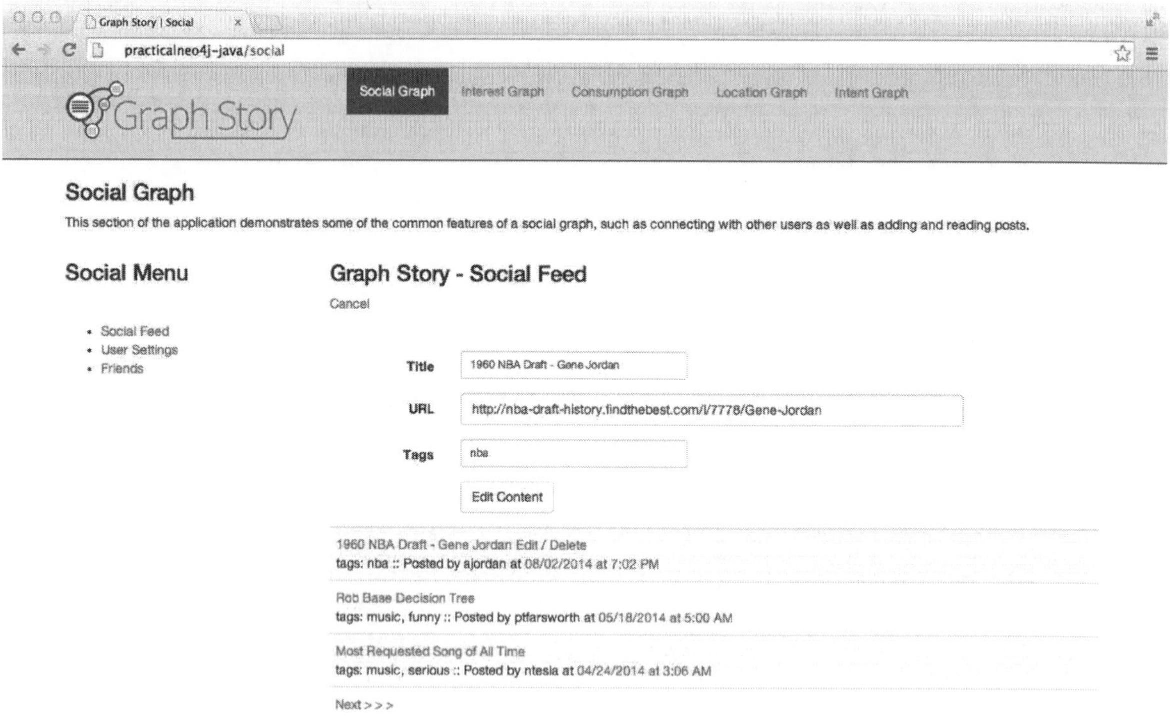

Figure 12-11. *Editing a status update*

The edit feature, like the add feature, uses a route in the graphstory application and a function in graphstory.js, which are edit and editContent, respectively. The editContent action passes in the content object, with its content id, and then calls the editContent method in ContentDAO class, as shown in Listing 12-32.

In the case of the edit feature, you do not need to update relationships. Instead, you simply retrieve the existing node by its generated String Id (not graph id), update its properties where necessary, and save it back to the graph.

Listing 12-32. editContent Methods in SocialAction and ContentDAO

```
@Action(value = "posts/edit", interceptorRefs = {
        @InterceptorRef(value = "cookie", params = { "cookiesName", "graphstoryUserAuthKey" }),
        @InterceptorRef(value = "json", params = { "noCache", "true", "excludeNullProperties",
        "true" }) },
        results = {
                @Result(name = "success", type = "json", params = { "noCache", "true" })
        })
public String editContent() {
        try {
                if (graphStory.getStatusUpdate() != null) {
                        graphStory.setMappedContent(graphStoryDAO.getContentDAO()
                                .editContent(
                                graphStory.getStatusUpdate(),
                                cookiesMap.get(GraphStoryConstants.graphstoryUserAuthKey)
                                ));
                }
        }
        catch (Exception e) {
                log.error(e);
        }

        return SUCCESS;
}

//editContent in ContentDAO
public MappedContent editContent(Content content, String username) {

String tagStr = trimContentTags(content.getTagstr());

Map<String, Object> contentMap = IteratorUtil.singleOrNull(cypher.iteratorQuery(
" MATCH (c:Content {contentId:{1}})-[:NEXTPOST*0..]-()-[:CURRENTPOST]-(user { username: {2}}) " +
" SET c.title = {3}, c.url = {4}, c.tagstr = {5}" +
" FOREACH (tagName in {6} |  " +
" MERGE (t:Tag {wordPhrase:tagName}) " +
" MERGE (c)-[:HAS]->(t) " +
" )" +
" RETURN c.contentId as contentId, c.title as title, c.tagstr as tagstr, " +
" c.timestamp as timestamp, c.url as url, {2} as username, true as owner ",
map("1", content.getContentId(), "2", username, "3", content.getTitle(),
                "4", content.getUrl(), "5", tagStr, "6", tagList(tagStr))));
ResultSetMapper<MappedContent> resultSetMapper = new ResultSetMapper<MappedContent>();
return resultSetMapper.mapResultSetToMappedClass(contentMap, MappedContent.class);

}
```

Deleting a Status Update

As with the "edit" option, when status updates are displayed, the current user's status updates will contain a link to "Delete" the status. Once clicked, it asks if you want it deleted (no regrets!) and, if accepted, generates an AJAX GET request to call the delete route and corresponding method in the ContentDAO class, as shown in Listing 12-33.

The Cypher in the delete method begins by finding the user and content that will be used in the rest of the query. In the first MATCH, you can determine if this status update is the CURRENTPOST by checking to see if it is related to a NEXTPOST. If this relationship pattern matches, make the NEXTPOST into the CURRENTPOST with CREATE UNIQUE.

Next, the query asks if the status update is somewhere the middle of the list, which is performed by determining if the status update has incoming and outgoing NEXTPOST relationships. If the pattern is matched, connect the before and after status updates via NEXTPOST.

Regardless of the status update's location in the linked list, you will retrieve it and its relationships and then delete the node along with all of its relationships.

To recap, if one of the relationship patterns matches, replace that pattern with the nodes on either side of the status update in question. Once that is performed, the node and its relationships can be removed from the graph.

Listing 12-33. deleteContent Methods in SocialAction and ContentDAO

```
@Action(value = "/posts/delete/{contentId}",
        results = {
                @Result(name = "success", type = "json")
        })
public String deleteContent() {
        try {

                graphStoryDAO.getContentDAO()
                        .deleteContent(
                                contentId,
                                cookiesMap.get(GraphStoryConstants.graphstoryUserAuthKey)
                        );

                Map<String, Object> msg = new HashMap<String, Object>();
                msg.put("Msg", "OK");
                graphStory.setMessage(msg);
        }
        catch (Exception e) {
                log.error(e);
        }

        return SUCCESS;
}

// deleteContent method in ContentDAO
 public void deleteContent(String contentId, String username) {
        cypher.iteratorQuery(
        " MATCH (u:User { username: {1} }), (c:Content { contentId: {2} }) " +
        " WITH u,c " +
        " MATCH (u)-[:CURRENTPOST]->(c)-[:NEXTPOST]->(nextPost) " +
        " WHERE nextPost is not null " +
        " CREATE UNIQUE (u)-[:CURRENTPOST]->(nextPost) " +
        " WITH count(nextPost) as cnt " +
        " MATCH (before)-[:NEXTPOST]->(c:Content { contentId: {2}})-[:NEXTPOST]->(after) " +
```

```
        " WHERE before is not null AND after is not null " +
        " CREATE UNIQUE (before)-[:NEXTPOST]->(after) " +
        " WITH count(before) as cnt " +
        " MATCH (c:Content { contentId: {2} })-[r]-() " +
        " DELETE c, r",
        map("1", username, "2", contentId));
}
```

Interest Graph Model

This section looks at the interest graph and examines some basic ways it can used to explicitly define a degree of interest. The following topics are covered:

- Adding filters for owned content
- Adding filters for connected content
- Analyzing connected content (count tags)

Interest in Aggregate

Inside the `interest` method of the `InterestAction` class, you will retrieve all of the tags connected to a user and their friends the `tagsInMyNetwork` method found in the `TagDAO` class. This is displayed Figure 12-12 in the left-hand column on the page.

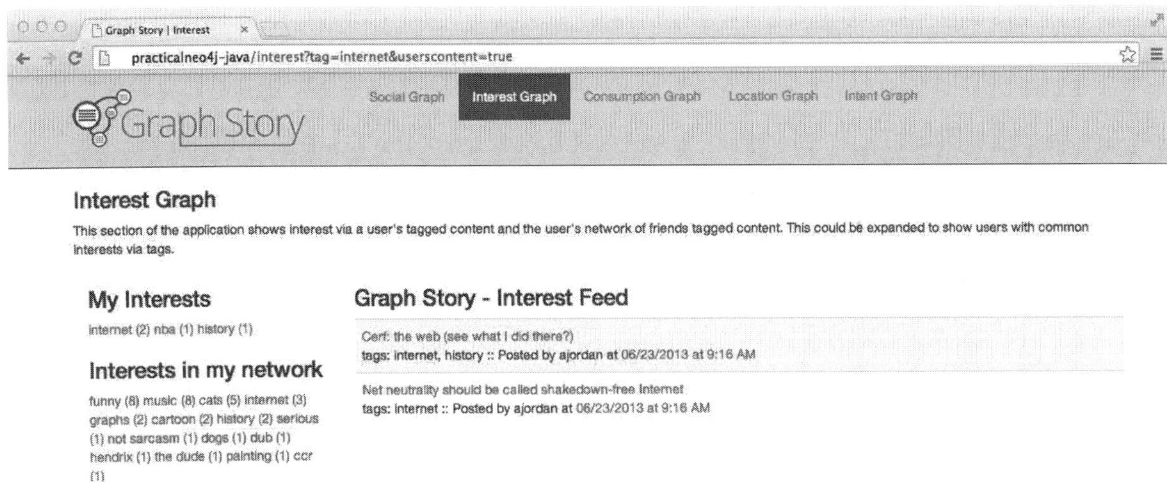

Figure 12-12. *Filtering the current user's content*

The markup is located in `{PROJECTROOT}/WebContent/mustache/html/graphs/interest/index.html`. The `tagsInMyNetwork` method uses two queries, which are shown in Listing 12-34. The `tagsInNetwork` finds users being followed, accesses all of their content, and finds connected tags using the `HAS` relationship type.

The userTags method is similar but is concerned only with content and, subsequently, tags connected to the current user. Both methods limit the results to 30 items. As mentioned earlier, the methods return an array of content and tags, which supports the autosuggest plugin in the view and requires both a label and name to be provided in order to execute. This autosuggest feature is also used in the status update form and search forms presented later in this chapter.

Listing 12-34. userTags and tagsInNetwork in the TagDAO Class

```
// returns just the current user's tags
public List<MappedContentTag> userTags(String username) throws Exception {
        ResultSet rs = cypher.resultSetQuery(
                " MATCH (u:User {username: {1} })-[:CURRENTPOST]-lp-[:NEXTPOST*0..]-c " +
                " WITH distinct c " +
                " MATCH c-[ct:HAS]->(t) " +
                " WITH distinct ct,t " +
                " RETURN t.wordPhrase as name, t.wordPhrase as label, count(ct) as id " +
                " ORDER BY id desc " +
                " SKIP 0 LIMIT 30",
                map("1", username));

         ResultSetMapper<MappedContentTag> resultSetMapper =
         new ResultSetMapper<MappedContentTag>();

       return resultSetMapper.mapResultSetToListMappedClass(rs, MappedContentTag.class);
}

// returns tags of the users being followed
public List<MappedContentTag> tagsInNetwork(String username) throws Exception {
        ResultSet rs = cypher.resultSetQuery(
                " MATCH (u:User {username: {1} })-[:FOLLOWS]->f " +
                " WITH distinct f " +
                " MATCH f-[:CURRENTPOST]-lp-[:NEXTPOST*0..]-c " +
                " WITH distinct c " +
                " MATCH c-[ct:HAS]->(t) " +
                " WITH distinct ct,t " +
                " RETURN t.wordPhrase as name, t.wordPhrase as label, count(ct) as id " +
                " ORDER BY id desc " +
                " SKIP 0 LIMIT 30",
                map("1", username));

        ResultSetMapper<MappedContentTag> resultSetMapper =
        new ResultSetMapper<MappedContentTag>();

        return resultSetMapper.mapResultSetToListMappedClass(rs, MappedContentTag.class);
}
```

Filtering Managed Content

Once the list of tags for the user and for the group she follows has been provided, the content can be filtered based of the generated tag links, as shown in Figure 12-12. If a tag is clicked on inside of the "My Interests" section, the getContentByTag method, displayed in Listing 12-35, is called with the isCurrentUser value set to true.

Listing 12-35. Get the Content Owned by the Current User Based on a Tag

```
public List<MappedContent> getContentByTag(String username, String tag, Boolean isCurrentUser) {

        List<MappedContent> contents = null;
        ResultSetMapper<MappedContent> mappedContentResultSetMapper = new
                ResultSetMapper<MappedContent>();
        try {
                if (isCurrentUser) {
                        ResultSet rs = cypher.resultSetQuery(
                        "MATCH (u:User {username: {1} })" +
                        " MATCH u-[:CURRENTPOST]-lp-[:NEXTPOST*0..]-p " +
                        " WITH DISTINCT u,p" +
                        " MATCH p-[:HAS]-(t:Tag {wordPhrase : {2} } )" +
                        " RETURN  p.contentId as contentId, p.title as title, p.tagstr as tagstr, " +
                        " p.timestamp as timestamp, p.url as url, " +
                        " u.username as username, true as owner" +
                        " ORDER BY p.timestamp DESC",
                        map("1", username, "2", tag));

                        contents = mappedContentResultSetMapper
                               .mapResultSetToListMappedClass(rs, MappedContent.class);

                        } else {
                               // this block is shown in Listing 12-34
                        }
                }
                catch (Exception e) {
                        log.error(e);
                }

                return contents;
        }
```

Filtering Connected Content

If a tag is clicked on inside of the “Interests in my Network” section, the `getContentByTag` method is called with the `isCurrentUser` value set to false, as shown in Listing (Listing 12-36)

The second query is nearly identical to the first query found in `getContentByTag`, except that it will factor in the users being followed and exclude the current user. The method also returns a collection of items and matches resulting content to a provided tag, placing no limit on the number of status updates to be returned (Figure 12-13). In addition, it marks the owner property as false.

Listing 12-36. Get the Content of the User's Being Followed Based on a Tag

```
public List<MappedContent> getContentByTag(String username, String tag, Boolean isCurrentUser) {

        List<MappedContent> contents = null;
        ResultSetMapper<MappedContent> mappedContentResultSetMapper = new
                ResultSetMapper<MappedContent>();
        try {
                if (isCurrentUser) {
                        // this block is shown in Listing 12-33

                } else {

                        ResultSet rs = cypher.resultSetQuery(
                        " MATCH (u:User {username: {1} })" +
                        " WITH u " +
                        " MATCH (u)-[:FOLLOWS]->f" +
                        " WITH DISTINCT f" +
                        " MATCH f-[:CURRENTPOST]-lp-[:NEXTPOST*0..]-p" +
                        " WITH DISTINCT f,p" +
                        " MATCH p-[:HAS]-(t:Tag {wordPhrase : {2} } )" +
                        " RETURN  p.contentId as contentId, p.title as title, p.tagstr as tagstr, " +
                        " p.timestamp as timestamp, p.url as url, " +
                        " f.username as username, false as owner " +
                        " ORDER BY p.timestamp DESC",
                        map("1", username, "2", tag));

                        contents = mappedContentResultSetMapper
                               .mapResultSetToListMappedClass(rs, MappedContent.class);
                }
        }
        catch (Exception e) {
                log.error(e);
        }

        return contents;
}
```

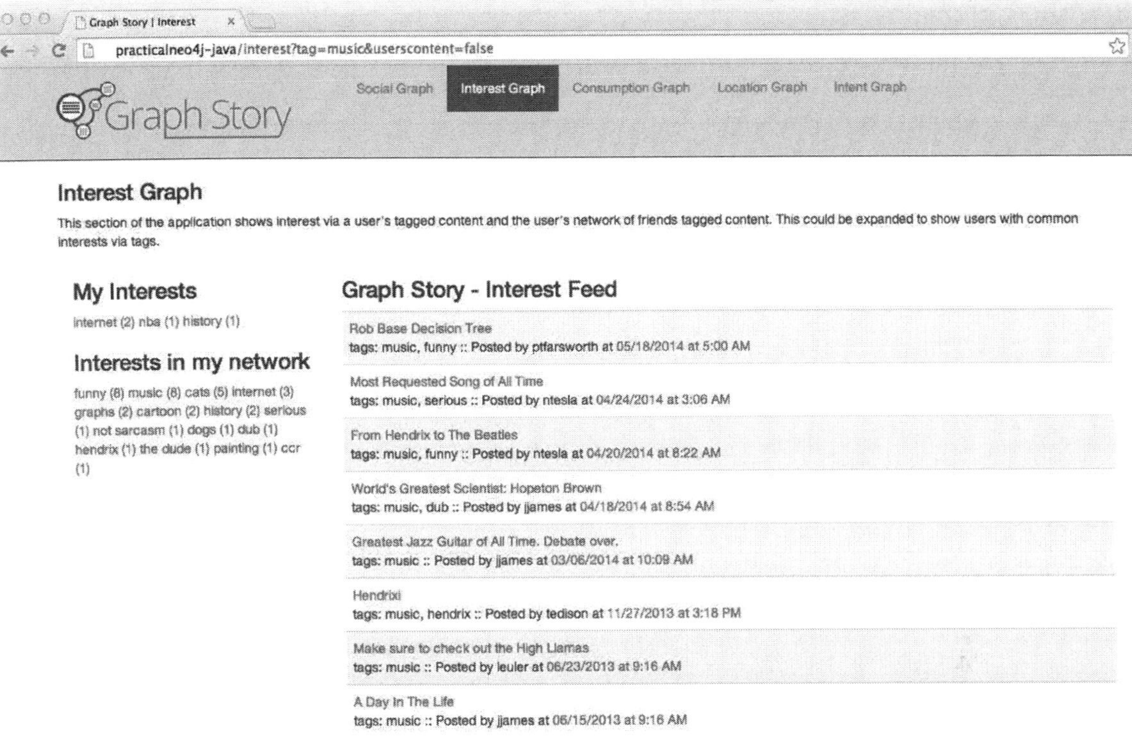

Figure 12-13. *Filtering content of the current user's friends*

Consumption Graph Model

This section examines a few techniques to capture and use patterns of consumption generated implicitly by a user or users. For the purposes of your application, you will use the prepopulated set of products provided in the sample graph. The code required for the console reinforces the standard persistence operations, but I will focus on the operations that take advantage of this model type, such as:

- Capturing consumption
- Filtering consumption for users
- Filtering consumption for messaging

Capturing Consumption

You are creating code that directly captures consumption for a user, but the process could also be done by creating a graph-backed service to consume the webserver logs in real time or another data store to create the relationships. The result would be the same in either event: a process that connects nodes to reveal a pattern of consumption (Listing 12-37).

Listing 12-37. Show List of Products and Product Trail of Current User OR Return Snippet of Products

```
//show products and products VIEWED by user
@Action(value = "consumption/{pagenum}", results = {
        @Result(name = "success", type = "mustache", location =
                "/mustache/html/graphs/consumption/index.html"),
        @Result(name = "page", type = "mustache", location =
                "/mustache/html/graphs/consumption/product-list.html")
})
public String consumption() {
        // returns a product list HTML snippet
        if (pagenum != null) {

                // set current page
                Integer curpage = pagenum;

                // get the list of products for this page
                graphStory = graphStoryDAO.getProductDAO().getProducts(graphStory, curpage);

                // increase the page count
                curpage = curpage + 10;

                // set the next page to call
                graphStory.setNextPageUrl("/consumption/" + curpage.toString());

                return "page";

        } else {
                setTitle("Consumption");

                // retrieve the first page of products
                graphStory = graphStoryDAO.getProductDAO().getProducts(graphStory, pageNumStart);

                // set the product trail
                graphStory.setProductTrail(graphStoryDAO.getProductDAO()
                    .getProductTrail(cookiesMap.get(GraphStoryConstants.graphstoryUserAuthKey)));

                // set the next page to call
                graphStory.setNextPageUrl("/consumption/10");

                return SUCCESS;
        }
}
```

Filtering Consumption for Users

One practical use of the consumption model is to create a content trail for users, as shown in Figure 12-14. As a user clicks on items in the scrolling product stream, the interaction is captured using `createUserView`, which ultimately returns a `list` of relationship objects of the `VIEWED` type.

In the `Consumption` section, take a look at the `createUserProductViewRel` method to see how the process begins inside the controller. The controller method first saves the view and then returns the complete history of views using the `getProductTrail method,` which can be found in the Product service class. The process is started when the `createUserProductViewRel` function is called, which is located in `graphstory.js`.

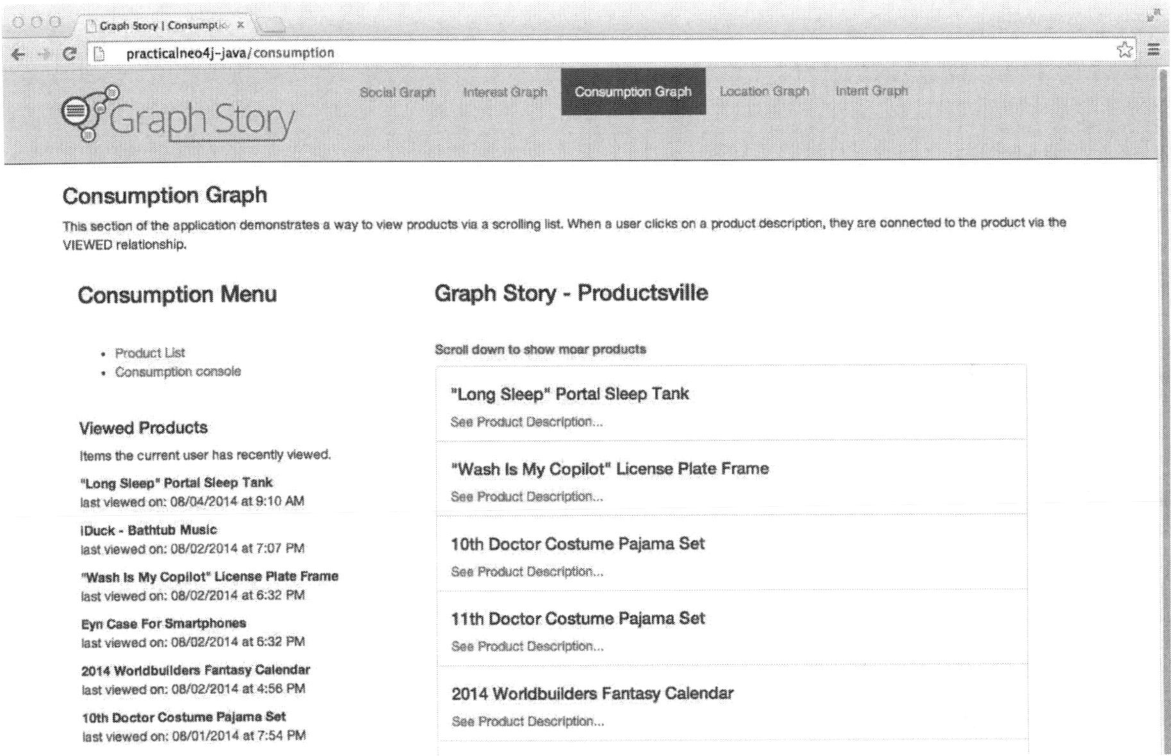

Figure 12-14. *The Scrolling Product and Product Trail page*

For the sample application, you will use the `addUserViewAndReturnProductTrail` method in the `ProductDAO` class to find the Product entity being viewed and then create an explicit relationship type called `VIEWED`. As you may have noticed, this is the first instance of a relationship type in the application that contains properties. In this case, you are creating a timestamp with a `Date` object and String value of the timestamp. The query, provided in Listing 12-38, checks to see if a `VIEWED` relationship already exists between the user and the product.

If the result of the `MERGE` clause within query is returns zero matches, then a map is created with key value pairs to create properties on the new relationship, specifically `timestamp` and `dateAsStr`. Otherwise, the query will update the existing relationship properties to their new, respective values.

Listing 12-38. Methods to Add a userview for Product

```
@Action(value = "consumptionview/add/{productNodeId}", results = {
                @Result(name = "success", type = "json")
        })
public String addUserViewAndReturnProductTrail() {
        try {
                 graphStory.setProductTrail(graphStoryDAO.getProductDAO()
                        .addUserViewAndReturnProductTrail(
                          cookiesMap.get(GraphStoryConstants.graphstoryUserAuthKey), productNodeId
                      ));
        }
        catch (Exception e) {
                log.error(e);
        }

        return SUCCESS;
}

// the method to add a user view in the ProductDAO class
public List<MappedProductUserViews> addUserViewAndReturnProductTrail(
        String username, Long productNodeId) {

        try {
                Date timestamp = new Date(dateAsLong);
                SimpleDateFormat dformatter = new SimpleDateFormat("MM/dd/yyyy");
                SimpleDateFormat tformatter = new SimpleDateFormat("h:mm a");
                String dateAsStr = dformatter.format(timestamp)
                        + " at " + tformatter.format(timestamp);

                ResultSet rs = cypher.resultSetQuery(
                        " MATCH (p:Product), (u:User { username:{1} })" +
                        " WHERE id(p) = {2}" +
                        " WITH u,p" +
                        " MERGE (u)-[r:VIEWED]->(p)" +
                        " SET r.dateAsStr={3}, r.timestamp={4}" +
                        " WITH u " +
                        " MATCH (u)-[r:VIEWED]->(p)" +
                        " RETURN p.title as title,  r.dateAsStr as dateAsStr" +
                        " ORDER BY r.timestamp desc",
                        map("1", username, "2", productNodeId, "3", dateAsStr,
                         "4", timestamp.getTime()));

                ResultSetMapper<MappedProductUserViews> resultSetMapper
                                = new ResultSetMapper<MappedProductUserViews>();
                return resultSetMapper
                        .mapResultSetToListMappedClass(rs, MappedProductUserViews.class);

        }
        catch (Exception e) {
                log.error(e);
                return null;
          }

}
```

Filtering Consumption for Messaging

Another practical use of the consumption model would be to create a personalized message for users, as displayed in Figure 12-15. In this case, a filter allows the "Consumption Console" to drill down to a very specific group of users who visited a product that was also tagged with a keyword (Listing 12-39).

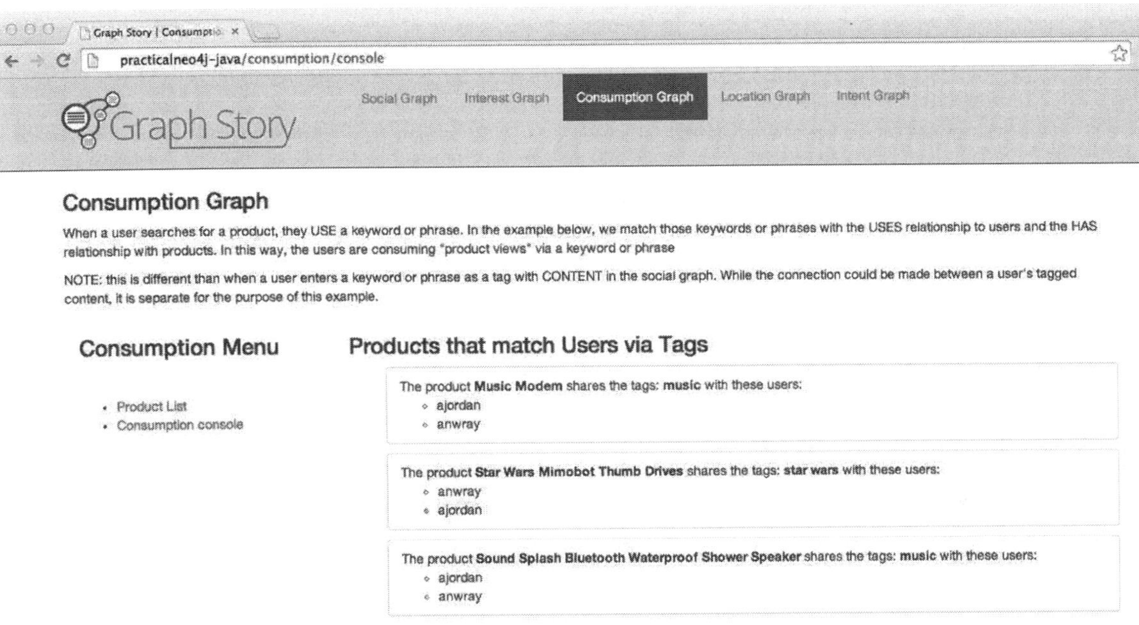

Figure 12-15. *Consumption console shows products connected to users via tags*

Listing 12-39. The `consumption console` Route and Methods to Get Connected Products and Users via Tags

```
// displays products that are connected to users via a tag relationship
@Action(value = "consumption/console", results = {
        @Result(name = "success", type = "mustache", location =
                "/mustache/html/graphs/consumption/console.html")
        })
public String console() {
        setTitle("Consumption Console");
        graphStory.setUsersWithMatchingTags(graphStoryDAO.getProductDAO()
                        .getProductsHasATagAndUserUsesAMatchingTag());

        return SUCCESS;
}

//tags that match products and users
public List<MappedProductUserTag> getProductsHasATagAndUserUsesAMatchingTag() {
```

```
        try {
                ResultSet rs = cypher.resultSetQuery(
                "MATCH (p:Product)-[:HAS]->(t)<-[:USES]-(u:User) " +
                " RETURN p.title as title, " +
                " collect(u.username) as users, " +
                " collect(distinct t.wordPhrase) as tags", null);

                ResultSetMapper<MappedProductUserTag> resultSetMapper =
                        new ResultSetMapper<MappedProductUserTag>();

                return resultSetMapper
                        .mapResultSetToListMappedClass(rs, MappedProductUserTag.class);

        }
        catch (Exception e) {
                log.error(e);
                return null;
        }
}
```

Location Graph Model

This section explores the location graph model and a few of the operations that typically accompany it. In particular, it looks at the following:

- The spatial plugin
- Filtering on location
- Products based on location

The example demonstrates how to add a console to enable you to connect products to locations in an ad hoc manner (Listing 12-40).

Listing 12-40. `location` Method for Showing Locations Nearby or Locations with Specific Product

```
// show locations nearby or locations that have a specific product
@Action(value = "location",results = {
        @Result(name = "success", type = "mustache", location =
              "/mustache/html/graphs/location/index.html")
        })
public String location() {
        setTitle("Location");
        try {
                mappedUserLocation = graphStoryDAO.getUserDAO()
                .getUserLocation(cookiesMap.get(GraphStoryConstants.graphstoryUserAuthKey));

                if (distance != null) {
                        if (StringUtils.isNotBlank(productNodeId)) {
```

```
                    graphStory.setLocations(graphStoryDAO.getLocationDAO()
                    .returnLocationsWithinDistanceAndHasProduct(
                            mappedUserLocation.getLat(),
                            mappedUserLocation.getLon(),
                            distance,
                            Long.valueOf(productNodeId)
                    ));

                    graphStory.setProduct(graphStoryDAO
                    .getProductDAO().getProductByNodeId(Long.valueOf(productNodeId)));
                } else {
                    graphStory.setLocations(graphStoryDAO.getLocationDAO()
                    .returnLocationsWithinDistance(
                            mappedUserLocation.getLat(),
                            mappedUserLocation.getLon(), distance)
                    );
                }
            }
        }
        catch (Exception e) {
            log.error(e);
        }

        return SUCCESS;
}
```

Search for Nearby Locations

To search for nearby locations, as shown in Figure 12-16, use the current user's location, obtained with `getUserLocation`, and then use the `locationsWithinDistance` method. The `returnLocationsWithinDistance` method in the `LocationDAO` class uses a method called `addDistanceTo`, which returns a string value of the distance between the starting point and the respective location (Listing 12-41).

Listing 12-41. The `returnLocationsWithinDistance` Method

```
public List<MappedLocation> returnLocationsWithinDistance(Double lat, Double lon, Double distance) {

        try {
                ResultSet rs = cypher.resultSetQuery(
                "START n = node:geom({1}) WHERE NOT(has(n.type)) " +
                " RETURN n.locationId as locationId, n.address as address, " +
                " n.city as city, n.state as state, n.zip as zip, " +
                " n.name as name, n.lat as lat, n.lon as lon",
                map("1", distanceQueryAsString(lat, lon, distance)));

                ResultSetMapper<MappedLocation> resultSetMapper =
                new ResultSetMapper<MappedLocation>();

                List<MappedLocation> locations = resultSetMapper
                        .mapResultSetToListMappedClass(rs, MappedLocation.class);
```

```
                // add the distance in miles to locations
                addDistanceTo(locations, lat, lon);

                return locations;

        }
        catch (Exception e) {
                log.error(e);
                return null;
        }

}
```

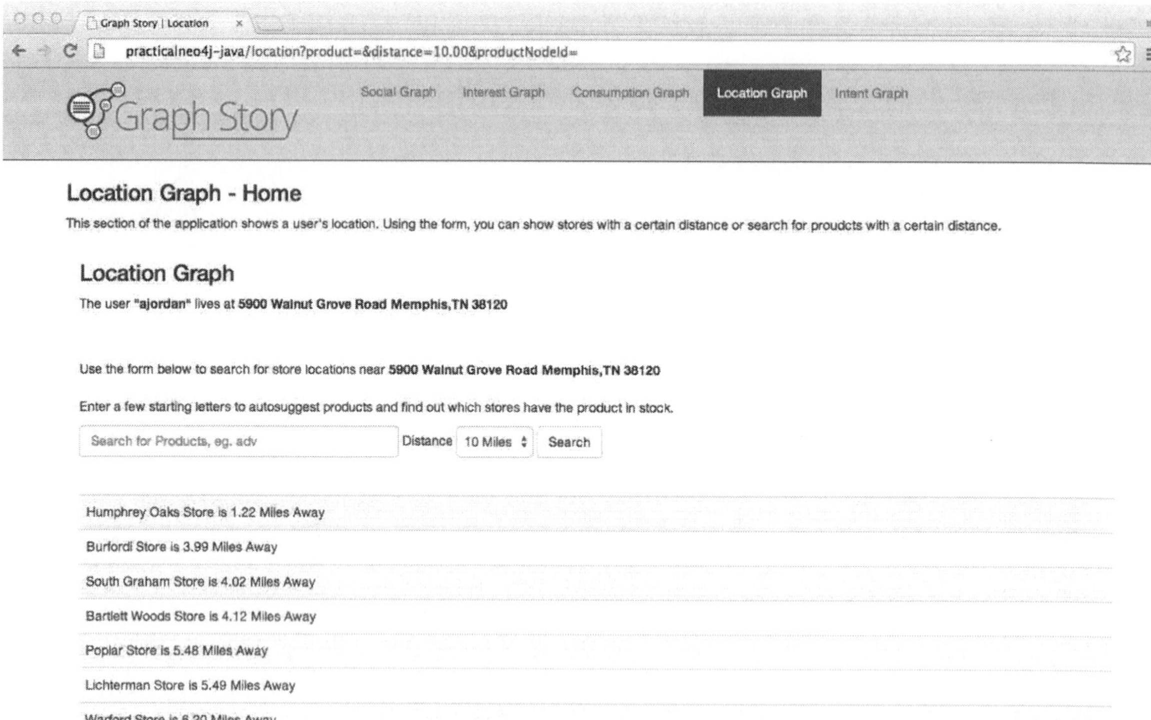

Figure 12-16. *Searching for Locations within a certain distance of User location*

Locations with Product

To search for products nearby, as shown in Figure 12-17, the application makes use of an auto-suggest AJAX request, which ultimately calls the search method in the `ProductDAO` service class. The method, shown in Listing 12-42, returns an array of objects to the product field in the search form and applies the selected product's productNodeId to the subsequent location search.

For almost all cases, it is recommended not to use the graphId as it can be recycled when its node is deleted. In this case, the productNodeId is safe to use, because products would not be in danger of being deleted but only removed from a Location relationship.

Listing 12-42. Search for Products

```
@Action(value = "/productsearch/{q}",results = {@Result(name = "success", type = "json")})
public String productSearch() {
        try {
                graphStory.setMappedProductSearch(graphStoryDAO
                        .getProductDAO().search(q));

        }
        catch (Exception e) {
                log.error(e);
        }

        return SUCCESS;
}

// search method in ProductDAO
public MappedProductSearch[] search(String q) {

        q = q.trim().toLowerCase() + ".*";
        try {

                ResultSet rs = cypher.resultSetQuery(
                        "MATCH (p:Product) " +
                        " WHERE lower(p.title) =~ {1} " +
                        " RETURN count(*) as name, TOSTRING(ID(p)) as id, " +
                      " p.title as label  " +
                        " ORDER BY p.title LIMIT 5",
                        map("1", q));

                ResultSetMapper<MappedProductSearch> resultSetMapper =
                        new ResultSetMapper<MappedProductSearch>();

                List<MappedProductSearch> mappedProductSearchResults =
                       resultSetMapper.mapResultSetToListMappedClass(rs, MappedProductSearch.class);

                MappedProductSearch[] mappedProductSearch = new
                        MappedProductSearch[mappedProductSearchResults.size()];

                return mappedProductSearchResults.toArray(mappedProductSearch);

        }
        catch (Exception e) {
                log.error(e);
                return null;
        }

}
```

Once the product and distance have been set, the search can be executed and the `location` method tests to see if a `productNodeId` property has been set. If so, the `returnLocationsWithinDistanceAndHasProduct` method is called from `LocationDAO` service, as shown in Listing 12-43.

Listing 12-43. The `returnLocationsWithinDistanceAndHasProduct` Method

```
public List<MappedLocation> returnLocationsWithinDistanceAndHasProduct(
Double lat, Double lon, Double distance, Long productNodeId) {

        try {
                ResultSet rs = cypher.resultSetQuery(
                " START n = node:geom({1}), p=node({2}) " +
                        " MATCH n-[:HAS]->p " +
                        " RETURN n.locationId as locationId, n.address as address, " +
                        " n.city as city, n.state as state, n.zip as zip, " +
                        " n.name as name, n.lat as lat, n.lon as lon",
                        map("1", distanceQueryAsString(lat, lon, distance), "2", productNodeId));

                ResultSetMapper<MappedLocation> resultSetMapper =
                new ResultSetMapper<MappedLocation>();

                List<MappedLocation> locations = resultSetMapper
                .mapResultSetToListMappedClass(rs, MappedLocation.class);

                // add the distance in miles to locations
                addDistanceTo(locations, lat, lon);

                        return locations;

        }
        catch (Exception e) {
                log.error(e);
                return null;
        }
}
```

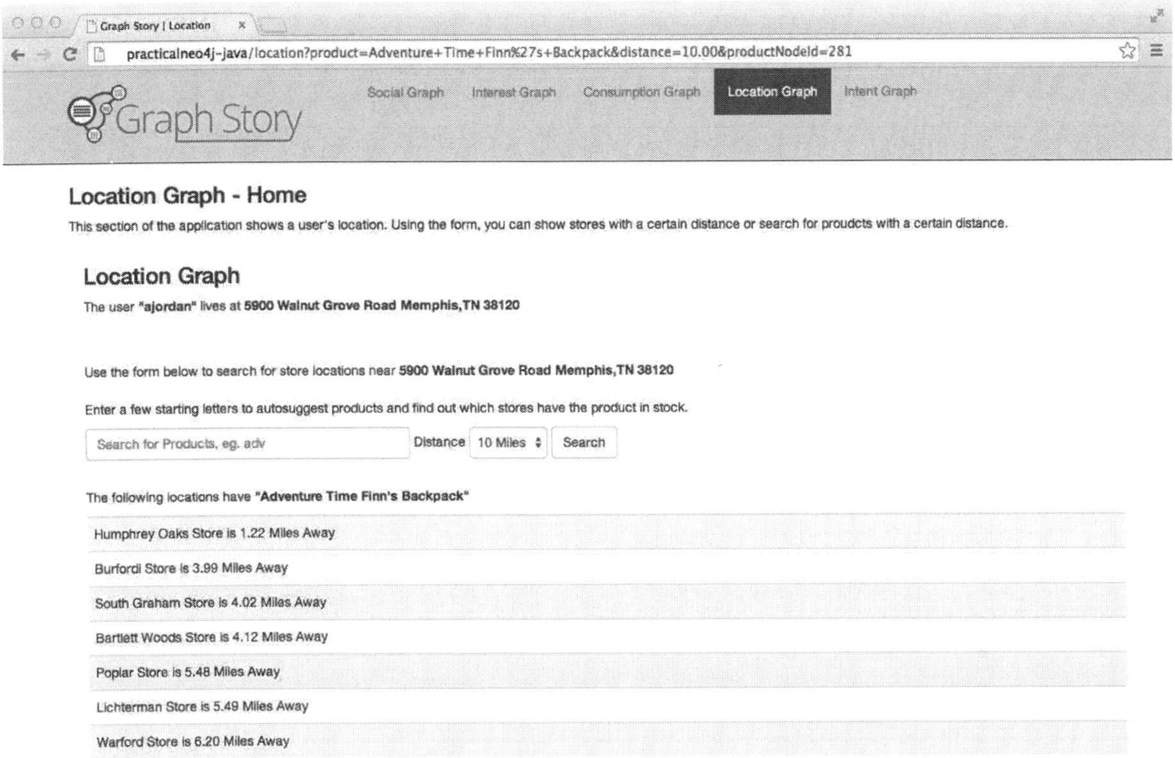

Figure 12-17. *Searching for Products in stock at Locations within a certain distance of the User location*

Intent Graph Model

The last part of the graph model exploration considers all the other graphs in order to suggest products based on the `Purchase` node type. The intent graph also considers the products, users, locations, and tags that are connected based on a Purchase.

Products Purchased by Friends

To get all of the products that have been purchased by friends, the `friendsPurchase` method is called from `PurchaseDAO` class, which is shown in Listing 12-45. The corresponding route is shown in Listing 12-44.

Listing 12-44. Purchases made by Friends Route

```
@Action(value = "intent", results = {
                @Result(name = "success", type = "mustache", location =
                        "/mustache/html/graphs/intent/index.html")
        })
public String intent() {

        setTitle("Products Purchased by Friends");
```

```
        try {
                graphStory.setMappedProductUserPurchaseList(graphStoryDAO
                        .getPurchaseDAO().friendsPurchase(
                                cookiesMap.get(GraphStoryConstants.graphstoryUserAuthKey)
                ));
                graphStory.setUser(graphStoryDAO
                        .getUserDAO().getByUserName(
                                cookiesMap.get(GraphStoryConstants.graphstoryUserAuthKey)
                ));
                }
        catch (Exception e) {
                log.error(e);
        }

        return SUCCESS;
}
```

The query finds the users being followed by the current user and then matches those users to a purchase that has been MADE which CONTAINS a product. The return value is a set of properties that identify the product title, the name of the friend or friends, as well the number of friends who have purchased the product. The result, as shown in Figure 12-18, is ordered by the number of friends who have purchased the product and then by product title (Listing 12-45).

Listing 12-45. FriendsPurchase Method

```
public List<MappedProductUserPurchase> friendsPurchase(String username) {
        try {
                ResultSet rs = cypher.resultSetQuery(
                "MATCH (u:User { username : {1} } )-[:FOLLOWS]-(f)-[:MADE]->()-[:CONTAINS]->p " +
                " RETURN p.productId as productId, " +
                " p.title as title, " +
                " collect(f.firstname + ' ' + f.lastname) as fullname, " +
                " null as wordPhrase, " +
                " count(f) as cfriends " +
                " ORDER BY cfriends desc, p.title ",
                map("1", username));

                ResultSetMapper<MappedProductUserPurchase> resultSetMapper =
                new ResultSetMapper<MappedProductUserPurchase>();

                return resultSetMapper
                        .mapResultSetToListMappedClass(rs, MappedProductUserPurchase.class);
        }
        catch (Exception e) {
                log.error(e);
                return null;
        }
}
```

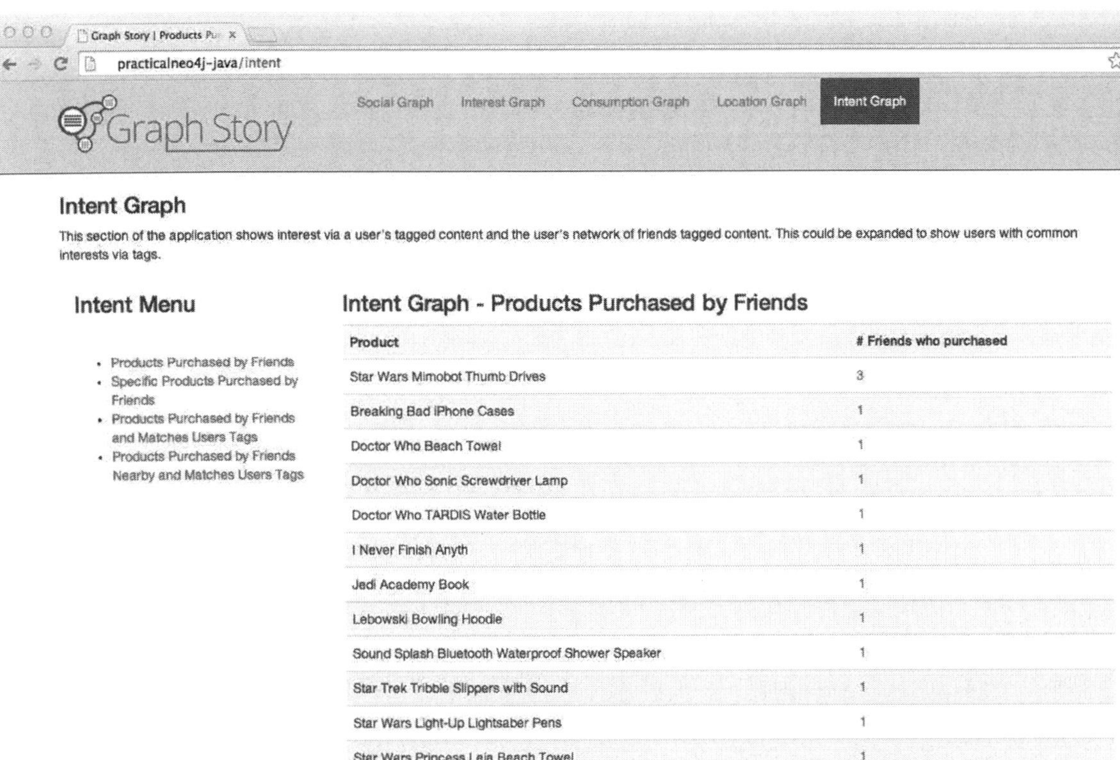

Figure 12-18. *Products Purchased by Friends*

Specific Products Purchased by Friends

If you click on the "Specific Products Purchased By Friends" link, you can specify a product, in this case "Star Wars Mimobot Thumb Drives", and then search for friends who have purchased this product, as shown in Figure 12-19. This is done via the `friendsPurchaseByProduct` method in `Purchase` service class, which is shown in Listing 12-46.

Listing 12-46. `FriendsPurchaseByProduct` Route and Method

```
@Action(value = "intent/friendsPurchaseByProduct",results = {
		@Result(name = "success", type = "mustache", location =
			"/mustache/html/graphs/intent/index.html")
	})
public String friendsPurchaseByProduct() {

	setTitle("Specific Products Purchased by Friends");
	setShowForm(true);

	try {

		if (StringUtils.isBlank(producttitle)) {
			producttitle = "Star Wars Mimobot Thumb Drives";
		}
```

```
                graphStory.setMappedProductUserPurchaseList(graphStoryDAO.getPurchaseDAO()
                        .friendsPurchaseByProduct(
                            producttitle,
                            cookiesMap.get(GraphStoryConstants.graphstoryUserAuthKey)
                    ));
                  graphStory.setUser(graphStoryDAO.getUserDAO()
                      .getByUserName(
                            cookiesMap.get(GraphStoryConstants.graphstoryUserAuthKey)
                      ));
        }
        catch (Exception e) {
                log.error(e);
        }
        return SUCCESS;
}
// a specific product purchased by friends
public List<MappedProductUserPurchase> friendsPurchaseByProduct(String title, String username) {
        try {
                ResultSet rs = cypher.resultSetQuery(
                "MATCH (p:Product) " +
                " WHERE lower(p.title) =lower({1}) " +
                " WITH p " +
                " MATCH (u:User { username : {2} } )-[:FOLLOWS]-(f)-[:MADE]->()-[:CONTAINS]->(p) " +
                " RETURN p.productId as productId,  " +
                " p.title as title, " +
                " collect(f.firstname + ' ' + f.lastname) as fullname, " +
                " null as wordPhrase, count(f) as cfriends " +
                "ORDER BY cfriends desc, p.title ",
                map("1", title, "2", username));

                ResultSetMapper<MappedProductUserPurchase> resultSetMapper =
                new ResultSetMapper<MappedProductUserPurchase>();

                return resultSetMapper
                        .mapResultSetToListMappedClass(rs, MappedProductUserPurchase.class);
        }
        catch (Exception e) {
                log.error(e);
                return null;
        }
}
```

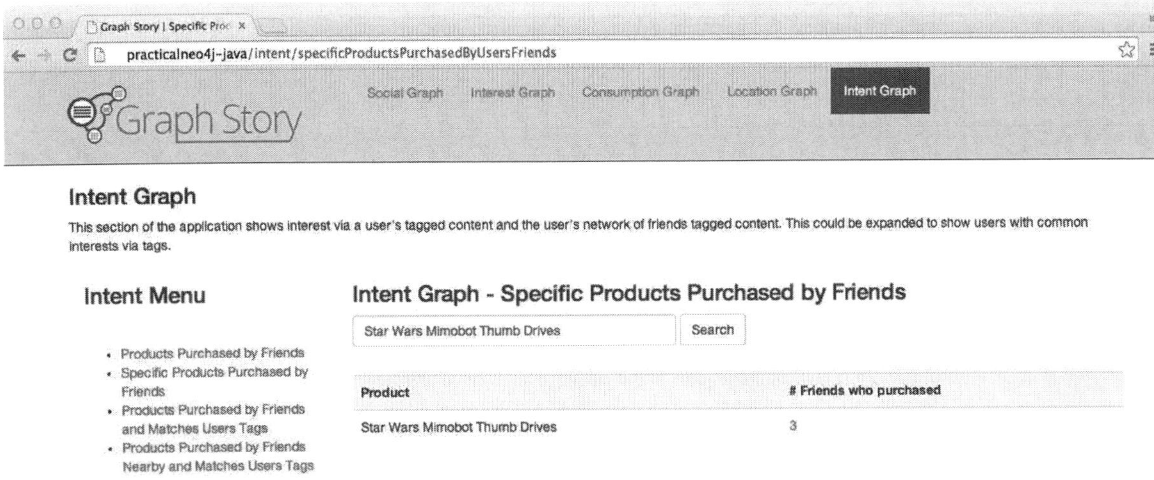

Figure 12-19. *Specific Products Purchased by Friends*

Products Purchased by Friends and Matches User's Tags

In this next instance, you will want to determine products that have been purchased by friends but also have tags that are used by the current user (Listing 12-47). The result of the query is shown in Figure 12-20.

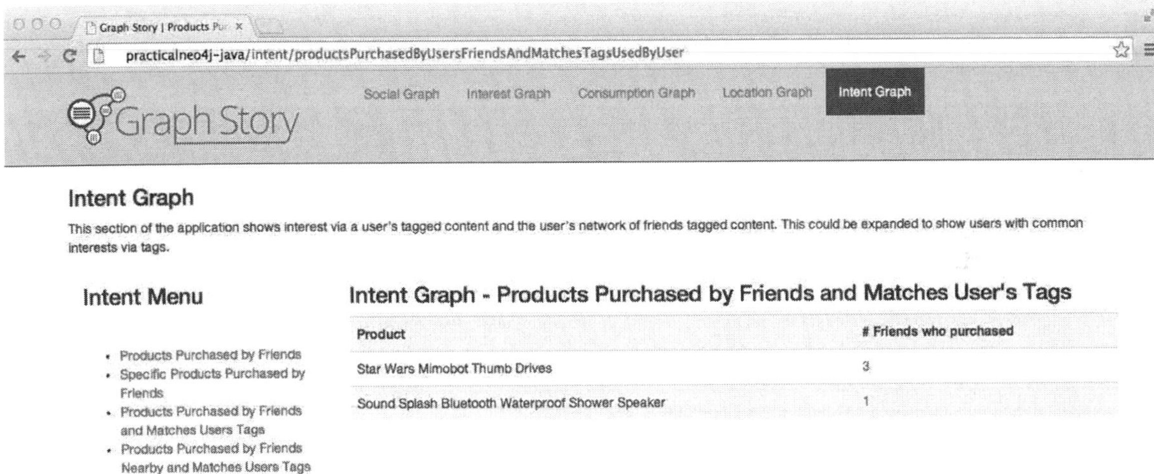

Figure 12-20. *Products Purchased by Friends and Matches User's Tags*

Listing 12-47. Product and Tag Similarity of the Current Users's Friends

```
@Action(value = "intent/friendsPurchaseTagSimilarity",results = {
                @Result(name = "success", type = "mustache", location = "/mustache/html/graphs/
                intent/index.html")
        })
public String friendsPurchaseTagSimilarity() {
        setTitle("Products Purchased by Friends and Matches User's Tags");

        try {

                graphStory.setMappedProductUserPurchaseList(
                        graphStoryDAO.getPurchaseDAO()
                        .friendsPurchaseTagSimilarity(
                                cookiesMap.get(GraphStoryConstants.graphstoryUserAuthKey)
                        ));

                graphStory.setUser(graphStoryDAO.getUserDAO()
                        .getByUserName(
                                cookiesMap.get(GraphStoryConstants.graphstoryUserAuthKey)
                        ));
        }
        catch (Exception e) {
                log.error(e);
        }

        return SUCCESS;
}
```

Using `friendsPurchaseTagSimilarity` in `PurchaseDAO` service class, shown in Listing 12-48, the application provides the userId to the query and uses the `FOLLOWS`, `MADE` and the `CONTAINS` relationships to return products purchases by users being followed. The subsequent `MATCH` statement takes the `USES` and `HAS` directed relationship types to determine the `TAG` connections the resulting products and the current user have in common.

Listing 12-48. The Method to Find Products Purchased by Friends and Matches Current User's Tags

```
public List<MappedProductUserPurchase> friendsPurchaseTagSimilarity(String username) {
        try {
                ResultSet rs = cypher.resultSetQuery(
                "MATCH (u:User { username : {1} } )-[:FOLLOWS]-(f)-[:MADE]->()-[:CONTAINS]->p " +
                " WITH u,p,f " +
                " MATCH u-[:USES]->(t)<-[:HAS]-p " +
                " RETURN p.productId as productId,  " +
                " p.title as title, " +
                " collect(f.firstname + ' ' + f.lastname) as fullname, " +
                " t.wordPhrase as wordPhrase, " +
                " count(f) as cfriends " +
                " ORDER BY cfriends desc, p.title ",
                map("1", username));
```

```
            ResultSetMapper<MappedProductUserPurchase> resultSetMapper =
            new ResultSetMapper<MappedProductUserPurchase>();

            return resultSetMapper
                    .mapResultSetToListMappedClass(rs, MappedProductUserPurchase.class);
        }
        catch (Exception e) {
            log.error(e);
            return null;
        }
}
```

Products Purchased by Friends Nearby and Matches User's Tags

Finding products of friends nearby who have purchased a product that also matches a user's tags is done by the `friendsPurchaseTagSimilarityAndProximityToLocation` method, easily the world's longest method name and is located in the `PurchaseDAO` class (Listing 12-49).

Listing 12-49. The `friendsPurchaseTagSimilarityAndProximityToLocation` Method in the `IntentAction` Class

```
@Action(value = "intent/friendsPurchaseTagSimilarityAndProximityToLocation", results = {
                @Result(name = "success", type = "mustache", location =
                "/mustache/html/graphs/intent/index.html")
        })
public String friendsPurchaseTagSimilarityAndProximityToLocation() {

        setTitle("Products Purchased by Friends Nearby and Matches User's Tags");

        try {

            mappedUserLocation = graphStoryDAO.getUserDAO()
                    .getUserLocation(
                            cookiesMap.get(GraphStoryConstants.graphstoryUserAuthKey)
                        );

            graphStory.setUser(graphStoryDAO.getUserDAO()
                    .getByUserName(
                            cookiesMap.get(GraphStoryConstants.graphstoryUserAuthKey)
                        )));

            graphStory.setMappedProductUserPurchaseList(graphStoryDAO.getPurchaseDAO()
                        .friendsPurchaseTagSimilarityAndProximityToLocation(
                        mappedUserLocation.getLat(),
                        mappedUserLocation.getLon(),
                        new Double("10.00"),
                          cookiesMap.get(GraphStoryConstants.graphstoryUserAuthKey)
                    ));
```

```
        }
        catch (Exception e) {
                log.error(e);
        }

        return SUCCESS;
}
```

The action method calls the `friendsPurchaseTagSimilarityAndProximityToLocation` method shown in Listing 12-50. The query begins starts with a location search within a certain distance, then matching the current user's tags to products. Next, the query matches friends based the location search. The resulting friends are matched against products that are in the set of user tag matches. The result of the query is shown in Figure 12-21.

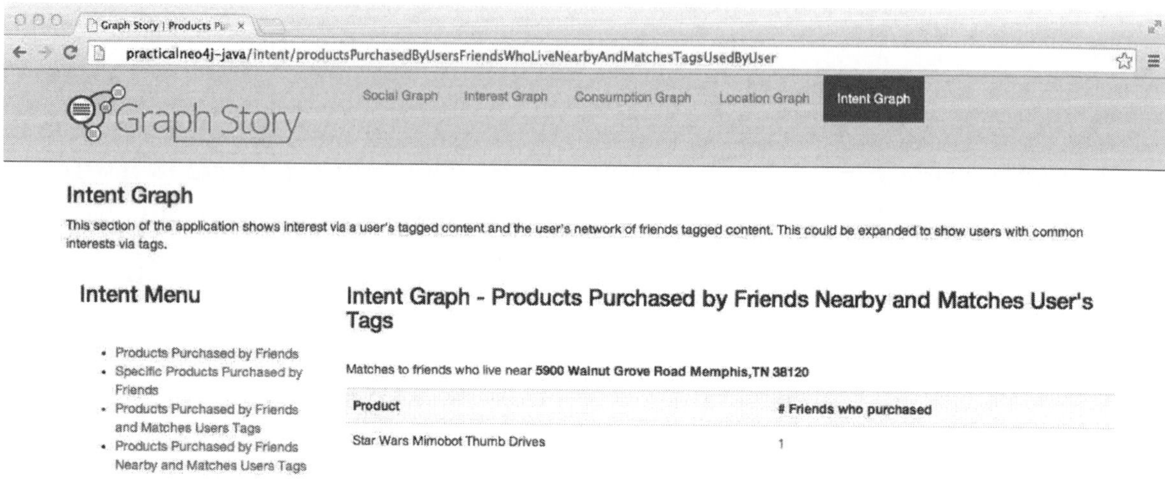

Figure 12-21. *Products Purchased by Friends Nearby and Matches User's Tags*

Listing 12-50. `friendsPurchaseTagSimilarityAndProximityToLocation` Method in the PurchaseDAO Class

```
public List<MappedProductUserPurchase> friendsPurchaseTagSimilarityAndProximityToLocation(Double
lat, Double lon, Double distance, String username) {
        try {
                ResultSet rs = cypher.resultSetQuery(
                "START n = node:geom({1}) " +
                " WITH n " +
                " MATCH (u:User { username : {2} } )-[:USES]->(t)<-[:HAS]-p " +
                " WITH n,u,p,t " +
                " MATCH u-[:FOLLOWS]->(f)-[:HAS]->(n) " +
                " WITH p,f,t " +
                " MATCH f-[:MADE]->()-[:CONTAINS]->(p) " +
                " RETURN p.productId as productId, " +
                " p.title as title, " +
                " collect(f.firstname + ' ' + f.lastname) as fullname, " +
                " t.wordPhrase as wordPhrase, " +
                " count(f) as cfriends " +
```

```
                " ORDER BY cfriends desc, p.title ",
                map("1", distanceQueryAsString(lat, lon, distance), "2", username));

                ResultSetMapper<MappedProductUserPurchase> resultSetMapper =
                new ResultSetMapper<MappedProductUserPurchase>();

                return resultSetMapper
                .mapResultSetToListMappedClass(rs, MappedProductUserPurchase.class);
        }
        catch (Exception e) {
                log.error(e);
                return null;
        }
}
```

Summary

This chapter covered using the Neo4j JDBC driver with examples of how to add and update nodes, create relationships and remove relationships, and add and remove labels on existing nodes. In addition, it presented sample code for creating features and functions around the Social, Interest, Consumption, Location, and Intent graphs.

Index

M

N, O

U, V

W, X, Y, Z